Practical Facilitation

A TOOLKIT OF TECHNIQUES

Christine Hogan

KOGAN PAGE

First published in Great Britain and the United States in 2003 by Kogan Page Limited
Reprinted 2005

120 Pentonville Road
London N1 9JN
UK
www.kogan-page.co.uk

22883 Quicksilver Drive
Sterling VA 20166-2012
USA

© Christine Hogan, 2003

The right of Christine Hogan to be identified as the author of this work has been asserted by her in accordance with the Copyright, Designs and Patents Act 1988.

ISBN 0 7494 3827 4

British Library Cataloguing-in-Publication Data

A CIP record for this book is available from the British Library.

Library of Congress Cataloging-in-Publication Data

Hogan, Christine (Christine Frances)
 Practical facilitation : a toolkit of techniques / Christine Hogan.
  p. cm.
Includes bibliographical references and index.
  ISBN 0-7494-3827-4
 1. Employees–Training of. 2. Business consultants–Training of. 3. Group facilitation. 4. Group relations training. 5. Communication in management. I. Title
  HF5549.5.T7H596 2003
  001–dc21

                                        2002156052

Typeset by JS Typesetting Ltd, Wellingborough, Northants
Printed and bound in Great Britain by Biddles Ltd, King's Lynn, Norfolk

Practical Facilitation

To my parents, Marjorie and Frank Hogan, who inspired and helped me to love learning and experimenting.
To my husband, Steve, who patiently mentored me through the trials of computing.
And to Katie, John and Gill, my wisdom friends who challenged my thinking and patiently gave me feedback.

Contents

in meetings 211; Agendas, minutes, timekeeping, sharing roles
and responsibilities 212; Encouraging dialogue rather than
debate 220; External versus internal facilitators 224; Evaluating
meetings 224; How to encourage resistant groups to use new
techniques 227; Technology 228; Conclusion 229

The author

Dr Christine Hogan is a professional facilitator, educator, consultant and author. She is committed to helping people to learn how to facilitate and to enhance innovations in facilitation through reflective practice, networking and research.

Her extensive consultancy work in Australia and Asia focuses on personal, organizational and community development. She has worked in Nepal, Mongolia, Malaysia, and has spent the past two years working in the Lao People's Democratic Republic.

She was a Senior Lecturer in Human Resource Development in the School of Management, Curtin University of Technology in Perth, Western Australia, where she coordinated graduate human resource development programmes and taught in the areas of facilitation and group process skills, conflict resolution and cross-cultural communication. She is now an Adjunct Senior Research Fellow of Curtin University of Technology and international consultant.

Christine is also author of *Understanding Facilitation: Theory and principles* (Kogan Page), a companion to this book which focuses on the theoretical background to facilitation. She has also published *Facilitating Empowerment: A handbook for facilitators, trainers and individuals* (Kogan Page) and *Facilitating Learning: Practical strategies for college and university* (Eruditions, Melbourne).

In her spare time Christine paints on silk under the name of 'Isadora', after Isadora Duncan, the famous educational innovator and dancer.

Christine would welcome feedback and dialogue about ideas in this book. You can find out more about her work and how to contact her by going to the following Web site: www.hogans.id.au

Acknowledgements

Many people have been involved in the development of this book. Nothing occurs in a vacuum; many authors, scholars, friends and facilitators and workshop participants have impacted on, or in some way contributed ideas to the book. There are too many of them to mention here, but I want to thank especially my wisdom friends, Kati and John Wilson, who not only mentored and supported me through my PhD, but also engaged in lively discussions, patiently read manuscripts and gave me feedback with love, hugs and humour.

Thanks to my adopted sisters, Gill Baxter and Carol Newton-Smith, for their support and laughs, and especially to Gill for expert counselling through the 'ups' and 'lows' of the writing process. Also thanks to my long term friend and mentor, Peter Frost.

One of the most difficult jobs is keeping a computer under control and formatting a book. Thanks to my husband and best friend, Steve, for his computer mentoring and for the thousands of times he carefully listened to and answered my queries with patience and clarity.

Thanks to facilitation students over the years and to members of 'Facnet', the facilitation network in Perth for all the lively discussions and support.

I am indebted to Sue Jefferies, a friend and colleague, for writing Chapter 14 incorporating her facilitation skills and experience with technology with distributed teams. Thank you, Sue, for this chapter and your contributions to this book.

I have, of course, utilized work from many sources which I have acknowledged in the references. There is now a wealth of information that has entered the 'common domain' of facilitation through Internet discussion groups. I have attempted to trace the sources of these ideas. If I have inadvertently missed or wrongly referenced works, please let me know and any error will be rectified in future editions of this work.

Thanks to Philip Mudd, publisher, Susan Curran, Fiona Meiers, Maria Devine and Russell Clarke at Kogan Page. I have really enjoyed working with you all.

Last but not least, thanks to my Mum for all her cheers and support through the years, and to my Dad who taught me so much. I wish they were both here to see the completion of this book, but I know you are with me in spirit always.

Christine Hogan

Introduction

Never doubt that a small group of thoughtful, committed citizens can change the world. Indeed, it is the only thing that ever has.

Margaret Mead

The futurist Robert Theobald proclaimed that the 21st century would be the 'healing century' (1998). If healing is to occur for all life forms and the planet, then we need to learn ways of communicating with and treating each other and our earth more humanely.

There is magic in facilitation, in capturing the ideas of participants and enabling individuals to harness their own energies, skills and group wisdom. It is much more than a toolkit or sewing box of group techniques and processes, even though this is the title of this book. At deeper levels, facilitation is about helping people engage in, manage, and cope creatively with the rapid changes within themselves, their communities and the globe. It is about creating new forms of and spaces for democratic decision making, to make a more 'civil society': that is, a relationship – 'a way of relating in the local and global community which fosters inclusive respectful, and responsible participation and peace' (Hanson, 1997: 56).

Various forms of facilitation have existed since people formed groups to live and hunt together. However, the demands of the 20th and 21st centuries have led to refinements and improvements of techniques and processes and the creative development of new ones. It is now possible to earn a living as a 'facilitator'. The more we learn, the more we know there is to learn about human communication and group work, so we need to reflect upon, monitor and conduct research into this field.

Facilitator toolkit or sewing box

The facilitator's toolkit or sewing box is a colourful, sparkling treasure trove. It is infinite in its delights, and continues to grow and expand with use. The more you put into it, the more you get out, which I have found is similar to the facilitation profession itself. The deeper you reach into it, the more you realize there is to learn, and the more profound the learning as a result. Experienced facilitators have literally hundreds of tools in their toolkits, and are selective in choosing when and how to use them because 'if your only tool is a hammer, all your problems will look like nails', and a hammer or a sewing needle are just that, tools which can be used to create wondrous furniture or superb cloth *or* to cause havoc. However, used sensitively and with skill, they may also be used to create magic, exquisite happenings borne out of the sheer creativity and joys of people who seek to make organizations, communities and the world better places for us all.

Many toolboxes and sewing kits have fixed drawers in the base. In these are the foundation tools and materials: they may not be used every day, but they are there when needed, and form the basis of our profession.

In the facilitator's tool/sewing box I believe there are four main base drawers. These were discussed in depth in my book, *Understanding Facilitation: Theory and principles*. I will briefly recap on these four layers to set the scene for this book.

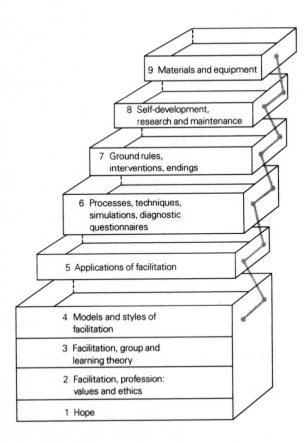

Figure 0.1   A toolkit: layers within layers

The base drawers

1   Hope

I started Book 1 with hope in the following words:

> The world needs more dialogue.
> Facilitators help people to engage in dialogue.
> Dialogue is a better way to solve disagreements than war.
> Facilitators therefore are involved in peace making and peace building.
>
> I have a dream.
> One day facilitation skills will be part of mainstream curricula in schools and colleges.
> One day there will be free speech for all.
> We will learn to talk instead of kill and bomb.
> We have the brainpower to do this.
> One day there will be world peace.

Before my mum died in London in 2000, she gave me her beautiful oak chest. She called it a 'hope chest', which was a traditional name for a dowry box where a woman would collect items of clothing and linen for marriage. A facilitator's tool kit is a kind of hope chest in which we constantly gather tools and techniques. Also our work is not value-free. It is based on hope for better forms of human interaction, better organizations and communities, and a better world.

2   The facilitation profession

Facilitation has grown up across the world, in numerous cultures and disciplines, to help groups clarify and solve problems resulting from dramatic social, cultural and technological change where old routines, customs and expectations are breaking down. In *Understanding Facilitation*, I described facilitation: its rise in management, education and training, and community development, and how different tools and techniques need to be developed and/or adapted in different cultures.

The rise of the profession and issues of values and ethics were discussed through case studies and coverage of how the International Association of Facilitators has developed a list of facilitation ethics and accreditation processes. I raised questions about how values and ethics may be monitored in this growing, exciting and diverse profession.

3   Facilitation and group theory

There is a vast body of literature that underpins the work of facilitators. As copious tomes have been written on this topic, I had to be selective and chose theories and concepts that have been useful to me in my facilitation work. I selected theories that are easy to recall and hence easy to put into practice.

4   Models and styles of facilitation

I described definitions and five models of facilitation: how they were developed and how they may be used to learn about facilitation. The first was designed by John Heron in the UK, between 1977–93 (Heron, 1989, 1993). The second was designed through discussion on the Internet between members of the International Association of Facilitators (IAF) and the Institute of Cultural Affairs (ICA) 1995–2000 (in the United States and across the world) (Pierce, Cheesebrow and Braun, 2000). The third was designed by A Glenn Kiser and takes a more linear approach to the stages of facilitation (Kiser, 1998). The fourth was developed by Hunter *et al* (1999) in New Zealand; and fifth, I offered a personal 'Living frame of facilitation'.

To illustrate the rise of the uses of technology for facilitators, I developed a model describing the technologies that were available to facilitators at the time of writing, and discussed the work of Gilly Salmon, who developed a model of competencies required by e-moderators (Salmon, 2000).

The upper drawers

This book, *Practical Facilitation*, complements the theoretical approach of *Understanding Facilitation*. The focus is on the contents of the 'pull out' drawers at the top of the tool/sewing box. They are the more visible aspects of the profession. As the title indicates, this book elaborates on the breadth, depth and diversity of a facilitator's toolkit. The book starts with consulting and contracting with clients, and ends with evaluating and ongoing learning and maintenance ideas for facilitators.

5   Applications of facilitation

Level 5 of the toolkit includes the variety of applications of facilitation. Facilitators as consultants (internal and external to organizations and communities) are 'called in' for various reasons:

- capacity building, developing creativity;
- team building, meetings, problem solving;
- conflict resolution, mediation and restorative justice;
- planning, organizational development and change;
- community planning, building, consultation and development.

Chapter 1 focuses on the process consulting work of facilitators. Like many writers, I found that the chapter grew and grew and grew. So I took out a section on international consulting and facilitation, which will be developed in another book.

6   Processes, techniques and simulations

Having determined what a facilitator is required to do, we then choose from our toolbox suitable processes, techniques and simulations. We may use diagnostic questionnaires on ourselves or with groups, to help to gain more information or patterns of information.

Everyone has to start somewhere, so Chapter 3 focuses on ways to help new facilitators build up knowledge and skills in facilitation. Facilitators have to accommodate diversity of learning, thinking and being styles of individuals, so Chapter 4 is somewhat larger because it elaborates on the joys of using methods to stimulate holistic thinking and learning, involving all the senses. Although cross-cultural issues are raised in almost every chapter, I have brought together key ideas in Chapter 5.

Chapter 8 focuses on practical processes for opening, planning and evaluating meetings. Chapters 9, 10 and 11 are devoted to processes for planning, creativity, problem solving and decision making respectively.

Chapter 12 is aimed at developing workable relationships in the workplace and community, and includes innovative work on restorative justice and community consultation.

Chapter 13 focuses on using the outdoors as a stage for facilitating personal development and teamwork.

I am indebted to a friend and colleague, Sue Jefferies, who wrote Chapter 14 which illustrates how facilitators can harness technology to enable distributed teams to communicate more effectively.

7   Ground rules, interventions and endings

The next level of the toolkit relates to how facilitators work with groups to negotiate ground rules and intervene when necessary to end workshops. Most facilitators have some forms of individual or group behaviour that they dread, so Chapter 6 is devoted to methods for preventing and/or facilitating inappropriate behaviours. Chapter 15 looks at the all too often neglected issue of how to end workshops effectively, and Chapter 16 is devoted to demystifying evaluation techniques.

8   Self-development, research and maintenance

Chapter 7 develops a variety of journal writing processes which may be used by facilitators to help participants' self-development, or by facilitators themselves to reflect upon, monitor and explore learning. Chapter 15 describes the many different ways of ending workshops.

Last, but not least, facilitators need to put time and energy into ongoing learning and research and maintenance of their health and well being, and suggestions are given in Chapter 17.

9   Materials and equipment

The physical tools of facilitation are mentioned where appropriate in context in the book. A list is contained at the end of Chapter 3.

Change

This book, like *Understanding Facilitation*, is a snapshot in time. New and exciting developments are going on in group work all over the world, and I know that as soon as I submit this manuscript I will be learning exciting new ideas and techniques from other facilitators, and will be trying to do new things and in different ways. I have included some Web sites, but know there are hundreds more. Daily some Web sites die and new ones appear.

Many people's ideas, books, videos and Web sites have contributed to my learning. I have tried to reference everything to provide the reader with resources. If I have omitted anyone I apologize; let me know and I will rectify the situation in the next edition.

I welcome dialogue on any issues in this book, or reminders of things I have omitted or should improve.

Happy facilitating!

1

Consulting with clients

A consultant is someone who does not know what he/she will be doing in six months time.

Source unknown

Introduction

This chapter focuses on the very important stages before a workshop, including making contact with clients (whether you are an internal or external facilitator, the principles are the same), conducting a needs analysis, contracting, preparing workshop plans and evaluations.

Types of consulting style

There are three types of consulting style, the 'expert', 'pair of hands' and the 'process' mode (Schein, 1987, 1988, 1999). I will briefly describe each in turn. However, this chapter and the rest of this book focus mainly on the 'process' mode.

Expert mode

First, in the 'expert' mode, a consultant is invited to look over an organization and/or problem somewhat like a doctor, point out what is wrong, and prescribe potential solutions or recommendations to the organization or 'patient'. This mode is fraught with difficulties, as workers and managers (in the patient role) are often reluctant to reveal deficiencies. Questionnaires and interviews designed by outside experts frequently do not ask the 'right' questions, and answers rarely reveal the whole story. Similarly, there is no ownership of the solutions proposed by the consultant.

Pair of hands mode

Second, the 'pair of hands' or purchase mode relates to the purchase of expert service/skills for a defined length of time: for example, IT specialists might be brought into a company for six months to write and set up a computer program specific to the organization's needs.

Process mode

Thirdly, the 'process' or facilitator mode highlights the role of a facilitator who works alongside managers and workers to help them identify and solve their own problems. The facilitator does not need to be an expert in the field, but needs to learn about the key players (in both the formal and informal hierarchy), the relevant 'language' of the organization, and relevant past history. The concept of 'process consultation' was developed by in depth Edgar Schein (1987, 1988, 1999) and later added to by Brendan Reddy (1994).

A process consultant is invited into a group to make thoughtful and intentional interventions into how the group is working, to help members become aware of their functioning, or to enable them to achieve task/s that they could not complete alone. If the process consultant starts to offer solutions, then he/she is acting as a manager, not a facilitator. It is this mode that is the focus of this chapter.

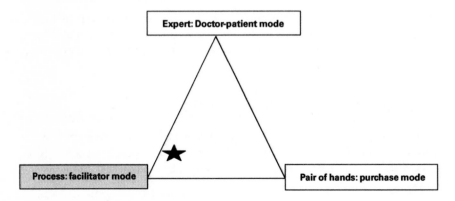

Figure 1.1 Types of consulting

Within the facilitator mode there are also different 'styles of facilitation', as discussed in *Understanding Facilitation*.

Process consulting

In 1999, Schein revisited his earlier works and highlighted 10 principles of process consultation. I have added ideas in brackets:

● Always try to be helpful (but not in a smothering, oppressive way).
● Always stay in touch with current reality. (Be calm and fully present, bearing in mind past and possible future scenarios.)

- Accept your ignorance. (You will be learning right up to the end of your consultation time and beyond. You will need to be able to cope with ambiguity.)
- Everything you do is an intervention. (You cannot 'not' communicate through presence, body language, words and deeds. You are being observed right from the first meeting.)
- The client owns the problem and the solution. (You cannot take over or get over-involved.)
- Go with the flow. (The Taoist philosophy of bending with the wind may save you some sleepless nights.)
- Be constructively opportunistic with confrontative interventions. ('Carpe diem': seize the day, but think before you leap as well as confront.)
- Everything is a source of data. (Take photos discreetly and with permission, and keep a journal and record as much as you can. Note and record intuitions. Keep creative journals (see Chapter 7). They are a wonderful record if you get called on to do future work with an organization.)
- Learn from inevitable errors. (See the 'Learning from mistakes' process described in Chapter 17.)
- When in doubt, share the problem. (You may need to be careful who you share the problem with: always have a 'critical friend', mentor or supervisor outside the organization.)

These 10 principles are useful guidelines for facilitators.

Choosing a facilitator

What makes an effective facilitator? What should managers look for in a facilitator? Sandor Schuman (1996) suggests that four basic skills should be looked for when choosing a group facilitator:

- **The ability to anticipate the complete problem-solving and decision-making process.** A facilitator should be able to take a strategic or helicopter view, but should not pre-empt the direction that the group might take. A facilitator needs to be able to change direction if that is the will of the group and within its values and guidelines.
- **The ability to use procedures that support both the group's social and cognitive processes.** The facilitator needs to have a variety of processes and techniques that help the group to think about issues at hand *and* be able to help individuals participate and listen to one another.
- **The ability to remain neutral regarding content issues and values.** The facilitator must always stay out of content. Once he/she jumps over the line into content, or advocates solutions, the facilitation role is broken. A facilitator may summarize and provide processes to enable groups to reframe ideas and information.

    If the goal of a workshop is capacity building and development, a facilitator will need to find out what people already know and build on this, then bring in new ideas, skills and materials to the group.

- **The ability to respect the group's need to understand and learn from the problem-solving process.** A facilitator should work as transparently as possible (hence the suggested 'Framework for workshop planning' using the headings content, process and time (Doyle and Straus 1976) shown in the box on page 33). You would not ask someone to go into a casino and play a game without knowing the rules. The same is true with workshops. Some processes are quite complex, and a facilitator needs to meet the participants' need to understand the processes, if not beforehand, then at least by the end. People need to be treated with respect, and be informed of the purpose of activities. They need to know why they are being asked to do something, and/or be involved in co-creating or adapting processes.

Comparison between external and internal facilitators

Facilitators may consult within their organizations or work freelance with many different organizations. Each role has its own advantages and disadvantages (see *Understanding Facilitation* Chapter 5). At times it is necessary for internal and external facilitators to co-facilitate to get the best of both their worlds and expertise (see *Understanding Facilitation* Chapter 7). An evaluation of each type of facilitation is given below.

The main difference is that external facilitators 'get to go home', but internal facilitators are involved for the long term. They have to pace themselves, maintain objectivity, confidentiality, navigate the politics, power structures and hierarchies, and at all times maintain limits and boundaries (Scott, 2000). Another way around this issue is to invite an in-house facilitator from a department who is not directly involved with a particular group. That way the facilitator knows the culture and language of the organization.

The rest of this chapter is written for external facilitator/consultants; however, many of the ideas are relevant to internal facilitator/consultants.

Making initial contact

Managers and/or groups frequently only contact a facilitator when they are in extreme difficulty and when all other means have failed to solve a problem. The contact person may be well informed, or in some cases may only be given a basic briefing, so it is important that a facilitator works like a sleuth to get to the issues at the base of the organizational iceberg. Just as in the medical model, the presenting symptoms may not indicate the real cause of the underlying problem. For example, a request for a stress management workshop may not be the solution when the work structures are constantly overloading people. Not all these issues are necessarily raised in public, but it is very helpful if you can find out about them.

The purpose of the intervention

The first contact is often a phone call with a direct invitation to a particular facilitator, or a call for tenders for an advertised piece of work. A few pertinent questions may save you a lot of time and energy, as the following story illustrates. Sometimes clients do not know exactly what they want. So it is useful to ask:

What is the purpose of the workshop?
What outcomes do you want to see after the workshop?
What kind of experience/s do you want participants to have?

When you receive the answers to these questions you may want to clarify by asking yourself and a client, 'Is a workshop the best way to solve xxx?'.

STORY: CHECKING FOR SENIOR MANAGEMENT SUPPORT

A person I knew rang me one day and the following conversation ensued:

John   Chris, would you be available to come to our organization to facilitate a workshop on empowerment?
Chris   Sure, I would love to, tell me more, but what is this workshop part of?
John   We just heard from another organization that your workshop was great and thought it would be a good idea.
Chris   Have you discussed the idea of empowerment with senior management?
John   Not yet.
Chris   Well, they need to be supportive and understand the ramifications of such an initiative. How about you get back to me when you have spoken to them, and perhaps we can all meet to discuss the aims and issues involved.
John   Sure, I'll ring you next week.

John never rang back.

Before the first meeting

Before the first meeting, find out what you can about the organization through your own network or the Web. Remember to triangulate: do not just use one source of information, cross-check. It is useful to find out as much as you can about the language of the organization, current issues, key players, and internal as well as external politics.

First meeting

Visits to offices/organizations beforehand are well worth the time and effort to:

- meet participants informally and vice versa;
- conduct a needs analysis;

- see/walk around and observe the working environment and ambience;
- observe the interactions between team members, managers and/or the general public: that is, codes of behaviour and organizational culture/s.

At the first meeting it is necessary to put yourself and the client at ease. Some initial smalltalk is often necessary (especially with people from Southeast Asia, who often think you are rude if you jump into business talk too quickly). You need to build rapport and trust before jumping into problems. However, this depends on the work culture: some people like to get down to business quickly.

Introducing yourself and establishing credibility

At a suitable point with clients you are going to need to be able to explain your facilitation background and how you work in order to establish credibility (without appearing to blow your own trumpet).

STORY: GENDER ISSUES: ON PROVING ONE'S WORTH

I always use the name 'Christine' and not 'Chris' in formal correspondence. There-fore there can be no mistake about my sex, which is often the case if I use the name 'Chris'. Noel, my boss in a consulting firm, asked me to discuss a deal with a glass company at Canning Vale, a suburb in southeast Perth. The managers perceived a problem with the productivity of their six shifts of workers. Each month, one day was devoted to a meeting of the shift team, comprising 12 men and their immediate supervisor. Senior management was concerned that these days were not being used productively, and I was informed that management wanted the men to be more actively involved in problem solving and decision making. I arranged an appointment by phone with the training manager.

I recall choosing my clothing carefully beforehand: plain trousers and a colour-ful top, but quite conservative by my standards. The office near the front of the huge car park was rather sterile. The secretary rang for the training manager, who greeted me with a helmet and ear muffs and invited me to walk through the fac-tory on the way to the supervisor's office. Moving gantries and fork lifts full of jangling crates and bottles clattered noisily above and on every side. I felt as if I needed eyes in the back of my head, there was so much heavy plant machinery on the move; it was so hot and noisy.

When I entered the supervisor's office, a number of men stood somewhat awk-wardly. I smiled as each introduced himself and shook hands. In Australia, some women tend not to shake hands; however, in England, my birthplace, women shake hands with everyone (except Orthodox rabbis). On arriving in Perth and noticing the cultural differences, I made a conscious decision to shake hands firmly with men and look them straight in the eye on first contact. I sensed that by not shaking hands, women do not get a chance to 'connect' with the men they meet. I have never noticed men reacting negatively to a firm handshake, provided I take the initiative.

The men uttered greetings and we sat down. There were the usual preliminary pleasantries and we started to discuss their issues. I sensed 'dis-ease'. I listened hard, but I picked up uneasy body language as they spoke to me. Some of the men looked down or shifted in their seats. I waited for a pause to intervene, while at the same time racking my brain for something to say to relieve the tension. I sensed that even though they knew a female consultant was being sent to them, they were not relating to me easily.

When my chance came, I joined the conversation. 'It's a while since I was in Canning Vale. Hasn't it changed with all the new factories going up?' Luckily one of them took the bait and asked why I had visited the area. I replied nonchalantly, 'I used to teach inmates at Fremantle Jail. They were a pretty rough bunch, some of them. My classes got very popular, and at one time I had up to 24 blokes in a room together. Sometimes I visited other prisons like Canning Vale or Albany to conduct workshops.' (Fremantle was a maximum-security jail, which was built by convicts in 1855 and closed in November 1991.) The impact of my comment was magical. One guy rolled up his sleeves, another coughed and moved his neck, another man leant forward. We were in business. At the end of our discussions they had agreed that I would facilitate six one-day workshops, one per month for each shift. These were to be conducted in their training room, a demountable building in the factory grounds.

Preparing a one-page statement of your facilitation values

A short one-page statement about 'how' you facilitate is really useful. There are many questions you can ask yourself, such as 'What central values guide your facilitation practice?' (asked by Dale Spender during the IAF discussions to develop a set of facilitation values). No one can pretend to be value neutral. Facilitation itself is not value-neutral.

A one-page handout containing a statement of your values and ways of working is useful to give clients. When formulating your statement of how you work, it may help to think about the answers to four deceptively simple but searching questions that Wayne Muller developed 'that reveal the beauty and meaning of our lives' (see the box below). You may need to tailor your statement according to the language of the clients you work with.

QUESTIONS THAT REVEAL THE BEAUTY AND MEANING
OF OUR LIVES

- Who am I?
- What do I love?
- How shall I live, knowing I will die?
- What is my gift to the family of the earth?

Source: Muller (1997)

In my statement I include my perception of the roles and responsibilities of the participants and the organizers. These are kept on computer and may be adapted. For example, I believe that participants should attend voluntarily, yet I know there are some workshops regarding new legislation or workplace practices where everyone must attend. Figure 1.2 is a sample which I adjust for different clients and situations. See also the International Association of Facilitators list of code of ethics, discussed in *Understanding Facilitation* Appendix 2 and available at: http://www.iaf-world.org/iafethics.htm

---

Figure 1.2   Code of roles and responsibilities

Christine Hogan

The philosophical basis of my work is as follows. I strive to help clients make their work places more productive, satisfying and enjoyable. I have a commitment to participatory learning and democratic decision making. My belief is that it is important for participants to find their own solutions to issues and projects. I contract with organizers beforehand and clarify workshop processes with participants, so that everyone is involved and owns both the content and the processes of the workshop.

My work involves 'holistic learning', that is, it attempts to involve the whole person and all the senses in the learning process. I have a commitment to ethical behaviour and mutual respect for individuals, opinions and different cultures. At any time I respect the rights of any participant who may wish to observe an activity rather than participate.

I am willing to share my observations of participants and their interactions and confront individuals, directly or indirectly as appropriate, if their behaviour is detrimental to the work of the group. If appropriate, I am prepared to recontract and change direction if that is the consensus decision of the group.

Roles of facilitator
My roles as a facilitator are to:
- develop processes for the workshop in conjunction with the organizers and/or participants;
- contract with participants to develop desirable codes of behaviour;
- explain processes to the group;
- negotiate/change or adapt these processes as required by the group;
- encourage participation from as many participants as possible and protect the choice of those who do not wish to participate;
- contract regarding use and changes of use of time;
- protect individuals from verbal attack;
- ask questions to illicit ideas, opinions and hidden agendas;
- ensure that ideas and decisions are recorded as accurately as possible;
- encourage ongoing feedback about the workshop/s;
- ensure that suitable formative and summative evaluation strategies are developed and ensure that collated evaluative information is fed back to the participants and organizers.

Assumptions
My assumptions are that:
- all participants will attend voluntarily;
- effort is made to cater for the special needs of individuals (language, food, furniture, space etc);

- effort is made to ensure that participants are not interrupted during the workshop;
- follow-up work and learning (based on feedback and evaluations) will be encouraged and supported with time and resources by the managers and the organization/s after the workshop.

Roles of participants
The roles of the participants are to:
- discuss, adapt and/or add to ground rules;
- think about their needs/issues beforehand;
- make their needs known to the workshop organizer, facilitator and/or group;
- bring necessary documents and/or ideas from other employees to the workshop
- listen to intuition and raise issues with group and/or facilitator contribute to discussions;
- listen actively to understand meaning and feelings behind words;
- ask for explanations regarding group processes and renegotiate where necessary.

Roles of organizers and/or management
The roles of organizers are to:
- brief all participants about the purpose of the workshop;
- ensure that all data from the workshop are collated, typed, distributed to participants and stored for later reference;
- liaise with the facilitator in the planning of the workshop to arrange adequate time to accomplish the goals of the workshop;
- organize a suitable venue, that is, large well-ventilated room with suitable tables, seating and wall space;
- ensure that all stakeholders are represented at the workshop (where necessary);
- ensure that managers are present for the whole of the workshop (where necessary, that is, to ensure that issues are heard accurately, responded to and where possible to support implementation of long-term changes);
- support participants in follow-up work after the workshop.

Contracting

Contracting is an important part of the facilitation process. Indeed the facilitation process starts with the first contact, whether it is by phone, e-mail, or whatever, and may carry on throughout the design and enactment of the workshop. Contracting in the facilitation sense does not have the closed finality and formality that is involved in a legal contract. (But it may, so check carefully what you sign.)

There are two levels of contract. The first is the contract you make with the client/organizers regarding content of the workshop, scope of the project, processes, costs and so on. The second is the contract you make with the participants on the day of the workshop regarding desirable norms, and if necessary, to modify direction regarding purpose and content.

The purpose of contracting is to determine:

- What is the purpose of the workshop (for the organization, managers, participants)?
- What are the desired outcomes and/or behaviours after the workshop/s?
- What are you going to facilitate (the topic/problem or issue)?
- How are you going to facilitate(the process/es)?
- How long are you going to facilitate (number of days)?
- Who is the client? Who are you going to facilitate? (Who is going to be directly involved?)
- Who are the stakeholders? Have all the right people been invited? (See Figure 1.3).
- What will happen to the data?
- How will you know if you have been successful? That is, how will you evaluate your intervention, and what resources are necessary to do this?
- How will the organization support participants to follow-up on agreed strategies?

Contracting involves clarification on both sides regarding expectations and perceptions of what will occur, and developing agreements. It is a chance for a facilitator and a client group to determine if there is a 'match' between the skills, values and style of the facilitator, and the needs and values of the client group.

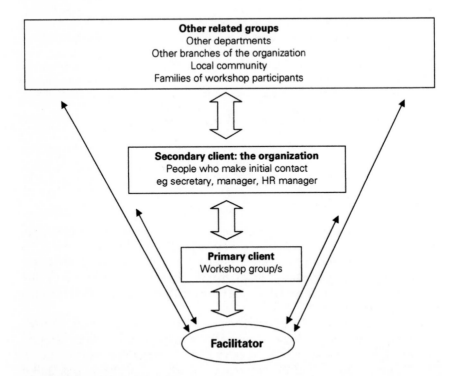

Figure 1.3 Who is the client?

Adapted from Schwarz (1994)

According to Schwarz (1994), the purposes of contracting are to:

- determine whether or not the client group from management downwards is committed to working on the issues at hand;
- enable group members to voice their issues first hand, and for them to see the facilitator and the way he/she interacts with others;
- develop trust: the group divulges some of its problems and what members have done so far to solve them. The facilitator divulges his/her experiences in this field. There is an element of risk plus the need for building empathy and support.

A 'contract' in this context is a letter of agreement. Some facilitators prefer not to use a formal contract, as they prefer to keep relationships with clients on an informal and high trust basis. Some clients (especially government departments) have programme contracts that they give to all consultants. Contracts usually contain:

- names of people involved;
- mutually agreed services;
- who will provide what service, materials and consumables;
- dates and deadlines;
- breakdowns of costs.

Some contracts include a cancellation clause.

The story so far

When discussing issues with a client it is useful to ask open-ended questions early on. Questions like 'Can you tell me the story so far?' are far less daunting for some clients than 'What is the problem?' Clients usually use storytelling devices, and may describe a critical incident or issues in a circuitous way. Often egos are at stake, so some issues may be covered or omitted completely. Remember, you are only hearing one side of the 'story'.

You need to listen actively to responses: with your head for issues, and your heart for feelings. There are many checklists of questions: one is reproduced below. Ask if you may take notes to ensure you get everything down. Taking notes allows silence and 'think time' for the client. Make sure you look up and maintain eye contact as much as possible. Watch his/her body language. Listen more than talk, and do not rush to conclusions on what interventions to make. You need to keep an open mind and stay flexible.

I only use a checklist like the one below at the end of the conversation, after the storytelling and our dialogue has finished, to see if there is anything I have not covered. If you go through the questions in order you may sound very mechanistic, and you may not listen properly and follow through on themes dictated by the client. Sometimes it is better to just let clients tell you 'the story so far', and to listen as stories unravel in a non-sequential way.

General questions for diagnosing the problems of the primary client

Adapted from Schwarz (1994: 53), Block (1999) and my own thoughts.

Identifying problems

- Can you fill me in on the story so far?
- Can you give me some specific examples of issues/problems?
- How many people are involved? Do they see this as an issue?
- Can you elaborate on. . . ?
- What is your hunch on what is going on?
- How widespread are the problems? Do they occur all the time, or only under certain conditions or with certain individuals?
- In what ways do members contribute to the problems? In what ways do you contribute to the problems?

History of the group and past interventions

- What is the history of the group? How has the membership and leadership changed?
- When did the problems begin? What else was occurring at that time or shortly before the problems began?
- What have you tried so far that worked? Did not work?

Consequences for group effectiveness

- What are the consequences of these problems?
- How do the problems affect the group's ability to produce quality products or deliver quality services or work together?

Potential causes – environmental, society, political

- Are there any external factors that could be influencing the group, for example a change of government and/or government policy; an economic recession; cataclysmic event?

Potential causes – process

- What do you think are the causes of the problems? What have you seen or heard that leads you to think these are the causes?
- How does the group solve problems and make decisions? Or are solutions dictated to them? Who decides who decides?
- How does the group communicate and manage conflict? Coordinate its work with others in the organization? Do any of these seem related to the problems you described? If so, how?

Potential causes – structure, organizational context

- Does the group have clear goals? Are members motivated by their tasks? Does the group have the right kind of members to do its work? Do members understand and agree on their roles? Do they have enough time to do their work? What kinds of behaviours do members expect of each other? What are the core values and beliefs that members share about work? Do any of these seem related to the problems you described? If so, how?
- In what ways does the organization help or hinder the group?
- Is there a clear mission and a shared vision? Is the culture supportive? How are group members rewarded? Does the group get enough information to do its work? Is there enough training and other resources? Appropriate physical space to work in? Do any of these seem related to the problems you described? If so, how?
- Can you give me an organizational chart and a list of roles and responsibilities of this particular group?
- How do you think other people in the group would identify the problems and their causes? Would others disagree?

Motivation and resources for change

- What have you tried so far that worked? Did not work? Why do you think X did not work?
- What have you tried to do to improve the situation? What were the results?

Experience with consultants and current request for help

- How do you think the group will feel about working with an outside facilitator on these issues?
- Have you used other consultants or facilitators in the past, either for this situation or others? What role did the consultant or facilitator play? What were the results?
- What did the consultants do that members liked or disliked?
- What has led you to contact someone now? What has happened or is about to happen in the group or organization?
- How did the idea to call me in particular come about? Who initiated it? Were group members consulted first? How was the idea received by other group members?
- How do you see me helping the group accomplish its objectives?

Outcomes

- What would success look like to you?
- What are your essential needs?
- What are your desirable wants?
- How can you/we measure success/outcomes?

Meeting the group

- When can I meet the group to hear their issues to enable me to plan the workshop? Or if this is not possible:
- Is it possible for me to conduct a needs analysis via e-mail/phone beforehand?

Confronting

- I might be wrong, but I have a niggling concern I'd like to raise with you. . . it appears as if your mind is already made up? (You may need to question and/or coach the client in what is possible, not possible within the ethics of facilitation.)

Ending

- What do you expect me to do after the workshop? (For example, reports, collations of evaluations, typing of data, follow-up work.)
- I'll need to go away and think about this. How soon would you like me to send you a proposed outline?
- Let's summarize what we've agreed upon so far.

The organizational structure

Ask for a list of the full names (and nicknames) of participants with their job titles, and a diagram of the organizational hierarchy or chain of command in the group or organization. This gives you an overall picture of the formal structure of the organization. There will, however, frequently be informal chains of command, roles and power cliques. Where possible, ask about the informal chains of command and linkages. This can be very instructive. In some organizations the informal structure can make the whole system unstable.

The organizational iceberg

It is important for facilitators to consider the depth of the intervention that is required. The metaphor of an iceberg is often used to focus on the issues. (See Figure 1.4.) As you go deeper down into the iceberg, the level of risk increases and the emotional work increases. A facilitator needs to be aware of his/her own skills and limitations, and lowest levels may be best left to qualified psychologists.

Listen to your intuition: confronting your client

During discussions, carefully tune into your intuition. There may be hidden agendas. If you have any doubts or concerns, voice them or go home, sleep on them, and later check them out with your client. Do not ignore them.

1. Goals and tasks of group members
Methods and outcomes

2. Overt issues of group members
Communication and decision-making patterns
norms, conflict, organizational culture

Surface of the water

3. Covert group issues
Power struggles, trust issues

4. Deeper history
Culture, deeply held beliefs, values,
assumptions, entrenched ways of
working, defence systems,
basic needs and fears

5. The unconscious
Not accessible to the group or
the facilitator

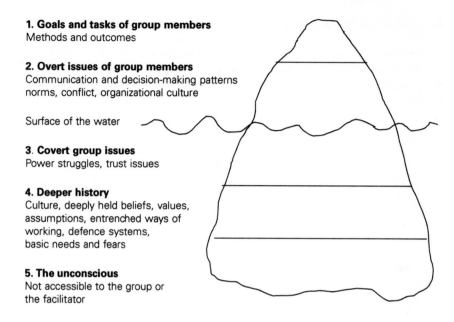

Figure 1.4   The organizational iceberg

Adapted from Schein (1988) and Reddy (1994: 700)

You have choices:

- Accept the workshop as requested.
- Renegotiate to include your suggestions for more time or whatever.
- Pass on to another more experienced facilitator.
- Arrange to do the workshop with another facilitator so you can learn new facilitation skills on the job.
- Withdraw. It may be better to withdraw at this point, than do so later, and lose face.

You can be even more assertive and openly confront your client. For example, you might say, 'May I confront you on an issue that is concerning me?' (Pause. . .) 'After all, that is why you are bringing in an outside facilitator, and I presume you are wanting me to do that at the workshop? (Pause. . . wait for agreement.) 'You say you want to involve your workers in planning xxx, but on so many issues it sounds as if your mind is already made up. For example, when you said. . . Or am I jumping to the wrong conclusion?'

Backing out gracefully

If necessary, this is the time for a facilitator to say, 'No thank you' if:

- the job does not require a facilitative intervention: workshops are not the most suitable interventions for everything;

- your intuition and inner alarm bells are ringing noisily;
- the job does not fit within your range of skills;
- the work requires more time than you can allocate;
- the timeline is unrealistic and the organizers refuse to extend it;
- the CEO indicates that he/she does not really want or value participation;
- the work does not fit with your values and ethical boundaries.

STORY: ETHICAL ISSUES

Here is a story from my early days as a consultant in a large consulting firm. (Some names have been changed.) One day my boss, Noel, called me into his office. 'I've got an interesting one for you here I think you'll enjoy, in Melltown. They want a strategic planning workshop. Go and see Mr Brown.'

Noel was right: I was excited. Fred Brown, a significant figure in Perth, at that time had a vision to bring together the three important retail zones of Melltown for a development plan. The problem was that visitors to Melltown only visited one of the three main centres: the port, the old markets or the modern shopping centre.

Our pre-planning discussions seemed to go well. Fred was enthusiastic, and when I sounded him out on using the search conference process he was receptive. 'Oh yes, I remember in the US we used that process, really good stuff, got people behind what we wanted to do. . . etc.' Immediately warning bells went off in my mind and I got a sinking feeling in my stomach. Did this man really want the participation of interested stakeholders, or was he just going through the motions? My gut feeling told me the latter. He sidestepped my questions regarding ongoing action after the workshop.

I drove back to my office and immediately went to see Noel. 'Do we have to bid for everything we can?' I asked, and explained my concerns. I didn't want to have anything to do with Fred, who by now I really distrusted. Noel was a very good mentor, and described various levels of consulting, including 'educating the client'. He suggested that I could refuse to put in a proposal, or write the proposal in such a way as to guarantee the ethical side of participation.

I went away and pondered on this dilemma. In the end I did submit a proposal. In it I made it mandatory to have a secretary with a laptop at the back of the room, to note down quickly all the data from the flip chart paper, so that all stakeholders would be able to go away with a copy of the raw data at the end of the day. (One of the big problems with this type of work is getting data to participants after the workshop, before the energy and momentum decrease.) I showed it to Noel, then sent it off.

I did not get that job, and I do not know what happened; however, I could sleep soundly at night. To this day I have an inbuilt warning system regarding the ethics of facilitation and possible manipulation of participants.

See *Understanding Facilitation*, Chapter 11 for a detailed discussion of facilitation and ethics.

Look for agreements and commitments from top management

Agree on goals, objectives, problems and issues (that is, what is the presenting problem and what are the underlying problems?). If you are invited to do capacity building or to change behaviours, be firm and pin down management to be clear about what participants should be able to do or behave after the workshop.

Check the role of the organization/organizers in terms of support and commitment. How will the support of top management be demonstrated at the workshop? Ensure that senior management are committed, and will either open/close the workshop, or be present throughout it if necessary. Check that staff will be made available to cover the phones so that participants are not interrupted.

For planning workshops it is necessary to have data typed and distributed quickly after the workshop. I now ask that a non-participant be present with a laptop, so that data from flip chart paper can be typed concurrently. (In cross-cultural workshops we have had two laptops, so data can be recorded simult-aneously in different languages and later 'back translated' before distribution.) If there are no laptops available, check who will be responsible for typing and producing the final report. Sometimes managers assume that the facilitator will do this. If you take on this role, be sure to add time for this into your costing.

Ask how management will be prepared to support participants making ongoing changes after the workshop.

Needs analysis: getting a broader picture

Go beyond just questioning one or two people regarding needs. Keep asking yourself, 'Who is the client?' Talk to participants, if possible face to face, if not by phone or e-mail. Summarize your findings to your original contact. As a 'process consultant' and 'facilitator', it is not your job to give solutions. Stay out of content.

You may not be able to make process suggestions without first going away and doing some research. Do not just accept what the client tells you; probe beneath the surface. Only one-seventh of an iceberg is above the surface, and it is the same frequently with organizations.

Evaluation

Discuss how the session will be evaluated at the planning meeting, in terms of:

- 'formative' evaluation as you go along at the end of each day;
- 'summative' evaluation at the end of the workshop;
- 'long term' evaluation three months after the workshop (see Chapter 16).

Most importantly, ask what will happen as a result of the evaluation. Very often evaluations are conducted but participants do not see the collated summary and do not see any changes in future workshops. As a result some people are understandably cynical of spending time on evaluations.

Negotiating a fee

> I must say I hate money, but it's the lack of it I hate most.
>
> Katherine Mansfield

If you are competing for a contract there may be a fixed fee. Alternatively you may be asked to give an estimated figure and then negotiate later, if you are offered the contract. In other instances you may have to negotiate up front.

Principled negotiation

The concept of 'principled negotiation' was developed at the Harvard Negotiation Project, and is described simply as 'getting to yes' (Fisher and Ury, 1981). It is based on being both 'soft' and 'hard': soft on people, but hard on issues. Principled negotiators are problem solvers who seek a wise outcome in an amicable and efficient way, using the four main concepts outlined in Table 1.1.

Table 1.1   Key concepts of principled negotiation

Concept	Explanation
1. People	Separate the people from the problem
2. Interests	Focus on interests, not positions
3. Options	Generate a variety of possibilities before deciding what to do. Invent options for mutual gain
4. Criteria	Insist that the results be based on some objective standard or criteria

Source: adapted from Fisher and Ury (1981)

People
Try to keep feelings and issues out of the negotiation. Of course your feelings will impact on whether you eventually decide to take the job if it is offered. Negotiators should be 'hard' on the 'issues' not on each other. Remember it is important to maintain good relationships in the long term.

Interests
Sometimes during a negotiation people forget the underlying issues. What is it that each party really wants?

Options
Develop options to choose from. Do not decide on everything at once. Look for what is useful/valuable for you and cheap for the other party and vice versa. There is rarely one 'right' solution.

Criteria

List issues that can be measured in figures: hours, costs, length of report, numbers of people, future work and so on.

During the analysis stage, gather as much information as you can. Make a careful list of your costs: preparation time, research data gathering costs and so on. Try to think from the other person's and/or organization's point of view. During discussions ask questions, listen and record answers. Address differences in perception and feelings. Reason and be open to reason. If necessary buy time so 'you' and 'they' can think about options. Once an amicable decision is reached, summarize agreements and send copies for everyone in writing.

It is normal for a client to think of additional needs later as workshops evolve. If other things are added, make a note. Never do things for clients that they can do for themselves. You may need to renegotiate the item, and the remuneration needed for the work involved. Conversely you may wish to point out the extra work but do it 'gratis' in the interests of future work and your ongoing relationship. In one organization, I agreed to complete some extra work and negotiated a free place in a forthcoming workshop with visiting Risk Management experts in return. (The workshop was worth $500 to me, and it cost the organization nothing to have me as an extra participant.)

Terms of reference (TOR)

Some organizations publicize terms of reference (TOR) indicating the scope of the work, timelines and a list of who is responsible for what, and invite applications. Sometimes a fixed amount is offered; other times applicants are invited to submit a detailed fee quotation. If you are asked to quote, you may find it useful to see if there are any guidelines. Or give a couple of quotes: the bare minimum would cost 'x' but with xyz as well it would cost 'xx'.

Deciding whether to co-facilitate

You may need to think about whether to facilitate alone, or with another facilitator from within or outside the organization or community. One problem for co-facilitators is the additional cost to the client. However, you may wish to work with another facilitator/s if:

- The group is extremely large.
- The workshop is likely to be stormy and emotional. You may need one facilitator to work with someone who is upset separate to the main group.
- The issues are very complex or are likely to be extended over many months, in which case it may be useful to train several facilitators.
- You want an outsider to take over a part of the workshop where you are involved in content: that is, to involve an internal and an external facilitator.
- There is an issue of gender, and it may be best to include a male and a female facilitator.

- There is an issue of seniority, and it may be best to include an older and/or more experienced person as well as the relatively junior one acting as the main facilitator.
- There is an issue in a specialist field. It may be best to include a person who understands the nature and language of the organization/community better that you.
- There is a need for a cultural and/or language interpreter/translator.
- There is an issue of insider political knowledge. It may be best to have a person who knows the power conflicts and their history.

If you do choose to work with a co-facilitator, remember to invest time and energy in setting ground rules, deciding on processes and structures. Research into co-facilitation by Marie Martin (Martin, work in progress) indicates that co-facilitation takes three to five times as long as single facilitation to set up, negotiate, organize and close/debrief at the end.

Dividing responsibilities

Table 1.2 is a checklist for materials and equipment, outlining who is responsible for what.

Table 1.2   Checklist for workshop preparation

	Information	*Name of person responsible*	*Done*
Start and finish			
Opening: name of manager			
Closing: name of manager			
Letter to participants			
Prior reading			
Participants please bring (diaries, data etc)			
Request participants to indicate special dietary or physical needs			
Administrative details			
Attendance sheets			
Name tags			
Special physical needs			
Catering			
Water/fruit juice			
Arrival tea/coffee			
Morning tea/coffee			
Lunch			
Afternoon tea/coffee			
Special dietary needs			
Fruit			
Handouts			
Workshop outline			
Evaluation sheet			

Table 1.2 *(Continued)*

	Information	Name of person responsible	Done
Other handouts			
Venue			
Rooms			
Room layout			
Semicircle of chairs			
Cafeteria style tables like spokes of a wheel			
Other			
Materials			
Flip chart paper			
Sticky dots (red, blue)			
Coloured card: colours, size, numbers			
Felt pens: red, black, blue			
Adhesive gum			
Masking tape: 1 cm wide, 2 cm wide			
Wide brown tape: 2½ cm wide			
Paper clips			
Bulldog clips			
Rubber bands			
Sticky-backed notes: yellow, blue, pink			
Scissors			
Stapler			
Other equipment			
Flip chart stand			
Overhead projector			
White board			
White board eraser			
Electronic white board			
Television			
Video recorder			
Digital camera			
Data show			
Lap tops			
Printers			
Sound/recording systems			

Participants

It is important that you check the attendance list. Do you have all the 'right' participants? Who are the stakeholders? Who has been left out? For example, do you need to invite: secretaries, cleaners, school keepers, parents, students, past clients, customers, members of the local community, children and teenagers? Yes, children and teenagers are often left out of decision-making processes that will impact on them.

Is the workshop compulsory or voluntary? Some workshops have compulsory attendance for training to do with new legislation, such as interview techniques or equal opportunity issues in the workplace. Discuss what is to be done regarding reluctant attendees. No one can/should be forced to learn and/or attend. Why?

Catering for diversity

Do not make assumptions about the group members; ask about disabilities. Many disabilities are not obvious. This information will be important when you are planning icebreakers and energizers. This will enable you to plan suitable icebreakers and activities that are inclusive of all participants. Hearing impairments are common with blue collar factory workers.

If the workforce is multicultural and/or multilingual, ask if some people will need to sit beside a friend who can translate when necessary. You may have to adjust your use of colloquialisms, and use written as well as verbal instructions.

Check food requirements. Increasing numbers of people require vegetarian food, while others may have allergies to wheat and/or dairy products.

Facilitator's roles

Check out the required roles of the facilitator. Are you being required to weed out hidden agendas? If so, how can you do this without compromising people who are willing to speak out? If management asks you to do something that it should take responsibility for, what will you do? I know of one organization that brought in consultants to break the news about redundancies, as managers were too scared to do the job themselves.

Advertising and promotion of the workshop

In designing the advertising of workshops, you must present the goals and processes honestly. For example, if you are advertising an innovative workshop with a variety of experimentation, you might want to add something like, 'This workshop is for the brave at heart, we will be experimenting in a number of areas,' or 'This course is for people who are experienced in interviewing techniques, but need to update as a result of recent changes to legislation in the area of. . .'. Let people know what they are 'buying into' so they can make informed choices. If there is a mismatch between the advertising and what is presented, people have a right to be frustrated.

You may also want to add ideas to ensure that all learning styles are represented, but you must deliver what you advertise. See Table 1.3.

Add information about the facilitator: your experience, style, and examples of past work in the area. This helps to establish your credibility with the group.

Table 1.3 Advertising messages

Advertising message	Learning style (Honey and Mumford, 1986)
You will be able to try out new strategies	Activist
You will be encouraged to think about your current work practice	Reflector
You will be given the results of the latest theories/ research on this area	Theorist
You will spend time discussing the relevance of the materials presented to your own work, and given opportunities to adapt ideas and develop action plans	Pragmatist

Making contact with the workshop group beforehand

Ask if it is possible to meet with the group members beforehand, to hear their version of what is needed. I often ask for a few minutes at the next staff meeting. This means that the individuals get to meet me beforehand, which makes the workshop easier as they are not meeting a complete stranger. Also I am less likely to miss issues. I usually pass around plenty of sticky-backed notes, and ask them to write one issue per note. This enables everyone to participate anonymously, and gives a first glimpse at the overall picture. Realistically, however, this is not always possible, in which case a needs analysis by e-mail or phone is the next best thing.

Summarize

During meetings, take time to look at your notes, read back ideas generated, pause. . . then listen again as more details flow.

Fees and costs

How much are you worth? This will depend on your amount of experience, reputation and what you are required to do, and the amount the client has to invest in achieving goals and/or solving problems. Some facilitators go with a straight market rate and charge the same amount per workshop day, which includes all preparation, meetings and so on. Other facilitators cost each workshop individually, and estimate an hourly rate for preparation and the like based on a formula. Remember you will not be available to work every day of the year.

Many people, including me, find it somewhat embarrassing to discuss money. Also it may be hard to know what to charge. Useful probing questions are 'What does your organization normally pay for a one day workshop?' and 'Do you have a fee structure?'

I used to feel very embarrassed about naming my workshop fee. A mentor advised, 'Do not say the fee first. Describe all the things you will be doing, then pause and say, 'For all this preliminary work *and* meetings *and* the workshop itself *and* handouts [pause] the total cost is $XXX.'

Companies on the whole do not hold workshops at weekends. This is good because we all need to value family/community time. Staff development I firmly believe should be valued as an integral part of the work place, and should be in company time. Most people probably can only 'charge out' their services for about 1,100 to 1,400 hours a year (Schaper and Volery, 2001).

CALCULATING FEES

Mary is a self-employed facilitator. She wants to earn a gross personal income similar to the one she earned in her last job in a company: $40,000 per annum. She operates her business from home, and estimates that it costs another $10,000 to cover expenses like stationery, phone calls, travel, insurance, Internet costs, books and so on. She therefore needs to earn $50,000 to maintain her income.

There are 52 weeks/year
Minus
   4 weeks holiday
   3 weeks public holiday
   4 weeks sickness
   1 week professional development

makes 40 working weeks per year.

Mary estimates that she can generate 1,200 hours work each year. Therefore her hourly rate will be $50,000/1,200. To be on the safe side, Mary should in round figures cost her time at $50 per hour.

A one-day workshop may take three days' preparation, research, meetings, reading, typing proposals, writing e-mails, making phone calls and so on. It would cost:

4 days x 8 hours per day = 32 hours
32 x $50 per hour = $1,600

Source: adapted from Schaper and Volery (2001).

Further information on costing

Web site: http://www.wa.imc.org.au/Benchmarking/Report.html

Cancellation issues

You may wish to discuss cancellation fees. This may sound harsh, but if you have refused work for a whole week to cater for a client who lets you down, you need to cover some of your time costs. Put agreements in writing.

Documentation of workshop data

Check how data will be documented and distributed after the workshop. Minutes need to be distributed quickly, within one week of the workshop, otherwise the momentum is lost. Ask:

- Who is responsible for typing up information on flip chart paper?
- Is it possible for a person who is not a participant to keep minutes on a laptop computer?
- Who will ensure accurate records/wall minutes are kept?
- Is there an electronic whiteboard?
- Who will disseminate data, and within what time, after the workshop?
- Is the facilitator responsible for producing a workshop report? If yes, what is the deadline and how many copies are required? (Time for this needs to be added into your budget).

STORY: CHECK WHAT IS REQUIRED BEFOREHAND

In a planning workshop in Lao PDR with 50 kindergarten administrators and teachers, we used two laptops: one with a Lao typist and the other with an English speaking typist. There were two facilitators: one Lao, one English (myself). I acted as co-facilitator, process adviser and typist. Issues were generated on cards in Lao. An interpreter sat beside me and whispered translations to me, but I was worried about the accuracy of her translation.

On the last evening of the three-day workshop the Lao facilitator back-translated the English ideas I had typed. We were both extremely weary, but we needed the data quickly. We also needed to work on it while it was fresh in our minds. The point is that we both made a mistake and had not realized that the contractor assumed we would write the reports. We had failed to clarify this issue, but we learnt from our experience.

Follow-up workshop

It is often useful for there to be a three or six-month follow-up workshop, to enable participants to give each other a progress report on the implementation and/or evaluation of strategies. This should be built into the contract. Often clients want to save money. However, you can still ensure that they set a date to meet autonomously to check on the rate of implementation of their action plans.

Checklist of agreements

At the end of negotiation it is useful to put into writing a list of agreement of who is responsible for doing what, when, and timelines. See Table 1.4.

Table 1.4   Checklist

Items	*Details*
Services to be provided	
Date/s of workshop and timelines	
Venue	
Preparation of venue	
Consumables to be supplied by	
Write up date/report	
Payment amount	
Payment due	
Cancellation fee	
Handling extra services	
Dispute resolution if required	

Converting a needs analysis to a draft workshop plan

Once you have conducted a needs assessment it is necessary to determine the overall aim of the workshop, then concentrate on planning processes that are most appropriate to enable the group to meet those aims.

Aims

An aim is usually written from the organization's point of view: for example, 'The aim of the workshop is to improve the effectiveness of weekly meetings'.

Workshop plans

A useful way to design a workshop is using the headings 'content', 'process' and 'time'. Facilitators need to develop a questioning framework to enable them to plan comprehensively for workshops and meetings. Frequently we focus on the content: that is, *what* is to be achieved? Rarely is enough time spent on *how* the participants will problem solve, plan and/or learn: that is, process, or on *how long* is needed to accomplish individual items. Doyle and Straus (1976) developed this in the context of meeting agenda preparation. It is directly suited to help facilitators plan workshops, so that they question themselves on exactly 'what' they want to achieve and 'how': that is, what process is going to help them facilitate the group to achieve its purpose.

I have found it particularly useful as a facilitator to frame the 'content' part as questions, and in my own version to add columns for group structures and equipment. See Table 1.5.

Table 1.5 Framework for workshop planning

Content What?	Process How?	Structure Grouping?	Equipment Materials?	Time How long?
1. What is the purpose of this workshop?	Explanation of purpose by the team leader or facilitator	Whole group	Handout of workshop plan Flip chart paper Masking tape Pens	9.00–9.10
2. What do you want to get out of today?	Paired interviews and round robin to collect ideas on flip chart paper Dot voting to rank order issues	Pairs Individual voting	Handout Coloured dots	9.10–9.20
3. How can we work together?	Contracting for desirable behaviours	Whole group	Flip chart paper Masking tape Pens	9.20–9.40

Source: Adapted from Doyle and Straus (1976)

How much information should be given to clients beforehand? Some facilitators have complained that on occasion they have submitted detailed workshop plans, did not get the job, but heard later that their ideas were used by the organization. Others say that such plans may be restrictive. It is a matter of personal facilitator style and experience, and the workshop focus and context.

Facilitators may wish to plan in different ways and use power in three ways:

● 'Hierarchical mode': that is, alone after consultation with clients. The framework can be circulated to participants for comment, to stimulate prior thinking and enhance ownership of the process. New facilitators tend to need more hierarchical plans, as it is harder to think creatively under pressure.
● 'Cooperative mode' with clients and participants.
● 'Autonomous mode': that is, delegated or seized planning power by participants. (For further explanation see the Heron model of facilitation styles, discussed in *Understanding Facilitation* Chapter 6.)

Jargon

Try to keep facilitator jargon to a minimum. Conversely, ask your clients about the jargon they use. You may need to develop a lexicon of 'in-house' terms, and/

or at the workshop keep a sheet of flip chart paper on the wall to build up new terms.

Questions regarding venue

Below is a list of questions to ask regarding the proposed venue:

- Is it possible for participants to meet off site, away from their normal workplace?
- Is the location easily accessible for everyone (public transport, parking etc)?
- What is the ambience like? Are there plenty of windows? Is the room light or heavy? Does it uplift or depress the spirit? Is the ambience oppressive: say, too corporate/plastic?
- Are the heating, air conditioning and ventilation adequate?
- Are the physical facilities right for the group and the processes you will use?
- Are chairs comfortable?
- Is there a large boardroom table in the way?
- What are the acoustics like? Is the location free from undue noise and other distractions?
- Can the space be used flexibly?
- Are there any 'house rules': for example, can flip-chart paper be displayed on the walls?

Second meeting: renegotiation

A second meeting may be required to fine-tune the structure (the content, process and time plan) and confirm and clarify understanding of issues. At the end of the contracting meetings the client and the facilitator should have:

- a clear summary of the desired outcomes of the workshop;
- mutual understanding of the possible problems/blockages to a successful workshop, and backup plans where necessary;
- an agreed list of roles and responsibilities.

The client should have plans to support, and to ensure that all relevant participants are invited with sufficient lead time to be present. These agreements may and often do change, but at least they are a start in achieving mutual understanding and support.

Preparing participants for a training workshop

If participants are not adequately prepared for a training workshop, some may arrive with 'the bulldog' look: that is, arms folded, passively aggressive, ready to take on the facilitator and the world in general. These people are often angry and do not want to be there. Sometimes there are people who feel hurt or devalued. Instead of being convinced by their managers that sending them on workshops is inviting their participation in decisions and/or investing in their skill development, some individuals see it as a punishment for not performing well enough, while others may think they know it all.

Figure 1.5 is an example of a 'pre-course questionnaire' which invites participants to talk to their bosses about their reasons for sending them on a course, ways of supporting them while on the course (for example, preventing phone interruptions), and methods for supporting their innovations and change on their return. The questionnaire also involves participants in thinking about what they personally want to get out of a workshop.

Only use this type of questionnaire if you are prepared to contract for individual needs at the beginning of the course. If you do not use the information, participants understandably will ask why they were asked to complete

---

Participants'
Pre-workshop preparation form

You are now booked into a workshop entitled   _____

Please ensure you complete this form and bring it with you on the first day of the workshop, as it will form the basis for you to get the most out of the programme. The facilitator will ask you to state your needs at the start of the workshop, and will endeavour, wherever possible, to ensure that the workshop is tailored to meet both your needs and the needs of your fellow participants.

Research shows that individuals and organizations get far more out of workshops when the participants and their managers thoroughly prepare aims beforehand and conduct a post course follow up.

Talk to your manager/boss/supervisor and ask the following:

1. Why am I being sent on this workshop? Is it:
- to develop my career path within the organization by learning new skills?
- to learn new systems or skills to maintain current performance levels?
- to get extra coaching – to raise my performance/skills in a particular area to an acceptable level?
- to ensure that my ideas contribute to future plans?
- to utilize my skills in problem solving?
- for any other reasons? _____

_____

2. What expectations do you have of me as a result of my attendance on this workshop? (That is, what changes in my behaviour will you expect to see?)

_____

_____

3. How will you support me in any changes I want to make (in my behaviour and/or work) when I return from the workshop?

_____

4. Is there any preparation you think I should do before the programme starts? (Other than completing this questionnaire or pre-reading sent out by the organizers.)

_____

5. When shall we meet on my return to:
● evaluate the workshop?
● agree on ideas for on-the-job application of new ideas/skills/strategies?

Questions to ask yourself

1. Why am I going on this workshop? What are my objectives?

_____
_____
_____
_____
_____

2. What arrangements and/or attitudes can I develop prior to and during the workshop to ensure that I get the maximum benefit from it?

_____
_____
_____
_____
_____

3. To what extent do I need to make time available in the evenings to revise notes or prepare materials?

_____
_____
_____
_____
_____

4. Do I need to make arrangements to cover my calls/work while I'm away?

_____
_____
_____
_____
_____

Please remember to bring this with you on the first day of the workshop.

Figure 1.5 Participants' pre-workshop preparation form

the forms in the first place. Niederman and Volkema (1999) surveyed 238 group facilitators, and found that, understandably, more experienced facilitators are likely to adapt agendas to take into account the needs of the group.

Preparing participants for an interactive meeting

Participants are better prepared for an interactive meeting if after your initial meetings with them, and before the meeting itself, they are sent a draft version of the meeting aims and stages using the headings content, process and time. This contributes to transparency and allows people to think about issues beforehand. Invite feedback by phone or e-mail.

The day before

The day before the actual workshop or meeting it is useful to ring the contact client and ask, 'Has anything changed since we last met?' If possible, visit the venue if it is new to you, and make sure you know how to work equipment beforehand.

After the workshop: follow-up with the client

Summarize evaluations from participants and your own evaluation, and send the summary and raw data to the client. If possible ensure that results are e-mailed to all participants. Some clients prefer to process their own evaluations. Follow up on feedback if necessary, and keep feedback on file for future use.

Mistakes and misunderstandings in consulting

Mistakes and misunderstandings between clients and facilitators may occur on both sides. Mistakes facilitators make when being engaged by a client include:

- not obtaining enough information from the client;
- failing to get to the real problem/hidden agendas;
- forgetting to check that all the people involved are invited;
- failing to check out the suitability of the room;
- agreeing to the client's suggested process when it may not be appropriate;
- not asking enough questions;
- forgetting to put agreements in writing;
- not allowing enough time for the chosen process/es;
- doing things for the group members that they should do for themselves;
- not allowing enough time for work after the workshop has finished.

Mistakes clients make when engaging facilitators include:

- asking facilitators 'to solve their problems';
- hidden agendas; going through the motions; window dressing;
- not including/allowing key stakeholders/decision makers to participate;
- giving unrealistic time frames for the desired outcomes; wanting a quick fix;
- not valuing the facilitator's services adequately;
- insufficient briefing;
- inappropriate facilitator for the job;
- insisting on inappropriate date/location;
- no allowance for research, training needs analysis/preparation;
- failing to be self-analytical;
- making an inadequate contract;
- continually adding to the original contract.

Keeping in contact with clients

Here are some tips for marketing your work:

- Design an interesting business card.
- Design different coloured business cards and give people a choice.
- Put your photo on the back of the card so people will remember what you look like.
- Design different business cards for the different kinds of areas you work in (easily printed now on personal computers).
- Join professional organizations in your field and consulting organizations.
- Keep an accurate, up-to-date database of names, addresses, e-mail addresses.
- Have a mobile phone so you are easily contactable (but turn it off when you are in a meeting with clients).
- Use an answerphone or phone and fax message service.
- Write journal and newspaper articles and give copies to clients.
- Write books or chapters in books.
- Produce audio and/or video tapes.
- Speak on local radio and television about a topic related to your work.
- Speak at conferences (but do not 'hard sell' yourself: get someone else to introduce you and give the accolades).
- Keep an up-to-date, one-page CV with a photo.
- Keep a list of workshops conducted in specific fields to attach to forthcoming proposals.
- Send clients a newsletter (by e-mail which saves trees) with ideas and tips and notes on your activities.
- Keep an up-to-date Web site (see below).

What other ideas can you think of?

Web site design

It is very useful to develop your own Web site. Here are a few pointers adapted from Elizabeth Castro's suggestions (2000). Ask yourself:

- What do I want to convey?
- Who is my audience?
- How can I tailor my content to appeal to my audience?
- How many pages will I need?
- Do I want readers to go through pages in sequence or be able to explore in any direction?
- How can I develop a simple naming system for my pages?

Hints

- Keep your Web site simple.
- Don't overdo the graphics, as your Web site will take too long to load and your readers will get impatient and move on.
- Once your Web site is established, keep it up to date.

Conclusion

In spite of all the ideas above, it is useful to remember there are many successful facilitators who do not have clear-cut business plans or fixed rates. Some facilitators who find the financial side of small businesses difficult and/or uninteresting often work in tandem with partners or colleagues who handle that side of the business. However, given all that, it does make sense to undertake courses in small business and/or consulting before giving up your 'day job'. When individuals hear about the 'feast or famine' issues in consulting, they may realize that the pressures are perhaps not for them, or conversely they may welcome the autonomy and the added adventures.

2

Beginning a workshop: contracting, icebreakers and developing trust

You only have one chance to make a first impression.

Source unknown

Introduction

At the beginning of workshops there is usually a need for introductions between participants and to find a way to 'break the ice'. People rarely get down to business immediately, even in established groups. The start of a workshop is like the overture in a concert, hopefully a relaxing taster or introduction of interesting things to come.

This chapter is divided into the following sections:

- preparation;
- introduction of facilitator and building rapport;
- clarifying the purpose of the workshop;
- contracting for needs and ground rules;
- the emotional side of group formation;
- icebreakers;
- learning names;
- building trust;
- forming small groups;
- energizers.

Many activities have been passed on around the world through networking and are now in the facilitation/training domain, so it is now difficult to attribute references for some.

Prepare: the P7 principle

There is an easy mnemonic I learnt from a friend and colleague, Peter Adamson, many years ago which might energize you as you wade through the hard work of preparing a workshop. It consists of seven words beginning with P:

Prior preparation and planning prevents piss poor performance.

If a workshop looks easy and effortless it usually means there has been a tremendous amount of forethought and preparation. There are no short cuts, but thorough preparation is useful investment of time and energy.

Room preparation

Wherever possible, facilitators need to assess the venue and the workshop room beforehand. The ambience is important. Although many workshops are conducted in hotels, my personal preference is for less formal situations. Ideally I prefer rooms that are light and airy, with windows so participants can see out to the sky, preferably located with an outside area for walks in the fresh air at breaks. I also prefer to have one long white wall for flip chart paper, cards and visual displays. Although some people prefer to have flip chart stands, I prefer to keep things simple (and there are times when stands are not available or sometimes they collapse!).

The day of the workshop

Readiness is a state of mind as well as arranging the physical layout of a room and equipment to suit your purposes. I like to arrive early, at least an hour and a half before the start time, to set up the room, music, flip charts and so on. Then I have time to centre (calm myself), have a drink and go to the washroom before participants arrive. I plan for some things to take more time than expected, as often rooms need rearranging and so on. One facilitator I met in the United Kingdom liked to 'clear the air' in a room before participants arrived. He would go to the four corners and invoke peace in case there were negative vibrations from previous occupants.

My aim is to ensure that when the first participants walk in the door I am finished preparing, so I can greet and talk to them. I find this most beneficial in that I can make links with some individuals before we start. I often glean useful information and/or stories about them and their organization. It also seems more polite: if I am dashing around the room moving furniture and pinning up paper, they may feel ignored and unwelcome.

Room layout

Regarding room layout, for small groups of up to 18 people, semicircles or circles are best. However, a big circle of 25 people can be quite intimidating for some, so it is best to divide the group around cafeteria-style tables organized like the spokes of a wheel pointing towards the front of the room. If there is space it is useful to have a semicircle of chairs at the front and cafeteria-style tables at back. The movement of positions and availability of flexible group structures can be very useful.

Music and mood

Music helps to 'fill a room' with welcoming sound. Of course tastes in music differ, but it does form a talking point and also means people do not have to whisper in a silent, echoey room. Some music can create a receptive, enthusiastic and energetic mood, while other quieter forms like baroque (Bach, Vivaldi, Telemann) can create a more reflective mood (see Chapter 4).

Refreshments

When we want to make newcomers to our homes feel welcome, we give them a cup of tea or coffee. The same applies for workshops. The act of pouring a drink enables participants to mix, socialize, and reduces tension. For 'non-morning' people, the early morning 'cuppa' is an important part of waking up. An urn bubbling away all day at a workshop is a welcome sight.

Food

People appreciate being pampered, but over eating stifles energy. At one of the best workshops I attended a local woman did all the catering, which included really interesting salads, fruit and breads, as well as an array of cold meats and cheeses.

Displays

Depending on the theme of the workshop, displays of pictures, posters and sayings can stimulate thinking and discussion. In rooms that are rather like concrete boxes I hang colourful sarongs. In one workshop I attended with Fran Peavey, I noted she asked participants to bring something to make the room feel more hospitable. Participants displayed their wares, and the results were delightful and creative. The variety of objects also stimulated conversations between strangers.

Developing presence

> If you walk, just walk.
> If you sit, just sit.
> But whatever you do, don't wobble.
>
> Unmon, a Zen Master.

In order not to 'wobble' you need to be thoroughly prepared, and the workshop room needs to be ready when everyone arrives. The idea of presence stems from the concept of 'aikido', the Japanese martial art. 'Ai' means harmony, 'ki' means energy and 'do' means the way. So 'aikido' means the harmonizing of energies of the body, mind and spirit. It means focusing your thoughts, feeling balanced and fully in the moment.

Centring exercise

A strategy that I learnt from John Heron, which I use with trainee facilitators, is to place your hand on your body's centre or 'hara' (your hara is a couple of inches below your navel) and say, 'I am present in my belly'. Place your hand on your heart and say, 'I am present in my heart'. Place your hand on your larynx and say, 'I am present in my voice' (you should feel your tone of voice start to drop). Place your hand on your forehead and say, 'I am present in my head' while realigning your head and shoulders and spine. Finally say, 'I am fully present' (Heron, 1999).

To centre yourself, at the beginning of a workshop or before making an intervention (see Chapter 6), take a few moments to breathe slowly and deeply. Say to yourself, 'I choose to be centred', or a mantra of your choice. Let your stomach muscles relax, unlock your jaws, and send your concentration to your centre. It helps if you place your fingers lightly on your 'hara' as a physical reminder.

If you are feeling centred and confident it also helps you to feel fully present. In that way you can then almost divorce yourself from your own issues, so you can focus totally on the group and the task at hand.

Getting attention

When you wish to start, you will have to gain everyone's attention. When you are ready to begin it is useful to take a deep breath to centre or ground yourself, and begin with a slightly raised voice and slow words. Often people realize it is time to settle down, and talking naturally diminishes.

A simple, unobtrusive way to attract attention in a very large group is to raise your hand in the air and invite others to do the same. Quickly others notice and copy, until you have everyone's attention. This strategy was used in cub groups, but is also used in environmental groups as a non-hierarchical way to gain attention.

Another way for fun is to have a collection of duck calls, gongs, bells or rattles. One strike of a small cymbal is useful to calm everyone down. Noise seems to diminish as the resonance of the cymbal fades.

Facilitator introduction and building rapport

During the introduction time it is useful to make time to explain:

- a little about your personality and background;
- your style of and background in facilitating;
- your expectations about how the workshop should go, regarding proposed processes (see questions and changes or agreement to these), but emphasize that outcomes will be generated by participants.

Facilitators need to build and maintain empathy: that is, rapport and connectedness with participants. We all build empathy in different ways; there are no hard and fast rules. Some people are naturally empathic; others need to learn to develop their own approaches. Think about facilitators/speakers you have observed who were naturally empathic. What were some of the things they did? How did you feel as a result? Think about people you have seen who were unempathic. What did they do or not do? How did you feel as a result?

I am not advocating that facilitators should be in the entertainment business or popularity stakes, although we do need fun exercises to energize and motivate participants. I am suggesting that there is a need to make connections as human beings before venturing into the journey of learning and discovery together. Developing empathy is normal, polite human behaviour in one to one and one to small group encounters in most cultures, so why shouldn't it be normal in one to large group situations? I have met facilitators who admit they have walked into workshops without building in time for icebreakers. I believe there are many possible reasons for this approach: shyness, keenness to 'get on with the job', nerves, unawareness, forgetfulness, and perhaps in a few instances, arrogance.

Building trust: Coke

Social relationships of all types rely on trust. Trust is fragile. It is built up slowly but may be destroyed in an instant. Once lost it takes time to rebuild, or may never be regained. Recent changes in organizations under a number of euphemisms like downsizing, rightsizing and restructuring may have eroded the trust of workers in management. Participants need to feel trust in the facilitator and the institutions involved in workshops. Trustworthiness builds when there is a perception of fairness and fair play.

The acronym 'Coke' was developed by Covello (1992) and Peters and his co-workers (1977) as a result of their research into how scientists, engineers and planners, in their roles as facilitators, can build trust and empathy with adults in community meetings about environmental risk and health issues. Sometimes meetings are attended by angry, frustrated and/or fearful people. Hence it is important that scientists, engineers and planners who facilitate these meetings are able to build and maintain empathy and trust. Covello and Peters and co-workers found that there were four main attributes of successful community facilitators:

C: Commitment
O: Openness
K: Knowledge
E: Empathy.

Their research indicates that empathy is the most important of the four attributes. Table 2.1 contains space for you to prepare your opening comments relating to the COKE acronym described above.

Table 2.1   COKE

Explanation	*Your ideas*
C Commitment: ● to the subject area; ● to facilitation; ● to participants etc.	eg 'I'm dedicated to trying to help participants be involved in decisions that affect them and their workplace.'
O Openness: ● approachability and contact in and out of the workshop room; ● openness to questions; ● ground rules.	eg 'Please feel free to ask questions or raise issues at any stage, or if you prefer, talk to me at the coffee break if you wish to raise an issue in private.'
K Knowledge: ● experience; ● research in the subject (don't overdo this, unless it is important to establish your credibility).	eg 'I've been involved in strategic planning work for. . . years.' eg 'I've been working and researching into the community impact of environmental pollution issues for xxx years.'
E Empathy: ● getting on the same wavelength as participants, making connections; ● building rapport.	eg in a room full of educators, 'My father was a school principal,' or in a room full of community workers, 'I used to work with unemployed': find some link with participants.

There are a number of aspects that impact on behaviour of both participants and facilitators during their first encounter; all feel some degree of tension or even nerves. Participants watch our body language and 'size us up' from the minute they see us, walking down the corridor, entering the workshop room, or even in the washrooms.

Some hints

There is a fine dividing line between saying too much and saying too little. Prepare what you want to say, but too much rehearsal may lead to a stilted introduction. I find it is best to be as natural as possible, and to bring in elements about my connections to the subject and the participants and myself, interspersed with information about the workshop.

Remember physical barriers: standing behind a chair or table creates psychological barriers. On the other hand, sitting on a desk may appear rude to people from some cultures.

Take your time, wait to get everyone's attention and talk slowly. Humour helps! An anecdote about your own experience as a participant (ie openness) can raise a smile. Your tone of voice is as important as your body language. If you say, 'This is my favourite subject' in a monotone, you will not be believed.

Look around the room at participants' faces. Make eye contact with as many as possible. Don't stare out of the window or down at the floor as you speak. Smile as you speak, when appropriate, but not if you are addressing serious issues, because if your body language and verbal messages contradict each other, the participants will notice immediately and distrust you. When all else fails, relax and enjoy yourself. Allow yourself to be 'you', at the same time showing your enthusiasm for the workshop topic and/or process.

The way you start a workshop sets the tone for consequent interactions between you and your participants. If you develop empathy with your participants, not only will they interact with you in a more positive way, they will also be more motivated about the workshop.

Introducing the workshop

> The best impromptu speeches are the ones written well in advance.
>
> Ruth Gordon

It may be useful to have a senior person to welcome everyone and briefly highlight the purpose of the workshop. This indicates commitment by senior management. I have emphasized the word 'briefly', as there is nothing worse than the beginning of a workshop being taken over by a manager who likes to hear his/her own voice and/or who may alienate the participants. If you suspect this may happen, either brief the person carefully or do not invite him or her to speak first.

The purpose of the workshop

> If you don't know where you're going, you may end up somewhere else.
>
> Source unknown

Display the purpose and workshop plan, written up on flip chart paper, as an aide memoire for you and the group. This means you don't have to go and look at notes. If the participants have contributed to the planning of the workshop, and seen the plan already, there is less likelihood of any surprises on the day of the workshop. However, it is often useful to fine-tune what the workshop is all about.

Most people have a strong inbuilt need for 'fair play'. Trust is built by being honest, open, accountable and transparent. If you are seeking 'substantive consensus', that is, that everyone agrees with decisions, it is important upfront at the beginning to decide what decision-making process you will use if consensus is not reached. Not reaching consensus is not 'bad' or 'failure'. In reality, in a pluralist society it is hard to reach consensus, but if people have been involved in developing and learning about the processes used, they are more likely to participate and accept the results. In other words, 'procedural consensus' is part of establishing trust. It means that the processes are fair and open.

Expectations

Next you need to find out what participants want to gain personally from a workshop, even if you have asked this before at pre-workshop meetings. Ask:

Why are *you* here today?
What do *you* want to get out of this session?

Notice the 'you' is in italics. I suggest the facilitator uses the pronoun 'you' rather than 'we' to differentiate the facilitator and participant roles. The issues and solutions of the workshop belong to the participants. If relevant, ask participants to refer to the pre-course preparation sheet outlined in Chapter 1.

Contracting

Group and individual needs

Even though needs analyses are often conducted before a workshop, it is often very useful to ask participants what they want to get out of the workshop. If this is posed as a question to the whole group, there is usually a long embarrassed silence. But if you ask participants to interview each other in pairs, lively discussions ensue. If the workshop is focused on capacity building, I distribute handouts with three questions, as shown in Figure 2.1.

Name _____

At the end of this workshop:

1. What do you want to be able to do? (skills)

2. What do you want to know? (knowledge)

3. How do you want to feel? (attitudes)

Figure 2.1   Handout for contracting for individual needs

The interviewer must write down the answers and hand back the sheet to the owner of the ideas. (These can also be collected later.)

Once both participants have had time to state their needs:

- Ask for one idea per couple and 'round robin' the group.
- List ideas on flip chart paper, leaving a 10 cm margin down the left side.
- Give participants three adhesive dots each and ask them to choose three separate items.
- Invite the whole group to go and place their dots on three different items on the flip chart paper down the left-hand side. (Remind them *not* to place dots on the white board as they are hard to remove! This happened once and the results were hilarious).

If you think people may be swayed by others seeing where they place their dots, and depending on the issues that may arise, you may want to number the topics, and ask people to write the topic number of each dot before leaving their seats to place their dots on the butcher paper. The data gathered gives the facilitator and the participants a clearer view of individual needs *and* the whole picture.

Contracting requires openness from the facilitator, and he/she may need to point out areas that may only be touched on, or that are outside the brief and/or skills of the facilitator. These things should be mentioned here, otherwise participants may have their expectations dashed, and a facilitator will lose credibility. Participants may then be cynical about the contracting process at their next workshop. Do not invite input if there is no scope for attending to individual and group needs.

Contracting for desirable ground rules

The way in which a facilitator starts a workshop sets the 'tone'. He/she can invite people to be open, to tell their stories, to state their needs. There can be implied commands: 'This will work well if today you. . .'.

All groups quickly develop 'norms', rules of behaviour which impact on the way people behave, interact and dress. It is useful to involve participants in generating and discussing ground rules. This process lets everyone know where he or she stands, and also helps the facilitator make effective interventions later on, if behaviour becomes dysfunctional. A list of ground rules is like a contract. (See Figure 2.2.)

As suggestions are generated, check that they are acknowledged and accepted by all the participants. Do not assume agreement. Ask:

- How does that sound?
- Can you live with this?
- Does anyone want to make any changes and/or additions to this?

For workshops that cover many days, it is useful to keep the ground rules on display at every workshop, and sometimes to review them and ask the group members to evaluate their progress in keeping to these rules.

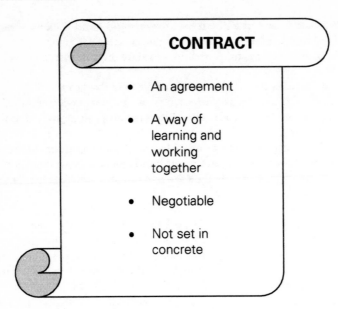

Figure 2.2   A facilitation contract

Here are some examples collected from many sources. You would not need to generate so many, but knowing that they exist as possibilities might be useful:

- Join in discussions.
- Be punctual. (If late, enter quietly; do not disturb others.)
- Start and end sessions on time.
- One person speaks at a time, no side talking.
- Actively listen to one another.
- Respect confidentiality: personal stories remain within the group.
- Turn off mobile phones and beepers.
- Respect difference in ways of being, values, ideas.
- Celebrate success.
- Have fun.
- Help the recorder to keep accurate wall minutes; check that your ideas are recorded as accurately as possible.
- Make needs known, for example for stretch breaks.
- Speak for yourself. Say 'I think/believe', rather than infer that the whole group thinks one way.

In workshops that require movement, ask participants to tell you quietly if they have any physical problems or if they are on medication. In this way if a participant has a disability you can cater for his/her needs without the rest of the group knowing there is a problem.

Discuss confidentiality issues. Ask individuals not to mention names of organizations or people, and to keep stories within the four walls of the room to preserve anonymity.

I find that contracting sets up dialogue between me and the participants about areas of mutual concern. Spending time on contracting is investment in the future, as participants and the facilitator know where they stand.

I usually add 'the right to say "no"' for discussion: in other words, any individual can decide to watch an exercise, not participate, if he/she so chooses. I add, 'Sometimes it takes more courage to say "No" than to go along with the group'. This issue is discussed further in Chapter 11.

Lastly, determine what are the rules for changing and/or adding to the rules. Add to ground rules as new issues arise. Use positive reinforcement: praise participants for ground rules they keep. Firmly draw participants' attention to ground rules that are broken. This can be done easily by merely pointing to a particular rule.

Energy levels

I find that when I am facilitating my energy levels are high. However, participants do need frequent breaks and/or changes of activity to enable them to maintain concentration. I find it useful to invite participants to let me know when they need a break. There are different sorts of breaks, all of which are useful:

- stand and stretch, or energizer;
- pause for a joke or silly question or anecdote;
- tea/coffee/loo breaks.

Psychological somnambulism

At the contracting stage of the workshop you may wish to invite a participant to strike a cymbal to remind all the participants to come back to the 'here and now' and stop 'psychological somnambulism': that is, sleepwalking during our interactions with others, so we are unaware of our behaviour, our motives and its effects (Heron, 1999).

Smoking

The laws in Australia now make smoking in most workshop venues illegal. Still, if this is likely to be an issue it may be useful to bring it up at the beginning, and to find an area outside for smokers, so that non-smokers are not subjected to passive smoking.

Alcohol

Drinking alcohol is a way of relaxing and socializing. Indeed it is often how workers socialize, do 'shop talk' and network. However, we know that it affects people by at first heightening and later dampening feelings. Excessive alcohol leads to headaches and muddied thinking, and behaviours different from 'normal', whatever that may be. Hangovers may also impact on the whole group during residential programmes. Colma Keating (2002) suggests that you openly discuss alcohol, and the individual responsibilities participants have to themselves and the group.

To contract or not to contract for ground rules?

To contract or not to contract is an interesting question. There are some facilitators who maintain that no ground rules should be drawn up, as they inhibit
true behaviours. They say it is better to let the group run its normal course, then
when and if behaviour becomes dysfunctional, intervene. I believe this can be
detrimental to the group and to some individuals. It leaves the facilitator having
to work from negatives rather than from positive behaviours which can be built
on. Often facilitators are called in when a group is dysfunctional, and I believe
the contracting stage is a chance to indirectly get the group to describe ground
rules (which they may never have discussed before).

The emotional side of group formation

Let us first look at feelings from the point of view of the participants. Ask
yourself, 'How do I feel when I join a new group?' Of course reactions will
depend on the type of group, but words like 'excited', 'anxious', 'shy', 'nervous'
and 'energized' may spring to mind. The sort of questions that may go through
people's minds when joining a new group are:

- Who are the others?
- What are they going to be like?
- Will it be useful?
- What will the facilitator be like?
- What are we going to be asked to do?
- Will I fit in?
- Will they like me?
- Will it be fun?
- Will I be able to meet people with similar interests as me?
- Will it be boring and a waste of time and money?

Icebreakers

Time spent on a well-chosen, suitable icebreaker is 'investment time' designed
to enhance effective interaction. An icebreaker is a short process or structured
activity, about 10–15 minutes in length, designed to:

- enhance introductions;
- put participants and facilitator at ease with one another;
- encourage early interaction (West, 1997);
- generate energy and enthusiasm for the work ahead.

Choosing appropriate icebreakers

There are many books and Web sites that provide a wide variety of warm-up
exercises. The problem is, there is rarely any accompanying evaluation of

possible serendipitous outcomes, so I have included a checklist to help you to choose exercises that are appropriate to your group and your own facilitation style. (Also see Chapter 5 on cross-cultural issues.)

If you consider how most people feel when joining a new workshop, it is often best to keep icebreakers as simple as possible: it is normal to feel awkward. It is also usual for the facilitator to feel some degree of anxiety, depending on the job in hand and the type of group. Emotions may build barriers between group members and/or between the facilitator and the group.

Bart Dahmer wrote an article entitled 'Kinder, gentler icebreakers' (Dahmer, 1992) in which he describes joining his wife at antenatal classes. When they were asked to meet another couple, find out about them, and introduce them to the group, he describes his embarrassment (and the other couple's) as he stumbled through half-digested information about a person he had only met for a few minutes. There is another issue with this common form of icebreaker. When a person is speaking, the participants obviously look at the speaker. They take in information about the person the speaker is describing, but attach the wrong face to that information. In addition, the people who are being talked about may feel irritated if their details are wrongly given to the group.

If the workshop content and/or processes are new for the facilitator, a simple, appropriate icebreaker serves to put the facilitator at ease too! As a facilitator I usually join in ice breakers (unless I want to observe dynamics or watch for safety reasons). I don't ask participants to do anything I'm not prepared to do myself.

As a rule, small group activities and those where everyone is engaged at once are least threatening, and should be used before you ask people to speak in front of the whole group. Try to link icebreakers to the theme of the workshop. So for example, at a creativity workshop you could bring in a variety of props such as hats and scarves, and invite people to introduce themselves in a creative way.

Imagine a video of icebreakers in your mind beforehand, so you can estimate their duration (which may cause you to eliminate some as too time-consuming). For example, if you want each participant to answer four questions about themselves you may need to allow about three to four minutes each. If there are 30 participants you could use up 90 minutes. It is useful if you go first, to give an idea of how much detail you require. You can tell participants, 'You have a maximum of four minutes each, after which I'll ring a bell so we can ensure that everyone has equal air time'.

Here is a checklist for evaluating icebreakers adapted from Pike and Jones work on effective training (1994):

- Does it help to bring people together physically, mentally (and perhaps spiritually)?
- Does it help people to be more comfortable with each other?
- Does it facilitate networking?
- Is it relevant to the workshop: can participants see a logical tie-in between the opening, icebreakers and the workshop itself?
- Does it maintain or enhance self-esteem?
- Is it fun for the facilitator and the participants?

- Does it arouse people's curiosity and energy?
- Will it include everyone?
- Is there enough space?
- Is it safe physically and emotionally?
- How long will it realistically take?
- Is it suitable for the size and composition of the group?

Introductions

It is useful to 'round robin' the group and ask participants to say their names, job role, and organization (if applicable). If the facilitator goes first, you can role model how long you anticipate this to take. As each person has spoken, thank him/her and repeat his/her name.

In larger groups this exercise may take too much time, so you can do an alternative exercise by asking, 'Hands up those from XXX area/department'. [Pause] 'Welcome! Hands up those from XXX area/department. . . Welcome. Have I missed anyone? … Oh, welcome. Where are you from?' In this way everyone in the room feels as if you have welcomed them, even if they haven't each had a chance to speak yet. Alternatively, ask people to introduce themselves to others at their table.

Humour

Humour is a major factor which increases enjoyment in groups. It can help people relax during an icebreaker and lift tension, or it can just be something that springs from the group as part of the general joie de vivre. Hopson and Scally (1981) suggested the following criteria. Humour should be:

- Inclusive. In-jokes by one group can exclude others. It should not be one group laughing at the expense of others. In this area racist, ageist and/or sexist jokes may be offensive.
- Well timed and intermittent. If the group goes into continual rounds of humour where people are trying to cap each other, people may go into 'flight'. Humour should lubricate the group's work, rather than 'clog the mechanism' (Hopson and Scally, 1981: 170).

See also the comments on humorous songs and so on in Chapter 3. West (1997) has gathered a variety of icebreakers and exercises just for pure fun.

Learning names

Many people, facilitators included, find it hard to remember names, especially when everyone is a little tense at the forming stage of a group. Do not assume that names are learnt immediately. It may take more than one activity before everyone learns all the names of the group members.

Remembering names

One way to help with memorization of names is to ask individuals to state their name and a mnemonic for remembering it. It helps if the facilitator is ready with his/her own example, such as, 'My name is Isabella, the name of a Queen of Spain,' or 'My name is Bevan and I've got a place reserved in heaven'. After an individual states his/her name, ask the whole group together to repeat the mnemonic for each person: for example, 'Hello Isabella, the name of a queen of Spain', 'Hi Bevan who's got a place in heaven'. An alternative is to use the first letter of the alphabet, as in, 'My name is Chris and I like chocolate', 'My name is Aphay and I like apples'. When everyone has spoken, round robin the group with everyone repeating the names and mnemonics.

It is useful to get everyone somehow to say something no matter how simple, within the first 15 minutes.

Name tag distribution

Distribute to participants one name tag each, *not* their own. If some people are late, give some participants one extra nametag. Ask participants to find the person who owns the name on the tag, and invite them to spend some time getting to know the person they meet. If any tags are left over, ask the people with the extra nametags to greet, and distribute them to, newcomers on arrival. (This has the added bonus that latecomers who may feel embarrassed are welcomed by a group member as well as yourself.)

Name meanings

See Chapter 5 on cross-cultural groups.

Throwing a ball

This exercise is useful after everyone has heard names once. It is best to divide participants into small groups of say six people. Ask them to 'number off' from 1 to 6 and remember their number. Remind people not to throw too hard. Use a soft ball or toy. The thrower says, 'I'm Chris, hello Jane,' and throws the ball to Jane. The catcher says, 'Thanks Chris, I'm Jane, hello Jim,' and so on. In Asia, it is easy to buy light bamboo balls in a variety of sizes that are usually used for street games. In one group, a man brought in a cuddly toy cat, called 'Tiddles', which the group threw to each other to learn names. The group named the activity 'Tossing Tiddles', which caused great mirth, and the cat was incorporated into a number of activities during the life of that group.

When the participants have learnt all the names in their small group, ask numbers 1 to 3 to move to the next group clockwise, and so on. Later you can ask an individual from one group to throw to someone in the next group, and the ball can be passed around the room, building up the complexity of the activity. More balls can be added to add humour, noise and a little chaos. (Make sure cups and saucers are out of the way.)

Continuum formation

Ask participants to line up in a continuum in a curve so each person can see everyone else's face. (Note that in some cultures, for example the Aboriginal culture, there are issues about meeting the direct gaze of others according to status and/or gender codes of behaviour.) You can ask participants to line up according to a number of different factors depending on the focus of the workshop, such as:

- Distance travelled to attend the workshop (shortest to longest).
- Alphabetical order of first names (A–Z).
- Sequence of birthdays starting from January to December. (Do not ask for age seniority. Why? See also Chapter 5 on cross-cultural issues.)
- From 0–100 per cent according to how much energy and enthusiasm they felt when they woke up that morning and realized they were attending a workshop that day. This activity is a useful way for facilitators to gauge feelings and attitudes of participants for the tasks ahead. In one workshop, a person who did not want to be present actually made his feelings known by opening the door and standing outside the room. This was really useful, since that resistance (its cause and possible solutions) could be discussed early on.
- Number of years experience in a particular field (from new to experienced people). (See also group formation at the end of the chapter.)

Occasionally a participant may stand in front of another person, so ask him or her to move along so everyone can see one another.

There are at least three issues of caution regarding the use of continua to sort people in terms of experience:

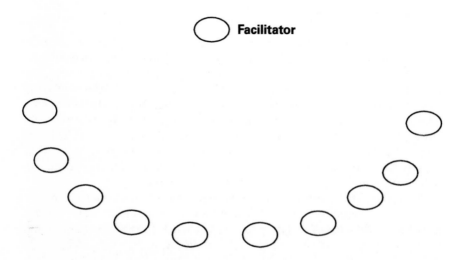

Figure 2.3   Continuum formation

- Be careful not to make assumptions. Remember that 10 years of experience for some may have been the same year repeated 10 times.
- In places where people are promoted by virtue of politics or connections, this could cause major embarrassment or resentment from some.
- It could turn out to be disguised age grading and embarrassing for some, especially if age is being used as a criterion when choosing candidates for redundancy in downsizing.

Point out how useful it is to have newcomers in the group, as they bring new perspectives, experiences and often ask useful and different questions, whereas the more experienced may take things for granted or because of ego, not wish to show their ignorance in front of others. Ross James adds a useful stage and adds up the total years of experience of each person in the whole group: see Chapter 5.

Cultural backgrounds: map of the world

Explain that the participants need to stand on an imaginary map of the world according to where they were born. Show them where the points of the compass are, north, south, east and west by pointing to each wall in turn. When people have found 'their birthplace' ask them to introduce their name, place of birth, and how they journeyed to the country you are now working in. Acknowledge people from other cultures or those who have a different cultural heritage as useful 'cultural advisers' to the group.

Group structures

The physical arrangement of groups will impact on the ensuing dynamics. Ask yourself:

- What is the purpose of the group?
- What do I want to achieve?
- How will I physically arrange the group members to enable them to achieve their task?
- What is the composition of the group (age, status, gender balance etc)?
- Do I want to involve the group in deciding about seating arrangements?
- Should I prearrange the seating (to bring some people together, or to split others)?
- What is the size of the group? (See also 'Group size' in *Understanding Facilitation*, Chapter 8).

Variations in size and layout

Small groups: dyads (2)

Paired discussions maximize interaction and are least threatening. This is especially useful for 'paired interviews' where one person listens and the other questions; then roles are reversed. This structure:

- helps quieter participants;
- maximizes participation and 'air time' per person;
- is very useful at the beginning of workshops when tensions are higher;
- helps meetings when discussions get 'bogged down'.

If there are two or more particularly vociferous power holders in the group, I try to ensure they are paired together.

Triads (3) and fours

Triads and groups of four also give more input and variety of ideas.

Circle of chairs

The circle represents the concept of equality (King Arthur seated his knights in a circle to eliminate the sense of hierarchy). Facilitator and participants have equal space and height. The circle is a feminine symbol, as opposed to straight lines representing the masculine. It is associated with the idea of a protected or sacred space where all participants are equal. (Traditional dances were circular in many cultures (Walker, 1988).) Circles are used for restorative justice and open space workshops, and concentric circles can be used to accommodate groups of up to 500 people (see Chapter 12).

A large circle of 25 people will feel intimidating for some participants, whereas a circle of about 15 people is much more intimate.

Semicircle or horseshoe

Participants sit in a semicircle focusing on the facilitator, who can record ideas on flip chart paper. This is a useful shape for the facilitator to direct attention and contentious issues on to flip chart paper, rather than for participants to direct them at each other, which may happen in circular formations.

Table groups

These are useful for small group discussions of five to six people. Participants can spread out materials and lean on a table (this often helps people with back trouble). Circular tables of a maximum of 5 feet are best to accommodate open interaction for up to eight people.

Three-ring circus

Three or more groups are engaged in different activities simultaneously. They complete different tasks, then at a given signal rotate activities, so that eventually all have visited each workstation. A flip chart stand is provided at each workstation. See Figure 2.4

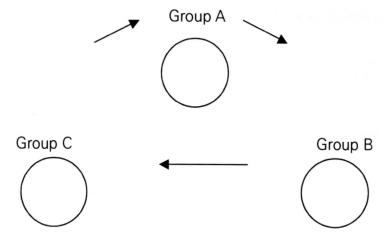

Figure 2.4   A three-ring circus

Processes for forming groups

It can be helpful to have a number of strategies to enable participants to form groups of different sizes, to reduce the risk of some people being left out, and to enable participants to work with people other than their friends or close colleagues. The easiest way to form ad hoc groups is to ask people to 'number off' according to the group size you want. For example, if you want to form groups of four people and there are 32 people in the room, ask one person to say 'one', the next 'two', then 'three' up to eight, then start again 'one', ' two' until everyone has a number. Ask the 'number ones' to raise their hands and spot one another, then indicate the part of the room you wish them to meet in. Repeat for each of the four groups. You can also use letters of the alphabet, fruits or even animals, and if appropriate ask people to make the noise of the animal to meet their fellow creatures. The resulting farmyard cacophony raises a laugh.

Self-select groups

Individuals choose the people they want to work with. These groups usually start with higher trust levels than groups where people do not know each other. However, individuals do not meet new people, and their creativity may be impaired by 'groupthink'. Individuals who are not selected may feel embarrassed.

Options groups

Either the facilitator or preferably the group generates topics, and participants 'vote with their feet' and join a group topic they feel passionate about. This maximizes motivation and autonomy.

Designated groups

The facilitator decides on small group composition based on the goals of the workshop. Or there may be a need to split up certain individuals or bring certain people together. In some hierarchical cultures it may be useful to put together people of the same rank.

Parts of a whole

Christmas cards, post cards or playing cards may be cut into the required number of pieces linked to group size. Or if you wish five people in each group, the different lines from various limericks may be used. (It is useful if you can find limericks (rhyming songs) that relate to the issues of the workshop.)

Forming pairs: opposites

Participants have to find their other half. Give all participants a note with the name of an item that has a pair, and ask them to find their other half. Examples include: 'gin and tonic', 'right and wrong', 'win and lose', 'husband and wife', 'male and female', 'yin and yang'. This icebreaker can be used to link up to the issues of extremes of thinking and dualism in Western thought. It may be used to initiate conversations on the differences between dialogue (that is, exploration of ideas) and debate, in which new ideas are often lost in heated win-lose tactics.

New groups from existing ones

To form the same number and size of groups as there are already, keep the participants in their current groups and give each person in the group a different number, colour or name from the other members of that group.

To form groups of a different size, keep the participants in their groups as before, making sure you have the same number of different numbers, colours or names as the number of groups you require. Organize the cards into order, for example blue, red, green, yellow, and repeat, or Smith, Jones, Patel, Lee, and repeat. Deal out the cards round the groups, carrying straight on from one group to the next. If the change is to larger groups, not everyone can be in a completely new group.

Forming groups with certain characteristics

You may wish to get participants into groups of varying sizes in an ad hoc fashion, or with various criteria in mind: for example a mix of learning styles, or cross-cultural groups (see Chapter 5).

Learning styles

If you wish to form groups with a mixture of learning styles it is useful to administer the Honey and Mumford 'Learning styles questionnaire' (1992) beforehand, and formulate groups with a mix of people whose dominant style is activist, reflector, theorist or pragmatist.

Team roles

Likewise the Team Roles Questionnaire (Belbin, 1993) may be used for formulating teams with mixed skills. Research by Belbin on teams and McCarthy (1980) on learning styles has shown that it is better to form groups with a mixture of learning styles/ways of being. This is similar to patterns in nature: monoculture is too unwieldy in times of disease or stress.

Note that these questionnaires are only a guide to behaviour. People are very complex animals and behaviour is always influenced by the environment and the topic in hand! Also take care that participants do not start to label one another, as this may limit their behaviour and thinking.

Mix of experience in a particular field

Ask participants to form a continuum, starting from no experience at one end of the room to 50 years experience at the other end. This technique is useful at the beginning of a training programme, where you are wishing to get an idea of past experience in a particular topic, and wanting to form work groups with people with a mixture of experience.

Mix of cultural backgrounds

Ask participants to form a continuum, starting from those born closest to the workshop location and moving to those born farthest away. If there are 32 participants and you want to have groups of four, ask them to number off from 1 to 8. Ask all the 'ones' to meet together, the 'twos' and so on, and you will end up with eight groups of four people with different cultural backgrounds.

Sameness

In some hierarchical societies or organizations it is often difficult for people lower in the hierarchy to speak, especially if their ideas are not the same as their bosses'. In Lao PDR we preordained the seating for small-group discussions with separate tables for government officials, upper management, lecturers, heads of department and so on. Each group was asked to generate ideas on cards, and all ideas were displayed on the wall. Lively and productive discussion ensued from people from all levels of the organizational hierarchy.

Tabling group information

We are similar in our differences and different in our similarities.

Michael Pearson

In some groups, I want people to pair up for special work as 'buddies' or in small groups. There is no easy way of choosing. Methods like assigning pairs, or pulling names out of a hat, take away autonomy. Michael Pearson has developed a technique to enable participants to learn about each other and make a more informed choice by mapping the group (Pearson, 2002) This information may be drawn quickly from the group and entered into a grid on a whiteboard. (An electronic whiteboard is especially useful, or a participant may help as scribe.) A selection of ideas is included below, more than might be necessary. Or you may wish to invite the group to generate the list. I have omitted a heading for 'age' as some people may feel embarrassed. (In Asia this is not the case, as people openly ask, 'How old are you?' as a means of working out seniority, which is partly based on age. This is to find out what honorifics or forms of address are required. Being older is an advantage.) This is similar to the idea of mapping cultural issues described in Chapter 5.

Magic carpet

Another more visual and creative way to help people speak about themselves is to ask participants to make a metaphorical 'magic carpet' or poster of

Table 2.2 Group information

Names / Information	Amy	Khim	Jen	Lila	Pat	Menga
Gender						
Born in						
Home suburb						
Favourite food						
Mother tongue						
Relationships: M or S						
Religion						
Work title						
Name of workplace						
Transport available						
Available to meet group (evening or weekend)						
Computer literacy						
Preferred learning style/s						
Recreational activities						
Hobby						
Personality						
Languages						
Music						
Sport						
Aspiration						
Children						
Pets						
Last holiday						

information about themselves, what they have to offer a 'study buddy', and what they are looking for in a study buddy or small working group. The topics to be drawn on the 'carpet' are best negotiated with the group. Some participants often find it easier to talk about themselves when holding up a sheet of flip chart paper, as participants look at the poster rather than the person.

Problem-solving activities

If your workshop involves problem solving, it is useful to use icebreakers that involve simple problem solving.

Broken knots

Ask the group to form smaller groups of 8 to 12 people. Ask them to extend right hands and link with another person, but not a person to their immediate left or right. Then repeat with the left hands. Now ask groups to untangle themselves slowly without letting go of hands. Warn them that they may need to loosen their hold of each other to allow for movement until they can untie their knots.

There are four possible solutions to the knots:

- one large circle with everyone facing in or out;
- two interlocking circles;
- a figure of eight;
- a circle within a circle.

Check beforehand that everyone can participate, and warn people to wear suitable clothing. In some multicultural environments it may be necessary to designate some all-female groups. The debriefing can be used in a number of different ways. Useful questions are:

- Did all people who made suggestions get listened to? If not, why not?
- How did you hinder one another?
- How did you help one another?
- What useful strategies do you want to incorporate into future exercises?

Then ask the participants to repeat the exercise, taking note of the desirable behaviours that were discussed.

Another well-known problem-solving exercise is the 'broken squares' simulation from Pfeiffer and Jones (1974). The advantage of this exercise is that it is conducted silently, so it is extremely useful in multicultural groups where standards of English vary.

Building trust

Trust walk

Tell participants they are going to undertake a trust walk with a partner. You can use blindfolds (I collect face masks on airplanes) or simply ask one person in each pair to close his/her eyes. The role of the guides is to give their partners an interesting and safe walk and help them touch, smell and hear interesting things. It is important that the facilitator stresses the trust aspect of the activity, as if this is betrayed the exercise could have a very negative impact, and monitor participants for safety.

After three minutes roles are reversed. Debriefing questions focus on:

- How did it feel to put your trust in someone else?
- Did you open your eyes or keep them closed?
- How did it feel to be responsible for someone else?
- What did you learn about yourself during this exercise?
- How can this group develop and maintain trust?

See Chapter 13 for more trust activities.

The mirror walk

Joanna Macy (1991) has developed a beautiful variation of the trust walk to develop our awareness of our interconnectedness with each other and nature. After describing the seamless links between living beings through the air and water, she invites participants to use the trust walk to see nature differently. The exercise is conducted in silence, and is best conducted in an outdoor setting, though it may also be used indoors.

In pairs, participants take turns to be led in silence, which allows people to use their senses. Their partners supply them with a variety of sensory experiences, such as a flower or leaf to smell, an invitation to feel the texture of a leaf or tree trunk, to hear the sounds of birds. At given intervals the guide adjusts his/her partner's head as if aiming a camera and says, 'Open your eyes and look in the mirror'. The other person opens his or her eyes for a moment or two to take in the sight. After the eyes have been closed, the sensory experience is heightened. The intense focus and awareness makes this a very powerful exercise.

It is useful to demonstrate the exercise first. In Thailand, Myanmar and Laos it is very disrespectful to touch a person's head as it is the most important part of the body. So invite participants to make their needs known to their partners regarding touch.

There is total silence except for the words heard occasionally, 'Look in the mirror'. After a predetermined time, make a sound and invite everyone to swap roles.

The SAID process is useful for debriefing. Useful questions include:

- What did you notice?
- What surprised you?
- What feelings came up as you were guiding, being guided?

There are often some very interesting insights gained from this exercise. I recall as a participant seeing a flower with such brilliant colour as never before.

In a variant, the person who takes a turn to close his/her eyes does so for a much longer period, and the lead person takes his/her partner to a beautiful flower or tree trunk, so that when the eyes are opened the person is only about 20 cm away from the flower. The person opens eyes only for a few seconds, and closes them again.

Building cooperation

It is useful to have an exercise that involves everyone working together (provided the group is not too large). I do not know the original source of the following exercise, but I know that the names Karl Rohnke, Kuon Custer Hunt and Barbara Steinwachs are linked to it, so thank you, wherever you are.

Bean bag balance

Ask participants to bring or find something to balance on their heads, such as a book or a purse (but not a hat). The goal is to cross a line about 10 metres away within three minutes, while adhering to the following ground rules:

- The items must be on everyone's heads when they cross the finish line.
- No one may hold the item in place.
- The owner may not touch his/her item: if it falls off someone else must pick it up.
- Everyone must step over the finish line at exactly the same time.

Some debriefing questions include:

- What happened? What did you do?
- Who 'won'? Why? How? (There are 'group wins' as well as 'individual wins' in the workplace.)
- Is the workplace sometimes like this (people move at different paces, with different skills and different burdens)?
- Are you used to helping others to complete tasks?
- What else could you have done to help them achieve the goal?
- Can you give examples of work situations where you have to help others to achieve a group goal.
- Is there a situation coming up where the learning from this activity may be applied?
- If yes, what will you do?

Eating together

Some food ideas that are simple (and might best be done outside) include having a meal with everyone around a table tied to the people on either side of them by the wrist. Cooperation and trust are required to eat!

Another variation is having a 'straight arm' meal: no one is allowed to bend his or her elbows. This means no one can feed themselves.

Energizers

Energizers are short exercises designed to raise the energy levels of the group. They may be used to:

- provide movement or action during flat or slow sessions;
- release tension in difficult or emotionally charged sessions;
- provide some fun and laughter;
- separate one session from the next;
- enable people to be physically closer (remember different individuals and cultures have differing comfort zones regarding proximity).

Criteria for choosing energizers

Here are some questions to ask yourself when choosing an energizer:

- How well do participants know one another?
- What stage of development is the group at?
- What stage of the workshop will you use it in?
- What is the background experience of participants?
- What is appropriate (there may be status issues)?
- Are there any potential age, gender and cultural issues?
- Will the dress of some participants, for instance saris, sarongs, tight trousers/ skirts, or high heels, inhibit their movement?
- Is the room temperature and weather too hot and humid for a lot of activity?
- Is the exercise safe? Is there enough room for the group members to move around?
- What mobility and medical considerations need to be considered? For example, a disabled person may feel awkward if he/she cannot join in. (Remember many disabilities are not obvious.)
- Do you feel confident with a particular exercise?
- Would you feel embarrassed if someone asked you to do it?
- Have you seen the energizer working before? What did you learn?

Singing songs

Songs can be fun, however, some people feel inhibited about singing, even with other people. Songs may be suitable for a later time in the workshop. Many people do not mind singing a song when the group members have become acquainted. One useful song that sets people laughing is the 'Smile Song', which is sung to the tune of 'John Brown's Body'. It is useful for stress management workshops, when introducing the concept of endorphins: that is, that changes in body chemicals are brought about by laughing, smiling, exercising and so on.

It isn't any trouble just to s-m-i-l-e,
It isn't any trouble just to s-m-i-l-e,
So smile when you're in trouble,
It will vanish like a bubble,
If you only take the trouble just to s-m-i-l-e

Haa ha ha ha ha-ha haaaaaa ha
Haa ha ha ha ha-ha haaaaaa ha
Haa-ha ha ha ha-ha haaaaaa ha
Ha-ha ha ha-ha ha ha-ha ha ha ha ha ha.

It isn't any trouble just to l-a-u-g-h,
It isn't any trouble just to l-a-u-g-h,
So laugh when you're in trouble,
It will vanish like a bubble,
It you only take the trouble just to l-a-u-g-h.

Haa ha ha ha ha-ha haaaaaa ha   Etc. . .

It isn't any trouble just to g-r-i-n, grin
It isn't any trouble just to g-r-i-n, grin
So grin when you're in trouble,
It will vanish like a bubble,
If you only take the trouble just to g-r-i-n, grin

Haa ha ha ha ha-ha haaaaaa ha Etc. . .

Dale Anderson (www.curtain-up.com/books.html)

Figure 2.5 The smile song

Energy check

To check energy levels, the facilitator draws a thermometer on the board and asks participants to write their names beside how they are feeling, in terms of 100 per cent energy to 0 per cent energy. This is useful after lunch or after afternoon tea, to gauge the energy levels of the group. See Figure 2.6.

Jokes and humour

Jokes and humour can be a delightful way of raising energies, oxygen flow and so on. Remind people to stick to the ground rules in case anyone is inadvertently offended.

Exercises

Short stretching exercises give a physical as well as mental break. Demonstrate slowly, and always remind people to do what is comfortable/natural for them, or to say 'no' if they wish.

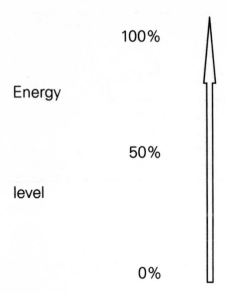

Figure 2.6   Energy levels

Useful references

There are a wide variety of resources available on icebreakers. See for example Barca (1993), Dahmer (1992), Forbes-Greene (1980), Jones (1995), Kirby (1993; 1992: 779), Newstrom (1998, 1991), Scannell (1994) (Sleigh 1996), Ukens (1996), and West (1997). Useful Web sites include http://www.nwlink.com/~donclark/leader/icebreak.html and www.albany.edu/cpr/gf/resources/Exercises.html

Conclusion

First impressions count. The purpose of the workshop should be clear, and time invested in generating ground rules. Icebreakers are an integral part of enhancing interaction among participants, and between participants and the facilitator. They need to be chosen carefully, and it is useful to keep a journal of activities that work and different responses to the same activity by different groups.

I have tried to give reminders of the many things to think about at the start of a workshop. There is no best 'way' or best process for opening workshops, but it is useful to have a kaleidoscope of strategies in your toolbox that may need to be adapted or changed on the day.

3

Basic facilitation toolkit

One ounce of practice is worth tons of learning.

Gandhi

Introduction

Newcomers to any profession often naturally feel a little daunted at first, since when applying for jobs the first things people ask are, 'How much experience have you had?' or 'What qualifications have you got in this area?' The result is that most people who are starting out feel like they are caught in a Catch 22 situation. So this chapter is designed to cover:

- basic questioning techniques;
- a generic debriefing process: the ORID process;
- the emotional tools of facilitation;
- adapting workshop plans;
- the physical toolkit of facilitators.

Chapter 17 gives you information on where to learn more about facilitation, self-assessment tools for facilitators and suggestions on how to maintain your health and well being.

Dances with participants: questioning and listening

What does dancing have to do with facilitation? Ideally workshops should be like a dance. Dancing is one of the most powerful forms of human interaction, partnership, learning and fun. In partner dances, one dancer leads, then the other. It's the same with facilitators and participants. Questioning and active listening skills are primary communication tools for facilitators and (also preferably for participants). Socrates (469–399 BC) was perhaps the first to point out that a question is a midwife that brings ideas to birth. He himself used to practice this 'art of intellectual midwifery'. (Chauderi, 1975: 30–34).

Facilitator questions

> One who questions cannot avoid answers.
>
> Source unknown

If we read or hear a question we cannot help but start to think about it. We may not be able to answer it, but most of us have a good try. Facilitators use questions to provoke reactions from participants, start discussions, enhance thought, check assumptions, confront, raise awareness, gather information.

Most processes start with questions. And there are many kinds. Likewise the ways of answering questions vary too. While trying to help groups adhere to the agreed ground rules, a facilitator needs to be aware of the diverse communication styles between different individuals and cultures. Communication may be direct, circular, fast, hesitant, ponderous and/or repetitious.

Open and closed questions

The two main kinds of question are 'open' and 'closed'. An open question opens up thinking and invites a variety of answers. A closed question on the other hand may only be answered by a 'yes' or 'no', or some similar brief statement. There are degrees of 'openness' and 'closedness'. For example, take, 'What do you think would be the best use of the time left?' versus a forced-choice closed question, 'Do you want to do xxxx or xxxx or xxxxx?'

Closed ⎯⎯⎯⎯⎯⎯⎯⎯⎯⎯⎯⎯⎯⎯⎯⎯⎯⎯⎯⎯⎯⎯⎯⎯⎯⎯ Open

'Does this make sense?' and 'Have I made myself clear?' are closed questions, and participants may feel awkward admitting that something does not make sense to them. Questions like, 'Any questions?' or 'Does anyone need some of the words or ideas here clarified?' are open and more likely to generate a response, as are ground rules like, 'There are no such things as stupid questions'.

Remember to count to 10 and allow participants some 'think time' before jumping into the silence.

Asking the 'right' questions

> The important and difficult job is never to find the right answers, it is to find the right question. For there are few things as useless – if not dangerous – as the right answer to the wrong question.
>
> Peter Drucker

It is useful to frame questions before a workshop and imagine the answers that might be generated. At the beginning of a process you might want to fine-tune questions 'cooperatively' with participants.

Asking the right person/s

Facilitator questions may also be targeted at different people, for example one person, a small group, or the whole group.

Probing questions

Probing questions enable the facilitator to gain clarity or to dig deeper into issues: for example, 'Can you tell us more about xxx?'

Naïve questions

Naïve questions are often welcomed by participants who feel shy of showing their ignorance, and can be used by the participants or the facilitator to clarify the meaning of certain concepts. For example, the facilitator might say, 'This is not my area. Can you explain this term please?'

Metaprocess questions

Alerting the group to focus on its process is called 'metaprocessing'. Bob Dick suggests that you 'inform. . . invite' (Dick, 1984). For example:

Inform:	It's half past three. That's half our time gone. There is still lots to cover.
Invite:	Can anyone suggest some way of speeding up the process?

You might also use this to listen and act on intuition:

Inform:	I'm a bit lost now. Something is happening.
Invite:	Can you tell me what is going on in the group?

Or 'inform. . . suggest. . . invite':

Inform:	It's half past three. That's half our time gone, but some people look a bit tired.
Suggest:	Shall we have a quick 10 minute break so you can stretch, get a drink and bring it back to the group so we can keep going?
Invite:	What do you think? Or are there any other suggestions?

Rhetorical questions

A rhetorical question is one that does not require an answer. Its purpose is to make a point or gain attention more effectively than with a plain statement. For example, 'What does dancing have to do with facilitation?' can have more impact than a statement, 'Facilitation is like dancing'.

Leading questions

Leading questions provoke a wanted answer. They are frequently seen in evaluation questionnaires, for example, 'Have you enjoyed today's workshop?' or 'In what ways was the workshop useful?' The latter question is fine as long as the opposite is also asked: 'In what ways was the workshop not useful?' This question is negative and may elicit some useful information. However, questions that ask for constructive suggestions for improvement can tap into the creative energy of participants: for example, 'How could the workshop be improved next time?' See also Chapter 11, Strategic questioning.

Further resources

See Hogan (1999) for processes to use to enhance questioning in adult learning situations.

Even Rudyard Kipling exhorted the values of questioning. I use his well-known poem to remind participants of questions to ask:

> **Six honest serving men**
> I keep six honest serving-men
> (They taught me all I know);
> Their names are What and Why and When
> and How and Where and Who.
> I send them over land and sea,
> I send them east and west;
> But after they have worked for me,
> I give them all a rest.
> I let them rest from nine to five,
> For I am busy then,
> As well as breakfast, lunch and tea,
> For they are hungry men:
> But different folk have different views;
> I know a person small-
> She keeps ten million serving-men,
> Who get no rest at all!
> She sends 'em abroad on her own affairs,
> From the second she opens her eyes-
> One million Hows, two million Wheres,
> And seven million Whys!

The 'she' mentioned by Rudyard Kipling in his poem could well be a facilitator! Note her seven helpers in Table 3.1.

Basic facilitative interventions

> Asking for help is the most dignified thing you can do on this earth.
>
> Source unknown

Active listening (listening with the head for information, and with the heart for feelings) and questioning skills are fundamental to facilitation. Some simple ideas are set out in Table 3.2.

Table 3.1   Seven helpers of facilitators

Who	Who is affected?
Who	Who has the problem?
Who	Who needs to solve it?
What	What do you know about it?
What	What are the causes and effects?
What	What can be changed about it?
What	What assumptions are you making about it?
How	How widespread is the problem?
How	How will you know when it has been solved?
How	How will you go about solving it?
How	How will you know if you are successful? Define this in terms of goals *and* processes used to achieve the goal/s
Where	Where does it fit into the big picture?
Why	Why is this a problem?
Why	Why do you want to solve it?
With what	With what resources?
When	When do you need to do this by?

Source: adapted from Hopson and Scally (1986)

Questioning processes

Two basic questioning processes follow. The 'ORID process' is central to all facilitation work as it is a generic debriefing tool, and the 'keys to understanding' provides questions that are like keys to open up deeper understanding of new concepts.

Table 3.2   Facilitative interventions

Type of facilitative behaviours	*Explanation*
Active listening	
1 Paraphrasing*	Facilitator states concisely the essence of the participant's message in his/her own words. For example, Facilitator: 'Let me see if I've got it right. . .'. Facilitator: 'It sounds like...' Facilitator: 'The picture you're trying to paint seems to illustrate. . .'.
2 Reflecting feelings*	'You seem puzzled about. . .'.
3 Reflecting meaning*	Facilitator mirrors feelings and meaning: 'You feel. . . because. . . is that correct?'
4 Mirroring	Use the participant's exact words, but not the tone. Mirroring develops trust, but don't use too often as you may sound like a parrot, or make the participant feel you are mimicking him/her.
5 Summarizing*	Facilitator selects relevant data systematically. 'One theme that seems to be emerging is. . .'. 'Let's recap on the story so far. . .'.

Type of facilitative behaviours	Explanation
6 Summarizing with participants	Facilitator uses cooperative mode: 'Can you help me summarize the main points here. . .'.

Probing

7 Drawing people out and probing	Facilitator: 'Tell me more.' Facilitator: 'Can you give me an example?' Facilitator: 'What do you mean by?' Facilitator: 'And. . . so . . . because. . .'.
8 Probing deeper thinking	Facilitator: 'Could you tell us what leads you to that conclusion?' 'If these are the presenting problems, what might some of the underlying issues be?'
9 Trying to get below the surface	'Why?'. . . wait for answer. 'Why?'. . . wait for answer. 'Why'. . . wait for answer.

Opening up thinking

10 Generate creative thinking	If there were no constraints. Facilitator: 'What are some ways you could. . .?' 'Tell us about your dreams about how you would like things to be.' See brainstorming, brain writing and round robin process.
11 Embedded questions	Facilitator: 'I'm curious to know. . .'. Facilitator: 'I'm wondering how you will use/adapt this at work.'

Keeping on track

12 Sequencing	If a number of people want to speak at once, indicate the order. 'Let's hear from Jane first, then Jim and then Prem.' It may be necessary to interrupt the sequence occassionally to let people respond to the last comment before going on to the next thread of conversation.
13 Tracking	Facilitator 3 steps: 'I'm going to step back and summarize. It sounds as if there are three strands here and I want to make sure I'm tracking them. The first seems to be about. . . the second. . . the third. . . Does it sound like that to you?'

Maximizing participation

14 Encouraging	Facilitator: 'Is this raising any questions in people's minds?' Facilitator: 'Who else has an idea? A lot of men have been speaking, let's hear from the women.' But be careful not to embarrass a quiet subgroup or individual into more silence. Dale Spender's research on gender and discourse in Australia points out that males tend to dominate conversations. This may also be a norm in other cultures.
15 Balancing	'Are there any opposing views?' (Shows facilitator is impartial and that all can speak.) 'Where do the rest of you stand on this?'
16 Making space	Watch body language of quieter people. If you notice a change of expression or a flicker in facial muscles, say, 'Joan, what was that thought?' and wait. Or round robin the whole group to make space for everyone to speak.
17 Intentional silence	Hold the silence in a group. Give people thinking time. Be careful: 'silence' does not mean consent. Quakers use silence: 'Let's have five seconds silence.' Keep your face blank, stay centred, pay attention and 'hold the space'.

Type of facilitative behaviours	Explanation
Listening for common ground 18 Summarize	Indicate you are going to summarize differences and similarities. Summarize differences. Summarize agreements, ie common ground. Check: 'Have I got it right?' Alternatively, get the group members to summarize differences, similarities etc.
Speeding up 19 Use the clock	Facilitator 'We've got five minutes left, have we heard from everyone?' 'Can anyone suggest how we can speed up the process?' 'Are there any things that need to be said before we finish?'
Challenges 20 Embedded commands	Facilitator: 'As you leave here tonight you can be *eager* and *energized* to start practising what you learnt.'
21 Use tone, pitch, rhythm	Facilitator: 'Could you. . .'. Facilitator: 'Would you. . .'. Facilitator: 'Can you. . .'.
Cognitive inputs 22 Embedded theory	Compose a story to bring an abstract theory to life.
Metaprocessing 23 Process discussions	Are you keeping to the ground rules? What is going on at the moment in the group?
Pinning down the wafflers 24 Gathering examples and perceptions	Asking people to be concrete and specific, to give actual examples to get away from sweeping generalizations.
25 'I' not 'we'	Asking individuals to use 'I think' rather than 'We all know that. . .'.

Types 1–4 are often designated as 'active listening skills' (Bolton, 1987).
Adapted from Kaner *et al* (1996: 41)

The 'ORID' or focused conversation debriefing process

A very useful debriefing process is the ORID questioning process, which is based on the Kolb experiential learning cycle (see *Understanding Facilitation*, Chapter 8). This process is simple, and you can practice it on a one to one basis with family and friends. It is also a simple tool to teach participants. In that way they learn to work in cooperative mode and debrief one another in pairs.

Author/purpose

This process was designed by Laura Spencer of the Institute of Cultural Affairs in the United States, to enable individuals to ask questions to make the most out of the wisdom and experience of others (Spencer, 1989). It was developed further by Stanfield (1997) who called it the 'focused conversation method'. See also the ICA Web site, www.icaworld.org/index.html

The beauty of this process is that it is fundamental to all facilitation. The purpose of the ORID process is to:

- provide facilitators with a framework that is based on Kolb's experiential learning model (Kolb, 1984);
- enable participants to reflect on an event or commonly shared experience, eg a lecture, a quotation, an article, television programme, a meeting, then interpret the experience, and decide what to do as a result;
- enable participants to listen to one another's perceptions and emotional responses, suspend judgement during the discussion, and as a result gain a broader and deeper understanding of an experience.

Size of group

This process may be used in many different formats:

- by a facilitator and the whole group;
- by participants in pairs: they interview each other;
- in small groups with a facilitator in each group;
- by a mentor to a mentee.

Materials

Flip chart, paper and pens to record responses.

Venue/layout

Semicircle of chairs, tables.

Stages

A facilitator leads the process by preparing, then asking, questions to which the group members respond. In introducing the process, the facilitator may wish to explain the rationale of the process, which is to obtain perceptions and learning from experience. Some facilitators prefer to explain the four stages so that participants more easily stay on task. (It is also useful for participants to learn processes that they can use in the future.) If a participant bypasses a stage, the facilitator calmly brings him/her back on task. Each participant is asked to give only one idea at a time, so that the participation of as many people as possible is encouraged.

Differences in perception and recall are acknowledged, and may be recorded on flip chart paper to keep track of ideas. The facilitator may wish to summarize or ask for further explanation.

There are four distinct stages of questioning whose first letters make up the mnemonic 'ORID':

- **Objective questions;**
- **Reflective questions;**
- **Interpretative questions;**
- **Decision questions.**

Questions need to be:

- preferably prepared beforehand, tailored with care and related to the experience itself;
- open-ended and specific;
- sequenced, ie start with easy questions.

If no one answers, wait, allow think time, repeat the question, or rephrase the question. If an idea comes up that is off the topic, note it on a separate sheet 'for attention later'. Invite participants to bring in opposing ideas: 'It looks as if there are three perspectives here. Are there any others?'

Objective questions: facts, data, senses

Objective questions are used to draw out the facts and observable data about the event. Participants learn that there are different perspectives of observable reality. Questions relate to thought, sight, hearing, touch and smell. For example:

- What images or scenes do you recall?
- Which people, comments or words struck you?
- What ideas/people caught your attention and why?
- What sounds do you recall?
- What tactile sensations do you recall?

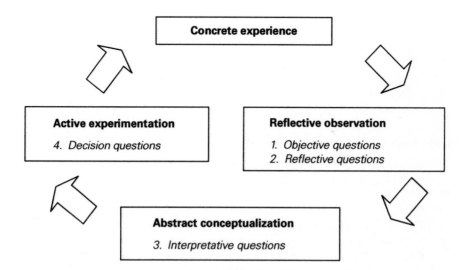

Figure 3.1 Relationship between ORID questions (italics) and the experiential learning model (bold letters)

- What were the other elements?
- What words jumped out at you?

Reflective questions: reactions, heart and feelings

Reflective questions relate to the affective domain of emotional responses moods and hunches. Examples include:

- How did this xxx affect you?
- Were you concerned at any time?
- Were you surprised at any time?
- Were you worried at any time?
- What was the high spot?
- What was the low spot?
- What was the collective mood of the individuals involved?
- How did the group react?
- Were you surprised/angered/elated/curious/confused/depressed by anything in the experience?

If individuals have difficulty identifying feelings, some suggestions could be put forward, for example, 'During the experience were you surprised/angered, intrigued/confused?' Frequently individuals respond to correct the questioner regarding the intensity of the feeling: for instance, 'No I wasn't angry, I was absolutely livid'.

Interpretative questions, critical thinking: so what?

The participants are invited to consider the value, meaning or significance of the event for them. This enables them to put their thoughts into perspective by hearing other people's viewpoints. For example:

- What was your key insight?
- What was the most meaningful aspect of this activity?
- What can you conclude from this experience?
- What have you learnt from this experience?
- How does this relate to any theories, models and/or other concepts?

Decision questions: now what?

Individuals and/or the group then have to make decisions on outcomes and determine future resolutions and/or actions. For example:

- What will you do differently as a result of the experience?
- Has this experience changed your thinking in any way?
- What would you say to people who were not there?
- What was the significance of this experience to your study/work/life?
- In future in how many different ways could you. . . as a result of this?
- What would it take to help you apply what you learnt?

Outcomes

The participants develop a shared understanding of the event and desired outcomes.

Advantages

This process stops meandering discussions that may lead nowhere. The process enables individuals to get to the heart of the matter, rather than reach superficial conclusions. The questioner uses a questioning framework to enable detailed reflection and learning. People frequently evaluate or judge events too quickly, without considering all the elements. Spencer outlined her perception of the process:

> It is simple because it follows a natural process – it does not have to be taught. It is sophisticated because it ensures that each step of the natural process is taken, thereby reaching a conclusion based upon the widest base of data possible.
>
> (Spencer, 1989: 48)

Frequently emotional or intuitive responses are not acknowledged. This process helps participants broaden their perspectives of an event and turn emotions into action.

> Emotions are important data. When taken into consideration in making a decision, they strengthen and support the decision. Ignored they usually jeopardize the decision.
>
> (Spencer, 1989: 48)

The method gives a structure to the debriefing process and prompts recall. A group can formulate a common strategy as a result.

Disadvantages

The disadvantages of the process are it:

- could appear awkward until the skills needed are internalized;
- may be time-consuming;
- requires cooperation of all other person(s) present.

Interesting points

This process may be used with families and friends on a one to one basis, or it may be used consciously in your own thinking, or in a journal process, writing down your own interpretations of events.

Variations

The process can also be adapted: for example, a large group is divided into four subgroups. Each is assigned to a work station that has a flip chart, on each of which are one of the four stages and key questions. All group members work concurrently, adding ideas to their group's flip chart paper for about 5 to 10 minutes. At the end of that time, the facilitator requests each group to move collectively to the next work station, where they add their thoughts to the next list, and so on until each group has worked at each of the four work stations. The facilitator then draws the whole group together to summarize the main elements of learning.

Keys to understanding new concepts

The next useful questioning process is called the 'keys to understanding new concepts'. Research by Sylvia Downs indicates that learners often confuse 'memorizing' with 'understanding'. Both are useful in their own ways. Memorizing is useful for surface learning of information we need for quick recall. But understanding is needed for learners to understand abstract concepts and to achieve 'deep' rather than 'surface' learning. In how many different ways do you develop your understanding of a concept? Try to list a few.

These keys were developed to enable you to unlock any concept. Therefore the keys will be useful for you in your work as a facilitator, to engage participants in analysing a concept in workshops. The keys can be used as an opener to find our prior learning about a concept. They can be used at the end, to find out if the understanding of the concept has been expanded. See Table 3.3.

Table 3.3   Basic forms of questions based on the keys to understanding

Key	Questions	How the keys help with understanding
Key no 1 **Purpose**	What are the reasons/ causes of XXX? What are the purposes of XXX? Why do. . .?	Encourages the learner to look beyond the obvious Enables learner to focus thoughts more accurately Many adults are pragmatic and like to know the purpose of things
Key no 2 **Viewpoints** **(other people's** **viewpoints)**	How is XXX seen by. . .? How does XXX look to. . .? How do you think your colleagues at work will react to XXX? How do you think customers will respond to XXX? What is the overall picture?	Enables people to walk in someone else's shoes See perspectives from inside and outside an organization Helps learners to develop empathy with clients/customers Develops helicopter vision of the whole
Key no 3 **Comparisons**	How is X different from Y? How does X need to differ from Y? Are there different forms of X for different purposes? How is a facilitator similar to and different from an elephant?	Enables participants to fine-tune a concept Prevents muddling with another concept Comparing similar activities can identify what learning needs to be transferred Comparing with a very different object can get participants to think creatively and/or differently about a concept
Key no 4 **Problems**	What are all the things that could go wrong with XXX? What could prevent these	By looking at problems learners are encouraged to look at the past, present and future

Table 3.3 *(continued)*

Key	Questions	How the keys help with understanding
	problems happening? What are the short-term problems? What are the long-term problems? How could you manage problems that are inevitable?	Learners start to anticipate and therefore prevent problems and/or manage them better
Key no 5 **What if?**	What if XXX were left out? What if XXX failed to arrive? What if a competitor developed XXX? What if XXX doesn't work? What if other people do not accept XXX?	Helps to develop understanding of issues that need to be tackled New equipment may not always work or be available, so this key gets learners to think about the practicalities This key may limit ideas if introduced too early
Key no 6 **Checks**	How can you measure if XXX is successful? What are the implications of XXX in the future?	Reminds participants to evaluate and look to the future Need some baseline data to compare changes with
Key no 7 **Experience**	What previous experience have you had of XXX? What have you heard about XXX?	Much of our social understanding comes from experience May give facilitator understanding of some misconceptions built on hear-say or limited prior experience
Key no 8 **Imagination**	Imagine an ideal XXX	If a person has no experience of a concept he/she has to use imagination to build the concept

Source: adapted from Downs (1995)

Developing the emotional tools of facilitation

Emotional intelligence has been cited as the next important area of human communication (Barbalet, 1998; Goleman, 1996, 1998). First, facilitators need to be able to identify, manage, and when necessary communicate, their own feelings; and second, they need to be able to help participants to identify, use and communicate their emotions to others to enhance understanding and empathy.

We are all experiencing a number of feelings all the time. We cannot 'not feel' something, while we are alive, that is. Until recently there seemed to be a barrier against expressing feelings in many homes and workplaces. Expression of feelings and intuitions has often been regarded as a sign of losing control, being irrational or over-emotional. The ideal managers and workers, it was thought, should be cool, objective and rational if they were to be effective.

Cultural and gender aspects

How we express our feelings is culturally and gender based. Every culture develops its own codes of behaviour, and sanctions against those who break those codes. Our parents, teachers, religious institutions and workplaces condition us on how we can or cannot behave. Indeed if everyone simply expressed everything, it could be argued that there would be total chaos.

There are also gender differences, in that it is more acceptable in the West for men than women to express anger and aggression, while it is more acceptable for women to express fear and to cry. In Southern European countries and South America, however, it is more usual for both men and women to express feelings openly. In Asia, losing one's temper also means losing face.

What causes feelings?

Feelings ebb and flow continuously, triggered by the world we live in. But we need to take responsibility for how we react to this world; in other words, we have choices. Feelings impact on our thoughts, actions and decisions. We often react to events in a split second, according to our values (deeply held beliefs) and feelings, thoughts and behaviours. As facilitators we need to be able to monitor our feelings, and not make quick or 'knee-jerk' reactions to participants if they exhibit inappropriate behaviour.

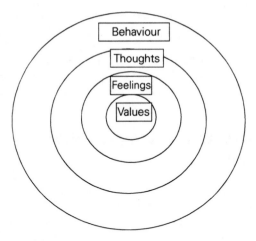

Figure 3.2 The relationship between outward behaviour and thoughts, feelings and values

Emotional intelligence

Emotional intelligence involves identifying your own feelings and reading the feelings of others. 'Know thyself', as Socrates put it. Self-knowledge, in the sense of an awareness of one's own feelings as they occur, is key to emotional intelligence. The development of emotional intelligence or competence or 'feeling literacy' is now recognized as a primary skill in the workplace, especially for facilitators and managers. These skills include being able to:

- identify and accept our feelings and patterns of feelings (those triggered from the past and those generated in the present);
- manage feelings and moods, rather than be ruled by them;
- choose whether or not to express feelings;
- choose where and how to express feelings;
- recognize when something or someone in the present triggers a past hurt and distress; that is, 'presses your button';
- appreciate that expression of emotions can be healing and/or improve mutual understanding and communication;
- show empathy to others and be able to reflect feelings back to them;
- help others to express feelings when appropriate in order to increase mutual understanding;
- recognize patterns or distress in ourselves, others, communities, organizations and society (Hunter, Bailey and Taylor, 1997; Macy and Brown, 1998).

Facilitators need to be self-aware, able to identify their own feelings and to manage them. If you find it hard to identify your own feelings, try:

- listening to your emotions;
- listening to your body;
- finding words to express your feelings.

Goleman (1996) identified four stages, shown in Table 3.4. It is easy to remember them using 'SOCS' as a mnemonic. When something happens, all sorts of emotions are triggered. Once we have identified those emotions, we need to think about the options we have, and the consequences of those options. Then we have to decide which solution will be most useful in the specific situation. For example, a participant might really irritate you. You need to think about your 'knee-jerk' reactions versus more logical reactions.

It can also be useful to use the notion of the stages with participants in workshops, to help them think about reactions to work events. There is nothing wrong with feelings like frustration and anger; it is what we do with those emotions that is important. They can be useful energizers for action to change the status quo.

Table 3.4 Taking charge of present feelings

Stage	*Question*
Situation	What is the situation and how does it make you feel?
Options	What options are available?
Consequences	What are the consequences of each option?
Solutions	Pick one or two best-fit solutions and develop action plans.

Managing your feelings at the beginning of a workshop

You can help yourself feel confident and at ease on the day of a workshop by:

- preparing very well;
- arriving early and getting organized well before the start of the workshop so you can relax and greet people as they arrive;
- dressing comfortably.

Clothing

There are no hard and fast rules on dress codes for facilitators, but your comfort is important. Facilitation is hard work, you need to be able to move around freely without restrictive clothing. You will be on your feet a great deal, so comfortable shoes are important. In a centring exercise in which I once participated, I noticed that in order to stand and centre, the women in the room who were wearing high heels had unconsciously kicked off their shoes. High heels mean that your centre of balance is pushed forward. For men, wearing a tie is equally restricting. The choice is yours, but you need to be aware of the impact of your dress on your comfort and well being.

Some theories of communication say that to be accepted, you should 'match' or reflect the dress of those you are working with. There is something to be said for this. In Laos I wear a 'sin', a wrap-over long skirt rather like a sarong. Lao participants have been very pleased to see that a Westerner enjoys wearing their traditional costume, and we have had long conversations about the colours, the style of weaving and where the garment comes from. It helps me build empathy with the participants. However, I love wearing unusual and colourful clothes brought from my overseas travels in my facilitation work (and leisure time) back in Australia. I feel far more energy in these brightly coloured clothes than in a traditional business suit. So I usually dress somewhat differently from the organizational norms. If you dress differently, you may have to work doubly hard to be accepted and/or taken seriously. What is interesting is the number of migrants who chat to me about my clothing, since many of them have given up their traditional dress in order to 'fit in'. Personally, I am rather sad that the colour and diversity of clothing in the world is being lost. So choice of clothing is partly a matter of preference and personal style and being yourself, partly functionality, partly fitting in and perhaps partly risk-taking.

Reading and reflecting the feelings of participants

Goleman describes a 'self-science course' for fifth-grade students, in which the students learn to identify their feelings each day. As the teacher calls the roll, each student answers, giving a number from 1 to 10 where one equals low spirits and 10 equals high spirits. For example 'Jessica, I'm here and I'm 10 today, I'm jazzed, it's Friday', and 'Patrick, I'm excited, and nervous, 8 today'. This is a useful exercise for new facilitators: at points during the day, describe to yourself how you are feeling and why.

Reflecting the feelings of others is an important part of active listening and assertive behaviour skills. Bolton (1987) suggests four strategies:

- Listen for feeling words, or if there are none, listen to the tone of voice for clues.
- Infer feelings from the content.
- Observe body language.
- Put yourself in the other person's shoes. How would you feel if you were experiencing the same thing?

Anger, sorrow, fear and guilt are natural responses to our problems and frustrations. Emotional discharges, like tears, indicate release of tension; they are healing. Likewise laughing and yawning are forms of discharge, and should not be taken as signs of indifference or boredom (Macy and Brown, 1998).

Helping participants to describe feelings about an issue

An exercise on stating feelings about an issue is useful in problem solving and decision making. Edward de Bono (1985) added a 'red hat' to wear when describing feelings in his 'six thinking hats process'.

The clichéd question, 'How do you feel about. . .?' is often greeted with stony silence. It is interesting to see how out of touch some adults have become in identifying feelings. However, you can make an educated guess at the feeling. For example, try, 'I imagine you feel really upset about. . .'. The person will feel heard, and/or correct you if you are wrong, saying something like, 'I'm not just upset, I'm very, very angry about it'.

Another strategy is to ask participants to complete the sentence, 'I feel. . . about this idea'. I have noticed that participants often start to say, 'I feel that. . .': in other words, they have slipped into their logical thinking frame of mind, as if 'I feel that' is synonymous with 'I think'. To help them I sometimes give them a list of feeling words (see Table 3.5), or pictures of expressions. Deal and Veeken (1997) have produced 'The Bear Cards', simple pictures of bears with a variety of expressions, as described in Chapter 4.

Words that describe feelings

The English language is rich in adjectives that describe the range and depth of feelings (see Table 3.5). We also have a useful supply of adverbs to describe the intensity of those feelings, like 'a little, somewhat, quite, very, really, deeply'.

Expression of feelings as healing

The expression of grief, fear or anger can be seen as healing, rather than 'breaking down' or 'losing control'. However, it is my belief that the facilitator needs to be skilful in steering group members between certain emotional tramlines or ground rules: most facilitators are not trained counsellors or able to deal with deep catharsis; the setting may not be suitable, and more importantly, participants may not have signed up for such an intervention. However,

Table 3.5 Feeling words

Happy	Sad	Angry	Confused	Scared	Jealous	Weak	Strong	Loving	Physical
alive	ashamed	aggressive	baffled	anxious	dissatisfied	apathetic	able	adoring	awful
amused	awful	annoyed	bewildered	apprehensive	distrustful	defenceless	active	affectionate	cold
blissful	bad	bored	chaotic	fearful	envious	deficient	assertive	caring	drunk
bubbly	deathly	cool	crazy	frightened	hurt	deflated	assured	cherish	drugged
calm	deflated	cross	dazed	horrified	insecure	disabled	bold	desire	dry
cheerful	dejected	disgruntled	disorganized	insecure	revengeful	emasculated	capable	ecstatic	energetic
delighted	depressed	disgusted	disoriented	jumpy	suspicious	exhausted	certain	empathetic	exhausted
ecstatic	disappointed	enraged	distracted	nervous	threatened	exposed	confident	enchanted	greedy
elated	dismayed	exasperated	distraught	panicky		feeble	courageous	erotic	hot
excited	dissatisfied	fed-up	disturbed	petrified		frail	desirable	fancy	hungry
feel good	distressed	frustrated	doubtful	shaky		fragile	determined	fondness	hurt
fine	disturbed	hateful	flustered	shy		gentle	eager	friendly	ill
glad	down	hostile	harassed	stunned		guilty	energetic	like	in pain
great	dreary	hot-tempered	helpless	terrified		ill	firm	passionate	itchy
joyful	embarrassed	impatient	lost	threatened		impotent	forceful	pity	nauseous
lovely	fed-up	indignant	misunderstood	timid		inferior	healthy	sexy	relaxed
loving	gloomy	infuriated	mixed up	worried		insecure	independent	sympathetic	restless
marvellous	grieved	irate	muddled			lethargic	intense	tenderness	sensual
peaceful	helpless	irritated	nonplussed			listless	positive	warm	sexy
pleasant	hopeless	livid	perplexed			passive	powerful		shivery
proud	hurt	mad	puzzled			pathetic	productive		sweaty
relieved	lonely	outraged	surprised			powerless	resistant		tense
satisfied	low	provoked	stunned			puny	secure		terrible
thrilled	miserable	riled	stupid			run-down			thirsty
wonderful	moody	seething	uncertain			sickly			tired
	negative	sore	undecided			unable			wet
	painful	stormy	unsure			unfit			
	self-pitying	stubborn	vague			useless			
	sober	uncontrollable				vulnerable			
	sorry					worn-out			
	terrible								
	unhappy								
	unloved								
	unwanted								
	upset								
	worthless								

Source: from Hopson and Scally (1982)

it is not unusual for a participant to show some distress in a group, and the facilitator needs to be able to handle such occurrences with empathy and compassion.

STORY: CONTINUUM EXERCISE GIVES VALUABLE INFORMATION

At the beginning of a workshop I asked a team to do the continuum exercise (described in Chapter 2) and to line up in terms of energy for the workshop. I noted that the female manager was down the low end of the scale. When I asked, she said, 'I'm feeling very weary this morning, just like a wet rag, not my normal self at all'. I was very surprised, as when she contracted with me to undertake the workshop she was bubbling with energy and enthusiasm. Her body language signalled she did not want to say more, so I moved to the next person.

At morning tea I sat with her and she started telling me of her sleepless night. Her son was in the navy, the Gulf War was about to break out, and he had been contacted to be ready for active duty. Understandably she was worried sick. She burst into tears, and I and another participant sat with her, just being with her and empathizing. After a while the sobbing diminished, and she dried her eyes and blew her nose. On returning to the workshop after morning tea, she explained her atypical behaviour to her team, who rallied around her. In this instance I do not believe she lost face. I think she gained face, she showed her humanity. Managers are allowed to be vulnerable and have feelings too. Her expression of her feelings was healing, for both her and the participants who were puzzled by her atypical behaviour. She did not allow her emotions to completely destroy her demeanour, she chose to move on, but at least everyone had a much clearer understanding of the causes of her atypical behaviour.

Distress recordings/patterns

Negative experiences cause distress, which may impact upon or scar our psyche in the long term. This past distress is like 'baggage' that we carry around with us. It can sometimes trigger us to overreact when we experience a similar situation, hear a word, smell something, or see a person and/or behaviour that reminds us of that past distress. The colloquial term is:

What presses your button?

We need to be able to distinguish between current realities and past distress or 'baggage'. We all have some distress patterns which may confuse us, make us forget reality, and/or prevent us from straight thinking. This is normal. Likewise participants may have their buttons pushed by you and/or other participants. As a result some anger may be displaced onto the facilitator. I saw one female facilitator at the beginning of a workshop say, 'Please note, I may look like your sister, or say something like your mother or school teacher or whatever, but I am not those people, I am me'.

> Anyone can become angry – that is easy. But to be angry with the right person, to the right degree at the right time, for the right purpose, and in the right way – this is not easy.
>
> Aristotle

STORY OF THE SAMURAI AND THE ZEN MASTER

A belligerent samurai, an old Japanese tale goes, once challenged a Zen master to explain the concept of heaven and hell. But the monk replied with scorn, 'You're nothing but a lout – I can't waste my time with the likes of you!'

His honour attacked, the samurai flew into a rage, and pulling his sword from its scabbard he yelled, 'I could kill you for your impertinence.'

'That', the monk calmly replied, 'is hell.'

Startled at seeing the truth in what the master pointed out about the fury that had him in his grip, the samurai calmed down, sheathed his sword, and bowed, thanking the monk for the insight.

'And that,' said the monk, 'is heaven.'

Source: Goleman (1996: 46)

Discharge of feelings

Many Western societies are rather oppressive about expression of feelings in families, schools and the workplace. In many parts of Asia, it is also regarded as rude to express openly feelings that might disturb the harmony of the group. Body language varies from culture to culture. Smiles usually represent open friendliness, but smiles and even laughter may also be used to cover embarrassment in some cultures. Feelings are discharged or vented in a number of different ways: see Table 3.6.

Table 3.6   Discharge of feelings

Kind of emotion	Manifestation during discharge
Boredom	laughter, talking, staring, dreaming, yawning (though yawning can also be release of other emotions too, eg disagreement, or a way of relaxing and getting more oxygen into the body)
Light anger	laughter, warm perspiration
Heavy anger	angry noises, violent movements, warm perspiration, tantrum, raging, temper tantrum
Light fears (embarrassments)	laughter, warm perspiration, fast walking
Heavy fears	trembling, shivering, cold perspiration, active kidneys, teeth chattering
Grief	tears, sobbing

Visual language tools of facilitation

The brain uses different pathways to process verbal and nonverbal information. A person who gets information from both channels has an easier time linking up the pieces.

Horn (1998)

Our brains can only hold in conscious thought a few ideas at a time. Hence telephone numbers are grouped in clusters of three or four digits. It is the same with conversations and threads of discussion. We need some sort of visual record to help us 'see the wood for the trees'. So facilitators keep 'wall minutes' to record the 'group memory'. The rationale for a group memory is to keep an accessible, agreed record of the discussion that can be easily referred to; a facilitator can backtrack and rerun the ideas from a meeting. But wall minutes must be used effectively. I have met some participants who say, 'Not another flip chart paper meeting! Why don't we just talk?' Some people are cynical if nothing comes of 'flip-chart paper workshops'. I find I need to outline the rationale and ensure that ideas are typed and distributed. Also, the people who want to return to 'just talking' are often the talkative ones who benefit most from that approach.

Writing can be time-consuming, and Doyle and Straus (1976) suggest splitting the role of facilitator and recorder. However, if you do this you must be able to trust the recorder to record all ideas, and not edit or omit ideas he or she does not agree with. So I suggest you occasionally look back at what the recorder is writing, as well as keeping eye contact with the group. (Yes, facilitators do have to have eyes in the back of their heads!)

Advantages of recording group memory

The group memory:

- Helps everyone to focus on the task.
- Helps the participants whose learning style is more visual than auditory who need to 'see' things (see Chapter 4).
- Allows participants to see both the content and process unfold, and how they reached a decision.
- Prevents overload of information; participants can relax.
- Frees participants from taking notes. However, some prefer to do this as a way of focusing their concentration.
- Enables participants to feel that their ideas have been heard and acknowledged by the group.
- Allows participants to check that ideas have been recorded accurately.
- Prevents endless repetition. (Allows the facilitator to gently confront: 'Have we got this issue already? If so, do you want to add anything else?')
- Allows graphic representation, diagrams linking ideas.
- Allows ideas to be stored between workshops and easily transported and displayed at the next meeting.
- Encourages people to participate: as they see ideas are acknowledged and recorded, they know their ideas are worth writing down.
- Enables ideas to be depersonalized.
- Increases the sense of accomplishment of the group.
- Enables people to see surface issues and then dig deeper.
- Enables latecomers to catch up without interrupting.
- Allows absentees to catch up and see the flow of information.

- Reduces ambiguity and misunderstandings later about decisions, dead-lines, names and responsibilities for actions planned.
- Flip chart paper is low cost and does not break down. It can be attached to trees, vehicles, office walls alike.
- Enables electronic minutes to be quickly reproduced on paper or elec-tronically and distributed.

(Based on Doyle and Straus (1976))

Hints for recording group memory

Anyone can learn to scribe. Here are some hints:

- Fold the flip chart paper beforehand, in half then in half again until you have creases across the page about 5 cm apart. These folds will be invisible to participants, but give the scribe useful writing guides.
- Listen and try to capture key words and phrases. Use cursive writing rather than print as it is quicker. (Practise at home if necessary.)
- Write legibly in letters at least 4 cm high. The size will depend on the distance from you to the farthest person in the room.
- Ask if everyone can read what you write.
- Use abbreviations and symbols, stars, arrows, circles, concentric circles (Sonneman, 1997; Margulies, 1992).
- Use red to circle or underline key ideas. Never write with pale yellow, orange or pink pens.
- Ensure that if you attach the sheet to a wall, you have a sheet underneath to prevent ink bleeding through and damaging the wall.
- If the group is working very fast, have two scribes. Or if there are two or more dominant ethnic groups, ask other recorders to scribe in the other main languages spoken.
- Use alternating colours to separate ideas. Black and blue are best. Hold the pens in your left hand with the caps facing down so you can swap quickly. Resting the pens in their caps stops you inhaling fumes and slows their drying out. (Mr Sketch pens from Sanford's are non-toxic and smell of fruit!)
- Ask long-winded speakers for help in summarizing their ideas, and do not worry about spelling. Remember the quote, 'I never trusted a man who couldn't spell a word at least four different ways' (Mark Twain).

Parking lot

One sheet of paper on the wall separate from the wall minutes is useful as a 'parking lot', a place to put odd reminders or issues to come back to later. This ensures that these ideas are minuted and are not forgotten.

Card sorts and storyboarding

Flip chart paper is great, but what if you want participants to be able to move around ideas: to cluster, sequence, or rank or eliminate ideas easily? Sticky notes and coloured cards are great for this. Card can be obtained cheaply as offcuts from printing companies. Cards can also be used to show pictures of events or a story, for example in planning a video. The Schnelle brothers (1979) have developed 'metaplanning' processes, dividing whole organizations into small groups, each with a board and cards. Cards are attached to large sheets of brown paper with adhesive gum. It is useful to have different colours of card or sticky notes for headings. First, data is generated on the cards; second, ideas are clustered into groups, and headings are given to groups and marked on different coloured cards. See the LENS process, described in Chapter 11.

Sticky notes

There are now a number of colours, shapes and sizes of sticky-backed notes available. These can be used in a variety of ways: to write one idea per note, and to cluster, rank or sequence ideas. Straker (1997) has written about a variety of techniques for using sticky notes for problem solving.

Storage

Store wall minutes and cards carefully. Make sure that cleaning people are told that even what appears to be tatty paper is valuable and must never be thrown out. I have heard some terrible stories, where facilitators have been almost in tears after three days' work has been lost.

There is more information in the section on graphic facilitation in Chapter 4.

Collecting the physical tools of facilitation

It is a good idea to compile a kit of useful items. I store most of the items listed in Table 3.7 in a plastic fishing tackle box which is easy to carry around. A collapsible trolley with wheels is a lifesaver for carrying equipment and saving your energy and back. (Watch the okey straps though, as accidents have been caused when they come undone under pressure.) There are also plastic tubes available for keeping flip chart paper dry.

Conclusion

This chapter has covered some basic techniques in questioning (see Chapter 11 for strategic questioning techniques). The keys to understanding were included as important questions to aid participants to unlock concepts. Finally the physical tools of a toolkit were listed. The next chapter is exciting as it enables you to delve more deeply into facilitation by stimulating all the senses.

Table 3.7   Tools of the trade

Items	*Uses*
Visualization tools	
Washable felt pens for whiteboard: black, blue, red, brown, purple	Preferably with wedge-shaped ends that make neat writing easier
Permanent non-toxic multicoloured pens for flip charts (Mr Sketch)	Useful for multicoloured diagrams, wall minutes
Coloured dots: blue, red, yellow	For straw voting, prioritizing, ranking and decision making
Sticky-backed notes Coloured cards	Metaplanning type card sorts
Stick-backed easel pads	Large sheets which are easy to display because of their self-adhesive backing
Static magic	Plastic sheets that can be used instead of a whiteboard. Also make useful projection screens
Box of transparencies	
Transparency pens	
Masking tape, adhesive gum, drawing pins, glue stick	For attaching papers safely to walls and each other
Rubber bands, paper clips, bulldog clips, stapler, staples and staple remover, scissors, Stanley trimmer	For collecting and storing information
Dice, balloons, small bamboo balls, matches, puzzles, fun bubbles	Equipment for experiential exercises, ice breakers and energizers
For emergencies	
Tissues, sewing kit, pain killers, indigestion tablets for your personal use only	For emergencies, I have had split blouses, trousers and have occasionally had a fast-developing running nose! Also tissues are useful if a participant gets distressed
Glucose tablets, Berocca tablets, mints	For times when energies lag
Electrical items	
Extension cords	
Thick, wide parcel tape	For securing electrical leads to floor
Power boards	
Double adaptor	
Tape/CD recorder	
Variety of music CDs	Set the scene, change ambience
Stopwatch or kitchen timer	Great for reminding you of time during small group work
Laptop	
Portable printer	
Creating ambience	
Flowers	
Sarongs on walls	
Balls, hats, bubbles	To stimulate fun and creativity

4

Processes to involve all the senses

Do not do unto others as you would that they should do unto you.
Their tastes may not be the same.

George Bernard Shaw

Introduction

This chapter focuses on a variety of approaches that a facilitator may use to enable individuals and groups to think more deeply and/or differently about themselves, their organizations, and/or communities through the use of multi-sensory techniques. These may include the enhancement of the aesthetics of the workshop 'space' and the incorporation of sounds, music, silence, movement, poems, metaphors, paintings, drawings, photos, card packs, spiritual and ritual dimensions in workshops.

The quote above from George Bernard Shaw is appropriate. Facilitators require a wide variety of strategies which may send them out of their own comfort zones in order to help others be in their comfort zones, and/or stretch out of comfort zones. The chapter gives an overview of:

- diagnostic questionnaires;
- aesthetics and space;
- sound: music, silence;
- poems, metaphors and stories;
- movement and drama-based processes such as role play and theatresports;
- visuals techniques: paintings and drawings, photos and card packs;
- spiritual dimensions;
- time.

Ways of describing differences in people: diagnostic questionnaires

There is a vast amount of research now available describing the different ways in which people perceive and process new information, learn and behave. We need to cater for these differences. There is no space to go into these in this book, but some are summarized and referenced in Table 4.1.

There are many personality, behaviour and learning style questionnaires that enable us to:

- know a bit more about what we're made of;
- know a bit more about who we are;
- know our preferred ways of behaving and reacting;
- know our strengths and how to amplify them;
- know our weaknesses and how to overcome them;
- identify and understand differences in others;
- communicate with others in the ways that they will hear us;
- resolve conflict by understanding others better.

They all have something in common: they are merely devices that simplify the incredibly complex nature of human beings. However:

Beware of facilitators and participants labelling themselves or others.

We need to use these questionnaires with healthy scepticism and remember that they are only tools, and are not infallible. The information you get is restricted to what has been asked for and how the person feels on the day they complete the questionnaire. Some people are so fed up of questionnaires they approach them with distain. It is important to note:

- that we are all mixtures of the terms cited;
- that we all change over time;
- we should not label ourselves;
- we should not label others;
- we need to value diversity and difference.

No two people are alike, and we can therefore assume that no two people:

- achieve at the same rate;
- have the same past experiences;
- achieve using the same study and/or learning techniques;
- solve problems in exactly the same ways;
- have the same repertoire of behaviours;
- possess the same patterns of interests;
- achieve to the same degree;
- are motivated to achieve the same goals;
- are ready to learn at the same time;
- have the same capacity to learn.

Coupled with the above are differences of culture. And within one culture there are many differences.

Now for the 'good' news:

- We have more in common with one another than differences.
- Luckily people in groups accommodate one another.
- We adapt to different situations.

Table 4.1 summarizes some of the varied questionnaires available.

Facilitators need to maintain a balance between using a variety of activities that stimulate different senses, learning styles, ways of being (sitting, moving, talking, being silent), and small and large group work. You will have your own preferred learning styles and you will need to stretch out of your own comfort zone at times in order to accommodate the people with ways of learning and being different from your own.

Aesthetics/space

The choice of venue is important; however, it is often not possible to obtain a space with the ambience you want. There are many ways of changing the 'feel' of a room. Ask participants to bring something along. The item may also be used as an icebreaker, as each person can be invited to say why the item is important to him/her. Alternatively, you can change a space by hanging a selection of brightly coloured sarongs around the walls. I find this especially useful when using a computer lab for electronic meetings in synchronous time.

I met a facilitator in London in 1999 who described how he would 'clear a room' of negativity before participants arrived by spiritually walking to the four corners of the room invoking positive energy. For my part, my practice involves arriving very early, setting out seating, equipment and playing calming music so that when participants arrive there is a calming mood, not the distractions and noise of moving furniture and getting organized, and I can focus positive, welcoming energies on individuals. I find I am more at ease if I have made some sort of contact with everyone before we begin. This, of course, is not always possible.

The layout of the room also sends messages immediately to participants. Rows show formality and hierarchy, while semicircles of chairs and cafeteria-style tables indicate informality (see Chapter 2).

Lighting

Expensive, plush hotels frequently have workshop rooms without windows, and while air-conditioned they often do not recycle air enough for comfort. Colour and light are important. Bright, cheerful surroundings uplift the spirit. For some people, it is important to be able to see the sky. In dowdy work environments people frequently become lethargic or even depressed (Hogan, 2000). In recent years it has been found that lighting from fluorescent tubes can be enervating. New developments in lighting that reproduces the spectrum of natural light have shown dramatic results in lessening depression or seasonal

Table 4.1 Ways of describing differences in people

Learning styles	Learning styles	Learning styles	Team roles	Neuro-linguistic programming	Multiple intelligences	DISC model of behaviour	Personality types
Kolb (1984)	Honey and Mumford (1986; 1992)	Hopson and Scally (1986)	Belbin (1993)	Grindler and Bandler (1979)	Howard Gardner (1993)	Performax in Hollier (1993)	Myers (1980) based on Jung's work
Concrete experience	Activist	Enthusiast	Coordinator	Visual	Linguistic	Direct	Extraversion–Introversion
Reflective observation	Reflector	Imaginative	Shaper	Auditory	Logical-mathematical	Influencing	Sensing–Intuition
Abstract conceptualization	Theorist	Logical	Implementer	Kinaesthetic	Spatial*	Stabilizing	Thinking–Feeling
Active experimentation	Pragmatist	Practical	Team worker	Olfactory	Bodily-kinaesthetic	Conscientious	Judgment–Perception
			Plan	Gustatory	Musical~		
			Resource investigator		Interpersonal (between people)		
			Monitor-evaluator		Intrapersonal (self-knowledge)		
			Specialist		Naturalistic		
			Completer				

affective disorder (SAD). Fluorescent light is the most nutrient-deficient of all artificial lighting devices. See the Web site http://maxpages.com/vitalite/ Health_And_Productivity

Constructing surroundings that are pleasing to you and your participants is important. If you want to stimulate creativity, make the space bright, colourful and stimulating. If you want to create a sense of serenity, make sure you choose and create a calm space.

Some groups prefer working outdoors. In this case facilitators need to find venues with outdoor areas that have suitable shady and/or covered areas depending on the climate. It is also important to have surroundings where people can sit outside to talk or take walks at breaks. Some people learn and think best when they are walking around.

Sound

Percussion sounds

Small cymbals or tingshaws may be struck for drawing together people's attention. One movement can generate a strong and penetrating sound which usually brings people's attention. Some people enjoy the sound, while I have found others are reminded of school bells.

Tingshaws may also be used to awaken people from 'psychological somnambulism' (Heron, 1999), 'a chronic habit in human behaviour: the tendency to fall asleep in interactions with others without the awareness of one's behaviour, its effects, and its motives. Hence we need, with much support rigour to help each other wake up from time to time.'

Music and the brain

Music impacts on our brainwaves, heartbeat, feelings and state of mind. Liz Brant and Tony Harvey (2001) investigated the uses of music for training, and include a CD with their book which contains a wide variety of music from different cultures for use in workshops.

Music as background

I frequently use music in workshop rooms to fill silence, to make people feel more comfortable when they walk into a room full of strangers. Instrumental music is best while groups are working, as lyrics can be distracting. When you use music as a background during small-group discussions it is best to use a straw vote to check whether all participants are happy with and not distracted by the music. If there are objections, then do not proceed. If there is acceptance, check with groups near the source of the music regarding their comfort with the volume (or show them how to adjust it if necessary).

It is useful to choose music that does not have a wide range of volume, as otherwise you will have to keep adjusting the volume. Some baroque, New Age music, flute and pan pipe music is useful. *The Routes: Africa, Asia and the World* and *Routes: Britain, Ireland and North America* (Nascente label) provide four CDs which give a comprehensive coverage of world folk music.

Making music and/or noise to stimulate discussion

I use music during group work to stimulate private discussions. After all, no one can hear the group talking next door; music gives a feeling of privacy and intimacy. I use music to calm people or myself after work, or to energize after lunch or during low energy periods.

Table 4.2 Examples of percussion instruments

cymbals	rattles in the shape of bananas	ocarinas
small drums	wooden water buffalo bells	bells
pan pipes	drum sticks	whistles
kazoos	zills (belly dancing cymbals)	tingshaws (cymbals)

I use the song 'Power to the people' by John Lennon as an icebreaker to intro-duce a workshop on empowerment (Hogan, 2000). I have a collection of small instruments in a box. I invite people to sing the song and to make a 'noise' to drown out the 'ghetto blaster'. (The challenge to make a noise is to stop people feeling they must 'perform' as opposed to have some fun.) I invite participants to choose what they would like to use. As I produce instruments participants often change their minds. The song usually creates quite a din. (I got the idea from this from my father. During Christmas parties in London when I was a child he would play his 78 rpm record of 'Marching through Georgia'. The whole family would march in a line all around the house making a huge racket. I think the wine and beer helped. We would blow on combs covered with tissue paper or use saucepans as drums. It must have been a bizarre spectacle.)

This icebreaker triggers many discussion points. The issue of choice (ie what instrument; the right to say 'no', that is, to participate or not participate; the extent of the risk-taking behaviour; dancing) all become useful triggers to tease out issues: for example, empowerment is about choice and about managing risks.

Music, singing and dancing unite us as human beings as methods to express meaning; exalt life and death; joy and sadness. The words of the song provoke the beginnings of understanding of the subtleties of the issues surrounding the concept of empowerment: power cannot come to the 'people' en masse until each of us takes the responsibility for our own empowerment.

Music to illustrate the stages of group development

Heron (1999) uses the metaphor of the four seasons to illustrate the stages of group development (See also *Understanding Facilitation* Chapter 8). I introduce this to groups by using overhead transparencies to illustrate the four seasons, accompanied by the music of Vivaldi's 'Four Seasons' and a voiceover description of each stage. See Table 4.3.

Table 4.3   The four seasons of group development

Season	Stage	Explanation
Winter	The stage of defensiveness	Trust is often low, anxiety is high. 'The ground may be frozen, and the weather stormy.'
Spring	The stage of working through defensiveness	Trust is building, anxiety is reducing, and a new culture is being developed. 'New life starts to break through the surface crust.'
Summer	The stage of authentic behaviour	Trust is high, there is openness to self and others, risk-taking, caring and sharing. 'There is an abundance of growth and the sun is high.'
Autumn	Closure	Participants gather to examine the fruits of their learning and to transfer it to their own lives. There is celebration and sadness in farewells. 'The fruit is harvested and stored, the harvesters give thanks and go their way.'

Songs and humour

Laughter is an important food. It is healing and nourishing for all the members of a community to burst out laughing until the tears run down their faces. We are not laughing at each other; we are laughing with each other (Vanier, 1979:135).

Dr Albert Ellis (architect of rational emotive therapy (RET)) uses songs to help people overcome their 'irrational beliefs'. Briefly, the ABC of RET is:

A = Activating events.
B = Belief systems including irrational beliefs (eg I must be perfect, I must not make a mistake, I must control everything that happens, ie 'must-urbation').
C = Consequences.

He suggested that when activating events (A) occur in our lives, the consequence (C) is we may feel anxious, depressed, or self-depreciating because of our (B) irrational beliefs. Ellis found that he could incorporate humour to help people see the silly side of their irrational beliefs (but not their personhood). To do this he wrote both humorous and serious songs so that people could sing these to themselves to reinforce a change of self-talk. Added to this, he had serious discussions to dispute a person's irrational 'musturbation'. His songs are copyrighted, but found in his chapter in Ellis (1987).

During workshops, facilitators can encourage participants to write their songs about their own issues. Consider the song in the box, about downsizing.

TUNE: MARCHING THROUGH GEORGIA

Every time I come to work
The change is all around me
Every day I cannot slow
'Do more' the call surrounds me
Don't know where we're go-ing
Don't know where we'll end up
I just have to keep go-ing.

Chorus:
Down size, down size
We've got to make a profit
Down size, down size
We're losing all our people
Never mind the human kind
We've got to join the rat race
We're not ro-dents, we're pe-ople.

Every time I tread the mill
I can't help but keep on thinking
Use more, pay more
The environment is fast sinking
Animals, birds are on the run
Species taken one by one
We know it's time to sto-p.

Chorus

Music to stimulate learning and improve brain functioning

Gary Kliewer (1999) reviewed the mounting, though sometimes conflicting, literature on the positive effects of baroque music (Mozart, Vivaldi, etc) on brain development and learning. The term, 'the Mozart Effect' was coined by French physician Alfred Tomatis. It appears that some of the works of Mozart (particularly the Sonata for two pianos in D Major) do have a profound effect on the brain, though no one as yet knows exactly. One suggestion is that patterns of loudness repeating every 30 seconds may trigger the strongest response in the brain, because many brainwave patterns also occur in 30-second cycles, and Mozart's music most often peaks every 30 seconds.

Gordon Shaw at the University of California found that nerve cells were connected together by various firing patterns and rhythms. When he converted these into sounds he found the sounds were somewhat similar to baroque and some eastern music. Playing baroque music appears to:

- help people solve spatial awareness tests more effectively (Holden, 1994);
- enable people with Alzheimer's disease to function more normally (Kliewer, 1999);
- reduce the intensity and frequency of fits in people who suffer from epilepsy (Kliewer, 1999).

So where does this lead us? Obviously more research is needed, but it appears that the use of music is a useful tool for facilitators.

Songs as stimuli for discussion

Vocals can also be used to start a session and generate discussion. What you choose will depend on the focus of the session, the demographics of the participants and your own taste. Generally I do not use 'songs' as background music in sessions, as the vocals may be distracting for some participants. For humorous songs see Peter Honey's *Songs of Life and Learning* (Honey, 2002). See also the Web site, http://www.djmorton.demon.co.uk/scouting/campfire.htm

Making music

Drum circles are increasing in popularity for team and community building. Drumming links us to the most fundamental of all rhythms: the human heartbeat. 'Rhythm', as Gabriel Roth says, 'is the mother tongue.' People of different cultures and belief systems are united by rhythm: even though rhythms in various cultures differ, we cannot not respond to rhythm. Clapping hands together is one of the first things taught to children.

Rattles and the like can be made easily and cheaply using tins, plastic bottles, gravel and so on. People can usually participate in some way of their choosing. Different instruments or types of jembe drums and other percussion instruments may be used in a variety of ways to:

- stimulate creativity;
- develop teamwork;
- let off steam and relieve stress;
- change mind/brain flow – rhythm is hypnotic;
- provide a process for team building (ie people must listen to ideas and make space for others to contribute ideas) and there is a tangible product at the end.

For further information check out the following Web sites:

http://www.fastcompany.com/feature/drums.html
http://www.drumcircle.com/arthurian/articles/communitydrumcircle.html

Table 4.4   Songs as stimuli for discussion

Topic	Song	Artist
Welcoming music	Walk right in	
	Welcome to my world	
	Hello, goodbye	The Beatles
Self-development	You're simply the best	Tina Turner
Boosting confidence	I got you (I feel good)	James Brown
	You've got a friend	Carole King
Visioning, planning, values	Imagine	John Lennon
	What a wonderful world	Nat King Cole
Empowerment/power	Power to the people	John Lennon
Restructuring	Breaking up is hard to do	Neil Sedaka
Career planning	Do you know where you're going to? (theme from *Mahogany*)	Diana Ross
Letting go, change	I'm gonna wash that man right out of my hair	*South Pacific*
Creativity sessions/ group work	Various drumming CDs	Gabrielle Roth
Moving on to new goals	We gotta get out of this place	The Animals
Ending	Breaking up is hard to do	Neil Sedaka
	50 ways to leave your lover	Simon & Garfunkel
	Goodbye yellow brick road	Elton John
	We may or might never all meet here again	Vin Garbutt
	Leaving on a jet plane	Peter, Paul and Mary
Conflict resolution	Give peace a chance	John Lennon
Optimism	Always look on the bright side of life	*Life of Brian*

Music as signals

Music can be used at breaks and after lunch to change energies. I attended one workshop where the same piece of music was put on at the end of all breaks, signalling to participants that there were three minutes to go if they needed to rush to the toilet.

Silence

Silence enables us to connect with our inner space. It is often seen as a void to fill rather than a space to relish. It may be used and/or interpreted in many ways as:

- a space between words;
- a space for thinking or reflecting after a question has been asked;

- a means to clear the mind (meditation);
- a means of encouraging thoughtful discourse;
- punishment;
- a way of freezing someone out;
- a means of coping with painful experiences;
- a part of rituals and retreats;
- living or companionable silence between people at ease with each other's company;
- dead or bored silence between people;
- oppressive, imposed by power holders and/or some regimes;
- an indication of dissent (while it is sometimes interpreted by others as assent);
- an indication of respect for the ideas put forward: ideas are being pondered upon;
- 'keeping mum' or keeping a secret;
- deathly silence 'as silent as the grave';
- a pregnant pause awaiting some to come out;
- disconcerting and an indication that someone is not participating in an electronic discussion group (see Chapter 14);
- a sign that something cannot be told yet: for example catastrophic experiences are often followed by silence, even up to 50 years in the case of many holocaust victims and some Korean 'comfort women'.

Quakers use the power of 'gathered silence', where people in stillness can attune to inner deeper knowledge to allow an eruption of what needs to be said out of the spirit. I incorporate a minute of silence at times to enable people to clear their thinking, calm down, take some space. This is particularly appreciated by people with more reflective learning styles.

The problem is that in the West even thinking about silence is uncomfortable for some, while others find silence restful. Silence is a means of slowing down for facilitators, and could usefully be regarded as a friend. It is active and purposeful, not an empty void. For facilitators who find silence difficult, writing on flip chart paper gives a legitimate act to fill the silence while people are thinking. The same could be said for researchers conducting interviews: the process of writing enables comfortable silences and think time.

As facilitators we ask many questions, but often allow very little time for space or response. During teaching practice I was taught to ask a question and then count to 10 before saying anything; I had to learn to 'ride the silence'.

Paulo Freire (1972) in *Pedagogy of the Oppressed* described the process of 'conscientization' (awakening to see the socio-political context of their learning) to enable the poor to look critically at their world, to break out of their 'culture of silence' and to take control of their destinies by developing a voice.

A silent workshop

William Rifkin describes a 'silent workshop' in which the facilitator is in a mime-like, silent, almost disengaged role. He uses this approach with trainers and teachers to give them insight into the relationships and issues of power, control and responsibility for learning. In a silent role, the facilitator is not involved in 'turn-taking', the mechanism that paces and gives participants place in the sequencing of communication. Normally facilitators/teachers are far more involved in 'turn-taking ' than they realize, and a silence workshop is a way of highlighting to everyone the power that the facilitator has (Rifkin, 1999).

Poems and metaphors

Poems may be used for opening or closing workshops and topics, or to enhance shifts of thinking. A favourite poem of mine is 'The Road Not Taken' by Robert Frost. I do not use this poem to advocate always taking the 'less travelled path', merely to consider the dilemmas involved in choices; the need to discover as many choices as possible in a situation; and to call for using intuition as well as data in decision making.

THE ROAD NOT TAKEN

Two roads diverged in a yellow wood,
And sorry I could not travel both. . .

I shall be telling this with a sigh
Somewhere ages and ages hence:
Two roads diverged in a wood, and I –
I took the one less travelled by,
And that has made all the difference.

Robert Frost (1969:105)

Metaphor and poeticizing

A metaphor is a figure of speech in which a word or phrase is applied to an object or action to clarify understanding of another, as in, '"I had fallen through a trapdoor of depression," said Mark'. Metaphors have been used throughout history by visionary leaders, teachers and speakers to engage people actively and shift their thinking and understanding about ideas. Metaphors involve 'the imaginative use of myth, allegory, fable to convey meaning' (Heron, 1989: 67). From a linguistic perspective, if the comparison includes the phrase 'is like' then the phrase is a simile, but most people use the term 'metaphor' to include similes.

Metaphors go further than models in helping us to understand phenomena, as they take us further into connecting with an idea and/or experience. 'A metaphor is the use of one subject to clarify understanding of another. Metaphors are not only verbal, but often are physical expressions of an idea like a dance or body sculpting' (Garmston, 1994a: 60). Metaphors can enable us to hear sounds in our heads or smell fragrances. They help us to see the big picture (Kaye, 1996).

As Crotty (1996: 281) explains, 'A more poetic frame of mind can go some way at least in. . . allowing us to break with conventional ways of seeing and describing things'. Metaphors help us to see a phenomenon from different perspectives, gather and present information in a different form. Morgan (1986) examined the use of different metaphors to make sense of the complex organizations in which we work. He harnessed the metaphors of machine, organism, culture, brain, hologram, and psychic prison to describe the multiple realities in which we experience organizations.

In outdoor learning situations the outdoor exercises serve as metaphors for work experiences (see Chapter 13).

Facilitators can ask participants to use metaphors as a way of establishing prior knowledge and/or feelings about a concept, or their organization. For example, I found the question, 'How is a facilitator like an elephant?' combined with the poem below useful when training new facilitators.

The poem 'Six blind men and the elephant' is a powerful stimulus for thought about perception. Some say the poem originated in Sufi stories of ancient Persia; others say the story came from China sometime during the Han dynasty (202 BC–220 AD) as 'Three blind men and an elephant' and was expanded to 'Six blind men' in the Indian version as a Buddhist and Jain parable. There is also a version in Africa, which illustrates the universality of powerful traditional teaching stories. An American poet, James Godfrey Saxe, wrote the version below (Fabun, 1968).

SIX BLIND MEN AND THE ELEPHANT

It was six men of Indostan
To learning much inclined,
Who went to see the Elephant
(Though all of them were blind),
That each by observation
Might satisfy this mind.

The First approached the Elephant,
And happening to fall
Against his broad and sturdy side,
At once began to bawl:
'God bless me! But the Elephant
Is very like a wall!'

The Second, feeling the tusk,
Cried, 'Ho! What have we here
So very round and smooth and sharp?
To me 'tis mighty clear
This wonder of an Elephant
Is very like a spear!'

The Third approach the animal,
And happening to take
The squirming trunk within his hands,
Thus boldly up and spake:
'I see,' quoth he, 'the Elephant
Is very like a snake!'

The Fourth reached out his eager hand,
And felt about the knee,
'What most this wondrous beast is like
Is mighty plain', quoth he;
''Tis clear enough the Elephant
Is very like a tree!'

The Fifth, who chanced to touch the ear
Said, 'E'en the blindest man
Can tell what this resembles most;
Deny the fact who can,
This marvel of an elephant
Is very like a fan!'

The Sixth no sooner had begun
About the beast to grope,
Than, seizing on the swinging tail
That fell within his scope,
'I see', quoth he, 'the Elephant
Is very like a rope!'

And so these men of Indostan
Disputed loud and long,
Each in his own opinion
Exceeding stiff and strong.
Though each was partly in the right,
And all were in the wrong!

James Godfrey Saxe (1816–1867)

An extra verse was added on a Web site (http://www.noogenesis.com/pineapple/
blind_men_elephant.html) from someone called Roger. It has particular relevance
today:

Moral:
So oft in theologic wars,
The disputants, I ween,
Rail on in utter ignorance
Of what each other mean,
And prate about an Elephant
Not one of them has seen!

Having read the poem 'The six blind men' I give facilitation students a picture of an elephant and some flip chart paper and pens. They draw an elephant and add ideas which flow easily, with laughter and humour. Compare the possible response to the bland question, 'What does a facilitator do?' Some of the ideas generated are cited in Table 4.5.

Table 4.5 Using metaphors of a facilitator and an elephant

Body part	Explanation
Skin	Thick, ability to take criticism, 'keeping ego in your pocket'
Head/mind	Remembering people and their needs, elephants never forget, wisdom
Size/body	Projecting a large vision, powerful, group maintenance, but not dominating, centred, 'distress-free authority'
Ears	Big ears to listen to everyone, continuous movement, keep it moving, active listening skills, listening for insights, flow, foresight
Eyes	Monitoring, being aware, observing, give direction, seeing potential
Tusks	Gentle probing, confronting, provide direction, hones in on issues, guidance, conflict resolution – putting out fires, firm authoritative/ground rules/power
Trunk	Flexible, speaking and being heard, sniff out potential problems, sensing 'vibes' and energy levels, keep moving, watering, drawing out people
Legs	Moves with the group, not too fast, using a theoretical basis for work
Tail	Always a bit left in reserve, as a fly swat to energize 'social loafers', isn't distracted by little irritations/problems, ties together linkage, humour, icebreakers
Feet	Stable, not treading on anyone's toes, group work from solid foundations, grounded with earth, stable, centred
Knees	Flexibility
Herd	Group ethics, loyalty, identifying with group
Stomach	Endurance and energy, has stomach for conflict resolution, knowledge storage, listen to gut feelings
Bum	Planning for bodily needs, comfort, toilet, stability
Back	Lifting people's sights
Large body	Commands respect but bulk appears gentle, ie 'distress-free authority'
Auntie	Pregnant and nursing elephants are helped by another female or 'auntie' just as facilitators are helped by co-facilitators, mentors and support networks

The sum of the whole is greater than the parts, and from these ideas participants can then go on to write their own definition of facilitation and their own metaphors. See Table 4.6.

Table 4.6 Examples of metaphors of facilitation

Metaphor	Explanation
Midwife	Facilitators are like birth attendants (midwives) because they have nothing to do with conception, and after the birth leave the family to get on with life, though they may make some follow-up calls: ie they help with the process but are not part of the content.
Gardener	Facilitators are like gardeners because they have to turn over the soil of the organization and help others to see into the organizational issues before helping new seeds/ideas to grow.
Court jester	Facilitators are like court jesters because they say the 'unsaid' and bring hidden agendas to the surface. They also use humour, props, antics, and provide a counterbalance to power holders, eg a court jester could, within reason, tactfully make fun of the king/queen.

Metaphors and organizations

A familiar metaphor used to describe organizations is the machine, but one metaphor may not be enough. Using such a metaphor may restrict people's thinking to focus only on mechanistic issues. Bolman and Deal (1997) opened up thinking by using four different metaphors to enable change agents to view all aspects of an organization (see Table 4.7).

Table 4.7 Four metaphors for reframing organizations

	Structural frame	Human resource frame	Political frame	Symbolic frame
Metaphor for organization	Factory or machine	Family	Jungle	Carnival, temple, theatre

Source: Bolman and Deal (1997)

Metaphors and job roles

Four simple questions are used on the Web site <http://www.learner.org/channel/workshops/nextmove/metaphor/metresults.php3> to enable people to describe and explore their job roles:

- What metaphor describes you as a. . . eg facilitator?
- Explain how this metaphor characterizes you as a facilitator.
- Provide an example from your facilitation experience that illustrates your metaphor.
- Do you think this metaphor influences or guides your facilitation? If so, how?

Other uses of metaphor

Facilitators can incorporate metaphors to:

- Invite participants to draw their organization.
- Gauge emotions and reactions at the beginning and/or end of a session, to gauge changes in responses: for example, draw 'anger' or 'conflict'.
- Find out the mood of the group: for example, draw how you feel right now.
- Engage people in holistic thought: 'Your organization is like your body; if you have a problem with muscles in one part, other parts of your anatomy will compensate. How does this relate to your situation right now?'
- Encourage participants to introduce themselves: say, 'Please introduce yourself and compare yourself to a bird/animal; song/sound'.
- Promote lateral thinking by linking one idea to another using synectic questioning (Gordon, 1961) and oxymorons (statements that sound self-contradictory, like 'organized chaos' and 'friendly fire').
- Confront a group: 'It appears to me that this group is behaving a bit like a dinosaur because I've noticed. . . What do you think?'

Framework of metaphor use

Akin and Palmer listed six ways of using metaphors for intervening in organizations. They warn that 'Metaphors are not simple, straightforward tools. They are more the frame than the picture. . . (and) should always be considered in relation to how and where they will be situated, never only on the charm of the metaphor itself' (2000: 77). I have simplified their frame to the four components described below.

1   Outside metaphor/high centrality of facilitator

A facilitator brings in a metaphor to give to participants: for example, the facilitator is like an elephant; the stages of group development are like the four seasons.

2   Inside metaphor/high centrality of facilitator

The facilitator finds or induces a metaphor from participants within the organization: for example, the facilitator used the kombi van metaphor for a speech.

3   Outside metaphor/low centrality of facilitator

The facilitator trains the participants in ways of thinking in metaphors. The facilitator provides details on how to think in multiple frames, and gives participants a framework, such as the four frames for 'reframing organizations' shown above in Table 4.7 (Bolman and Deal, 1997).

4   Inside metaphor/low centrality of facilitator

The facilitator helps participants to find their own metaphors for their organization by inviting them to complete the sentence 'My organization is like a. . .' Methods are then compared and used as a springboard for identifying core values, vision and strategies to work towards that vision.

Table 4.8   Framework of metaphor use

		Metaphor source	
		Metaphor created **outside** organization and imported	In use **inside** organization or inducted from participants by facilitator
Centrality of facilitator	**Facilitator chooses** metaphor and directs how it should be used	1	2
	Participants choose metaphor and direct how it is used	3	4

Source: adapted from Akin and Palmer (2000)

Some guidelines for using metaphors

Care should be taken in choosing metaphors. Akin and Palmer (2000) suggest four main traps:

- **Use of specific metaphors in 'inappropriate' ways.** If you are using metaphor to describe changes, be careful to pick a suitable metaphor. A metaphor to promote gradual evolutionary change is not suitable if you wish to promote fast radical changes. A metaphor may have limited use, and you may need more than one; a machine does not adequately describe an organization. Some people may have little familiarity with the metaphor: for example when working in equatorial and monsoonal lands, I do not use Heron's metaphor of the Four Seasons to illustrate the stages of group development.
- **Some metaphors are ambiguous.** The metaphors of 'hard' (technical, analytical) skills and 'soft' (interpersonal) skills are misleading, in that many managers avoid the so-called soft skills area because it is far harder to learn and practice people skills effectively.
- **You cannot change organizational metaphors at will.** Metaphors become part of the fabric of organizations and entrenched through routines. Strategies to shift thinking may be required.
- **Do not put all your ideas into one basket/metaphor.** Multiple metaphors are needed: for example, human resource metaphors are needed alongside the mechanistic metaphors.

Metaphors, like stories, have hooks. The interpretation of metaphors is personal: all individuals will interpret metaphors in different ways, and will generate metaphors for their own learning, and the perceptions of all need to be valued.

Stories

The oral tradition is one of the oldest forms of communication. The first teachers used storytelling. It was/is the way in which members of a culture come to know where they come from, why they are here, where they belong, and how to live in daily life in the larger group. Stories contain and direct group members' behaviour.

The greatest teachers were storytellers: for example Sophocles, Vivekananda, Mohammed, Buddha, Jesus and Tagore. Their stories were often not based on true happenings, but used as a metaphor for learning. Story is both a window and a mirror: it shows us something new about our lives and/or our world, and offers a reflection of what is.

Types of story

There are many different types of story:

- Social stories connect us to our culture and teach us how to behave.
- Personal stories and anecdotes are used to learn about each other and build trust.
- Family stories tell us about heroes, heroines and villains.
- Myths, magic, mystery, fairy stories work at a deeper psychological level and teach us how best to deal with goodies and baddies, beasties and dragons. To teach and/or to initiate deep changes, the facilitator needs to work at this level.
- Teaching stories tell us how to do and not to do things. The books of the great religions of Hinduism, Islam, Buddhism and Christianity are full of teaching stories.

There are more superficial stories:

- Jokes are often stories where we 'send ourselves and each other up'.
- Spin-doctors are employed to change stories of organizations and politicians.
- Urban legends or myths.

Reasons why facilitators use storytelling

Why tell stories? People like them. They like to tell their own stories and they like to listen to them. But we don't all have the same levels of skill to tell or listen to them. Storytelling not only calls for a combination of skills, it is an art form. Stories take us back to childhood. The traditional children's stories are related to the world and help children understand life through the adventures of archetypal figures, for example the hero, the martyr, the wanderer, the magician, the warrior, the orphan, as described by Pearson (1991). The stories become a release from 'private fears or wonderings' (Wilson, 1979: 4). They connect us as human beings: 'Story telling embraces the past, present, and the future of all the races of the earth' (Wilson, 1979: 83).

Vision and mission statements do not come to life until there are stories woven around them. Facilitators can use stories at the beginning of workshops to elicit values and/or create a pattern for the learning and interacting. If a facilitator tells a personal story from his/her life there is a sense of self-disclosure and trust. Facilitators need to choose stories carefully. People are quick to realize when a story is not 'authentically' chosen and told.

In organizations and society, stories play a dual role: they act as powerful directives for members' behaviours, and they can also teach specific lessons. They are the 'glue' that holds the culture of an organization together. The stories provide a blueprint for 'the way we are in this place', how we deal with things here, what is 'ok' and 'not ok'. They articulate the way in which the organization is special, different from other organizations. These stories are for the most part unconscious. At a conscious level, stories can embed values, articulate vision and give meaning to events. With constant restructuring stories are lost, and so is part of the organizational fabric.

Stories may be used to confront behaviour. They enable us to hold up a mirror, to confront and tell the truth in a more palatable way.

JEWISH TEACHING STORY

A young woman called Truth was wandering naked and forlorn through the forest. She came to a village and knocked on the doors of houses. But the inhabitants were scared of her nakedness and they shooed her away and closed their doors.

Later that night, Parable found her huddled, cold and shivering. Parable warmed her and clothed her in story. Parable fed her and sent her out again into the forest.

The second time Truth knocked on doors in the village, the villagers greeted her and were delighted with her and invited her into their homes and hearts.

(Told by Marie Finlay, storyteller)

Affective domain – linking emotions and common experiences

'Deep' as opposed to 'surface' learning involves people tapping into the feeling domain (Biggs and Telfer, 1987; Ramsden, 1992: 415). Pure cognitive thinking is not enough: 'When a story is performed with style, emotions come to life in the audience. Even just listening to a story, as compared to a lecture, combines the processes of receiving and making sense of the material' (Rosen in Boje, 1991: 17–71).

Storytelling evokes a different response from participants in workshops than do more analytical approaches. For example, in a workshop to facilitate the development of a policy on the handling of violence in a hospital, I sought to bring the rationale within the policy to life. I asked the group, 'Are there any stories you have got of ways in which violence occurred and was dealt with "well" and "not so well"?' The results were stories told from the heart, with great feeling and emotion for the perpetrators, victims and onlookers. As one story was told, people 'hooked in' their experiences. When I suggested a stop for lunch, there was a consensus to continue: 'Just a bit longer as this is so interesting'. In other workshops when I asked questions like, 'Can you describe case studies/critical incidents of xxx in this organization?' the results tended to be very analytical, logical and interpretative.

Humorous stories with a message

Humorous stories can also make many points which otherwise might sound negative and get people's backs up. Roger Smith (2000) gives a superb tongue-in-cheek executive summary of a consultant report of a work study. The idea may be easily adaptable to other situations. It has some wonderful messages for people who want to quantify everything. See also the power of humour and laughter (Hogan, 2000).

CONSULTANT'S REPORT RECOMMENDING IMPROVEMENTS TO A SYMPHONY ORCHESTRA

- For considerable periods the four oboe players had nothing to do. The numbers should be reduced and the work spread more evenly over the whole of the concert, thus eliminating peaks of activity.
- All the violins, 12 in number, were playing identical notes. This seems unnecessary duplication. These staff numbers should be cut drastically, and if more volume of sound is required it could be obtained by means of electronic amplification.
- Much effort was expended in the playing of demi-semi-quavers. This appears to be an unnecessary refinement, and it is recommended that all notes should be rounded up to the nearest semi-quaver. If this were done it would be possible to employ trainees or lower graded employees more extensively.
- There seems to be too much repetition of some musical passages: for example, no useful purpose is served by repeating on the horns a passage that has already been handled by the strings. It is estimated that if all the redundant passages were eliminated the whole concert time of 2 hours could be reduced to 20 minutes and there would be no need to waste time on an intermission.
- On methods there are several criticisms where engineering principles could successfully be employed. It was noted that the pianist was carrying out his work as a two-handed job and was also using both feet for pedal operations, but in spite of this it was noted that some notes called for excessive reaching, and it is suggested that the keyboard could be redesigned to bring the notes within the normal working area.
- Obsolescence of equipment is another matter of concern, as it was noted that in the programme that the leading violinist's instrument is hundreds of years old. If normal depreciation had been employed, this instrument could have been written off and more modern equipment purchased.

The foregoing suggestions were discussed with the management in the person of the conductor, but he was of the opinion that the implementation would probably affect the box office. He, of course, has great difficulty defending his position because it involves nothing more than waving a baton at the orchestra members, who already have the score in front of them and could perform adequately without his distracting movements.

In the circumstances I have discounted his comments and suggest that, even if the box office is affected, I am sure the great savings arising from putting my recommendations into effect would cancel out any losses caused by lower attendance. (Adapted from Smith, 2000)

Charismatic techniques

Heron (1993, 1999) describes 'charisma' in terms of personal power and presence which are set into dynamic interaction with others. The idea of presence stems from the concept of 'centring' which is based on one of the key concepts of aikido, the Japanese martial art developed by Morihei Ueshiba (1893–1969). 'Ai' means harmony, 'ki' means energy, and 'do' means the way. Aikido means 'the harmonizing of energy'. The skill of centring and being present in the here and now helps us to bring into alignment our body, mind and spirit (Crum, 1987).

Bending time and space

Using charismatic techniques, a storyteller can by using charismatic centring techniques change time and space in a room. 'Charismatic time', described by Heron (1993), is slow, incorporates extremely long pauses, and lulls the listener into a different time and space. It enables the storyteller to tap into different levels of consciousness using 'distress-free authority' (that is, the facilitator needs to be fully present). Normal speech in 'clock time' on the other hand, is fast and jerky.

STORY: THE EMPEROR'S NEW CLOTHES

Once upon a time, there was an Emperor who loved new clothes. One day two rogues came to the town. They pretended to be weavers and told everyone that they could make the most beautiful clothes in the world, even clothes that were magical and could only be seen by those who were wise and fit to hold office.

The Emperor decided that if he wore such clothes he would be able to see who was unfit to hold office, as they would not be able to see his clothes. Members of the court visited the king and could not see the clothes, but did not dare to say so as they did not want to appear stupid and they feared losing their positions.

The Emperor visited the weavers to oversee their progress. The only problem was that when the clothes were 'finished' he also could not see them, but he did not want to say so, so he gave his approval. The weavers, being mischievous, even persuaded him to wear them for a procession in a forthcoming festival.

On the day of the procession the courtiers arrived early. They exclaimed how wonderful the emperor looked and escorted him to the procession. The streets were lined with people. As the procession passed people waved and hoorayed, 'How handsome the Emperor looks in his new clothes! What a beautiful cloak!' (Storyteller: use charismatic time)

'Why – hasn't – the – emperor – got – any – clothes – on?' giggled a very small boy in the crowd.

'Don't be silly', said his father, lightly cuffing him over the head.

'Yes, it's true,' laughed someone else, 'He hasn't got any clothes on!'

Gradually the whispers spread among the crowd until they were falling about laughing.

'He's got nothing on!'

The Emperor was most put out, as deep down he knew it was true, but he couldn't admit it. So he held his head even higher than usual and continued with the procession. His courtiers continued to carry his cloak all the way back to the palace, and the weavers escaped with their money.

The story describes different perspectives: those of the Emperor, the swindlers, the ministers, courtiers, the citizens, and the boy. It illustrates the problem of being swept along by events or fads (such as in management techniques). Until the boy spoke out everyone was affected by 'groupthink' and was afraid to 'blow the whistle' or 'go against the flow'. The courtiers were afraid of losing their jobs. It was an oppressive system that they all colluded with. This brought about lies, traps and collusion in a false reality. They cheered, but what were they cheering at and why?

The small boy breaks the mould by asking the unaskable (a strategic or change question). The story raises the issue of unquestioning enthusiasm for something new, or the so-called wisdom of others or gurus from afar. Fear is also an underlying theme of the story: fear of losing power, of appearing foolish, was disempowering for both the Emperor and the courtiers.

The ability to ask questions, to make people stop and think, is liberating (Ghaye, Gillespie and Lillyman, 2000). One of the key arts of facilitators is to find the 'strategic questions' that make people stop what they are currently doing and examine the status quo. (See Chapters 3 and 11.)

Influence and persuasion

Storytelling is a very useful tool in the workplace. Participants in meetings can use a powerful story to influence and persuade. Managers and leaders frequently use 'transformational' or 'charismatic' skills to motivate workers to follow a mission or goal (Conger, 1989), but they need to use the right metaphors. Mission and vision statements are often clinical and non-motivating, and eminently forgettable. If they are expressed as a story, however, the impact is very different, as illustrated by the great leaders of the past, like Martin Luther King in his 'I have a dream' speech. Anita Roddick was highly skilled in enthusing Body Shop workers by the stories of her travels and experiences with tribal peoples. She had her own video company, so monthly 'stories' could be sent out to 1,000 Body Shops in 30 different countries, containing not only her own stories, but also those of employees and their innovations. When customers buy Body Shop products, some buy because of the environmental stories linked to the products.

Learning, memory and recall

Psychologist Renee Fuller (Zempe, 1990) suggests that story may be the building block of human learning, an easy, natural way for humans to acquire information, ideas and concepts. Belbin, Downs and Perry (1981) described 'Kim's game', a storytelling strategy which was described by Rudyard Kipling (1908) to aid memorizing. In this activity, 30 items are placed on a table and participants are invited to look at them, then turn away and see how many they can remember. The facilitator debriefs the exercise by listing all the different memorizing methods used by participants. Those learners who use 'mentally active' methods are most successful.

Belbin *et al* suggest that if things to be memorized are incorporated into a story, people remember easily. For example, items to be remembered could be placed in a story that involves walking through a large Greek or Roman palace and identifying 'items' along the way. They suggest that the facilitator explain how 'verbalizers' and 'visualizers' memorize in different ways: verbalizers tell a story, visualizers see the story in their 'mind's eye'. Both visualizers and verbalizers will be particularly helped by the use of stories, and then should 'self-test' themselves at regular intervals. Another factor that influences the success of memorizing is the mental state of the learner. Stories can help increase relaxation during memorizing.

Stories teach non threateningly

John Cleese learnt that he could teach people very dry management tools and techniques through story and humour (see Video arts productions). In this way faults and poor practices are pointed out in an indirect non-threatening way.

Storytelling is a gregarious activity. Stories contain 'hooks' that link into the listeners' experiences. Stories enable us to know 'we are not alone'. Carter Liggett at the Pacific Graduate School of Psychology in Palo Alto, California theorizes that during a story, listeners experience a biochemical change involving decreases in the hormone cortisol and increases in the concentration of immunoglobulin A. These changes show up in the saliva of listeners, and are signs of a story's capacity to relax listeners and engage the right side of the brain, the wellspring not only of imagery but also of our capacity to deal with change (Garmston, 1994: 60).

Heron (1989) believes that telling a quick tall or outrageous story, or even a funny comment, is a valuable facilitation tool in causing an 'emotional shift' in groups. Everyone laughing together unites the group, increases oxygen flow, defuses tension and helps people return to a problem at hand.

Adult learning theory

Scherrie Foster, a storyteller (Zempe, 1990) states that the storyteller's goal is to allow people to establish a sense of community and to share openly experiences related to the told story. Knowles (1984), describing adults or andragogical learning, maintained that adults learn best when new information is added to their previous experiences. In fact adults *are* their experiences, and if a facilitator does not value them and allow adults to express some of them, they may feel irritated, unvalued and even indignant. Storytelling is central to the peer learning process which is a feature of the learning organization. Until new learning is integrated into the learner's past stories, it is not an integrated part of the learner.

Stories stimulate the listener to think at the time, and also later, on a conscious and subconscious level. The purpose is not to tell people what to think, but to create a space for them to think in.

Organizational life and empowerment

Just as individuals are products of their stories, so are organizations. Maintenance of stories helps to add stability and purpose to departments and organizations. Yet in these days of 'turbulence', 'restructuring' and 'downsizing', stories are lost and/or different stories are told. 'Without air our cells die. Without a story ourselves die' (Postman, in Zempe, 1990: 44). The major stories circulated at this time are stories of decline, injustice and despair. Many individuals are left alienated, depressed and even ill. Management frequently dismisses or represses these stories; there is no opportunity for them to be told.

Telling our stories to others helps to integrate the story's meaning; the intrinsic form in a story can transmute chaos and restore a sense of belonging. Even the most painful of experiences are in some way redeemed when they are told as stories (Salas, 1993: 19).

Internal and external facilitator/consultants who have knowledge of an organization's stories can more effectively tailor their interventions in the change process. The current climate of 'downsizing' and changing roles requires people to take on change, manage themselves through the process, and often manage others. In the absence of adequate information, people need a structure to make sense of their experiences, to add order to the chaos, to contain them in their work and lives.

When individuals are stressed because of impending 'downsizing' or 'retrenchment', frequently they are not given an opportunity to vent their hurt. Healing cannot occur until these stories are told and heard. Once this is done, then stories of competence and vision can be mobilized and a new culture built.

Some stories cannot be told until enough time and space have elapsed and adequate healing has occurred. For example, distance from a traumatic event may be necessary, as evidenced by the recent Korean and Dutch women's stories of the atrocities committed against them by the Japanese army 50 years ago in the Second World War.

The hero/heroine's journey

I describe in detail uses of the hero/heroine's journey for facilitators in *Facilitating Empowerment* (2000), so I will only briefly summarize Joseph Campbell's ideas here. 'The hero's journey' may be used to enhance the empowerment of others so that they can see their situation in a different way, as an archetypal journey. Archetypes are deep and abiding patterns in the human psyche that remain powerful and present over time. Joseph Campbell (1973) describes the stages of the universal journey and the adventures, joys, mistakes, challenges and dangers that face the hero at each stage. The hero/heroine is the person who takes off on a series of adventures beyond the ordinary, either to recover what has been lost, or to discover some life-giving elixir. The metaphor may be used in many facilitation scenarios to enable people to manage change, risks and transitions. For further information see Hogan (2000). The hero's journey metaphor can also be illustrated through movies like *Star Wars*, a modern myth.

Star Wars (original version)

Star Wars is a film directed by George Lucas. It follows the journey of Luke Skywalker, son of a Jedi knight, from a callow youth to Jedi knight. During this transformation he is aided by many allies, spiritual, human and mechanical. He is trained in the ways of a Jedi knight and carries with him the power of the Force, a universal energy, the force of the light. The enemy is the Empire, the force of darkness, embodied in the Empire and the fiend, Darth Vader, a former Jedi who has 'gone over' to the dark side. Finally Luke destroys the Death Star, the war machine of the Empire, and returns in glory, to be decorated by Princess Leia.

Linking to this well-known story, facilitators can invite people to tell personal stories. In describing for example the role of Ben Obi Wan Kenobi, participants can identify people in their lives who played the role of helpers/mentors. What was the gift they gave? What meaning does this have for the present situation? This questioning is repeated at various stages.

Exercises in storytelling techniques

Preparation

First of all have a clear purpose, then find the story. Choose a story that you enjoy and want to tell, and that your listeners can relate to, and remember a story consists of a beginning, a middle and an end, and usually there is a problem to be solved.

The beginning must be an invitation, to draw people in. Set the scene and make sure the context is clear. This allows the audience to join with the visions of the teller. Make sure you allow adequate time to develop this well. In the middle the problem emerges, a dilemma is created: again one that the listeners can relate to. At the end or climax is the resolution of the problem. Make this clear, as it offers listeners new ways of thinking about an issue. This is a learning/teaching point. It is also a letting go, where the audience must be in no doubt that the story is over.

There is a storyteller and a listener. The story does not exist without listeners, so keep them in mind! Learn your story in whatever is your preferred way. Some people read their stories over and over, others prefer to tell them to anyone who will listen, some put the story on tape and play it to themselves in the car, or when they are going to sleep, and others do all of these!

Learn the first and last lines by heart. This will get you started if you are feeling nervous, and allow you to end in a way that is clear to your audience. Then tell the story in your own way.

Exercises in a workshop situation

1 Warm-up

This is a non-threatening and enjoyable warm-up for people for whom the story process is new. Choose a partner and decide who will be the storyteller first, and who will be the 'giver of words'. The giver of words asks the storyteller, 'Tell me a story about. . .'. The storyteller begins, and the other puts words into the story at a reasonable pace. The words can support or challenge the storyline, and the storyteller must react and adjust the story accordingly. After three minutes, partners change roles and repeat the process.

During the reflection time the facilitator asks, 'What was the most difficult part of the exercise?' 'Why?' 'Who supported, who challenged?' 'How was that?'

2 Retelling

This activity is useful in developing active listening and a storytelling ability in the participants. Retelling in threes is less threatening for beginners. One person tells a story, the others listen for the content and the feeling. When the story is finished, the two listeners stand, link arms and jointly retell the story. Each of the group tells and retells a story.

In the debriefing the facilitator asks, 'What was it like to have your story told?' 'What was it like listening to a story, knowing that you were going to have to repeat it next?'

3 Creating the myth

Work with the image, the feelings that the image engenders. Decide on the time: present, past or future. What is the landscape, how does it reflect the mood, feeling? Who are the characters, the heroes, villains and magicians? Use 'story' language. Remember that a story has a beginning, a middle and an end, and that the ends aren't always tidy. Begin with 'Once upon a time. . .' or something similar.

Storytelling is an underestimated but powerful facilitation tool. Storytelling techniques can be learnt and practised by anyone. They are free in the monetary sense, but you may need to gain permission to use 'traditional stories' from some ethnic groups.

Using the stories of participants

Many organizations use case studies to teach participants how to diagnose issues and problem solve. Mumford (1999) suggested that 'case studies are dead, it's like dissecting corpses'. What he meant is that case studies are often written to teach certain points, date quickly, and often do not relate to the lives of the participants. As a result they can be analysed dispassionately, and while a participant may recommend, 'The manager should go and have a heart to heart with that staff member,' indeed that participant may not have a clue as to the interpersonal skills to go about such an intervention.

For examples of such case studies see the Web site http://www.mcsj. unisa.edu.au/current_articles.htm

Consider a facilitator who brings the case alive, saying, 'Would you come out and be the manager, John Smith, for a few moments? Choose someone to play the part of the staff member, Peter. Should you meet with him/her? And if 'yes' where is most appropriate? Would e-mail or a phone call do? Why not? What other options are there? How are you feeling about going to see this person? What do you think would be a good opener? Right, let's give this a go.' Later the facilitator can add, 'Has anyone got any other ways of saying this?'

Now consider a further step into the reality of the participants. The facilitator might say, 'Has anyone got a past or current story relating to xxx? Can you tell us about it?' (John, say, does so.) 'Thank you, John. What questions would the group like to ask John?' (The facilitator waits for questions and discussion.) 'Now let's role play an important turning point in the story. John, would you like to watch or have a role? Who else would like to join in?' And after the role play, 'What theories does this illustrate? What theories does it not illustrate? Can you draw up a framework, model from this?'

Tips for facilitators

- Prepare your stories carefully at first. Practise at home or in the car or in front of your cat or dog!
- Use your intuition to build in a story at the right time for your group. If it feels wrong, then save it for another time.
- Collect stories from a variety of different cultural backgrounds.
- Always give participants a chance to tell their own stories.
- Explain to participants why you use storytelling as a teaching-learning tool.
- Ask a colleague to watch you tell a story so you can get feedback.
- Practise using charismatic time (Heron, 1999).

Further references on storytelling

Chan and Mauborgne (1992) describe Chinese stories of leadership. Estes (1992) describes stories to help women get in touch with the power of their wild side. McCann and Stewart (1997) use animals as a basis for cautionary tales about management based on Aesop's fables. Simpkinson and Simpkinson (1993) focus on stories that transform and heal. Kaye (1996) provides a very readable account of myths and stories and metaphors in organizations. Hogan (2000) outlines traditional stories including, 'The women's wish', 'Who will bell the cat?', 'The old man and the horse', 'How Yu Gong moved the mountain', 'The listening prince', 'The tale of the sands', 'The good man', and 'The children's story'. See also Chapter 12, 'The story of the hundredth monkey'.

Movement

If I could tell you what I meant there would be no point in dancing it.

Isadora Duncan

Any kinds of movement create changes of energy. Some people actually think better when moving around (often to the chagrin of their teachers in the past). Energizers can shift thinking, energies and so on: see Chapter 2.

Physical movement can be used to shift frames of being and thinking. For example, if group members are locked into a certain way of looking at things, or are locked into storming behaviour, exchanging seats or standing and walking out to a space together can change the group dynamics dramatically.

Some people have a mix of 'naturalistic intelligence' (see Gardner above) and think and learn through movement. They often say things like, 'I think better with the wind in my brain'. See also Chapter 13 on outdoor learning.

Drama-based processes

There are now a wide variety of drama techniques that have developed in recent years:

- role play, such as hassle lines;
- theatre of the oppressed (Boal, 1992);
- theatresports (Martini and Foreman, 1995);
- international playback theatre network: http://www.playbacknet.org/;
- psychodrama (Moreno).

Each has its own uses and sets of ground rules, which are too diverse to enter into here. Suffice to say that training is required in these tools and techniques, as some can trigger deep distress. Facilitators are not therapists. (See *Understanding Facilitation*, Chapter 11 on Ethics).

Role play

Role plays are simulations of real or imagined events. I find it most useful to build a role play from participants' stories. Participants learn by acting out the behaviours they found difficult to deal with, and hence experience some elements of role reversal/seeing how people react to their behaviours, and by observing the protagonists in action.

Uses

Role plays are particularly useful for learning interpersonal skills and for raising concerns regarding gender and race issues. They often generate some 'ahas' or insights (Mumford, 1999). They are not so useful in groups with a resistance to take risks and low trust, especially if there is a mix of managerial levels in an in-house programme. Also if the verbal or English skills of some participants is low there may be problems. Role plays can be used to bring case studies to life.

Some dos and don'ts of role play

There are a few basic points to remember. People have to feel safe to undertake role plays, so always invite rather than coerce people to 'have a go'. Role plays in groups of three people, with one person observing (with feedback guidelines) maximize participation, and this is the least threatening group structure to use. Move participants into a different space for role plays, so that at the end as they move back to their own 'places' they shed their roles in time and space.

Always give or ask the 'actors' to take on a different name. At the end 'actors' need to 'de-role', that is, shed the role taken and resume their normal persona. If this does not take place, their peers may attribute some of the behaviours to them personally. You can prompt de-roling by saying, 'Thank you, George, for role playing difficult participant behaviour. I'm sure we've all met characters like Fred in our workshops at some time.'

Debriefing role plays

The debriefing session is the most important part of a role play, and assists participants to learn from experience and transfer that learning to their own lives. The ORID discussion process is very useful for this (Chapter 3). Once participants have discussed their learning, the facilitator I believe is morally bound to, first, help individuals to de-role and come back to the 'here and now', and second, ensure that participants do not continue to assign characteristics of the role to the person.

Four key facilitative questions can help with this. In the following example 'Mrs Jones' is a role-play name and 'Mary' is the real name of the participant:

> Mrs Jones, do you have anything to say to your co-role players?
> Mary, are you ready to rejoin the group (ie to go back to her original chair)?
> Mary, have you anything you would like to say to Mrs Jones?
> Mary, can you describe two ways in which you are different from Mrs Jones?

These questions can be applied to each role player in turn.

Another useful activity is to get everyone to stand, shake their bodies, run their hands down their arms and legs, and flick off the role. This change of space and energies also helps to de-role and bring everyone back to the 'here and now'.

Circus and juggling

Don't let gravity bring you down

Reg Bolton

Circus techniques have been highly successful as a means of enhancing community development in Australia, the United States and the UK (Bolton, 1987). The social benefits of bringing together different strands of a community to achieve a local performance are obvious, and this often results in positive media coverage of young and old collaborating and working together. There are always jobs available to suit people of all ages and fitness.

Learning to juggle promotes mind/body harmony, fun, perseverance and improvisation. Juggling is a useful ice-breaker for executive development programmes or to help human resource developers learn about different learning styles.

Circus activities 'work' because there is an element of magic and achieving the 'impossible', and most of all because they are fun. On long-term workshops, participants may wish to put on a show. Performing something for others is a gift. You can perform things in groups that you cannot do alone. Juggling can be made easier using small scarves (which slow down the process), and mistakes can be laughed off by blaming a 'sudden gust of gravity' (Bolton, 1998).

Playback theatre

Playback theatre is a form of storytelling and improvisational theatre in which participants tell stories from their lives and watch them enacted on the spot. Playback theatre has been used for over 40 years. The facilitator is called a 'conductor' who questions and reflects back understanding in order to give the actors enough material to improvise from. There is no judgement, no construct of one truth, or one right way to be or do (Pearson, undated).

The storytellers who step forward from the group of participants to divulge their experiences show courage. The teller chooses the actors for the roles in the unfolding story. Frequently there is accompanying flute or percussion music. Other participants watch and engage as they see the experiences of others; there is learning and insight, a chance to see things from different perspectives, to hear stories that are similar to and different from their own multiple realities.

Playback theatre has been used in hundreds of different settings and five continents in organizations, schools, prisons, communities and clinical settings. A useful Web site is the International Playback Theatre Network, www. playbacknet.org. Rea Dennis is currently conducting her PhD research project into the efficacy of playback theatre. She welcomes dialogue on a discussion list: to subscribe e-mail r.dennis@social.uq.edu.au

Playback theatre can also be combined with open space technology workshops, as illustrated in the following story.

Story: Combining playback and open space

Recently, I attended a National Conference with over 200 International Student Advisers from across Australia and Southeast Asia. The organizers planned a participatory opening morning, as opposed to the normal top-down formality of keynote speakers. The first session comprised playback theatre. The conductor asked participants first of all to focus on key words that described their difficulties getting to the conference. The actors jumped into various mimes and stances. Then the session progressed to playback theatre based on the stories of International Advisers who try to cope with ever-increasing numbers of students and concurrent critical incidents. I saw people who were very weary at the end of the year with tears of laughter in their eyes.

After the break chairs were reorganized into concentric circles and I facilitated an open space technology session (see Chapter 12). It was the first time that there had been a break in tradition from the normal 'academic' style conference. I was gratified by the response; about 30 groups formed and later entered their ideas on four laptops. Data was posted on walls and later sent out to their e-mail discussion groups. By lunch on the first day, participants had already started to network with people with similar interests. The noise in the restaurant at lunchtime was deafening, very different from the reserve I have noted previously on the first day of conferences.

Theatresports

Theatresports is another improvisational theatrical movement. Keith Johnstone, a director and writer at the Royal Court Theatre in the late 1950s, invented improvisational games as a means to overcome his writer's block, and free his creative process. Theatresports is a worldwide organization, whose aim is to promote performance and training in improvisation. There are Theatresports leagues throughout Europe, North America, South Africa and the Antipodes. Facilitators can use many Theatresports exercises as icebreakers and interactive energizers, creativity exercises and the like (Foreman and Clem, 1995).

Psychodrama

Psychodrama is a specialized form of role play developed by Jacob Moreno, a Viennese psychologist who contended that people could gain more from acting out their problems than from talking about them. The process digs down into deep layers of the past. Psychodrama can also help people to change roles, and was developed initially for Viennese prostitutes wanting a change of direction in life. Moreno and his family were prolific writers, and there are many Web sites on this topic. Psychodrama should only be used by trained and supervised specialists, and with the open and agreed acceptance of the participants.

Imagining

Facilitators can invite participants to 'imagine' they are their organizations, their problems and so on. Michael Polanyi, a Hungarian physicist and philosopher cites in *The Tacit Dimension* (1966) examples of science being a 'participatory' act. Keller followed this idea (1983: 198) and studied the work of the scientist Barbara McClintock, who said of the corn plants she was studying, 'I know them intimately and I find it a great pleasure to know them'. Indeed, many discoveries have been made by people imagining they were the objects of their research, wherein the gap between the 'knower' and the 'known' diminishes and enables new insights to emerge.

Films

There are two main types of films/videos, first, those that were designed as training videos, and second, commercial full-length films which are useful as observational learning. Third, there are films made by groups as a superordinate goal and/or teambuilding exercise. For example, at my university the first-year coordinators from five business schools came together to make a video about a 'video shop' as a case study story for students to analyse in their first semester. The making of the film was great fun and a fantastic exercise bringing together people from five different teaching areas (who scripted and acted in the video).

Training videos

The Abilene Paradox (Timmons, 1984) deals with the management of agreement in organizations. It demonstrates the fact that mismanaged agreement is as dangerous to organizational effectiveness as excessive conflict, because it can lead the organizations toward inappropriate goals. *Inside Story: Facing the demons* (1999) concerns restorative justice facilitation between perpetrators and victims and their families. *Methods* (1965) is a classic showing different styles of leadership with preschool children (and research ethics). In *The Music Paradigm* (1999) Roger Nierenberg conducts the BBC Concert Orchestra and describes to managers how an orchestra is like a metaphor for an organization. Other useful training videos are listed on page 475–76.

Commercial full length films

A good Web site for reviews and parts of scripts is http://www.filmsite.org/

Among films you might find useful are *Twelve Angry Men* (1957) which deals with jury decision making, *Dead Poets Society* (1989) on facilitating learning and autonomy, *She'll Be Wearing Pink Pyjamas* (1984), an outdoor programme for women, *Lord of the Flies* (1963), *The Dish* (2000), the story of the Australian team responsible for tracking (and temporarily losing) the space flight that put Armstrong on the moon, and *The Navigators* (2002), directed by Ken Loach, about privatization of rail track maintenance work in the UK and the impact on the group dynamics of the track gangs and on safety.

Visuals

Surfacing the culture of the organization

Here is a simple exercise to help to bring issues to the surface.

> Close your eyes. As you think of your organization, what image arises? Is it an animal, an object, a colour? Draw the image. Find a partner, discuss your image and how it reflects the organization as you see it.

The facilitator debriefs this exercise by asking individuals to show and explain their drawings. If the participants are from the same organization, commonalities of images may occur. Perceptual gaps may occur between people from different levels of the organization. Individuals often want to tell the story behind the image drawn.

When facilitators invite participants to draw an idea, there is often some resistance, as many people believe they cannot draw. However, even the simplest of symbols can portray very powerful messages.

Drawing

Betty Edwards (1988) explored the use of drawing to explore human emotions. In one exercise she invites participants to fold paper into eight segments, and to use pencil to draw, mark or make lines to depict various feelings, suggesting that the whole of the section could be used, or part, and the point or side of the pencil, heavy or light. There is only one ground rule: participants are not allowed to draw pictures or symbols, just lines.

1. Anger	2. Joy	3. Peacefulness	4. Depression
5. Human energy (power)	6. Femininity	7. Illness	8. Your choice

Figure 4.1   Drawing feelings

She suggests that facilitators use the following ideas to help participants:

> Read the word in the first rectangle: anger. Think back to the last time you were really angry. Without using words at all, even to label the event or the reason for your anger, feel within yourself what that anger was like. Imagine you are feeling the emotion again, that it flows first from deep inside, then into your

arm, down into your hand, and into the pencil, where it emerges from the point of the pencil to record itself in marks that are equivalent to the feeling – marks that look like the felt emotion. The marks need not be done all at once, but can be adjusted, changed, erased if necessary in order to achieve an image of the emotion that seems to fit the emotion as it feels to you. (Edwards, 1988: 67–68)

Drawings make feelings visible. One thing that is noticeable is the similarity of the images. They form a useful basis for discussion. Alternatively drawings may also be used to illustrate changes in perception. For example, asking individuals to draw their perception of concepts like 'conflict' or 'anger' at the beginning and end of a course on conflict resolution are useful tools to monitor shifts in thinking.

Visual language: charts and pictures

Robert Horn wrote about *Visual Language* (1998) and described the power of integrating words and pictures. He cited the work of Richard Mayer, who tested how well volunteers could understand the working of a bicycle pump or a car's brakes from verbal descriptions alone, pictures alone, or both simultaneously. Participants could recall details equally well from any of the three types of presentation, but when they had to apply their knowledge, those given both picture and words came up with 50 per cent more correct answers than the other two groups.

Other forms of visuals are useful:

- fishbone diagrams for plotting the causes of a problem or effects of a problem on key branches, eg people, environment, methods, equipment, policies;
- Gantt charts;
- mind maps and mindscapes;
- flow diagrams;
- argumentation mapping: charting ideas, eg using Six Thinking Hats as a mind map;
- mandalas and domain mapping (see Chapter 7);
- force field analysis;
- multi criteria decision grids (see Chapter 11).

Metaphor mapping

It can be very interesting to ask participants to draw their perceptions of their organization using symbols, squiggles and so on.

STORY: DRAW YOUR IMAGE OF THE UNIVERSITY

Some years ago, I asked new postgraduate students to draw their perceptions of the university. One drew a telephone handpiece dangling off the hook. Another drew a person's head and hands creeping up over a huge brick wall: strong images of how alienated they felt. The power of the images, however, was shown when I described them at a senior Quality Committee Meeting which among other things was addressing service to students. One top official immediately tried to 'shoot the messenger', and jumped down my throat, saying, 'How dare you say that, Chris!' A noisy argument ensued as other colleagues jumped to my defence. When it died down, I continued to elaborate on what the students had said about the images, and we were able to discuss what the images meant. As a result the staffing levels and training of student services personnel was increased.

In the facilitation of a community meeting to design a local park, I was lucky enough to have an artist working beside me drawing simple stylized pictures of the desirable images that children and adults described after a creative visualization session.

The following story illustrates how constructing a visual representation of communication patterns showed the group what was happening. It occurred during a community workshop to enable stakeholders and community members to be more effective in dealing with domestic violence.

STORY: COMMUNICATION PATTERNS AND STRING

After lunch the participants focused on their current communication patterns. I asked them to recount a story from finding a domestic violence victim. Depending on who was first on the scene, the communication patterns got really complicated. We could not see the wood for the trees. I tried to draw the evolving patterns on the board. It did not work. I had a flash of inspiration and asked for some string. One woman went off to her car. Meanwhile, the participants wrote on sticky-backed notes the names of each agency, and spread them out on the floor. The string arrived and the participants started weaving a kind of web. Every agency seemed to be involved to some degree, but noticeably few lines of string involved the police.

There was one of those sudden 'ahas' that sometimes occur in groups: an epiphanic moment. The police said, 'There we are, that's what we keep telling you, why don't you involve us more?' Explanations arose regarding the communication patterns, particularly of many male police. The lack of trust was discussed, and some useful dialogue ensued, so I sat down and let them go uninterrupted. I was pleased to see 'hidden agendas' flowing out freely. Trust appeared to be building.

Milly Sonneman's text *Beyond Words* (1997) provides useful techniques for using symbols on flip chart paper, which enable facilitators to learn the art of 'graphic facilitation' to draw out or illustrate ideas easily and quickly:

> When I began adding graphics and colour and using various formats to represent ideas, the whole way that my group reacted to the process underwent a major shift... graphically record a group discussion allows different people to absorb new information in the way they're most comfortable with – some respond best to the image maps, some prefer to concentrate on the words.

> Ronald Galbraith in Sonneman (1997)

Table 4.9 Visuals: the language of complexity

Pluses	*Minuses*
Simplify ideas	Don't show all nuances of information
Clearly show ideas	Don't show fine detail
Show complex ideas that words cannot describe	Need someone who can write/draw quickly and clearly, ie facilitator may need someone to help draw graphics, or invite participants to draw
Allow participants to skim quickly	
Show relationships between ideas	
People are used to taking in information visually now via television, computers etc	
Show the overall or more balanced picture	
Stimulate emotions	

Word provides basic autoshapes, but Milly Sonneman helps you to draw them in front of groups. Better still involve participants who can draw (look for the people who love to doodle).

Technology can help too, such as electronic whiteboards, or laptops plus projection panels. Computer programs like PowerPoint, Sketch (which transforms freehand sketches into more polished drawings), Mind Maps Plus, and Axon Idea Processor can be useful.

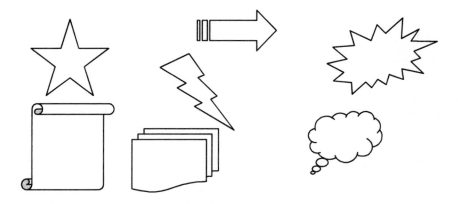

Figure 4.2 Examples of autoshapes

Mandalas

Mandalas are pictures that incorporate concentric circles, which are one of the most potent of human symbols. The outer circle represents the universe. Carl Jung believed that mandalas were a means of returning to inner harmony and exploring the human psyche. From Tantric beliefs to medieval Christianity to American Indian cultures, mandalas have been a source of reverence, inspiration, meditation and healing.

Mandalas are basically a representation of the universe, and may be used as a means of free drawing after meditations, or adaptations like 'domain mapping' may be used for plotting the various aspects of one's life (see Chapter 7).

Paintings

Many pieces of artwork can be used to open up discussion. Your choice will depend on your tastes and what pieces of art stimulate your own thinking. Here are some examples:

Table 4.10   Art to generate discussion

Issues	Painting	Artist
Gender	Frida and Diego Rivera	Frida Kahlo
Dual cultural heritages	The Two Fridas	Frida Kahlo
Pain	The Broken Column	Frida Kahlo
Distress	Weeping Woman	Pablo Picasso
Reflecting on learning at the end of a course/work	The Gleaners	Jean-François Millet
Conflict/war	Guernica	Pablo Picasso
Creativity/leisure	Children's Games	Pieter Breughel the Elder
	The Creation of Adam	Michelangelo
Change, engulfing issues	The Great Wave of Kanagawa	Katsushika Hokusai
Work	The Shearing of the Rams	Tom Roberts
	Industrial landscapes	L S Lowry
Mind stilling	Buddhist tankas	Various
Relationships: love	The Kiss	Gustav Klimt
Relationships: sorry	Breaking the News	Frank McCubbin
	Sculpture	
Relationships: love	The Kiss	Auguste Rodin
Reflection: thought	The Thinker	Auguste Rodin

Fractals from the Web

Colourful pictures of 'fractals', curves or geometrical figures, each part of which has the same statistical character as the whole, may be printed from the Web and used to stimulate discussion during workshops. See the Web site, www. fractals.com/fractal_gallery/krueger/91.1/2ceab.gut

Cartoons

Cartoons are very useful tools for putting hidden agendas firmly on the table. When people can laugh at themselves and their own idiosyncrasies there is a shift in awareness and acceptance, and even perhaps acknowledgement of the need for change. Scott Adams in the Dilbert series has parodied the management fads and corporate rhetoric of mission statements, downsizing, rightsizing (1996) and the future of work and society (1997). Michael Leunig, Mary Leunig and Ashley Brilliant cartoons are worth collecting, while the Kliban cat cartoons are useful in multicultural settings as many do not contain dialogue or show gender. (However, I found that in Mongolia cats are not very popular animals!) If you use cartoons in handouts you may need to obtain copyright permission.

Mask making

> Give a person a mask and he/she will tell you the truth.
>
> Oscar Wilde

I attended a workshop in 1991 in Canada, at a conference of the Organizational Behaviour Teaching Society, in which Dr Carolyn Egri and Professor Peter Frost engaged a large group of organizational behaviour lecturers in mask making in order to explore the links between shamans and OD specialists, and to provide a vehicle for self exploration.

1   Opening time and space

First they asked us to gather around in a circle, and we did a slow dance anticlockwise to create the 'space' for the ritual of mask making. (At the end, we repeated the exercise clockwise to close the 'space'.)

2   Slides and readings

Second, they showed us slides of the elements of air, sea, earth and fire, and we listened to their descriptions of the links between shamanism and personal and organizational change. Shamanism appears to have been one of the world's oldest traditions, common to all cultures. The roles of shamans were to restore balance and harmony, initiate change, be journeyers in time and space. They were not leaders of their communities. They lived on the fringes of society, simultaneously observing the internal mechanisms of their community and the changing external environment, similar to the roles of many facilitators (Egri and Frost, 1991).

3   Mask making

Masks help us to perform various roles. They have been part of all cultures throughout history. We need to know what different kinds of masks are available and the consequence of each. We were provided with cardboard, scissors, paints, glue, feathers, glitter, beads, material and left to our own devices for 20 minutes to make a mask that represented ourselves and the masks that we wear. Music and the burning of scented candles were an integral part of the scene setting.

At the end of the exercise each person spoke for two minutes about his/her mask (front and inside) to a small group. No discussion or interpretation was allowed, only active concentration on each person as he/she spoke.

Photos

Polaroid and now digital cameras are useful tools for photographing participants at the beginning, end or during workshops. Copies can be sent to everyone as e-mail attachments, as memorabilia or to help everyone learn names at the beginning of courses. Groups may arrange their own photos, edit and delete in camera, and compose new shots according to what they want to convey. I find that people respond well to having 'power over' the images that are being made of them.

Participants may also be asked to photograph concepts in groups. For example, the participants may be given the task of illustrating the concepts of 'team work', 'leadership' and 'creativity' in teams of five. Each person has to take one shot of each concept. Then each group selects their best shots which are pooled, displayed and discussed.

Digital cameras were used at the Asian Facilitator Conference in Penang (2001) to capture conference highlights, and were shown using Mircosoft Power Point and a large screen (and greeted with much laughter) as part of the ending rituals.

Photolanguage Australia

Our society is more visual than every before. *Photolanguage Australia* (Cooney and Burton, 1986a, 1986b) is a black and white picture set designed to facilitate communication by enabling individuals to articulate ideas, experiences, feelings, values and associations that have been triggered by the images. The 130 images represent various aspects of the human condition. The set can also be extended, depending on where a facilitator is working. (Sets are available in the Philippines.) It may be used for a wide variety of sessions including starting and finishing courses, values clarification and team building. Photolanguage was originally developed in France by Pierre Babin in 1968, as a tool for communicating with 'visually-oriented' youth.

Using photos does not require high levels of 'visual literacy' as you are not asking participants to analyse the photos, merely to react to them spontaneously. The process of holding up a photo also diverts the listeners' eyes from the speaker, so this process often helps shyer participants to speak. Some people say, 'I don't know why I chose this photo, but it spoke to me', and then suddenly they speak straight from the heart, while others explore meaning intuitively.

I used the set with a group of Aboriginal people during a course on 'Internalized racism'. The set of photos includes pictures of the many different races who live in Australia. There were pictures of Aboriginal people and ancient rock carvings. I watched curiously to see if those images would be chosen, but they were not. I later asked them why and someone responded, 'I chose the pictures that related most to my experiences here; however, I noticed that there were pictures of Aboriginal people and I was pleased. We don't normally see positive images of ourselves; we are so often omitted or portrayed negatively.'

The photos may be used in a number of ways, for example to elicit responses to:

- How are you feeling at the beginning of this course?
- Where do you feel your group is heading? And where would you like your group to be heading?
- How do you feel about your career/life at this time?
- What do you think you got out of this course personally?

While living in Lao PDR, I developed my own sets of photos using a digital camera so that participants could select from images of their own culture. In developing the sets I asked local people to evaluate my images and to add to my shooting script, so I covered their values from their perspectives.

Photos from the Web

You can download a wide variety of visuals from: http://www.webshots.com/

One colleague, Maria Martin, used the metaphor of the 'journey' for a conference presentation and workshop. She knew that many of the participants were owners of kombi vans. She found a site on kombi vans on the Web (www.vintagebus.com) which includes a huge number of photos of kombi vans inside and out, in all sorts of locations (including the bottom of the sea). She incorporated these into a very memorable session.

Card packs

There are a variety of card packs available. Card sorts provide participants with a means to move, shift, cluster and build ideas. Card sorts have an element of playfulness, and playing cards are universal.

Power cards

In *Facilitating Empowerment* (Hogan, 2000), I incorporated 60 power cards into an 'empowerment cycle' to make power visible, accessible, and to encourage people to talk about how power is used and/or abused in organizations. The cards are easy and cheap to photocopy so that participants may have their own 'pack' to take home.

Creativity cards

The *Creative Whack Pack* (von Oech, 1992) consists of a deck of 64 cards, each bearing a specific creative strategy, based on the idea that sometimes people need a whack on the side of the head to jolt them out of habitual thought patterns. I find the graphics somewhat 'aggro', but the descriptions and stories

Figure 4.3   Facilitating Empowerment

on each card are useful. The 64 cards are divided into four suits (each comprising 16 cards): Explorer, Artist, Judge and Warrior. According to von Oech, these represent the four roles (or types of thinking) of the creative process.

Explorer
The Explorer is the role for discovering the resources you'll use to create new ideas; the Artist is your role for transforming resources into new ideas. The cards in the Explorer suit highlight places and ways to find new information.

Artist

The Artist is your role for transforming your resources into new ideas. The cards in the Artist suit provide you with idea-generating techniques.

Judge

The Judge is the role for evaluating ideas and deciding what to do with them. The cards in the Judge suit lend decision-making advice.

Warrior

The Warrior is the role for implementing ideas. The cards in the Warrior suit give you the 'kick' you need to get your ideas into action.

You can view the cards on the Web at: http://www.kinecomm.com/java_example2/CreativeWhackPackHelp.html

The Bears

The Bears card pack (Deal and Veeken, 1997) illustrates a wide range of feelings through pictures of bears. The cards have no written interpretation of the feelings, and are useful in cross-cultural groups. In my experience they elicit humorous responses, but enable many people to voice and discuss feelings, which for some may be difficult.

Strength cards

The Strength cards (Deal and Veeken, 1992) contain both words and pictures of animals, illustrating 48 strengths. The Web site of St Lukes Innovative Resources contains many interesting resources: http://www.stlukes.org.au (e-mail: stlukes@ruralnet.net.au).

Strengths in Teams card pack

These are 28 pictures (A4 size) of people, demonstrating qualities and values of successful teamwork which may be used for teams to evaluate their strengths and areas for improvement (Deal, 1999). Also available from St Luke's Innovative Resources.

Spiritual dimensions of facilitation

Spirituality is an emotionally loaded word. For some it triggers links to bureaucratized, patriarchal religions or half-formed New Age mysticism. The Latin origin of the word 'spirit' is 'spirare', meaning, 'to breathe': the life force within us (Neal, 1997). By spirituality, I mean a sense of unity with the earth, universe, and all living things, together with links between the past, present and future. For some, there is a spiritual dimension to facilitation. We are all spiritual beings operating in this world, and we have certain ways of behaving, some of which are productive and some counterproductive. The facilitator works with these behaviours, but always honours the whole person or the spiritual beings in the group. That might sound a bit esoteric, but that is really what it is all about (Hunter, Bailey and Taylor, 1993:199).

Increasing interest in spirituality

Judith Neal (1997) gives an overview of literature, suggesting three reasons for the increasing interest in spirituality in the workplace:

- **Demographics.** Baby-boomers (people born after the Second World War) are now reaching middle age, examining their achievements and purpose in life in relation to the idealism of their younger years.
- **Turbulent change.** Downsizing and restructuring changes have left many employees scared and feeling devalued and dehumanized. The time that those with formal employment spend at work appears to be increasing (as opposed to the literature in the 1970s which foretold a shortening of the working week).
- **Turn of the millennium.** This caused many to reflect on the progress and horrors of the 20th century and imagine new goals for the future. Likewise, the events of 11 September 2001 when the World Trade Center was obliterated in New York, and subsequent talk of war and labelling of countries by politicians, have shaken individuals into reflecting on their own lives and the world order.

Futurist Joanna Macy calls this period 'The great turning' (Macy and Brown, 1998), while Robert Theobald calls this period 'The healing century' (1998). Both have developed rituals and processes to enable people to reflect.

At the present time there appears to be a shift in thinking in the West, in that there is a plethora of books currently being published on bringing back some kind of spiritual sense into the workplace (Bolman and Deal, 1995; Kornfield, 1994; Muller, 1997; Hillman, 1996). This is not 'spirit' in the religious sense, but recognition of the interconnectedness between the individual spirit, team spirit and organizational spirit, and earth spirit.

Guidelines for facilitating with a spiritual purpose

Judith Neal (1997) suggests five guidelines for incorporating a spiritual perspective into the teaching of management education, which may be of use to facilitators with a similar purpose:

- **Know thyself.** Facilitating provides many experiences to become self-aware. Examine why and how you do what you do and invite others to do the same.
- **Act with authenticity and congruency.** Be yourself. Do not build up the power of the facilitator role, use power with rather than power over others.

- **Respect and honour the beliefs of others.** It can be risky to mention the word 'spirituality' in some groups. If there is climate of trust and openness, then when appropriate, it may be useful to open up dialogue about the variety of belief and non-belief systems held by participants.
- **Be as trusting as you can.** Trust involves trusting yourself, your inner voice, and intuition for guidance to do the best you possibly can for your participants.
- **Maintain a spiritual practice.** There is a wide diversity of spiritual practices, from spending time in nature, meditation, to reading inspirational literature, yoga, writing a journal and shamanic practices (Egri and Frost, 1991).

Rituals and ceremony

Rituals and ceremonies are symbolic acts that focus on achieving some connection with each other, tradition and/or nature. They are an integral part of our daily lives and are part of our social behaviour as humans (Beck, 1990). They are a means of celebrating life itself.

The increased pace of life in the West, and the 'time is money' syndrome, have meant that rituals are often a neglected part of our society. We often forget, do not find enough time, or are not permitted to celebrate fully milestones or successes, or mourn our losses. Rituals may be created or may develop over time unconsciously. In recent years, many people have reclaimed their right to lead, co-create or reinvent their own rituals in their work, community and spiritual lives.

All cultures have some sort of rituals that have evolved over time: ways of opening, closing, celebrating birthdays, successes, transitions and so on. Animals too conduct rituals with the seasons. A facilitator may choose to introduce a ritual or invite group members to co-create rituals to mark significant events. (See Chapter 15 on Endings). Rituals make use of symbols, fantasy, myths, stories and metaphors. Beck (1990) describes the five kinds of rituals in Table 4.11.

Table 4.11 Types of ritual

Type of ritual	Examples
Beginnings	Start of a new group, project, organization, home
Mergings	Joining of groups, partnerships. Relationships with plants, animals, environment
Cycles and celebrations	Sundowners, the weekend (thank goodness it's Friday (TGIF)), birthdays, Christmas celebrations, end of Ramadan, Festival of Lights, annual review/reports, phases of the moon
Endings	End of a group, project; exams, leaving friends/organization, mourning the loss of a friend/relative/colleague
Healings	Coming together to support planetary healing, to help each other during a redundancy and/or restructuring

Guidelines for creating rituals

There are no hard and fast rules for creating rituals, but here are some suggestions. Be true to yourself and the purpose of the group. Always ask yourself, 'What is appropriate for the purpose of the group, its members, the time and place?' Explain the purpose of the ritual to the group and ensure you have consensus. Involve group members in co-creating or adjusting the ritual to make it 'fit' for them. If something 'feels' wrong, then listen to and use your intuition and the intuition of others. Use your creativity and imagination; use poems, stories, myths. Choose words with care. Use charismatic time (see above). Don't take yourself too seriously, allow for emotional switching and humour. Too much ritual can overload a group and may contribute to its stagnation, but too little can leave a group impoverished (Heron, 1987).

I believe we can learn many things about rituals from other cultures that have sustained the use of their rituals through time. There is one greeting ritual from the Masai tribe (I believe). When someone visits a tribe, instead of going immediately into discussions they are allowed to acclimatize for a day, then they are welcomed:

> I saw you coming from afar,
> I see you now
> and you are beautiful.

I have seen this greeting incorporated into a circle of participants, where the facilitator welcomes the first person, who turns to the second, and so on around the circle. The honouring of each individual and being told you are 'beautiful' is a very interesting sensation.

In Laos, there is a custom called a baci or su-kwan ceremony, a pre-Buddhist ceremony that is still commonly practised in Lao PDR today. It is used in organizations to greet newcomers or say farewell to departing friends, celebrate successes or New Year. (It is also used in families and communities.) Su-kwan may be interpreted as 'the invitation of the kwan' or 'the calling of the kwan'. The kwan are 32 spirits believed to watch over the human body's 32 organs, which are thought to constitute a person's spiritual essence. The baci ceremony is a ritual binding of the spirits to their possessor, and is a means of expressing goodwill and good luck to others.

A respected person performs the ceremony, invoking the kwan in a loud song-like voice. He calls on the spirits to cease wandering and return to the bodies of those present. He then asks the kwan to bring well being and happiness, and to share in the feast that will follow. After the invocation to the kwan is finished, the celebrants take pieces of cotton thread from silver platters covered with food, and tie them around each other's wrists to bind the kwan in place. While tying the thread, they wish one another health and prosperity. Some of the threads must be left on for three days; when they are removed they must be broken or untied, not cut. (Adapted from Bankston (1995).)

The purpose of the baci is to maintain the balance of good relationships with one's colleagues and neighbours as well as with all things. The ritual opens a moment in time and space for people to say the unsaid while tying the threads around each other's wrists, to show appreciation of each other, and to communicate on a different level. It is an opportunity to restore harmony. Some people may express platitudes, but in the baci ceremonies I observed (I participated in many of them from 2000–01), the Lao people undertook the rituals with a combination of respect and humour. On one occasion when the person who was conducting a ceremony forgot his words, they laughed and someone slapped a glass of beer into his hand, saying, 'Have a drink, this will help'. He laughed and easily continued. There was not the imposed rigid seriousness or pomp commonly associated with more formalized rituals. Rituals do not have to be 'heavy', indeed they are often improved by someone who lightens proceedings by some sort of comment which generates an 'emotional shift'.

I am not advocating the slavish copying of arcane rituals of other cultures, merely illustrating one that I found moving and useful: individuals going up to one another and wishing each other well, the tying of string, the seeing of the string on your wrist for days after the ceremony as a reminder of the wishes of those who chose to speak to you and so on. We have to create and/or find our own stories, myths and rituals.

Holistic rituals

'This is me', a holistic exercise (involving all the senses)

Holistic exercises are those where there is an attempt to involve the whole person: the head or thinking side, the heart or emotional side, the body, and the 'self' or spiritual side.

STORY: EPIPHANIC MOMENTS

During 1992, I was reflecting on the way I present myself to others. I always try to dress brightly and/or differently. I have never owned a tailored business suit. I was thinking about personal image and style as a facilitator. I was wondering if what I did was contrived, or a mask. What was the real me? I was also talking in depth to a visiting professor from America, Jo Garcia. He was of Puerto Rican origin, raised in the slums of New York. He was also struggling with the sense of who he was: American or Puerto Rican? Frequently he said people made him feel guilty that he had not devoted his life to helping other poor Puerto Ricans 'make it' like he had.

I had invited John Heron to Perth in mid-1992, and both Julio and I attended John's workshop. At the end of the second day, John invited us to join in a circle as follows:

- **Stage 1: One whole.** Arms down and palms facing out into the group say, 'I am'.
- **Stage 2: Collective.** Join hands and make a 'wush' sound, walk into the middle and raise arms and say, 'We are'.
- **Stage 3: Individual affirmation.** Walk back and with arms crossed across our own chests say, 'This is me'.

We repeated this three times. At the time I just enjoyed the celebratory feel of the exercise, but that night as I was doing some photocopying for John, my tired brain was wandering over the day's events, and suddenly there was a rush of 'understanding' or 'insight', and an acceptance of 'This is me'. That is, what I present to others is me. It was an epiphanic moment: an acceptance of myself as I am, instead of what others want me to be or how I think I should be to fit into the norms of the business school where I worked.

I recalled that my mother told me, 'You've always been dressing up ever since you were a kid'. So I had just continued that 'free child' side of myself. It was also perhaps my 'rebellious child', in that I refused to comply with the more serious 'power' dress codes of the business world. It has also occurred to me that the one freedom that women have in the workplace that most men have lost is permission to dress in a variety of ways and to be colourful. I have often noticed since my days working in Fremantle jail that if I dress brightly, it lifts the spirits of people I have contact with. I was saddened when the business school decided to have a uniform for support staff, then rather alarmed when many academics also started to wear the uniform. I wonder if dressing alike leads to thinking alike? I value diversity, colour and creativity in all its forms.

The interesting thing is that Julio also was stimulated by this exercise. He told me of his insight and acceptance that he could fit into and value both his Puerto Rican background and his middle class, white academic career. He also shed his guilt that he had not become a social worker among Puerto Ricans.

I used the exercise later with a group. One young Thai woman confided afterwards, 'You know I have never held hands with a strange man before. Just wait till I tell my father in Bangkok!'

I use variations of the exercise in some contexts. Some people react with laughter, or embarrassed smiles; others appear confused or seem to go along with it. What surprises me after workshops is when people later tell me how some exercise, or something I said, made a huge impact on them. It brings it home to me constantly the responsibility that facilitators have, and the need for constant reflection on one's work and motives.

This short exercise can be very affirming or threatening. The questions all facilitators must ask themselves are:

- Why am I using this exercise?
- Is it appropriate to this particular group of people?
- Is it appropriate to the stage of group development, the goals of the group, the time of day/evening?
- Do I feel comfortable with it? Is it within my facilitation style?
- How can I involve the group in adapting or co-creating the ritual so everyone is comfortable with it?

Slavish copying or use of processes from a myriad of available texts without critical forethought may lead to undesired results. The ground rule, 'You have the right to say "no"', plus a trusting, supportive environment to support that norm are important. See Beck and Metrick (1990) for further ideas.

Eating together

I note that some organizations want to have short (40 minute) lunch breaks at workshops, or if we have an hour, some participants dash off to their mobile phones or computers (if the workshop is on their 'home turf'). It is almost as if some are afraid to relax and communicate over food. I recall being a participant at one of Fran Peavey's workshops. Everyone brought food for lunch: we ended up with a veritable feast of foods of every colour and texture and taste, *and* had an hour and a half in which to take walks together or sit under a tree. It also gave Fran a chance to have a break away from us.

Eating together as a community event combines the joy of eating and drinking with the joy of meeting. A meal relaxes body and spirit. Preparing, passing food and cleaning up together encourage communication (Vanier, 1979).

Celebrating

Facilitators and groups require times to celebrate successes, relax and let go. I heard once of a group that also celebrated mistakes: that is, they were celebrating what not to do next time. Celebrating helps us to sweep away the irritations of daily life and forget our quarrels, at least for a while. There are so many things to celebrate: anniversaries, traditions and rituals. We can give thanks for what we have, what we have achieved, and for the journey – the process (Vanier, 1979). (See Chapter 15 on ending workshops.)

> We should always remember that there is a time for everything – a time to walk and run and a time to stand still, a time to discover and a time to choose, a time of adolescence and a time of maturity. We should never force a plant to grow more quickly than it does naturally – that hurts and destroys it (Vanier, 1979: 63).

Conclusion

This chapter covers a diversity of ideas. Some may feel new and/or strange. However, as facilitators we have to stretch out of our comfort zone to help others to feel at ease and to learn. In the next chapter I turn to the needs of cross-cultural groups.

5

Cross-cultural and diversity issues

> None of us – not even the most erudite knows more than a miniscule faction of what there is to learn of the totality of this complex process [cross-cultural communication].
>
> E T Hall

Introduction

Facilitating mixed cultural groups offers stimulating ideas and different perspectives but does require more facilitative attention to catering for the needs of diverse groups. There are both advantages and disadvantages of groups with high levels of cultural diversity. In *Understanding Facilitation* Chapter 9, I explored 'dimensions of cultural' characteristics that help make cultural characteristics more visible.

In this chapter I draw on my experiences in cross-cultural groups in Australia and also in the 'South': developing countries, namely Nepal, Mongolia and Lao PDR. The chapter includes:

- a diversity checklist for workshop design;
- opening ceremonies;
- ice breakers and energizers;
- hints to improve facilitator language;
- experiential learning: the transitional learning model/process;
- myths;
- giving and receiving feedback across cultures: the mirroring process;
- creating value with diverse teams: the MBI model/process and the cross-cultural card sort game.

Diversity checklist for workshop design

The following checklist includes questions for facilitators to think about when planning and evaluating workshops with regard to the gender, race, age, disability, sexual orientation, and cultural background of participants. The questions are adapted from a handout from the Teaching and Learning Committee, University of Western Australia (1999).

Diversity checklist for workshop design

1 Workshop design

In designing a workshop do you:

- consider the participants' gender, cultural background, learning styles, health and disability status, English language proficiency, values and experiences?
- include opportunities for a positive engagement with people from other cultures, practices and life expectations?
- seek assistance in workshop design from facilitators or others with specialist expertise in diversity work?
- include examples, reading which reflect a diversity of perspective?

2 Content

Regarding the content, do you:

- acknowledge the diversity of knowledge and experience of your participants?
- use examples/case studies/stories that are free of negative stereotypes or assumptions?
- use their examples/case studies/stories as a basis for discussion?
- examine the implications of diversity as part of the organizational issues being examined?
- encourage participants to recognize and understand different ways of knowing?

3 Delivery

In your facilitation do you:

- provide participants with a range of different learning opportunities?
- encourage participants to know and actively listen to each other?
- avoid negative or potentially offensive stereotypes or assumptions?
- encourage participants to use their backgrounds as a learning tool?
- speak in plain English and explain acronyms and unnecessary colloquialisms?
- actively discourage language or behaviour which is racist, sexist and homophobic?

4 Evaluation

In evaluation design, do you:

- provide participants with opportunities to give you feedback early on regarding your pace, volume and use of language?

- provide participants with a range of different anonymous and/or informal feedback mechanisms?

Opening ceremonies

In many countries in southeast Asia it is normal practice to open workshops very formally. Often large banners denoting the purpose of the workshop, agencies involved and the date will be hung behind an elevated platform. Important people will be seated at a top table (rather similar to formal weddings) bedecked with flowers. Opening speeches are very formal, starting with the highest ranking person. Welcomes and thanks are given to key people (giving face). The whole process may take up to an hour. Participants may be seated in rows or down long tables, with people of lowest rank furthest from the top table. These cultural mores are strong, and facilitators often have to accept and work around them, and build in extra time for them. It is useful to call a short break at the end of speeches, to enable everyone to stretch and rearrange tables and chairs into a format more conducive to an interactive workshop.

Icebreakers and energizers

One of the problems of many books on icebreakers produced in the West is the need for materials and/or handouts. Paper and equipment may be in short supply, or copying facilities hard to find or too expensive in the less developed world, so it is useful to build up a variety of activities that need little or no preparation.

Pass the blob

It is useful to have a range of nonverbal activities for cross-cultural groups. A useful icebreaker is 'Pass the blob', in which the facilitator explains that he/she has a blob that needs to be passed around the group. Quickly participants catch on to how they can either carefully, playfully, carelessly pass on the blob (or even drop it and scrape it together). This exercise causes laughter and can lead to later discussion on how we pass information and new ideas around the organization.

Pass the clap

Another quick activity is the 'Pass the clap' exercise. A facilitator turns to another person who must clap at the same time as the facilitator. Once 'caught' he/she turns and passes the clap to the next person in line. The next person receives the clap by clapping exactly at the same time as the sender. When everyone has got the idea the clap can be passed across the group. People must pay attention in order to be ready to clap together.

The thunderstorm

Another useful exercise, particularly relevant in monsoon countries, is 'The thunderstorm' (source unknown). The facilitator tells the group that he or she will demonstrate noises of the rise and then decline of a storm. As the facilitator starts a movement, each participant in turn copies and continues to make that sound. When everyone is making the first sound, the facilitator changes to the next sound, and each person in turn copies and keeps on making that sound. The sounds are made as follows and build up to a crescendo:

- Rub thumbs against opposing fingers.
- Rub fingers on palms of other hand.
- Click fingers.
- Pat hands on thighs.
- Stamp feet.

Then reverse the order as the storm dies down:

- Pat hands on thighs.
- Click fingers.
- Rub fingers on palms of other hand.
- Rub thumbs against opposing fingers.

Lastly, the facilitator stops, and each person stops in turn as the storm goes away.

Learning names

It is quite hard to learn names that sound different and are written in a different script from your own language. It helps if you have large place cards drawn up, with participants' names in English facing the front and their names in their own language and script facing them. If appropriate, I take a photo early on so I can review faces and names before the next day or workshop.

Name meanings

It is useful if individuals can introduce their name and the name they like to be called (and its pronunciation). Many people from southeast Asia, South America and Africa have names that have a meaning, so you can help them feel at ease by asking them to tell the group the meaning behind their name. To help Westerners you can add an alternative request, for example to explain why their parents chose that name.

Age

In Asia, asking the age of a relative stranger is normal and not regarded as rude as in the West. At one Organizational Behaviour Teaching Conference in the United States, I recall being very surprised, after the opening speeches, when the organizers asked 300 people to arrange themselves into age groups in ascending order up the stepped lecture theatre. I remember being shocked and disconcerted, but soon noticed that the elderly delegates from China quite happily climbed up to the back of the auditorium. The organizers interrupted us in the middle of the activity and asked people to return to their places. They quickly debriefed, and explained that they used the exercise purposefully to shock us: to make us aware of the potential for making some people feel uncomfortable when asked to disclose their ages. However, for me the learning was that in some cultures this was not an issue; indeed, as 'seniors' the Chinese delegation knew their age gave them status and respect, and they were proud of their seniority. In many countries, people ask you your age so they know how to address you (as of higher or lower seniority).

Singing songs

In many Asian and African cultures, singing songs are a pleasant way to start a course. Not only is singing an integral part of many of these cultures, but the rise of karaoke in southeast Asia has increased the popularity of singing in public.

At the beginning of a workshop in Kuala Lumpur, I was quite nervous. The heavy wooden desks were immovable in a training room. I faced a large group of veiled Moslem women sitting in straight rows. The introduction was of course very formal and respectful. I asked if they would be kind enough to sing me a traditional Malaysian song, and was quickly amazed at their smiling faces and lack of inhibition. Their singing helped to put both me and them at ease with one another. In Laos, in large workshops, participants from each province took turns to sing songs. Sometimes latecomers were asked to sing a song as a 'penalty', although it was accomplished with much more ease that in the West.

Another variation is to invite participants to make up their own songs about the topic. Sometimes it helps if you provide a well-known tune, such as 'Frere Jacques'. I have been surprised at how well known this tune is, and even found members of the Shan tribe in an isolated village in Northern Thailand singing to this tune in their own dialect (because of the influence of missionaries).

In the box is 'The choices song' which I wrote for an empowerment workshop in an Asian context. Better still, invite participants to write their own (see also Chapter 4).

THE CHOICES SONG

(To the tune of Frère Jacques)

We have choices, we have choices
What are they? What are they?
Get them all to-ge-ther, get them all to-ge-ther
One two three, four five six

What do we want? What do we want?
Can I see? Can I tell?
Dream your dreams to-day. Dream your dreams to-night
One two three, four five six

What can help us? What can help us?
Think wide-ly, think deep-ly
Many powers to u-se, many powers to u-se
One two three, four five six

Who can help us? Who can help us?
Day by day, month by month?
Let us help each o-ther, let us help each o-ther
One two three, four five six

Think of context, think of context
Move with care, move with care
Li-i-ttle by li-i-ttle, li-i-ttle by li-i-ttle
One two three, four five six

Some-times prob-lems, some-times prob-lems
Face them now, face them now
They will not defeat us, they will not defeat us
One two three, four five six

We can do-it, we can do-it,
Step by step, step by step
Joining hands to-geth-er, joining hands to-geth-er
One two three, four five six.

In Lao PDR, a common practice is to invite participants from each province to start the day off with a joke. This works well, but be prepared for some surprises: in some cultures, jokes may be far more risqué and politically incorrect than would now be acceptable in the West.

Map of the world

An interesting cross-cultural icebreaker is to ask participants to go and stand on an imaginary map of the world according to where they were born, with north being the front of the room, south at the back and so on. Then ask each person to introduce him/herself and give a few pieces of information about his or her birthplace.

Forming cross-cultural groups

It is useful to be able to form cross-cultural groups quickly and easily without causing embarrassment. Ask the participants to line up according to their place of birth. Start on the left side with the workshop venue, and instruct that the area on the far right is the farthest away from the workshop venue. Some chaos will ensue while people try to sort themselves out. Then ask participants to introduce themselves, and give a little information about where they were born.

To form groups, start at the end of the left end of the continuum (ie those born closest to the workshop venue) and ask individuals to 'number off' from say one to five if you want five groups in a room of 25 people. Ask all the number ones to raise hands and spot each other, then number twos and so on. You will find there is a mix of ethnic background in each group.

Once cross-cultural groups have been formed, a facilitator needs to help these groups explore and value their differences and similarities, and develop codes to enable them to work together. (See the work of Distefano and Maznevski (2000) later in this chapter.)

Analysing videos

Ellen Summerfield (1993) analysed over 70 films that can be used in cross-cultural areas. She maintained that films speak to the emotions as well as the intellect, and provide an entry point into controversial topics that otherwise might be too uncomfortable to handle. Films are valuable since they can be used to recognize and unlearn stereotypes. Another advantage is that in real life you cannot stop the action and replay (even in role plays re-enactments change tone, expression and meaning), whereas videos and the freeze frame capability allow us to analyse interactions in depth.

Notable recent examples include *Bend it Like Beckham* (Brits and Indians in London), *Gung Ho* (Japanese managers and American autoworkers), and *The Scent of the Green Papaya* (life in Vietnam). See *Management Live! The video book* (Marx, Frost and Jick, 1991) for more useful videos.

A Tale of O (1979)

Written and narrated by Rosabeth Moss Kanter, this cartoon is a timeless classic which explores the psychology of being the only 'O' in a group of 'Xs' in a light-hearted way. It can be used to raise issues of difference by reason of race, sex, religion, language, size, job, physical appearance and/or disability.

Language

There are many English accents: British, Australian, New Zealand, American, Canadian, plus a variety of regional accents which may make English difficult to decipher. If you have a group with participants of mixed English speaking ability, you do not want to slow down too much, as you may sound stilted. However, some hints below will help your participants to understand you better.

If you are facilitating alongside an interpreter, see *Understanding Facilitation* Chapter 9.

Hints

Write key words and instructions on the board or on flip chart paper. Verbal instructions are easily misunderstood or missed, as it takes a few seconds to 'tune in' to an instruction.

Use short sentences; break your sequence at logical points, such as at the end of a phrase, clause or sentence. There is a 'happy medium'. If you stop after very short sentences you may lose the attention of native English speakers in your audience. It is very easy to end up with a very long sentence, so go back and say, 'In summary what I am trying to say is. . .'

Rephrase clichés: for example, instead of 'at this moment in time' use 'now'. Instead of 'window of opportunity' use 'good opportunity'. Instead of 'level playing field' use 'everyone has the same opportunities'.

To make a specific point, slow down, stress the key words, or repeat, 'This point is important, so I'll say it again', or 'Let me just repeat this point'.

Discourse/sentence markers

Speech is punctuated by discourse markers to signal to listeners that you are moving to a different stage in your instructions: for example, 'Next I would like to introduce you to a process which was developed in the UK. It has six stages which I will explain in turn. First. . . Second. . .' or 'In summary. . .'.

Generating questions

Make questions acceptable when ground rules are negotiated at the start of a workshop. Signal at the beginning that you welcome questions: 'All questions are useful', or 'There is no such thing as a stupid question'. Provide participants with 'safe' opportunities for clarification and/or elaboration, such as, 'Turn to your neighbour and list any areas you would like me to repeat or explain further.' Then use a round robin to gather questions from each pair.

Facilitator questions

Keep questions simple and straightforward, for example, not, 'You've finished, haven't you?' but, 'Have you finished yet?'

Building confidence

Before dividing up a class into small groups for discussions, explain that at the end you would like all members of the small group to come out to the front to share the feedback with the whole group. This gives everyone a chance to stand with peers, share responsibility, and to say a little or a lot.

Check understanding

Check understanding regularly. Do not use closed questions like, 'Do you understand what you have to do?' as you will probably be answered with a nod. It is better to ask, 'Can you summarize what you have to do?'

Raising awareness at the contracting stage

Plurality is a strength for some groups and a problem for others. It depends on the goals of the group and its group process. At the outset, it may be useful to ask how the issues of communicating across cultures can best be addressed. If there is a minority of participants who need help with English, it may help if they are each seated next to a personal interpreter.

The facilitator also needs to model behaviours that value and celebrate the efforts of non-English speaking participants.

Translating concepts and meaning

A language and its associated vocabulary and speech structures control and limit thought patterns. New words are added and old ones discarded. Most of the management and facilitation terms in English have been created in the last 50–100 years. The word 'facilitation', coming from the French 'facile', is about 25 years old. Even terms like 'facilitation' mean different things to different people.

Consider facilitating in countries where these concepts and their related labels/words do not exist. First, there may not be any one suitable word (the concept of facilitator in Lao covers a line of print). Second, there may be a word in another language: for example 'power' in Malay is 'kuasa', but in the traditional sense, the meaning of power is that it belongs to God. Malays have a saying, 'Men plan and god decides'.

A way around this issue for facilitators is to ask:

- What does power mean to you?
- What does power mean in your culture?
- Can you describe, draw concepts such as 'power', 'empowerment'?
- Describe to the group what you have drawn.
- What do the others think?
- Do different sectors of your community view power differently?

Misunderstandings

When we lived in Hong Kong, we found that if we asked secretaries to perform a task by a particular date, they often replied, 'I will try'. I used to feel frustrated if the task was not completed, until I learnt that, 'I will try' was meant quite literally, and instead of telling me they were too busy (which could be perceived as saying 'No'), they used the word 'try' to mean exactly that: the intent was there, but there was no agreed promise.

Silence

After a facilitator has explained an exercise and asked for clarification questions, does silence mean, 'Yes, I understand'? Often it does not, but some participants in every culture are embarrassed to admit their lack of understanding. So the facilitator needs to consciously watch eye movements and body language for signals of non-understanding. But body language is ambiguous at the best of times, let alone across cultures.

Basic conversation in other languages

Australia is a largely monolingual society. Many languages are spoken by our indigenous and ethnic communities, but in cross-cultural groups there is an expectation that English will be spoken. Anglo speakers often perceive they have the advantage over foreigners who cannot speak English. In fact this is a fallacy, as Anglophiles often miss important nuances of information through this complacency.

Colourful flags concept

Renford Reese developed the 'colorful flags human relations modules' in schools in the United States in 1993. His idea was to encourage face-to-face active engagement in cross-cultural groups. His materials can be easily adapted by facilitators for adult learners.

The philosophy of the 'colourful flags' is that lack of dialogue leads to mistrust and misunderstandings between people from different cultural groups. (See Figure 5.1.) If individuals can start a dialogue, they will have a far better chance of understanding one another. It is a proactive-interactive approach. One of the causes of ethnocentrism is when one group of individuals see themselves as part of the 'in' group or the 'right' group. They see others as the 'out' group. We cannot assume that bringing people together with simple icebreakers will automatically result in fruitful mixing or the development of deeper relationships.

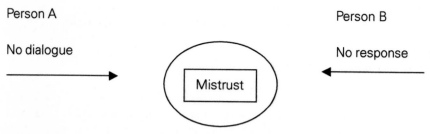

Figure 5.1   Lack of dialogue

The colourful flags approach suggests that participants in multi-cultural groups should at least make the effort to learn five basic greetings of co-participants (plus the meanings and difference in usage or non-usage):

● Hello. How are you?
● What is your name?

- Thank you. You are welcome.
- Please. Excuse me.
- Goodbye. Have a nice day.

The processes that result give an advantage to the bilingual and/or non-Anglo participants who become teachers. It does not matter whether participants develop perfect pronunciation; it is the attempt that counts. Indeed it is the mistakes that generate laughter and are the 'hooks' that encourage further dialogue.

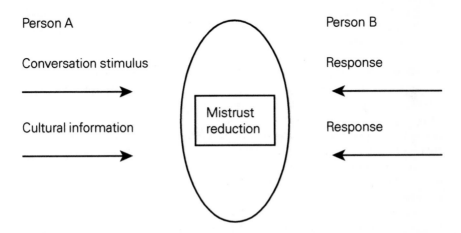

Figure 5.2 Conversation and contact

During the learning process participants start to engage with one another: one person is teaching and another is being taught, and everyone is engaged in the dialogue of learning (Reese, 1997). Laughter and humour can develop (provided that people are laughing 'with' and not 'at' each other), and participants can learn with guidance to give one another positive as well as constructive feedback.

Web sites:
http://www.class.csupomona.edu/colorfulflags/index.html
http://www.csupomona.edu/~rreese/MULTICULTURAL.html
http://www.csupomona.edu/~rreese/BRIDGING.html
E-mail: colorfulflag@csupomona.edu

Experiential learning

Those who know do not speak; those who speak do not know.

Chinese proverb

Members of different cultures tend to stereotype one another. 'The other group members won't speak out or ask questions' is a very culturally biased and blaming accusation. When I hear it, it reminds me of the analogy of finger pointing: if you point your finger at a person, remember that three fingers are pointing back at yourself. There appear to be at least three questions worth exploring here:

- Why are 'the other' members not participating? What is it about the group dynamics that makes them uncomfortable and wary? Remember in some countries people have learnt to survive by being very careful about what they say and do.
- What is participation? Remember you do not have to be continually vocal to participate. People can be silent and reflective, and be thinking about issues far more than a person who is talking for the sake of gaining attention or limelight.
- What are the ground rules? If you have included 'choices' such as 'the right to participate and the right to remain silent', then it is important not to start 'blaming' people who do not participate.

I have found that most participants from different cultures delight in experiential learning activities provided that certain conditions exist:

- a climate of trust in each other and in me;
- a safe environment;
- a build-up of exercises in pairs, then fours etc;
- explanation of the purpose of exercises;
- support and active involvement of senior officials;
- the opportunity to observe if preferred.

Context

Most people, if they are outnumbered by people from another culture, are naturally wary while they try to work out the norms or 'ways of doing things around here'. Participation rates depend on context: who is present, power differentials, the facilitator and how he/she builds a climate with feelings of trust. If a trusting environment is established and suitable processes are used, people of most cultures will participate, if and when they feel safe (Hogan, 1982).

Past experiences

Some participants may have had negative reactions from fellow participants in the past regarding their level of English and/or accent. It is important that facilitators do not accept rudeness and/or intolerance, and work to maintain ground rules of respect and acceptance. It is useful to remind English speakers of the difficulties they might face if they had to present or talk in a language other than their own.

Difficulty of breaking into discussions

Turn-taking in group discussion is hard for non-English speaking people as it requires very quick thinking and interjections into the flow of a discussion. Also in many cultures interrupting is considered very impolite (especially if a person older than yourself is talking). Therefore the facilitator needs to set up processes that help all participants to take turn, and carefully explain these ground rules and the reasons behind them. Putting an individual on the spot may increase nerves, however. Paired discussion and brainwriting are useful processes as they take the pressure off and allow 'think time' and 'writing time' (see Chapter 10). Brainwriting helps those participants who have been taught English mainly by reading and writing. Building up to small group discussion in fours or fives helps to build confidence. However, I still find it useful to invite everyone to help me encourage others to voice their thoughts.

Some participants may not know what phrases are used in English to intervene in a discussion, so it may help to have these written up on flip chart paper:

- 'Yes, I agree. However. . .'
- 'I think. . .'
- 'Excuse me, I would like to add something here. . .'
- 'Just a moment. Mary that is a really good point, but I think. . .'
- 'That's a useful point. Have you also thought of. . .?'

Sometimes our stereotypes about people of different cultures get jolted as the next story illustrates.

STORY: A SEARCH CONFERENCE IN HONG KONG

When my husband Steve and I lived and worked in Hong Kong, there was a general stereotyping of the Chinese students by the majority of 'gwailo' (foreign devil) staff. I used to overhear comments like, 'Chinese students rote learn; in fact, whatever you say they will write it down'. Other lecturers used to bemoan, 'Chinese students do not question or think critically'. Sadly, similar comments can still be heard in my own university today.

There were some lecturers, however, as this story shows, who were willing to use this negative stereotyping as a trigger for change, rather than continuing the rhetoric that the Chinese students were deficient. Donald Plate, a Principal Lecturer in Quantity Surveying, had just introduced a new course entitled 'Professional Diploma in Quantity Surveying'. Donald was concerned by the narrow educational subject range and limited general horizons of Hong Kong students. Donald had a desire to give first-year students more responsibility for their learning in a Liberal Studies unit. The rationale for this unit, in which there was no set curriculum (this would be developed and run by the students themselves) had been accepted.

Donald and his staff agreed to utilize me as a facilitator of a 'search conference' (see Chapter 9). I suggested that we should take the students off campus to a 'live-in' site at Po Lin Buddhist Monastery on Lantau Island in the second week of semester.

I facilitated many icebreaker activities on the first evening, and we started the search conference the next day. The students eagerly participated. At morning tea, I noticed that Donald was walking along shaking his downcast head. I was busy moving flip chart paper around and preparing hurriedly for the next session, but was concerned. I asked Steve (who was a lecturer in surveying) to find out if he was all right. Steve returned smiling, saying, 'It's all right, he's just dumbfounded. You've just broken all his stereotypes about Chinese students in 24 hours. He said in all his 11 years of working in Hong Kong that he has never seen Chinese students participate like this.'

Donald was also impressed with the quality and depth of their understanding. In the discussions in answer to the questions, 'What are the qualities of an educated person?' they showed maturity beyond their years, and indicated that they knew full well that memorization of facts was not the goal of learning.

Marks for participation

In some educational institutions, marks are allocated for verbal participation. I am philosophically and morally against this. While it can be argued that marks are useful motivators, such incentives may disadvantage minority groups and some quieter people of all cultures. Also what criteria are used: number of comments, length of comments, or quality of comments? And how can one person keep a record of such comments?

Sensitive and controversial subjects

Discussions sometimes focus on topics that may be uncomfortable for some participants to discuss in public. For example, discussion on religion, women's, men's and gay rights may be very difficult for some. Issues on human rights may also cause discomfort, especially when young people know they are going to return to countries where freedom of speech is not allowed. Areas where ideas polarize can also cause groups to split. Promote the awareness that in many areas there are no absolute' right' answers, but many shades of grey. If topics are contentious, but valid to the learning process, then a facilitator can help by encouraging others to share their culture's points of view. However, within one broad cultural group there can be many variations: for example, within Moslem groups there are differences of opinion on when Ramadan begins and ends.

Some participants find it exciting to discuss issues that are taboo or contentious in their own culture, as a way of making meaning for themselves. The ground rules are changing in so many cultures. It helps if a facilitator encourages participants to turn on the 'light' rather than the 'heat' (Rochfort and Blanchard, 1996).

The transitional learning model

In the next section I describe a 'transitional learning model' devised by an Australian colleague, Dr Ross James, to encourage participation and involvement in experiential learning in many cultures where education is delivered via the formal, didactic or 'banking' approach to learning (described in *Understanding Facilitation* Chapter 3). Indeed didactic strategies were encouraged by traditional and colonial rulers in Asia and Africa. There is understandably resistance by some participants when faced with more risky, experiential and learner-centred strategies, especially if there is potential loss of face in front of more junior colleagues.

Ross James developed his model, to encourage participation in experiential activities via safe transitions, during his work training health professionals and as radio programme producers in Pakistan and other countries throughout Asia. The model has six stages, and is designed to enable learners to make easy transitions in stages from lecturer-centred to learner-centred learning (James, 2000).

Years of experience icebreaker

One activity that Ross uses to set the scene is to ask everyone to line up according to their years of experience in the field they are about to study. Individuals introduce themselves in turn, and the number of years is noted on the board. These are then added up. This activity is partly designed to show that there is a wealth of experience in the room. It is also a needs assessment, and enables the facilitator to find out pockets of expertise that can be incorporated into the class. The facilitator also adds his/her experience, qualifications and so on to gain credibility and status in the group, which is important in high power-distance societies.

The next stages that lead the group to be more participatory and autonomous are self-explanatory and are described in Table 5.1.

Two major concepts strengthen the facilitation process of the transitional learning model. The first is that the learner is firmly positioned as a participant in, and a catalyst for, change. The model gives priority to learners (objects of learning) being facilitators (agents of learning), and the facilitator (an agent of learning) being a learner (an object of learning). The second important concept is what Ross calls the 'quality check'. The quality check is conducted at the end of each transition. It is a series of questions to stimulate discussion, reflection and action on the learning process; it is not an assessment of participants, but an assessment with participants.

The questions are associated with each transition, so their emphasis and direction will conform to the purpose of each transition, and be specific to the task being learnt. Also, a set of questions will be constructed for the facilitator and another set for the learner.

As an example, quality check questions for the cognitive transition might look something like this.

For facilitators:

● What happened in terms of the group dynamics of the small groups and their interaction with each other?
● What do you think about this result?

Table 5.1   Transitional learning model

Transitions and activities	Impact
1 Projective Participants project their ideas and opinions onto a concept, product or situation – a role play, case study, story, demonstration – and/or recall past experiences. For example, 'Think of the worst radio interview programme you have ever heard. What was so awful about it?'	*Participants* practise critical reflection and realize they have valuable experiences to build on. They engage in a non-threatening way with the facilitator. Criticisms are 'out there', not of self or others in the room. They learn they can learn from each other. *The facilitator* records all ideas on flip chart paper and *can* assess attitudes, biases, aptitude and assumptions. He/she can observe group dynamics, opinion leaders, and perhaps points of disagreement.
2 Cognitive The facilitator integrates and reorganizes the responses into a framework. For example, he/she organizes the information generated into all the competencies needed to conduct an interview, and adds research and/or information from his/her experience.	*Participants* are reassured by the facilitator's depth of knowledge and experience. *The facilitator* demonstrates expertise and maintains and enhances credibility by pulling together ideas into a framework This stage maintains cultural expectations of the facilitator's status and authority.
3 Application How can the ideas described in phase one be put into practice? For example, participants learn how to use a microphone or how to construct questions for an interview.	*Participants* engage in experiential learning and practise the skills and knowledge outlined in phase 2. For example, writing objectives to describe the correct use of microphones and/or using a microphone. *The facilitator* uses practical activities to involve learners and maintain interest and energies.
4 Synthesis The facilitator leads a discussion on a hypothetical problem situation. For example, how can an interview manage an antagonistic interviewee?	*Participants* collaborate to solve problems and experience teamwork. *The facilitator* assesses learning, and adds new ideas when necessary, which reassures the learners and facilitates collaborative group work.
5 Group reinforcement In pairs or small groups, participants work on a project: for example to prepare and conduct a small radio interview using all the skills and knowledge discussed above, so they can demonstrate what they have learnt.	*The participants* gain confidence in problem solving, decision making and organization of a group project. *The facilitator* assesses learning and is available to answer questions and act as a coach when required.
6 Self-direction Individuals now take responsibility to complete a project alone to demonstrate their own competence. Each person demonstrates his/her radio interview to the whole group.	*Participants* have more confidence and have accumulated learning from the previous transitions. *The facilitator* assesses individual learning.

Source: adapted from James (2000: 38)

- How well did participants demonstrate their understanding of the various aspects of program planning?

For participants:

- What new ideas did you gain from other small groups as they presented their work?
- Were their presentations appropriate for the situation?
- What did you think about the group dynamics of this activity?
- How difficult was it for your group to apply the theory to the task assigned?

Myths

There are many myths and generalizations that develop about the ways in which we do things. As the learning styles research indicates, some people of all cultures prefer to engage actively in learning (that is, some are more activist and some prefer to reflect). Likewise there are some people who like mind mapping as a form of taking notes and developing ideas, and others who prefer to make long lists, as the following models and stories illustrate.

'Asian' students do not like mind mapping: myth

I have noted that some of my Western colleagues make assumptions about rates of participation and learning styles of overseas students, as is illustrated in the following story.

STORY: ATTITUDES TO MIND MAPPING

At the beginning of 1990, as part of my coordination duties I went to Kuala Lumpur (KL), Malaysia to oversee the students there who were undertaking the organizational behaviour classes.

One class on mind mapping, in a stepped lecture theatre, was very interesting. I searched for a topic to which I thought the students would relate easily. I said, 'Why don't you give me ideas for a party or celebration, say at the end of Ramadan (the major Moslem event of the year), or for Chinese New Year. I'll mind map your ideas on the board for you.'

Next day, students arrived with their homework. They had applied the principles of mind mapping more quickly and enthusiastically than many of my Australian classes. 'Why didn't our lecturers teach us this?' one Malaysian student said almost angrily. I explained that my teachers at school did not teach this to me either, and in life we would constantly learn new things that we wish we had known earlier.

Later, in Perth, I encountered an Australian staff member who was blocking the introduction of mind mapping to all organizational behaviour classes. She commented, 'My overseas students at the other campus will not be able to cope with this'. 'Why not?' I asked. 'It won't fit with their cultures.' 'That's odd. When I tried this in Hong Kong and Malaysia, students were enthusiastic, and like down here, some students in the long term found it really useful, and others were ambivalent. Are you sure it's not your own feelings towards mind mapping?' She laughed a bit shamefacedly, nodding her head.

I often had to confront staff members directly or indirectly regarding using more varieties of strategies in their teaching and stretching their own comfort zones. It is not easy to change if you have been teaching in a particular way. I knew that if staff members were not enthusiastic about, for example, mind mapping, they could adversely influence the reactions of students. Lack of conviction is easily manifested by using half-hearted introductions that then lead to a self-fulfilling prophecy and stereotype, 'Overseas students do not like mind mapping'.

Giving and receiving feedback

The following account describes an early experience in Kuala Lumpur when I was trying to get feedback from a group of trainee facilitators (Malay and Chinese) participating in a one-week course.

STORY: TRYING TO GAIN FEEDBACK

At the end of the first day, as is my usual habit, I invited participants to complete a formative evaluation questionnaire. I explained its purpose, and that I would collate the ideas overnight so that we could create a picture of the group members' reactions to the day. As a result we would all have feedback on how we were working and learning together, and could change direction and/or emphasis if necessary. I promised confidentiality, and invited them to choose whether or not to put their names on the sheets. That night I avidly pored over their responses in my hotel room, and as per my promise, fed back the results on handouts, plus my perspectives, the next day.

Imagine my surprise at lunchtime when I bumped into Mr Wang. 'Ah, your course is going very nicely. I have spoken to some of the participants. Just one point: some of them find you hard to hear. At the end of sentences you drop your tone and volume, and with the air conditioner's noise, they cannot make out some words.' I thanked him and made a mental note to also speak louder and not drop my tone. I mused, 'Why couldn't they give me that feedback anonymously in writing the night before?' In some ways, working with a group of cosmopolitan and in many ways Westernized Malaysians was disconcerting for me. I made assumptions. What I realized was that the 'Western-ness' was superficial, and deep down their behaviour patterns were of course still Malay. Indirect feedback is more culturally correct for them. I wondered how many of our facilitation methods translate to their culture. So I constantly asked them, 'Can you use this method here? Would you need to adapt this to your culture?'

Feedback and context

I was invited with six other colleagues to teach in Mongolia in 1997 and 1998. I heard later that one of our mature female students faced imprisonment. (Luckily she had the support of the female lawyers association of Mongolia.) She had spoken out against the government, which was trying to suppress discussion about the worsening economic situation and the problems of street children. I recalled a discussion on giving and receiving feedback. One of the students commented, 'Giving feedback is dangerous'. This really made an impact on me, as the Western model of open feedback is expounded in so many books, forgetting the context, and that in some countries and regimes people learn not to give feedback in order to survive (or if you do give feedback, you toe the party line).

Metaphors and feedback

In some cultures I have observed the use of metaphors to give quite direct feedback. For example, in Lao PDR I was a guest at the signing of an MOU between two government departments. At the end of the formal proceedings and the press and photography session, wine flowed and playful discussion started (it was 10 am). One official then jokingly said to the head of the other government department, 'We've just signed an MOU, but our department has already finished so much work for your department without payment. . . We are already working in third gear of a car, you are still driving in first gear!'

Storytelling to enhance cross-cultural communication

In teaching a class on cross-cultural communication, I use storytelling as a device to promote attitude change. For example, in trying to alert people to the hurtful impact of cross-cultural misunderstandings, stories of racism told by classmates can have a far more dramatic impact than a cold, logical analysis of the causes of racism or case studies in books. Conversely, stories written by people of different ethnic backgrounds can enable the reader to enter into the minds of people of different cultures more easily (Harris, 1991).

Facilitating bi-cultural groups

The following story concerns a workshop for a western embassy (called Fellang Embassy). It comprised 'Fellang' staff and local Asian staff called 'Asio' for anonymity.

STORY: EMBASSY ANNUAL RETREAT

Before a bi-cultural annual three-day retreat between Asio and Fellang Embassy staff, I made time to visit every group at four separate times, in their offices and different locations in the SE Asian capitol. This gave me an opportunity to observe them interacting and see their codes of behaviour. The group comprised the widest range of power differences I had every encountered, as it comprised the Ambassador and the drivers.

I gathered stories from the last annual retreat, on what went well and what did not, and why. For example, one Asia staff member said, 'They (the facilitators)

Wall minutes: English   Wall minutes: Asio

Figure 5.3   Room layout

made us sit in a big circle (25 people). They then picked on individuals in turn to speak. We didn't like that.' Large circles of 25 people can be nerve-racking for some people. I decided to sit people in tables of six people like the spokes of a wheel, to enable small group discussions in twos, threes and fives, and so that each group could choose a spokesperson to feedback ideas to the whole group when necessary.

One of the goals of the workshop was to enhance communication across the organization, so I mixed the groups on purpose by putting out name cards (which I could also read at a distance), even though I was instructed by the 'contact client' to let people sit where they liked. (I likewise changed the groups for the following day.)

The pre-workshop meeting ensured that the participants all had the opportunity to state their needs for the workshop, and they all saw me. I had a chance to learn some names and build some rapport. I gave each person some sticky-backed notes to write his/her needs anonymously, and invited individuals to speak in turn to ensure that each had the opportunity to speak, before the workshop. I also gave them my e-mail address, to open up communication for those who felt intimidated at the first meeting.

I had to assert my needs to maximize group effectiveness. For example, I found that some participants spoke very little English. I requested that handouts should be translated and show English down one column and Asio beside it down the other, rather than that the two languages use separate handouts. The Asio language spreads out more than English, and this makes it difficult to direct people to look to the same spot on different handouts.

I was given excuses from the Fellangs: 'There isn't time, and the Asio staff can manage OK'. I insisted. In other workshops I also met resistance from the Asio who spoke good English, who resisted translating for their colleagues who did not speak so much English. I think they wanted to be seen to understand more English than their colleagues did as a matter of pride, as English was seen as the prestige language.

There was also resistance (from the Fellang staff) to working bilingually, as translating takes time. I was lucky that within the Asio staff there was a very talented woman who spoke fluent English. We co-facilitated with humour, and used two areas for wall minutes: one in Asio, in landscape format, and one in

English, in portrait format. Ironically, I noticed as we got going that working as a co-facilitating team did not slow communication as much as I had originally thought. Indeed the Asio verbal translation took the same time as it took me to write up participants' comments in English.

We took along Asio dictionaries, and sat Asio participants with little English next to a bilingual helper. Some of the Lao drivers found some of the Asio words in handouts needed explanation, and the dictionaries allowed them to find meaning if they felt embarrassed to ask questions.

I tried to find non-verbal activities to eliminate the problem of language (the 'Broken square' problem-solving exercise was great for this). I used many paired exercises so that people could discuss ideas in Asio if they wished. I also invited participants to join in cross-cultural pairs for the Trust Walk. Where touch was involved, I invited people to join with people of the same sex.

At the end of the first day, I distributed a formative evaluation questionnaire to check out my perceptions and misperceptions. Some unspoken issues came out. I was intrigued to note the number of Asio who wrote on their feedback sheets, 'She treats us with respect.' I did not really get to an explanation of what they saw me doing, but it seemed very important to them. Evaluations included, 'Sometimes the Fellang show anger and frustration if we (Asio people) try to ask questions', so the Lao people were getting double messages. One of the Fellang pointed out, 'I get fed up the way some of my colleagues keep saying the Asio won't ask questions or speak out. It is culturally biased and blaming.'

Next day these comments provided everyone with useful food for thought and talk. I illustrated the blaming in role play with my Asio colleague, saying that if I blamed her (pointing a finger at her), three fingers were pointing at me: I was to blame too. Everyone laughed. At the end of the workshop, a Fellang told me I was culturally insensitive, since pointing a finger is regarded as impolite in Asio culture. I later returned home with many of the Asio participants in a minibus, and found it useful to go through the feedback sheets with them for added clarification and understanding. They commented, 'No, we were not offended as we understood that you were demonstrating a point. However, if you had shaken your finger at us (they wagged their fingers at me) it would have been different. We would have been very offended. That would have gone right inside us' (they pointed to their hearts).

It is important to note that trying to do things 'right' doesn't mean you never get it wrong. I think, however, people of different cultures are on the whole very understanding, provided foreigners or 'the other' show willingness, respect and a desire to learn.

Needless to say, some hidden agendas were always present. The issue of power was never openly addressed, although I did mention it in a debriefing session. Any efforts at increased openness are underpinned by the issues of who the employer is: that is, who holds the power to give and retract job contracts. It was the Fellang and the aid agencies. So the Asio staff at any time might be asking themselves, 'If I speak out will they:

- renew my contract?
- be offended?
- hold it against me?
- still like me?
- think I am rude and disrupting the harmony of the group?
- lose face?'

Some interesting information evolved when the issues of delegation were discussed. For example, a delegated task may never 'get done' if the:

● task is culturally inappropriate;
● task is perceived to be politically dangerous;
● process suggested by the *fellang* (foreigner) is culturally inappropriate;
● process suggested by the *fellang* is perceived to be politically dangerous.

We cannot assume that because someone is not speaking they are not participating. One senior and very intelligent Asio man sat and listened and chose not to speak. He said, 'I am a lot older. I have very different ideas to those suggested here, but I choose not to say. It's OK.' We have to respect his decision and right to say 'No' and not participate.

Facilitating cross-cultural feedback

In Nepal in 1996, I was invited to facilitate a 'communication workshop' in a Danish development agency, between the Danes and their Nepalese office staff and Nepalese agencies. All participants spoke good English. I used a process which I think is called a 'mirroring process'. I do not know its source. I will describe the process and then discuss some of my observations from the workshop.

Mirroring process

Author/background

Source unknown.

Purpose/rationale

In this exercise, participants are asked to hold up a metaphorical mirror to the 'other' culture so that people of that culture can learn more about how they behave and communicate (Hogan, 1996).

Size of group

Thirty to forty maximum, divided into groups of four to five people formed of homogeneous cultures.

Materials

Butcher paper, felt pens, masking tape, pens and writing paper for each participant, adhesive gum. A large blank wall. Props: scarves, local cloth, hats and so on.

Venue layout

Open space for role plays, chairs in a circle. Space for small group discussions.

Time

About 15–20 minutes preparation. Five minutes for each skit. One hour for debriefing and discussion.

Establish the ground rules

It is important to focus participants on issues, not people. If some team members cannot attend it is very important to discuss with those present how they will brief the absentees later back in the workplace. This is because some of the participants' behaviours may change as a result of the workshop.

Explanations might go as follows: 'Please be as open, honest and sensitive as you can in the way you express your feedback. This is your opportunity to learn a great deal about one another, so that you can improve communication and processes in the future.'

Stages

Give participants the instructions shown below, and instruct each group that they will be asked to report back to the whole group using drawings, role play and storytelling.

- Draw the characteristics of the 'other' culture using symbols, coloured pens.
- What aspects of the 'other' culture do you like/admire?
- What aspects of communication with the other culture do you find difficult to understand and/or appreciate? Please give specific examples/stories.
- What suggestions do you have to improve communication between members of your respective cultures?

Outcomes

This activity leads to increased awareness of the 'other' and may take a group to a new level of understanding.

Advantages

This process helps to open up communication between cultural groups, to raise issues to the surface in a playful way. This process can also be used for any bipolar issues, such as parent and child, male–female, or old–young.

Issues are presented in a variety of creative ways using props of clothing and objects. Skits produce a lot of laughter (sometimes from the humorous situations, sometimes tinges of embarrassment). The humour and costumes allow people to take on the roles of court jester, and in some instances enable groups to move from the 'norming' (polite) to 'performing' stage of group development

(Tuckman and Jensen, 1977), where it is permitted to openly disagree and discuss differences. Where role play is used, the facilitator later asks each group to state verbally the points they were trying to get across to check for accuracy (especially as some of the role plays were in Nepali!).

From these issues the group generated a list of 'Hints for improved communication between Nepalese and Danes'.

Disadvantages

The process could lead to polarizing the two groups into 'them' and 'us' if time is not spent in the debriefing to highlight, 'How can you use the information gained to enable you to work better as a team?'

Discussion of the mirroring process

At the beginning of the workshop there was a ground rule established to identify 'issues not people'; however, occasionally participants needed reminding if they suddenly mentioned a person's name or mimed mannerisms of a particular person. For example, a laughing Nepalese participant said, 'When I had to go to Michael's house to get a lift to this workshop I was most embarrassed when he kissed his wife goodbye in front of me. I didn't know where to look I was so embarrassed.'

There were shrieks of laughter from some members of the group, and one Nepalese person quickly interjected, 'We do enjoy kissing in private,' followed by more laughter. Michael had just stepped out of the room. However, the point was made, and later that evening there were long discussions between Danes and Nepalese about how strong affection is shown in Nepal. It raised the point that with some (though not all) issues there is no compromise: 'When in Rome, do as the Romans do'.

A number of points were raised that could not be discussed fully, as some people were not present. The workshop group comprised people from many different organizations. I considered it unethical to discuss the behaviour of individuals from the Danish group if they were not there to discuss and/or explain their behaviour. I explained this reasoning to the group members and asked them to discuss issues, which on the whole they did.

Briefing absentee people who were involved in the issues raised

On day Five, at the end of the workshop, I raised the issue of briefing people who were not present, and participants agreed to brief colleagues on their return. However, as I was an external facilitator there was no way for me to monitor that this did happen, apart from ensuring that minutes of the meeting were circulated quickly, with as much detail as possible, to important 'others'.

There were also a number of new 'in phrases' generated at the workshop which would immediately evoke laughter and understanding, and which would need to be explained. For example, there was a cross-language pun that had arisen when I was explaining that there should be more open and constructive feedback, accompanying comments like 'tik' (Danish for good) and 'tikcha tikcha' (Nepali for OK) when things were OK.

Use of own language for small group work: responsibility of the 'receivers'

During the second group work exercise, with groups comprising either all Danish or all Nepalese, participants were invited to speak in their own language to lend a feeling of intimacy and also speed up the communication process. It was difficult, if not impossible, to listen to group progress unobtrusively to check whether the group members:

- had properly understood the instructions;
- were on task or in 'flight';
- were 'stuck';
- were preparing inappropriate responses.

It was the responsibility of participants to seek help from the facilitator. One group did misunderstand the instructions and did seek clarification.

Role play and storytelling

In general, I found that Nepalese people reacted far more positively to role play and storytelling than Westerners (though there was not any observable resistance by the Westerners present, as role play was a technique they used in their development work). Nepalese people find it very hard to give direct negative feedback; however, in the role plays they were able, through storytelling and mime, to bring out some very strong issues that up until then had not been raised.

The request to start stories, 'Once upon a time there was a group and/or organization in which. . .' worked well. Many individual short stories and anecdotes were shared, including one of a Danish participant who had fallen badly and cut his hand, and who had been emotionally hurt and appalled when a passing Nepali had burst out laughing. Immediately people in the room started laughing also, and long explanations were given by the Nepalese about their childrearing customs which always encourage them to laugh and look on the brighter side of things. Eventually the Dane shifted slightly in his anger and misunderstanding (and the participants also wiped their tears of laughter from their eyes!).

Listening skills

In hierarchical 'high power-distance' cultures like India and Nepal (Hofstede, 1980), individuals are prone to listen more carefully to people of high status.

Therefore it was necessary for the facilitators, like myself, to give information about their achievements in order to establish credibility. This felt difficult to me, as according to Australian and Danish 'low power-distance' cultural norms, such details may actually alienate participants. Therefore I decided not to add any further information than was given by the organizer: that I was a visiting Senior Lecturer from a university in Australia.

In order to enhance the active listening skills by the participants, the facilitator used the story of the 'Sounds of the Forest' (Hogan, 2000) and used many of the storytelling techniques described in Finlay and Hogan (1995). The pace of delivery was slow, with many hand gestures using Nepalese symbols: mountains, monsoons and rice. At the end the participants burst into spontaneous applause.

The workshop generated many recommendations. However, these recommendations need to be put into action by the participants themselves, and they need to be discussed openly with colleagues who were not present at the workshop. There were also three key issues between both cultures:

- the need for more trust from both groups;
- the need for more open constructive feedback as well as positive feedback, such as the 'tik/tikcha' pun mentioned above;
- the different levels of power between the two groups, where the Danes were donor givers with the power to terminate contacts, and the Nepalese were donor receivers.

These are big issues. However, identification and open discussion were a first step to reconciling these 'hidden agendas' which were underlying much of the communication between the two groups, and indeed much of the communication between members of countries in the so-called developed world and the developing world.

Lastly, as food was a focus of life for both the Nepalese and Danes, the group identified a food metaphor: 'Aim for chicken tikka masala' (a feast of tandoori chicken in a rich spicy creamy sauce, that is, synergy of cross-cultural groups) 'not dhal bath' (everyday food: rice, dhal and vegetables equals compromise). The explanation was to aim for synergy (ie $1 + 1 + 1 + 1 + 1 = 9$, not 5). Synergy is the creative potential in fully 'performing' groups: when a group of individuals come together and the sum of the output is greater than what they can achieve alone.

Creating value with diverse teams: mapping, bridging and integrating (MBI) model

I will now turn to the research by Joseph Distefano and Martha Maznevski (Distefano and Maznevski, 2000) who concluded that diverse teams tend to perform either better or worse than homogenous teams, with more of them performing worse than better. The two researchers divided multicultural teams into three categories (destroyers, equalizers and creators), which I will describe in turn:

- **The destroyers.** The destroyer teams are dysfunctional when the formal leaders make decisions without genuine discussion among members, and as a result destroy value rather than create it.
- **The equalizers.** The equalizer team members smooth, compromise and suppress any differences in ideas and perspectives. 'We suspect that most culturally diverse teams that think of themselves as "doing well" are really equalizers' (Distefano and Maznevski, 2000).
- **The creators.** The creating teams do more than use buzz platitudes like 'we value diversity'. They actively explore their differences like a jazz ensemble. From their observations of these teams Distefano and Maznevski developed the MBI approach: that these teams actively:
  - Mapped and tried to understand their differences;
  - Bridged their communication and took differences into account;
  - Integrated team-level ideas by carefully monitoring participation patterns, solving disagreements and creating new perspectives.

MBI is a mnemonic for the first letter of each stage.

Mapping to understand the differences

The important aspect of mapping is to find out which differences will make a difference to interactions and decision making , for example cultural values and thinking styles. 'Most global teams do not take the time to map cultural differences up front; they just rely on broad generalizations (stereotypes) that they have heard' (Distefano and Maznevski ,2000). There are many visual methods to map cultural differences:

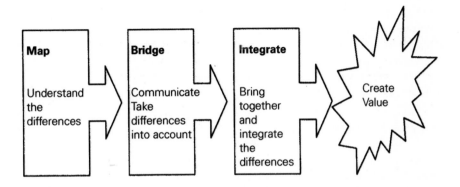

Figure 5.4   MBI approach to create value in diverse teams

- mirroring process (described above);
- cross-cultural card game (described below);
- using a table of cultural dimensions to stimulate discussion;
- videotaping meetings and analysing interactions.

Cross-cultural card game

Asma Abdullah and Peter Shephard (2000) have developed a colourful and useful 'cultural card pack' comprising 48 cards clustered into eight key concepts (see Table 5.2). In this cross-cultural game, players explore what these assumptions are, and become familiar with a list of cultural concepts which they can use to evaluate others from different cultures, not as 'good' or 'bad', but just 'different'. The main objective of this game is for players to acquire a language of neutrality, and begin to describe cultural differences and similarities as a result of their cultural and mental socialization and programming in their early years, or as members of a group. The card game helps participants address questions like:

- How and why are people different?
- How and why do some people like to work in groups and others alone?
- Why do some people build relationships before getting the task done?
- What are our hidden cultural dimensions and underlying assumptions?

These concepts are explained in *Understanding Facilitation* and in Abdullah and Shephard (2000), Hofstede (1980) and Hall (1990). See also the Web site http://asma.braindominance.com/game.htm

Table 5.2   Eight cultural dimensions

Culture A (more Eastern or Asian)	Culture B (more Anglo-Saxon or Western)
Harmony Harmony with the world	Control Control over environment
Shame Sense of shame drives actions	Guilt Sense of guilt drives actions
Relationship Relationship before task	Task Task before relationship
High context Circular indirect speech	Low context Linear direct speech
Polychronic time	Monochronic time
Collectivism Group loyalty interdependence and collaboration: 'We'	Individualism Independence and competition: 'I'
Hierarchy High power distance, and difference in status and wealth accepted and tolerated	Equality Low power distance. Inequalities minimized
Spiritual/religious	Secular

Table of cultural dimensions

A table of cultural dimensions like the one in Table 5.2 can be distributed as a tool for mapping discussions, acknowledging that terms like 'Asian' and 'Western' are gross generalizations and that all cultures have many differences between individuals, age groups, regional differences and city–rural diversities. After explaining each term, ask each person to tick his/her overall preferences.

The cultural iceberg

Another useful tool to stimulate discussion is the model of the cultural iceberg. Like the metaphor of the organizational iceberg described in Chapter 1, it can be used as a starting point for discussion.

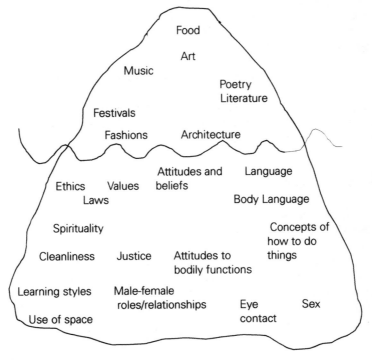

Figure 5.5   The cultural iceberg

Adapted from Brislin

Bridging to communicate across differences

Bridging to communicate across differences requires trust building, the development of ground rules, and motivation and confidence to discuss differences openly. Team members need to learn 'decentring', a skill similar to empathy and role reversal, but that requires individuals to suspend judgement and to value difference: that 'Difference just is. It is a fact of life'.

Integrating and levelling differences

Participants need to then 'recentre' and build new ground rules and processes based on what they have learnt during the mapping process, in order to:

- manage participation;
- resolve disagreements;
- build on ideas.

'People with different cultural values tend to subscribe to vastly different norms for participating', so Distefano and Maznevski (2000) suggest:

- Rotate a process leader or observer.
- Vary modes of meeting and sharing information: for example, solicit ideas before a meeting via e-mail, talk to staff in hallways to get the ideas, have buzz group discussions during meetings, have frequent breaks in meetings.
- Map ideas.
- If conflict occurs, go back to decentring to talk about problems.

The MBI model is a set of principles for helping teams to develop their own best ways to perform well. It may be applied to debriefing a meeting or for analysing a videotape of a team meeting.

Conclusion

Cross-cultural communication is a huge field. In this chapter I have given suggestions on designing workshops that include a diversity of participants, as well as workshops that focus on cross-cultural issues. There is scope for great learning, as well as misunderstandings, which may be minimized if facilitators pay attention to language and cross-cultural dimensions. A number of processes have been described to aid facilitators, including the transitional learning model, the mirroring process and the MBI model.

6

Difficult situations

Beam me up, Scottie.

A command from *Star Trek* to get back to the mother ship and safety.

Introduction

What may be regarded as difficult situations or inappropriate and/or stuck behaviour depends on the context, composition and history of a group, its purpose, the ground rules, and the style/s and experiences of the facilitator. What is inappropriate in one group or culture may be perfectly acceptable in another or in the same group, but at a different stage of development.

Ideally, a facilitator should be centred, in the moment, in tune with the group, and so on; however, there will always be occasions when 'the wheels fall off' in a workshop. By that I mean the dynamics change, 'buttons are pressed' (perhaps yours and/or those of some or all of the participants), and you will not feel centred.

In this chapter a number of strategies are described:

- preventing inappropriate behaviour;
- deciding who and what to confront;
- the intervention cycle;
- generic confronting skills and techniques;
- confronting the whole group;
- confronting a small group;
- generating your own strategies;
- making the best of a situation.

Preventing inappropriate behaviour

You will need a variety of tools and techniques, and if one doesn't work try something else.

Question: What is the definition of insanity?
Answer: Doing the same thing over and over again expecting different results.

Before the workshop begins

One facilitator colleague described a situation where at the start of a meeting one participant arrived and walked to the back of the room away from the group. The facilitator spotted this and immediately confronted the person, asking him to join the group.

Contracting

Preventing inappropriate behaviour begins at the contracting stage, with the primary client and the participants before the workshop (see Chapters 1 and 2), and then contracting with participants at the start of a workshop. This gives you power later on if you see behaviour that is contrary to the agreed desirable norms.

Story: Two strikes and you're out

A friend of mine was facilitating a group of geologists. There were two females in the group. At the contracting stage, someone suggested and they all agreed to the ground rule: 'No sexist or racist jokes; two strikes (two offences) and you are out'. In other words, you will get two warnings and at the third offence you will be asked to leave. We know that we all sometimes inadvertently make socially unacceptable comments, but some people are so used to doing it that they don't even realize who they might be hurting. This is especially true if those people do not react. (As a coping mechanism many people do not want to 'rock the boat' for fear of further recriminations.)

As the workshop progressed, it was obvious that some of the male participants had no intention of even trying to keep to the ground rule. So after the agreed two warnings, when a participant made a third racist comment the facilitator asked him to leave, and he did. 'After all', the facilitator said later, 'They agreed to the ground rule. There was no trouble after that.' The female participants later thanked the facilitator for making a stand.

What this story illustrates is the power that ground rules give to the facilitator, provided that ground rules are:

- Generated and agreed to by the facilitator and participants (in cooperative mode). An imposed list of ground rules does not have as much strength, though time constraints may require that ground rules are imposed hierarchically by the facilitator.
- Displayed clearly on flip chart paper for all to see.
- Referred to by the facilitator.

People often challenge the facilitator near the beginning of a workshop (storming stage). This is normal.

Who and what you should confront

Sometimes people who are difficult to get along with are our best teachers.

Anon

Most participants leave facilitators to confront inappropriate behaviour (in Heron's hierarchical confronting mode). However, once desirable codes of behaviour have been developed, facilitators can encourage participants to take some responsibility for confronting each other (cooperative and or autonomous confronting). Facilitators may need to confront:

- resistance;
- avoidance;
- blocked behaviour/thinking;
- inappropriate behaviour;
- inappropriate dress;
- inappropriate language.

Who you confront

Who do you confront? Start with yourself first. Then analyse the extent of the inappropriate behaviour.

The publications on confronting are mostly culturally based in the West. Confronting in front of the whole group could be very embarrassing for

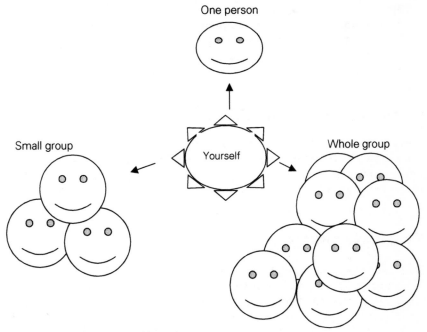

Figure 6.1   Who do you confront?

participants from Asia who value group harmony, and this may cause loss of face for both participant/s and facilitator. Decisions facilitators have to make include:

● to confront or not to confront;
● to confront in front of the group or to one side, at, for example, a coffee break;
● what strategy/ies to use: what to say and do, especially in terms of context and the cultural composition of the group;
● when to confront – timing;
● where to confront.

You also need to decide on whether to confront one, two or all three of the following:

● yourself;
● issues being avoided;
● the rigid behaviour;
● the source, such as limited learning objectives, cultural norms, past distress.

Facilitators need to decide on the confronting mode: should confronting be done in hierarchical, cooperative and/or autonomous mode?

● **Hierarchical:** you directly interrupt the behaviour and point out the issues.
● **Cooperative:** you do this with the group members. You ask first, gather their views, give your own, then have a general discussion.
● **Autonomous:** self and peer confrontation. You set up an exercise in which participants confront each other in small groups. Or set up an exercise in small groups in which individuals take turn to confront themselves on what they are avoiding.

Confronting yourself first

How can you confront others if you cannot/will not confront yourself first? It is useful for you to identify your fears regarding dysfunctional behaviours, such as fear of a verbal personal attack against you, and the behaviours that irritate you, or 'press your button', and stimulate some past distress.

The intervention cycle

There are three basic steps in diagnosing and intervening in dysfunctional behaviour (see Figure 6.2). Generally speaking, group members rely on the facilitator to intervene (although in groups which have developed the use of 'cooperative' and 'autonomous' power modes this may not be the case). Facilitators need to observe behaviour and compare it with the established

1,2,3 = Diagnosis steps; 4,5,6 = Intervention steps

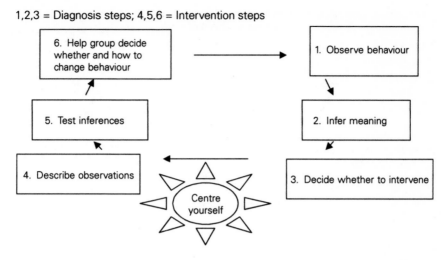

Figure 6.2   A diagnosis-intervention cycle

Source: adapted from Schwarz (1994: 127)

ground rules. Then there is the choice on whether to intervene or not. (The undesired behaviour may be temporary.)

There is a need to first 'confront yourself'. Ask yourself, is this behaviour 'pressing my button?' and triggering some past emotional distress? You could be transferring past negative people or hurts to the current situation. If the answer is 'Yes', then take time before confronting. Between stages 3 and 4 it is useful to 'centre yourself': take a deep breath to calm and help your thinking. Do not intervene as a 'knee-jerk' reaction, it is best to think first. Respond to the current behaviour, not your past issues/hurt. Be fully present in the here and now when you confront, to avoid 'pussyfooting' or 'clobbering' the person and/or group you are confronting. See Figure 6.3.

Why people withdraw from a group

People who leave a group may have one or more motives. They may withdraw to:

- protect themselves if things feel unsafe;
- vent emotions – have a weep in the toilets;
- indicate their anger/frustration exasperation and storm out;
- deal with an issue by flight rather than fight ('If I had stayed I would have. . .').

Participants may withdraw physically from a group, and usually give a reason to the facilitator and the group: their needs have been met, and/or pressing business requires their energies elsewhere.

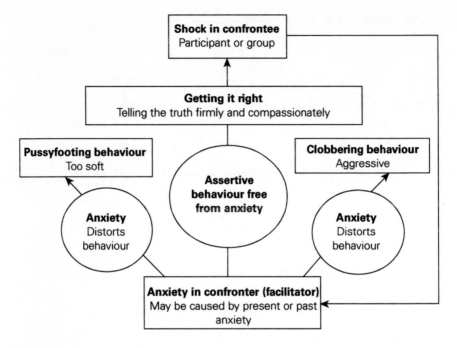

Figure 6.3   The process of confronting

Adapted from Heron (1999: 183)

Leaving a group without giving a reason can be a powerful and symbolic gesture of dissatisfaction with the status quo. Storming out may be very disarming for the rest of the participants (hence the 'Acts of god' process has a ground rule that everyone should stay throughout the process).

There are many ways of withdrawing. For example, people may stay silent and cut themselves off mentally from events. It may be a safer option for them, in some contexts. Some people may understandably fear retribution from a power holder in the group if they criticize the status quo.

If a participant feels threatened or uncomfortable with what is happening in a group at that stage of his/her life, it may be a very healthy thing to withdraw. If he/she is feeling vulnerable it may be useful to discuss options:

- Have a break and return.
- Stay and observe the group.
- Go back to the workplace.
- Go home.

Sometimes people who have left in a rage return once they have calmed down, as they do not want to miss out on what is going on.

Dealing with anger

All emotions are valid. With anger there is energy, and for the most part at least a person who vents his/her anger is acting authentically and providing you with a great deal of information. If people express themselves violently, this is because of an anguish that we should respect. People who shout are not necessarily cantankerous or destructive. They may feel wronged; they may be going through a difficult time; they may be on the verge of healing or commitment, for this too brings forth anguish. In any event they are suffering. If we respond too abruptly, we will not help them to become free and move towards a greater peace and harmony with the life of the community, its structure and its authority (Vanier, 1979).

Inform-invite confronting

A useful way to test your inferences or assumptions is to use two stages: 'Inform, invite' (Dick, 1984):

Facilitator: (*inform*)   'I've noticed xxx happening, which seems to be contrary to the ground rules generated at the beginning.'

Facilitator: (*invite*)   'What have you noticed?' (pause) or 'Do you agree?'

At times a facilitator may have a 'gut' feeling or hunch that something is wrong, but not know what it is, or what is causing it. For example:

Facilitator: (*inform*)   'I'm not sure what's going on here. The group seems different since lunchtime.'

Facilitator: (*invite*)   'Can anyone help me identify what's going on in the group right now?'

In other words, you invite comments and questions.

Generic confronting skills and techniques

Here are some general tips:

- Try not to take the inappropriate words or behaviour personally. Participants may be angry at someone or something else, but may be taking it out on you.
- Listen actively. Show the person you understand. Let him or her know he/she has been heard: summarize what he/she has said and repeat it back; ask questions for clarification, or give meaningful looks and sounds to let him/her know you're listening. Explain you would like to list the issues on flip chart paper so you can ensure that all problems are noted and addressed. Often all a difficult person wants is to be heard and understood.

- Use your empathy skills: saying, 'I know how you must feel' may evoke the angry response, 'No you don't, you are not me!'
- Imagine you have a coat of armour so that verbal attacks bounce off rather than infiltrate your psyche.
- Speak slowly and carefully. Stay cool. Breathe deeply. Once you've identified what is wrong, address the ground rules and/or values you feel were violated. Or state the boundaries of the workshop.
- Define your boundaries. Let participants know clearly exactly what you will and will not tolerate and why. If they know your limits, they may not be as likely to test them.
- Change the environment. Ask the person to talk to you outside, or ask the group to take an early break so you can talk to him/her alone.
- Later find ways to let go of your frustrations (see Chapter 7 and 11).

Facilitators have their own styles of dealing with issues, but here are some basic tools and techniques.

Confronting the whole group

When I contract with new facilitators at the beginning of a course, 'dealing with difficult participants' and 'increasing confidence' are two of the major items that always come up. Indeed they often speak of the 'group from hell' or the 'participant from hell'. I explain that 'behaviour is caused' and that people are not 'difficult' all the time (usually!) and refocus on 'dealing with difficult behaviours' and their causes.

I introduce them to the 'Acts of god' process first, before we do anything else: 'Here is the 'Acts of god' process that you can always fall back on, no matter what, but you must remember the five levels.' Then I share an anecdote: 'Once a past student rang me in my office saying, "I'm in the middle of a workshop, and it's not working. I suggested Acts of god and they agreed, but I cannot remember all the levels, so I called a coffee break. What are they?"' Students usually identify with the fright of forgetting under pressure and laugh. This seems to defuse some tensions.

As there may be religious participants who get annoyed by the term, I explain that it is an insurance term and not related to God. Hence it is spelt with a small 'g'. Even talking about difficult behaviours appears to develop stress in some student facilitators. I can feel the ambience of the room changing. When facilitators are stressed and on the spot with a group, it is sometimes difficult to think straight, so I suggest that they should keep a small notebook in their toolkit with reminders. I'm keen to help facilitators learn processes and procedures that will help them and will build their confidence. They may never need the process, but if they do it is there. Once facilitators have the confidence to confront groups regarding the real problems that need to be addressed, they can then choose from a menu of processes, adapt them and/or generate their own.

I will first describe the stages of the 'Acts of god' process and illustrate its use with a story.

Table 6.1   Confronting strategies

P: participants
F: facilitator

Type of facilitative behaviour	Explanation
1 Confronting the group with its own resistance. Embedded challenge, arousing curiosity	F: 'I'm not sure if you are ready for this yet.' Wait for participants to ask what it is, then tell them, and wait for their response. This sort of statement triggers people's curiosity. When they have heard what you suggest, they often agree to try something out, or suggest useful modifications.
2 Back off	If a suggested process is rejected, back off and suggest it later but reframe it.
3 Confronting individuals with their own resistance	F: 'Do you think there may be other ways of looking at this issue?' If the answer is 'Yes', 'What would you suggest?'
4 Responding to participants' generalizations	P: 'I don't know what to do.' F: 'What would you do if you did know?' P: 'I can't.' F: 'What stops you?' P: 'It won't work.' F: 'What aspects of it won't work?' P: 'We've tried that before.' F: 'What is different about the situation now?' P: 'I haven't learnt anything.' F: 'Anything?' P: 'I don't know what to do.' F: 'What would you do if you did know?'
5 Distortions	P: 'You make me so angry.' F: 'How do I make you angry?'
6 Embedded confrontation	Use a story to reflect back to the group some observed behaviours. See Chapter 4. For example, use 'The tale of the sands' in Hogan (2000) during change and transition workshops.
7 Resisting debriefing sessions	If some individuals want to focus constantly on just activities/simulations with little debriefing they may: ● have strong activist and low reflector learning styles (Honey and Mumford, 1992); ● fear discussion of deeper issues regarding themselves and their relations with others; ● be very high on the 'playful child' scale in transactional analysis terms. Draw the Kolb Experiential Learning Model on the board. Point out that missing out on aspects of the learning cycle may inhibit learning.

Table 6.1 *(continued)*

Type of facilitative behaviour	Explanation
8 Acknowledge and channel negative energy	F: 'Thank you for reminding us of the drawbacks. The group members need to be aware of all points of view, otherwise the group could fall into 'group think'. Why don't we use a PMI (the pluses, minuses and interesting points) to make sure we note all perspectives?' (Alternatively, use the six thinking hats.)
9 Place challenging quotes around the walls	'If you are not part of the solution, you may be part of the problem.'
10 Listen to and use your intuition	F: 'I may be wrong but . .'. F: 'For what this is worth, right or wrong, my impression is that. . . What do you think?'
11 Insults	P: 'This is a load of rubbish!' F: 'Thank you for your openness. Can you tell us why?' F: 'What do you suggest?'
12 Bring in the rest of the group	F: 'What do the others think?'
13 Resistance to 'reflecting' or resistance to 'theory'	Draw the Experiential Learning Model on the board (see Chapter 3). Point out that missing out on aspects of the learning cycle may inhibit learning.
14 Silence	F: 'Let's take one minute of silence here just to still our minds.'
15 Ignore the bait	Ignore the behaviour. Keep going, it may stop.
16 Emotional switching	Make a joke so that people laugh: cathartic release of tension.
17 Challenge	F: 'Did you come here to have your thoughts/values challenged, or did you come here for more of the same?'
18 Indirect confronting	F: 'It's after lunch and the next part of the discussions are crucial. Anyone can sabotage, that's easy; anyone can have quick aside chats to their neighbours. The real challenge is to give this part of the day your fullest energy. Can I have your commitment to that please?'
19 Controlled scream to vent your anger	Only to be used in extreme circumstances! Clench hands and let out a short but controlled, deep roar. Then when you have shocked everyone to attention, pause, then say how you feel: 'I'm angry because. . .'. See story 'The scream' on page 187.
20 Leave the group to sort something out autonomously	F: 'I'm just going to the toilet', or 'I'm going to step outside for five minutes so you won't be influenced or intimidated by my presence. When you have reached a decision please come and get me.'
21 Hold up yellow and red cards	Yellow and red cards are used in soccer and football rules to signal non-sporting behaviour. In some groups holding up cards might be humorous, relevant and useful.
22 Point to the contract of desirable group behaviour on the wall	Say nothing, just draw people's attention to the norms being broken.

Acts of god process

Author/background

This process was developed by Bob Dick in Queensland (1991) to enable a facilitator to confront a negative group and to marshall the energy of negativity in a productive way. In April 1998, I met Bob at a workshop and took the opportunity of asking him why he developed the Acts of god process. He thought for a moment and laughed. 'It was because I was desperate. I do some of my best work when I'm desperate. My arousal goes up, and so does my energy and creativity.'

Purpose/rationale

Many groups fail to move forward because of overriding negativity and hidden agendas. This workshop technique was designed to enable a group of people to focus cooperatively on their problems, and where possible to take action. It also enables participants to identify areas that are unchangeable and beyond their control.

Size of group

Groups of up to 30 people are most appropriate.

Materials

Flip chart paper, felt pens, masking tape, pens and writing paper for each participant, adhesive gum. A large blank wall.

Venue layout

Participants sit in a semicircle facing the facilitator and wall.

Time

Two hours minimum. The action planning stage may require future workshops.

Stages

Establish the ground rules

The role of the facilitator is to remind people of the ground rules at the beginning and to enforce them assertively during the process:

- Describe behaviours and issues, rather than naming or blaming individuals.
- All participants must contribute issues as clearly as possible.
- Everyone must remain until the end of the workshop.

Raising issues

Issues may be raised by brainstorming (which may mean that some people's ideas do not 'get heard') or by using the nominal group technique, as follows. Ask participants to write down individually a list of their issues/concerns. (Allow 5–10 minutes for this.) Then ask each participant to give a single response. Confront gently if a person tries to give more than one response at a time. Write up each issue clearly on butcher paper. Leave a left-hand margin of about 20 cm. Round robin the group until all ideas have been generated. Only allow one issue per person at a time. Do not allow any discussion or criticism of ideas at this stage.

Table 6.2 Flip chart layout of ideas

Category 1–5	Issues, concerns, problems
	Not enough information on the next project
	Ineffective meetings

Categorization of issues

Explain that there are five categories of issue, and write these on butcher paper clearly in front of the group. Explain that some are called 'Acts of god', and that this relates to the English phrase used in insurance policies and has nothing to do with religion:

1. Acts of god that you have to live with.
2. Acts of lesser gods you probably have to live with, but at least you can communicate your complaint/s to them.
3. Issues that you share with others, for example in another department of the same organization, and can resolve jointly with them.
4. Issues that are yours to work on, but for which you need help (maybe consultancy/training from an outside organization or from a different department.
5. Issues that you can work on yourselves without help.

Ask the participants to go through the list of complaints in turn and classify them according to the criteria described above. Write a large number 1, 2, 3, 4, 5, on the left column to identify these items. Do not allow any discussion to 'solve' the issues yet. It may be difficult to achieve consensus on some items, therefore if necessary allow a classification to cover two categories, such as 1/2.

Action planning

This section is very important. Place another sheet of butcher paper alongside the first and write the heading 'Action plans'. Remind the group about the 5WH mnemonic for action planning, from the first letter of the question words:

- What are you going to do?
- Why are you doing it?
- When are you going to do it?
- Where will you do it?
- How long will it take?

Another way of remembering this is to use the *Six Honest Serving Men* poem by Rudyard Kipling in the *Just So Stories*.

Table 6.3 Action plans

Level 1–5	Issues, concerns problems	Action plans
3	Not enough information on next project	Jo to see director before Friday and report back to next meeting on 3 May
4	Poor meetings	Toni to obtain three proposals/costs for training in meeting procedures and make recommendations at next meeting 3 May
1	Ineffective director	All to learn to cope with him/her

Group members should be encouraged to give themselves permission 'not to take action' at the present time. For participants to decide not to act is just as powerful in some instances as to act, and is very different from vacillating. The external economic and/or internal political climate may not be conducive for a successful outcome.

If nothing can be done about an 'Act of god number 1' it may be necessary for the group to decide to 'learn to cope with it' rather than to continually use up negative energy about something that is totally beyond their control. The fifth level can form the basis for the next meeting at a later date.

Outcomes

The outcomes are that members of a group have directly tackled their problems and focused energy on solving them rather than moaning about them.

Advantages

During the process negative comments, feelings and hidden agendas are vented. As a result energies are focused into formulating positive outcomes. Participants themselves usually feel more 'empowered' in that they have taken responsibility for their own problems. The important thing for upper management is to ensure that issues are dealt with quickly and positively.

Disadvantages

The Acts of god process has to be handled carefully, in that participants need to focus on issues and not personalities. The facilitator must guard individuals from attack. The process requires plenty of time to formulate action plans, therefore do not use this process towards the end of a workshop or meeting. The story below illustrates one time when the Acts of God process helped me turn the energies of a negative group.

STORY: USING THE ACTS OF GOD PROCESS
IN A PLANNING WORKSHOP

Bud, my colleague and education officer-friend in Fremantle jail invited me to facilitate a strategic planning workshop with prison education officers from across Western Australia. I enthusiastically agreed, as I was keen to find out about changes in the jail education system since my departure for Hong Kong in mid-1981.

We met with a few of his colleagues to plan the session, which appeared on the face of it quite straightforward. A venue was chosen 'off site' in the northern suburbs of Perth, and participants were flown into Perth the night before from the small, outlying country prisons.

I talked to Bud about a week before the workshop. Everything appeared to be falling into place logistically. However, on the day of the workshop, the group members' energies appeared low. I battled on until morning tea. It is common for a group of people in such stressful jobs to unwind by letting out their frustration during a workshop like this, a kind of 'communal catharsis'. However, the energy just was not there for looking positively into the future. I called a halt and confronted the group. 'I might be wrong, but I sense something isn't working.' They agreed and 'let out' that some very recent administrative changes had really made them all frustrated and angry.

I suggested the 'Acts of god' process. I explained the process in outline to the group members and asked them if they would be willing to spend some time on it. They agreed, so I kicked off the process. 'OK, what issues have you got?' Pause. . . uneasy silence. . . wait. One woman spoke out angrily. 'We work in a bloody jail!' My immediate inner response was to laugh, it seemed so obvious. Luckily as I felt my facial muscles change I was already spinning around to write on the flip chart paper, so I managed to control my inappropriate grin as I was writing. Then I composed myself, turned back to the group, and with a straight face said, 'Yes, what else?' Individuals shouted out their issues. Their raised volume and tones indicated underlying frustrations and anger. I kept reminding myself, 'Write it up on the paper. They are not angry with you; they are angry at the system.' Their issues rolled out for 15 minutes, then the pace slackened, the volume lowered, the anger diminished somewhat.

I went to the next stage of the process. 'OK now you tell me which category/ies you think each issue fits into. 'Where does 'We work in a bloody jail' fit for you?' 'It's a number one of course. We have to live with it.' 'Really?' Questioning pause. 'Well, hang on a minute. We don't have to work in a jail, we could work somewhere else.' The discussion continued, and at the same time the participants seemed to be reclaiming their power in a system which was systematically depowering them and what they stood for. Times had changed in their world since I had left. Education in prisons was less valued. There had been numerous cutbacks, and rehabilitation of criminals was deemed less important, and perceived as a cost rather than as an investment for the future safety of society.

Another way to confront a whole group and quickly change the dynamics is to use a 'controlled scream'. It's a risky tactic, as illustrated in the story below.

Story: The scream

I once worked with unemployed youths, and attended a residential life skills workshop. During the workshop, we were involved in a number of activities such as giving and receiving feedback, plotting our lives, and to managing life transitions. The weekend flew. People talked long into the night.

The last incident of the workshop was especially intriguing. We were sent off to complete a group activity and agreed to come back at 4.00 for the ending. However, we got so involved that every group was late back. Mike Jones, the facilitator, was furious. He stood silently in front of everyone, clenched his fists and let out a controlled roar. There was immediate silence. Then he spoke calmly. 'You have sabotaged the last part of the workshop as we have a commitment to finish at five o'clock. We now cannot do the last activity.' I was stunned. The ambience of the room changed immediately. I thought to myself, 'He's lost it, he can't handle it. He's spat the dummy.' I've often wondered what the last activity was, and about appropriate methods of confronting participants when they break the contracted group norms. Later I observed another facilitator use a 'controlled scream', that time in frustration with a group of unemployed youth (Hogan, 1988b).

I later realized a controlled roar/scream was a legitimate tactic, but it is risky as it can be so easily misconstrued by group members, especially those from Asia who perceive that the facilitator has lost face.

Going with the flow: changing the workshop plan

> The best laid schemes o' mice an' men
> Gang aft a-gley.
> (The best made plans often go astray)
>
> Robert Burns, 'To a mouse' (1786)

In Chapter 2, I described planning workshops with input from participants under the headings 'content', 'process' and 'time'. There are occasions when a facilitator has to drop plans and renegotiate the workshop purpose and use of time with the participants. At times, to stick to a preconceived plan when something good or bad has happened is inappropriate. Participants need to discharge feelings first, then may be more ready to tackle the task ahead.

STORY: CHANGING THE FACILITATOR'S SCRIPT

One group, middle managers in a government organization, arrived for a two-day course entitled 'The Organized Manager'. They looked very miserable. I greeted individuals as they arrived, inviting them to help themselves to coffee, and pointing out the direction of the coffee room. As each arrived I received a sort of grunted 'Hello'. No one seemed to want to look me in the eye. When I opened the course I took a deep breath and launched in with an enthusiastic welcome, desperately hoping that things would improve. The atmosphere was thick and heavy and I ground to a halt. 'What's wrong?' Pause. I scanned each of them in turn. Silence hung thick and heavy for what seemed like an eternity. Slowly, one member spoke up. 'Well, Chris, we are going through a restructure at the moment, and things are so uncertain that we don't even know if we will have jobs next week. So this course just feels like a waste of time, to be honest.'

I took a deep breath and sympathized, and asked others to speak. Similar laments came out, indicating deep fears, frustrations, a sense of failure, concern for families, doom and gloom. This gave me time to think. I knew it would be suicidal to continue the course as planned, so I decided to take a risk. 'Well, it seems as if while you are here it might be useful to focus on your present dilemma. Why don't we change the schedule to look at 'managing transitions'? What do you think?' The ambience of the room changed a little. 'What sorts of things do you mean?' 'It would entail looking at the stages of transitions: managing emotions; action planning. . . that sort of thing.' I paused. Silence. 'Seems OK, we've got nothing to lose after all.' I noticed a number of nods. I checked with everyone with my eyes. 'Right . How about you all get a cup of coffee while I nip upstairs for some materials?'

We spent the whole day on ways of managing transitions. I used exercises from the chapter from Hopson and Scally (1980) 'How to make and gain from life transitions', that I had learnt about when working with the long-term unemployed.

We had a very emotional day. People were metaphorically 'bleeding'. Participants told stories and opened up to one another, probably more than they had ever done before. They were so vulnerable. I empathized and told them of my experience of being laid off in a past position, ironically working with the unemployed. They were surprised. I have found that participants deem a course facilitator to be totally successful in life: they are surprised when some self-disclosure occurs. It's important not to dwell on oneself for long, I believe, but it helps build empathy and may open the floodgates of emotions.

By mid-afternoon we had been through the stages of transitions (see below) and a 'Fantasy Friday exercise', a creative visualization of a wonderful work day five years in the future (see Chapter 9). Each person had looked at strategies to manage the current transition and/or to start to look for other work. One person indicated he had always wanted to move to Margaret River anyway, and this might be a good opportunity. At the end of the day I spent time on 're-entry' strategies: that is, to re-enter their homes and families empathically, as I was concerned that they might drop their new plans on their partners without discussion.

At 4.30 on the first day I re-contracted for day two. 'Given that no matter what, you will need some more organizational skills whether you are in your present job or in another, do you want tomorrow to concentrate on 'The Organized Manager' programme?' There were enthusiastic nods. 'OK, which aspects of the programme would be most beneficial to you, given that we have got one day?' Negotiations took place and we started packing up. But the group did not disperse quickly, as was normal on day one of a course; they chatted to each other and to me. There were very different energy levels to the start of the day.

Weeks later I received mail from some of the participants, thanking me for the workshop and detailing the changes they were making to their lives.

After hearing the story above, some people have queried my decision, in case I was held accountable for not fulfilling the workshop contract. If that had happened, I would have been ready to give my reasons, and if necessary to call on the group members. That is not to say that you can do anything and everything, just because people agree. I felt that the changed plan that day modelled what an 'organized and sensitive manager' should do: attend to feelings and concerns, then people are more likely to be able to tackle their work effectively and efficiently.

The transition stages that I used to generate discussion are cited in Table 6.4. I linked these to the mythic Hero's Journey described by Joseph Campbell (1973) where a person is called upon to be something 'more than they currently are' and go on adventures. The possible stages that people in transition may experience (though not necessarily sequentially) are shown in the table, and are easily remembered via the mnemonic 'daddac', a word made from the first letters of each stage.

Table 6.4 Stages of transitions (daddac: first letter mnemonic)

Denial	I don't believe this
Anger	Look for someone to blame
Discussion	Look at options
Depression	Withdrawn, quiet, anger, feel there are no options
Acceptance	May not be in agreement, but are prepared to move on; aware of choices; letting go of the past
Celebration	Moving on, celebration and welcoming of new ventures

Dangers of going too deep

In the 1960s and 1970s there was a trend for 'encounter groups' in which facilitators encouraged people to say exactly what they felt about each other, directly to one another. This led to some major problems and hurts. Facilitators, I believe, need to keep to the top three levels of the organizational iceberg described in Chapter 2. Ned Ruete (1999) in an e-mail discussion group commented:

There are some powerful weapons out there that the untrained can stumble upon and make some real trouble with. When I took the NTL lab 'Training Theory and Practice', pairs of participants prepared and presented experiential learning sessions. One session was on the differences that our socio-economic background make in how we approach the world today. The presenters decided to help us remember our background by taking us through a guided visualization of our childhoods. *Bad idea*. It took the professionals who were teaching the course an hour and a half to talk some of the participants down from the feelings this visualization brought up. What causes feelings?

Experiential learning often engages people's emotions. Facilitators are not therapists. It is important for facilitators to be clear about what they have been contracted to do *and* for participants to know what they have agreed to participate in. (See *Understanding Facilitation*, Chapter 11).

Confronting a small group

Sometimes it may be necessary to confront a small group as the following story illustrates.

STORY: TWO MISMATCHED PARTICIPANTS

When I worked at the Australian Institute of Management I always enjoyed facilitating the 'Advanced Train the Trainer' five-day course, since it focused on group work facilitation. Or rather, I did until one group arrived, comprising of two friends from a mining camp, Bill and Ben. They had been sent to Perth at the last minute, as the two people who had booked were sick. As a result, there was a mismatch of expectations. I described the focus of the course and they looked rather puzzled. Throughout the contracting stage they kept casting glances at one another and smirking. I could not work out what was wrong, and as they were not disturbing the rest of the group, at that stage I decided to ignore the behaviour.

At morning tea I asked them what was wrong. They were instructors of people who use heavy machinery. The two appeared to think the course was a sequel to the 'Train the Trainer', a sort of 'How to do presentations even better', or 'How to tell 'em louder and clearer' was how they put it. I tried to explain that there were other ways of teaching people than the traditional 'show and tell', but they were clearly not convinced. At lunchtime I invited one of the male consultants to 'call in' to the group to reinforce my message about interactive learning, which he did. However, even a male 'ocker' voice failed to convince them.

When I went home on the Monday night I was distraught. In desperation I rang Noel, my boss at home. He was far less concerned than I was. He offered me three alternatives to give the two men the next day: first, to stay and actively and positively participate; second, to stay and complete different work in another room; third, to fly back directly to work at their mine site, and their company would receive a refund. I mused over the three choices and prepared some extra work in case they decided on option two.

The next morning, I took them to one side and described the dilemma. The second option appealed, but somehow their curiosity seemed to be aroused as to what they would be missing if they left the main group, so I described the day's activities. I left them in a room to think, but asked them to make a decision before we started at 9 am. To my surprise they decided to stay with the main group. I restated the ground rules, that they were to enter into it with a 'positive outlook and be prepared to give things a go', and they agreed.

Gradually as the week went on they became more and more enthusiastic. On the last day, they volunteered to undertake a role play of the 'silent demonstration process' (Downs, 1981). They dressed up in chefs' costumes and superbly showed the group how to make peppermint creams, but teaching only in response to the questions of the group members. By the end of the course they were wrapped with the concept of experiential learning and questioning, and behaved like the converted 'doubting Thomas' in the Bible!

Generating your own strategies

Once you have read this chapter it may be useful for you to think ahead to possible situations, and prepare yourself mentally with different strategies. Many new and experienced facilitators understandably have some underlying fears or concerns. Below is a list generated by participants in my facilitation classes. Take a look at them and add your own if they are different. Then think about strategies you can use to develop positive self-talk, and actions you could take if an incident did occur.

Making the best of a situation

I used to be a perfectionist, but I stopped because I wasn't good enough at it.

Anon

Billy Connolly, the comedian, started his performing career as a folk singer and banjo player. During one of his first solo songs he was telling a tale of a saint sailing from America to Ireland. About two verses in he stopped, completely flummoxed through nervousness. 'I've forgotten the words' he explained to the audience. . . 'but it's about a guy who is sailing. . .' He abandoned the song and

Fears and concerns	What can you say to yourself? ie positive self-talk	What could you say/do if it happened? ie have a variety of responses ready	How will you know if you are successful?

Figure 6.4   Common fears and concerns

made the best of the situation by telling a story instead of singing. As he gained momentum he embellished the narrative and performed a flourish on his banjo at the end: 'Dum diddly ah dum, ding din!'

It was so successful, he gained admiration and new friends that evening and embarked on a career as a comedian and story teller (and part-time banjo player) (Stephenson, 2001).

> Necessity is the mother of invention
> When in doubt call 'time out'.

Conclusion

Facilitation work requires us to work with a wide spectrum of people. That is what makes it so exciting. There are no set recipes for dealing with inappropriate behaviour, but the stories and strategies above provide a smorgasbord of techniques. After a critical incident it is useful to note the story, and if you are still upset later, deal with your feelings in a productive way. See Chapter 17 for ideas on ongoing learning and maintenance.

7

Creative and reflective journal processes

It's the good girls who keep the diaries; the bad girls never have the time.

Tallulah Bankhead

Introduction

All professions develop forms of reflective practice; it is not new. Reflection can happen 'on the run' almost simultaneously with an experience, or it can be a deliberate activity performed after an event (Schön, 1987). Journal writing is a recognized way of recording and reflecting on events. Sometimes they are called 'learning reviews' or 'learning logs'. This chapter focuses on creative techniques in writing. Various issues will be addressed including:

- what is a creative journal?
- journal writing strategies;
- writing blocks and how to overcome them;
- reviewing your journal;
- uses of creative journals;
- evaluation of journals writing for participants and facilitators;
- tips.

Journal writing includes a number of writing processes which may be used by:

- facilitators to monitor their own learning and development;
- participants in workshops to log and explore new learning;
- individuals for self-development, pursuit of goals, project management, action learning and research, to explore life transitions, to explore problem solving techniques (see Chapter 11);
- individuals to explore inner life or growth;
- small communities to monitor their own growth, process, learning and development (eg eco-villages).

The development of creative journals

Ira Progoff (1992) warned against the potential narrowing effect of using journals in a self-contained way, such as a narrow logging of events like the diaries many of us kept as children. These are static tools. Progoff suggests that journals should include creative techniques in order to stretch our thinking and take us out of our fixed attitudes and ways of being. So this chapter is devoted to illustrating creative journal writing techniques.

Creative journal writing began in the 10th century, when Japanese ladies of the royal court developed the diary into a form of self-expression and explored their fantasies as well as perceptions of reality. Early healers in Europe (who at that time were predominantly women) kept diaries containing information about herbs and remedies, much of which was lost during the tragic 'burning times' in the Middle Ages (Rainer, 1985). The process has been used for a variety of purposes. Leonardo da Vinci, Anne Frank (1945), Samuel Pepys (1983) and Anais Nin (1966–76) kept journals of reflections, questions, dreams, problems and creative solutions. Many included sketches, symbols and diagrams of their ideas.

Creative journal writing is a tool, a learning mechanism which involves many different writing techniques to enhance reflection and creative thought. It is not a learning log or traditional diary. The creative journal process is designed to encourage the use of a variety of creative as well as analytical methods of thinking. David Tripp (1993) uses journal writing very successfully with trainee teachers.

The aim is to enable you and/or your participants to monitor learning goals, processes and progress; interrelate ideas; develop understanding of yourselves at home and at work; describe learning plateaux and blocks and how you overcame them, and free up the writing process so that it can become a source of freedom, relaxation and fun. The journal can include phrases, passages, words, quotes, sayings, dialogues, drawings, doodlings, sketches, scribbles, cartoons, collage, mind maps, mandalas, prose and poetry, graphs and charts, colours, images and symbols.

The learning process is captured in the journal:

> Physical growth is easy to recognize, but personal growth is inward and elusive. In the metaphor of Lao Tse, it is evanescent, like smoke going out the chimney. We know it exists, but its shape keeps changing. It has no shape that we can fix in our mind; we cannot contain it in any mould. We know it is real, but soon it has disappeared and is beyond us.
>
> (Progoff, 1975: 18)

The type of journal-writing book depends on personal preference. However, an A4 blank book or loose-leaf file allows freedom of space and movement. A variety of plain, lined, coloured and white paper, coloured pens, scissors and glue are useful. A small pocket notebook is also useful to record impromptu ideas during the day.

I write a computer journal so that I can quickly add odd thoughts about groups as they come to me at the end of the day. However, I find a paper journal is more freeing for experimentation and creativity. My anthropologist friends, Kati and John Wilson, keep a small tape recorder to record ideas, and hunches from their different perspectives every evening when they are working as consultants.

Various journal writing strategies

Getting started

Creativity and reflection are enhanced by creating a relaxing writing environment. Some people like to write when there is soft orchestral or New Age music in the background (see Chapter 4). This will vary according to people's specific needs. It is important to enter into a positive frame of mind by saying to oneself:

> I can and I will give this session my best attention and motivation. I wish to achieve increased learning about myself. I wish to increase my health and well being and learn more about the world I live in. I will try to concentrate fully and work to my capacity, not pushing too hard nor being too soft, but extending as far as I can into my learning.

Remember, if concentration is difficult it may be better to do something else and come back to writing at a later time!

Doodling

Lucia Capacchione (1979) encourages doodling as a way of warming up to the writing process. Some people find it useful to accompany this activity with music and even a small dance around the room before they begin! It is also a way of invoking the creative child within, to play with colours and just let shapes happen. When the doodling is complete, look at it and record responses.

Make a mark

One art therapist I knew always started off by encouraging us to 'make a mark' on the paper. In other words anything, just to put your own 'self' on the paper and then you have started.

Stepping stones

This process refers to the idea of stepping stones across a river, each of which represents significant milestones that have enabled us to reach the present moment. Some stones may represent a pleasurable achievement, others a painful experience or failure, others joyful transitions, travel or relocation to a new abode or workplace. Progoff (1975) suggests limiting the number of stones to about 12.

Dag Hammarskjold in his autobiographical book, *Markings* (1964) describes the metaphor of a mountain climber who leaves markers up and down the mountains climbed, including in valleys and ravines. Stepping stones are simply 'significant markings'. Progoff (1975) describes stepping stones as a time-stretching process which enables individuals to think in chronological time: that is, objective sequencing of events and qualitative time. Next Progoff suggests the use of subjective perception by giving meaning and value to 'special' events, picking on certain stones that stand out and describing their significance.

Critical incident or event analysis

The phrase 'critical incident analysis' unfortunately is sometimes misunder-stood, in that people perceive it as being a 'major' or 'negative' event. David Tripp (1993) later decided to use the term 'event analysis' to suggest the small incidents of everyday life. They may be positive or negative; for example, incidents:

- that did not go as anticipated (either better or worse);
- that reflect and or challenge the values or beliefs of the person;
- that allow learning to be identified;
- that need further exploration through comparing experience with theory;
- to develop new models and hypotheses.

He suggested using a questioning approach to analyse 'events':

- What is important about what happened?
- What do I think is most useful for me to work on?
- What do I need to do to improve my performance?
- Why did it happen?
- What could I do about that?
- What are the pluses, minuses, and interesting points about each strategy?
- What strategy is most appropriate?
- Which should be described first?
- What else does this incident indicate?

You can also use the ORID discussion process (see Chapter 3).

Dialoguing

Dialoguing is an imaginary conversation or script. In the 1960s Gestalt thera-pists began using the technique. It is a relationship and meeting between the writer and an aspect of your life. Dialoguing may be between the writer and another person (living or dead), a work (such as an assignment or text), his/her body, events, institutions, animals, a problem or fear, religious, racial or cultural heritage. For example, a participant who was in touch with her fear when contemplating abseiling for the first time decided to confront the cliff (see Chapter 13).

One participant wrote a dialogue with a 'path not taken' in her career, and examined her attitudes to things that did not happen, which she needed to let go of since they were no longer obtainable. She then examined the positive aspects of the path she did take.

Unsent letter

Rainer (1985) suggests that it is useful to write unsent letters when confrontation is impossible, for example when the person is unavailable, or if such communication is rude or inappropriate, or might cause harm. Rainer warns about the overuse of this technique, if the writer is avoiding being open with another about an important issue that is obstructing the ongoing development of their relationship. One participant sent an 'unsent letter' to her husband, and also one to herself to investigate learning plateaux.

Mind mapping

Mind mapping is a learning tool that utilizes key words, colour, symbols and arrows to connect related ideas. Space does not permit a detailed description here. The reader, however, may consult Buzan and Buzan (1993), Hogan (1994), and Marguilies (1992), for further information. In journals I have also used the four squares of the experiential learning cycle as the key start areas of a mind map.

Mandalas

Pedler, Burgoyne and Boydell (1986) and Capacchione (1979) advocate the drawing of mandalas or domain mapping to help develop centredness through drawing. A mandala may be used for plotting networks: those people who are closest and those farthest away, and/or the segments of your life. Pedler *et al* called the latter, 'domain mapping', a diagram which resembles a pie cut into segments, with you at the centre. See Figure 7.1.

1. In the first ring write domains of your life, eg work, family and home, leisure, health and/or people in your life (Pedler *et al*, 1986).
2. In the second ring write key words to give an overview about how you are now.
3. In the third ring note your intentions, eg keep same, try to improve.
4. In the fourth ring note alternative strategies:
    - Change situation: be proactive, do something about it.
    - Change yourself: change your attitudes.
    - Change your relationship to the situation: live with it.
    - Leave the situation: move on in a constructive way.
5. In the fifth ring choose strategies.
6. In the sixth ring note first steps.

The advantage of seeing your life, organization or community in a circle is that it enables you to see where you are putting energies and if you are keeping a balance.

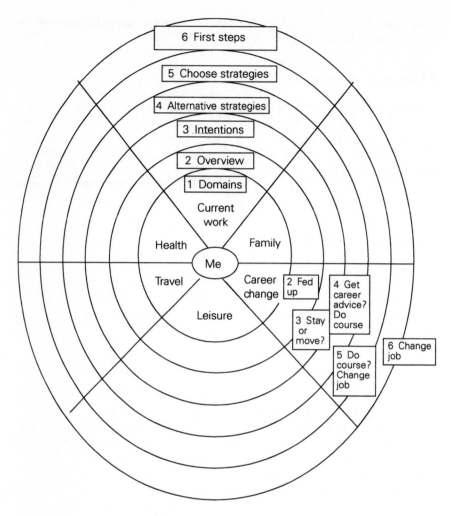

Figure 7.1   Domain mapping

Source: adapted from Pedler, Burgoyne and Boydell (1986)

Writing blocks and how to overcome them

> What you have experienced no power on earth can take from you.
>
> Friedrich Nietzsche (1844–1900)

Experiential learning and journal writing involves participants in all of Honey and Mumford's (1986, 1992) learning styles. They invite participants to have a variety of experiences, which appeals to those who have a preference for being Activists; the reflection stage appeals to the Reflectors; the generalization stage appeals to the Theorists, and the application stage appeals to the Pragmatists. Participants who have a strong preference for a particular style may experience resistance or blockages to developing a lesser-used style of behaviour. However, as Honey and Mumford (1986) suggest, it is useful for everyone to have learning versatility and be able to use all styles, so that we stimulate all parts of our brains.

Rainer (1985) describes the 'internal censor or internal critic' who in trans-actional analysis terms represents fears about 'OKness', about the quality or style of writing or who may represent the 'critical parent'. One participant commented, 'I didn't get blocks very often, but if I did I found doodling very useful to loosen myself up.' Others commented, 'Doodling somehow paints a picture' and 'I just babble on for a while and before long I was writing a lot' and 'If I get a block I just leave it until the atmosphere is more positive. I put the stereo on, good music and wine provides a pleasant atmosphere and thoughts flowed.'

Frequently, they and I observe a change in writing style and freedom:

> Just picking up my journal the other day I read what I wrote in the initial two weeks. Phew. . . I mean, you can almost notice how the change takes place weekly. Also the manner in which I write now about events certainly is different. For instance, there is not much fear about what I want/should do. . . in retrospect the initial fear has turned into a triumph for me.
>
> Samir

Another supervisor realized that writing blocks were normal. In this instance he came to understand that it is not 'how you feel' but 'how you feel about how you feel' that is important:

> Now if I get a block I will most probably think that it's OK, it's normal, it happens to everyone, I would feel quite easy about it and I would just write about the block and free myself!
>
> Wong

One participant described her fear at the beginning:

> I felt scared that I would be unable to tap into my creative side (I know I've got to) so I sat down and wrote my favourite quotes throughout the journal, so I would come across them as I added to the diary at a later date. Why? Ownership!
>
> Marie

One way of overcoming blocks is to write freely and intuitively without paying attention to grammar or spelling. Another way is to make a list, start mind mapping or to do a meditation exercise on the issue. Rainer (1985) suggests a number of strategies:

- **Write about the block.** Write about the symptoms of the block, for example, 'When I sit down to write my hand becomes heavy like a weight on my mind which stops me from writing. I can feel it now like a weight on my back.'

- **Dialogue with the block:**
  Me: Oh, it's you again.
  Block: Yes, and you are stuck on me again.
  Me: Why do you bug me?
  Block: Because you let me get the upper hand.
  Me: Aha, but not this time.
- **Write about your fear.** It is useful to ask, 'What am I afraid to say?' and then write it down. If you expose it head on, the fear is removed.
- **Make a deal with the block and/or critic.** Ask, 'What am I afraid to write?' If it is so bad then make a deal with it, write it down and then throw the piece of paper away.
- **Circumvent the block with an altered point of view or audience.** Another way to trick the internal critic is to alter the writer's point of view: instead of writing in the first person using 'I', start using 'he', 'she' or 'it'. Or you can change your audience: instead of writing for the facilitator, write as if you were writing for your most supportive friend – yourself.
- **Constructive blocking.** Some blockages may be useful. They may indicate tiredness and that the writer needs a break. Or they may indicate that something has been blocked for a long time.
- **Preventative strategies.** One way is to write in fourth gear: so fast that blockages do not have time to catch up the writer.

Learning blocks and how to overcome them

Learning blocks are a natural part of lifelong learning. Frequently blocks prevent the learner from deeply analysing an event. Tripp (1993) suggests using the 'Why? challenge' process to push through these blocks:

> Another simple form of analysis which can be far-reaching and sometimes quite devastatingly dramatizing in its effects, is like Sophocles to ask, and go on asking, the question, Why? When we do this we do not go for ever, but we may go on for a long time before we find that underlying our action or idea is one of two things: a normative statement or some form of reification. In effect the end point is the same: we see things are as they are because we choose to make them that way. In practical terms, if we ask 'Why?' for long enough, we end up saying either, 'Because that's how it ought to be' or 'Because that's how it is' (Tripp, 1993: 29–30).

The next stage involves really asking why 'that's how it is' and whether 'it' can be changed even in some small way. This process, as Tripp points out, can be quite disturbing when an individual realizes that his/her perceived lack of choice may have been a rationale or ego-defence mechanism (Rosenberg, 1967). Empowerment is about 'choice':

> There is always an alternative, and we can choose. None of the alternatives in some situations may be desirable, but it is the knowledge that there is always a choice that heralds the beginning of self-empowered thinking (Hopson and Scally, 1981: 57).

The realization of 'choice' may be blocked. I have recently been involved in workshops on domestic violence. Some women who were subjected to violence as children have developed a placating, coping mechanism in order to survive, as they could not leave the family situation. In adulthood, when faced with similar problems with violent husbands, some use the same coping strategies. They forget that as adults they have the choice of leaving, even temporarily, to show that violent behaviour is unacceptable. Progoff gives the analogy of sunlight dawning:

> The soil of our lives is loosened and softened. The solid clumps of past experiences are broken up so that air and sunlight can enter. New harnesses come in and have a fertilizing effect. Soon the soil becomes soft enough for new shoots to grow in. That softness inside of us is a new feeling, and it opens new possibilities.
>
> (Progoff, 1975: 100)

One participant wrote:

> I have undertaken the greatest learning experience of my life. Controlling what I learnt, how much I wanted to learn and my degree of success. Initially I was resistant to the process. . . I kept going although at a distance. . . reading and then suddenly I became focused. Experiential learning took place by challenging the traditional learning methods and involving myself in risk management.

Another participant wrote:

> The use of the journal initially presented a major blockage. This was the 'stranger' threat. It was the perceived tool that had the potential to unlock some inner secrets such as my original perceptions of early childhood, the pain of interpersonal relationships gone wrong, the agony of personal and professional self-doubts. All the little 'checkpoint Charlies' I had designed to prevent a breaching of my own 'Berlin wall' were in themselves in danger of being breached. Out of this bubbling cauldron of negativity, fears and cynicism came an acceptance of the journal. It became a friend, a secret closet one could open at any time and into which frustrations (and there were a lot) could be unloaded and then close the door.

Reviewing your journal

It is useful to review your journal. Lucia Capacchione (1979) believes it provides a new sense of perspective and reveals patterns, cycles and periods of insightfulness. She suggests many different ways of reviewing, including read segments to yourself aloud and/or taping and playing back segments. She also suggests keeping a summary log with dates and a synopsis in chronological order. For example:

February 26	nervous, concerned powerless
March 2	better, wrote contract
March 9	depressed, contract to be rewritten, under stress
March 11	rewritten contract, more confident, clearer aims.

This process can be used to highlight certain aspects: for example, some journal keepers highlight feelings, others highlight events and others learning issues.

Issues

Self-development requires participants to confront themselves. Some find this process very rewarding, others find it extremely difficult and at times painful, as many past issues are recalled. Some individuals find self-analysis and/or disclosure threatening. Therefore a facilitator has to be aware of and be equipped to facilitate the affective/feelings domain, to enable participants to work through these issues. One participant wrote, 'I was worried and confused, I just stared at the page'.

Some participants feel trapped by the issue of correctness: 'I kept wondering if I was getting it right'. Others felt trapped by their own stereotypes: 'Journal writing was meant for writers and artists and I am concerned as I do not consider myself to fit into either of these categories. . . as a result I did not take it seriously and tended to neglect it'. Some participants thrive on writing freedom, while others find lack of structure a threat at first. One participant wrote at the beginning, 'I feel frustrated. My learning before has been more structured. I feel silly with the results.' Later the same participant wrote, 'I have thoroughly enjoyed doing the journal. It's helped me to free up a bit. I would like to continue with it after the workshop. I look forward to other journal experiences.'

Many participants indicated a change in perception during workshops. At the beginning one participant commented, 'Oh no! I felt perplexed, powerless, unsure and listless. I felt that I didn't have any control over the situation. To begin with I put it out of my mind.' Later she said, 'This isn't so bad. . . it's a little stilted, but okay. . . this could be interesting. . .' At the end she wrote,

> I have thoroughly enjoyed the journal and I believe have taken to it like a duck to water. . . maybe my 'free child' revisited or visited for the first time! It has assisted me to clarify thoughts, ideas, concepts/strategies and 'capture' feelings as they're brimming or blocking further learning. I've especially enjoyed the buzz of a little creativity coming out of me.

Some participants had had negative previous experiences with journal writing, and overcame this block by choosing a journal book that was totally different in character to those used before. 'I went and bought an exercise book and deliberately covered it in a colour I liked so it would hide the pain somewhat.'

Some participants had had positive experiences of previous journal writing, and directly transferred their previous techniques to this assignment, 'Oh great, a journal again! I had to keep one when I was doing my Diploma in Education.' The same participant wrote later, 'Only recently it has dawned on me that it has to be creative. . . the one I had done before was just notes of my learning. I enjoyed the various processes to extend my reflections.'

Journal writing does not appeal to everyone, especially if they do not normally reflect formally and/or have difficulty with writing. (Remember some people have some very complex coping strategies to mask illiteracy or writing problems.) Individuals who are not native English speakers should be supported to write in their mother tongue.

Uses of creative journals

Journal writing includes a number of writing processes which may be used by:

● facilitators to monitor their own learning, hunches and development;
● participants in workshops to log and explore new learning;
● individuals for self-development, pursuit of goals, project management, action learning and research, to explore life transitions, to explore problem-solving techniques (see Chapter 11);
● individuals to explore inner and/or spiritual life or growth;
● small communities to monitor their own growth, learning and development (eg eco-villages).

Journal writing may be used to motivate participants to reflect carefully on the experiential learning experiences in workshops (and in the workplace), so that they are more able to develop self-directed learning and critical thinking. Verbal debriefing and group discussions in workshops are useful, but I believe the learning process is enhanced by a more private, in-depth reflection when learners are free to be and confront themselves. The journal process is a means to an end. The end is deeper and more long-lasting, learning about themselves. Some people boast about having 20 years of experience; however, all too frequently this means one year repeated 20 times over. Length of experience does not necessarily denote learning. 'One of the most important areas of learning for adults is that which frees them from their habitual ways of thinking and acting, and involves them in what Mezirow calls "perspective trans-formation"' (Boud, Keogh and Walker, 1985: 23).

Journal writing encourages 'deep' and 'achieving' rather than 'surface' learning:

> The deep approach is indicated by an intention to understand the material to be learnt, together with strategies such as reading widely, using a variety of resources, discussion, relating the unfamiliar to the familiar, reflection, etc. An intention to reproduce the material to be learnt and avoid failure through focusing on specific detail using rote learning strategies characterizes the surface approach. The achieving approach is exemplified by an intention to excel by using highly organized learning processes. The surface and deep approaches relate to the content of the material, while the achieving approach relates to the particular learning context.

> (Dart and Clarke, 1991)

Evaluation of journal writing

Advantages of journal writing for participants

According to Mumford (1999), people with a more 'reflective learning style' tend to like journal writing more than people with a more activist style. Those people with more pragmatist leanings like to build in practical tools to help them transfer learning to their work and home lives. This enables participants to see how life situations link to theories in texts. As a result they have an opportunity to delve not only into their thoughts, but also into their feelings about abstract theories. Those with more theorist tendencies like to build in models and charts so they can see things in a logical way.

Journals allow people to confront their own ways of thinking and/or being and explore their own practice in a way that they might not feel safe with in the whole group discussion.

Journal writing may also be used as an empowering self-counselling skill, 'an instrument for life' (Progoff, 1975: 9). The techniques once learnt may be used in times of stress, conflict and difficulty, or in gentler times for quiet reflection and learning. It increases self-reliance. 'I use it to get rid of frustrations I felt about my work and the weak and watery boss,' said one participant.

The journal is a useful record for future reference. Participants can start to identify patterns of behaviour. For example, when glancing through my journals I found that before risk-taking I always hesitate at the last moment, and I have learnt through positive self-talk to take the responsibility for pushing myself through that block. Journal writing also enables participants to look back on their progress.

Participants gain a learning tool which is transferable to a variety of situations later in college, work or home life. One participant wrote, 'I am happy having learnt this technique, I now feel that journal writing will form part of my life as it is an effective tool for self development which is an endless process'.

Journal writing at first is time-consuming, as it forces participants to integrate course material, reading and theories, as well as past and present experiences. This could also be regarded as a positive. Participants at first find it difficult to choose one critical incident to work on in depth. They tend to try to describe everything in workshops superficially.

Disadvantages of journal writing for participants

Some participants have had poor experiences of journal writing in the past. For example, one participant described how she kept a journal at school and confided in it her hatred for a particularly distasteful nun. The nun saw her writing in it and demanded to see it. The participant ran home (with the nun in hot pursuit) and tore out the offending pages. Her parents were summoned to the school. This participant overcame the resulting negative blocks by obtaining a journal that was totally different in size, shape and colour to her previous one. She also wrote an unsent letter to the nun in question.

Journal writing requires patience and persistence.

Advantages of journal writing for facilitators

Journal writing is a useful tool for facilitators to monitor their own learning, as well as intuition and hunches. The 'learning from mistakes' process can be used in a journal after workshops that have been problematic (see Chapter17).

It is a useful process to build into workshops, as participants often say at the end, 'We needed more time to think'. It also gives the facilitator breathing space and often triggers ideas to emerge.

Disadvantages of journal writing for facilitators

Journal writing is time-consuming and very hard if you are busy. It requires patience and persistence.

Uses of journal writing

I have used journal writing with managers as an adjunct to outdoor development programmes (see Chapter 13), assertiveness and 'train the trainer' programmes conducted through the Australian Institute of Management. One participant wrote to me months later and said, 'Just thought you would like to know that I'm still using the journal process. . . it's useful'.

Mumford (1987) and Honey (1989) in the United Kingdom use journal writing with managers on training programmes:

> Our own common experience in management, and for those of us prepared to read, the research on what managers actually do, show that reflective analytical processes are not widely valued or implemented across the range of management skills. It is not surprising they are not identified as a crucial learning skills.
>
> (Mumford, 1987: 101)

Management is frequently perceived as an active activity with little time for reflection. Mumford (1980: 94) points out that this is a myth, and that heart-searching and recrimination about failures do occur, but, 'Successes are examined for learning even more rarely – partly because examining the causes of successes would sometimes show how fortuitous success was'.

Tips

For participants

These tips have been collected with the help of participants:

- Identify a time and place to write.
- Get into the writing habit, do not put it off and miss out stages of your development.
- Stick at it: 'If at first you don't succeed, try, try, try again.'
- Record experiences as soon as possible after they happen (carry a small pocket book all the time).
- Do not try to describe everything.
- Release the 'free child' and suppress the 'critical parent' within you (Stewart and Joines, 1987).
- If you get stuck, go for a walk or have a cup of tea.

For facilitators

Based on my experiences I would suggest:

- Orientate participants carefully and explain the purposes of journal writing and how it relates to adult learning.
- Provide a variety of journal writing processes, as participants relate to some processes more readily than others.
- Encourage flexibility in how participants make entries into their journals.
- Sometimes negative past experiences may block the writing process. Invite participants to describe these negative past experiences and how they overcame them.
- Encourage participants to share parts of their journals with trusted peers so that they can give one another feedback and learn from each other.
- Encourage participants to reread their journal entries and add to past events in the light of time, as frequently patterns of behaviour are identified.
- Encourage participants to record critical incidents, and reflect more deeply.
- Allocate time during a workshop for journal writing and ensuing dialogue.
- Journal writing can be linked to learning styles and the experiential learning process.
- Participants should be invited to record 'content' knowledge/observations as well as 'process' knowledge/observations.
- Writing blocks should be discussed openly and participants be encouraged to share how they overcame them.

The video *Creative and Reflective Journal Processes for Students and Managers* (see References) may be useful.

Conclusion

In this chapter I have described journal writing techniques that may be used specifically for journal writing or as a part of general workshops. Journal writing is not for everyone. Writing blocks and resistance by some participants (or yourself) are normal, and strategies to overcome writing blocks have been suggested.

If you wish to use journal writing for your own professional development, see also the 'Learning from mistakes' process in Chapter 17.

8

Facilitating meetings

The foundation of all meetings is listening to the ideas of others.

Source unknown

Introduction

This chapter has been written with the intention of encouraging facilitators and meeting participants to experiment with a variety of meeting processes. In order to do this effectively, participants need to be informed about the functions of the processes and their uses. This will encourage the trust and participation which is necessary for effective meetings.

This chapter contains:

- discussion of Robert's rules and interactive meetings;
- common problems;
- methods to improve productivity and collegiality in meetings;
- strategies to encourage resistant groups to use new techniques.

Robert's rules

Formal meetings procedures were developed by Major Robert in the United States, who researched British parliamentary procedures and published his own manual in 1876 'to assist an assembly to accomplish the work for which it was designed, in the best possible manner. To do this it is necessary to restrain the individual somewhat, as the right of an individual in any community, to do what he pleases, is incompatible with the interests of the whole' (Robert in Patnode ,1989: 14). These rules were later entitled 'Robert's Rules of Order' and formed the basis for formal meetings in the Western world for over 100 years. These rules are well documented (Robert, 1985; Robert's Rules Web site: http://www.robertsrules.com).

In the nineteenth century, when Robert was compiling his 'rules', the environment was relatively stable and there was plenty of time for lobbying and arguing inside as well as outside the meeting room. This process also exacerbated the problem of hidden agendas. Decisions were made slowly after

Table 8.1   Advantages and disadvantages of Robert's Rules

Advantages	*Disadvantages*
Well-known ground rules for behaviour	Tends to create factions
Useful to control large groups	Many creative alternatives lost by voting
	Often chaired by a non-neutral manager
	Win–lose debating and point scoring
	Inhibits exploratory dialogue

lengthy argument and debate. Here the proposer of an idea frequently argued adamantly about the virtues of his/her idea, and a disbeliever tried his/her best to demolish the idea (and sometimes the person as well!). This resulted in a win–lose approach to decision making, and frequently innovative or different ideas were lost if they were proposed by quieter or less articulate participants.

Common problems in meetings

Dominators and repetition

The Schnelle brothers in West Germany recorded meetings to measure 'interaction density', or the number of utterances per hour. They estimated that in most meetings only about one-third of the members are actively involved (though we should not jump to the conclusion that people who do not speak are not involved mentally). In Figure 8.1 you can see that out of 15 participants, speakers A–D have the lion's share of the air time, while the majority E–O have substantially less time. The Schnelle brothers found that the inclusion of a 'moderator' or facilitator could help to give a better distribution of active

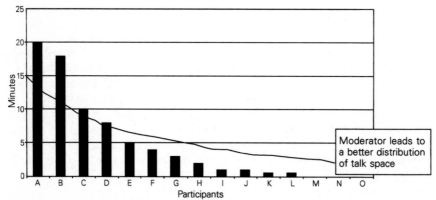

A, B, C etc represent the individuals in the meeting

Moderator leads to a better distribution of talk space

Figure 8.1   Measurement of talk time in meetings

Source: adapted from Schnelle (1979: 11)
NB: Moderator = Facilitator

participation (see curved line). They also found that the use of visualization techniques such as ideas on cards reduced the repetition of ideas and discourse 'going around in circle,' and as a result freed up more air-space.

Gender issues

Meanwhile, Dale Spender in the 1970s and 1980s in Australia (Spender, 1996) was researching gender issues by tape recording women and men talking in meetings and students in classrooms. She found that:

- Men talked more in mixed-sex conversations.
- Men determined the topic – women accommodated what men wanted to talk about – and it was often about themselves.
- Men interrupted more (98 per cent).
- Men appropriated women's ideas.
- The most common way that men interrupted, and took over the topic, was through a corrective device – of correcting women – often by such statements as 'What you mean is' or 'I think you'll find', or in some circumstances, 'You are wrong.'
- Women apologized to men again and again.
- Women asked men questions to which the women already knew the answers in order that men should look knowledgeable, while women appeared to be in need of information.
- While the majority of men defined a good conversation as one where they had the floor, most women thought a good conversation was one where everyone had a turn.

When Dale Spender was challenged about her findings, teachers and others repeated her research and found many similar results. Belenky et al in the 1980s (Belenky *et al*, 1997) proclaimed boldly that 'women's ways of knowing' were very different from those of men, and based on different life experiences, ie, that acculturation process and educational institutions were usually based on a male view of the world. Similarly Carol Gilligan (1982) pointed out that research has been based on data taken mostly from men. For some women and some men, issues like 'finding a voice', and 'being heard' make participating in meetings difficult. It is important that facilitators of both sexes bear this research in mind when observing meeting processes, and if necessary give a group feedback on their patterns of communication or 'mis-communication'.

Methods to improve productivity and collegiality in meetings

Opening meetings

Always start meetings on time. Why? Because if not the latecomers are 'rewarded' and the punctual people are 'punished'. It is important to make the key purpose of meetings clear (verbally and in writing, both handouts and on a whiteboard).

Some groups learn to have a few minutes silence to:

- leave behind outside issues;
- focus positive energies on to the issues at hand;
- focus on the 'here and now' of the group.

Agendas, minutes, timekeeping, sharing roles and responsibilities

Of course it is important that the meeting organizer provides participants with 'think time', provided that he/she sends out detailed agendas well in advance of the meeting. Frequently agenda items, which are cryptic in nature, are ambiguous and/or misleading. This is because they are usually single words, for example 'communications'. This word immediately is hooked up to thousands of different ideas in our individual brains. For example, to one person it could mean 'How can we improve inter-departmental communication?' To another it could mean 'How can we get more telephone outlets?' If agenda items are phrased as a question instead of a cryptic clue, the readers' minds are immediately set into action to help solve the issue. For example:

1. How can we raise money for the wotnot event?
2. Which project/s should we support?

Question 1 is an open-ended question which could have many 'right' answers. Therefore a process like brainstorming, which would encourage creativity, would be most applicable. This process was developed by Alex Osborn, an advertising executive, in New York in 1938. This process is described in Rawlinson (1979). Brainwriting is also a useful tool (see Chapter 10).

The generation of ideas needs to be followed by prioritizing the most suitable by dot voting (everyone is given five dots and asked to vote for five separate solutions). Dick (1984) suggests the use of different coloured dots for 'cyclic' voting in force field analysis. Step 1, use one colour for the most important items; Step 2, use another colour for the easy items to change; and Step 3, use a third colour for the best items to act on immediately.

Question 2 calls for a comparison and/or evaluation of two or more separate projects or ideas. Here it is useful to use an evaluation process developed by de Bono (1987) called PMI (pluses, minuses and interesting points). A decision matrix can be drawn up, and all participants are asked to focus on the advantages of an idea (even the antagonists), then the disadvantages, then the interesting or unusual features of an idea. In this way the energy of the group is directed towards analysing each idea on its merits. An idea is evaluated without its being linked to a particular person in the group. Many innovative ideas have been lost merely because people have ditched the idea of a person who is unpopular in the group.

It is also advisable to think through the most useful process to use to address an issue and the time designated to it (see Table 8.2).

Table 8.2   The layout of agendas in interactive meetings

Content (What?)	Process (How?)	Time (How long?)
How can we raise money? (Toni)	Presentation of issue	9.00–9.05
	Brainstorming	9.05–9.25
	Dot voting and prioritizing	9.25–9.35
What are the advantages and disadvantages of each proposal?	Pluses, minuses and interesting points.	9.35–9.50
	Decision making.	9.50–10.00

Notice that the name of the person responsible for raising the agenda item is also responsible for a brief five-minute introduction of the issue to the group. This saves time searching for the 'owner' of the issue, and eliminates participants asking, 'What does this mean?' By making processes visible to the group, there is joint understanding not only of the agenda, but also of how the group will tackle an issue. This enhances trust and more open communication.

Breaking down agenda items

It is useful to tackle agenda items in stages. First, as indicated above, invite the person who raises the item to make a five-minute introduction to the problem or issue. Often participants jump into giving solutions, and sometimes solve the wrong problem! The facilitator might ask the rest of the group for feedback, for example, 'Is this the whole problem?' 'How widespread is the problem?' 'What are the causes: long term and short term?' 'Is this a problem on the rise or on the decline?' Then the group can usefully shift to the next stage of problem solving: 'In what different ways can we solve this problem in the short and long term?' A list of ideas might be generated, or if creative solutions are called for, brainstorming or brainwriting might be appropriate. Then action planning can take place. See Figure 8.2.

Changing meeting structures and settings

Traditionally all meetings are conducted with participants seated round a long rectangular table, which provides a needed support for weary elbows and a resting place for papers, pens and cups of tea. The term 'board meeting' comes from the traditional board of wood and trestle.

However, this format has some undesirable side effects. Participants closest to the chairperson can more easily be heard. There is a friction of distance, and participants at the extremities often doodle, dream or read. The body language of participants can be open to misinterpretation. Individuals may be actively participating while remaining silent and doodling. In fact, drawing is a way of concentrating for some people. Unfortunately, there is no perfect method of ensuring that people are listening and participating all the time.

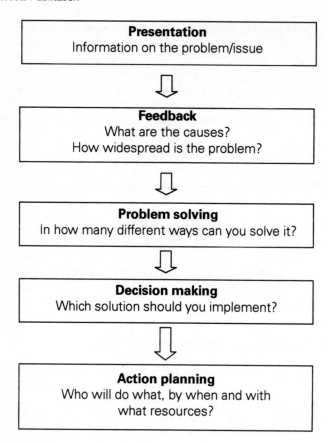

Figure 8.2   Stages in dealing with an agenda item

Figure 8.3   Traditional meeting layout

Eye contact is almost impossible between people who are sitting on the same side of the long sides of the rectangle. If two people become locked into debate, a 'toing and froing' and repetition of argument may ensue. Followers of the debate resemble fans at a Wimbledon tennis match, straining to follow the fast-moving ball, with heads turning left then right as the 'game' unfolds. Doyle and Straus (1976) recommended that the table should be removed and that participants should sit in a semicircle facing the wall minutes (the board should be taken out of the board meeting).

Likewise, the Schnelle brothers recommended a semicircle of chairs and breakaway groups behind, so that people can divide into small discussion groups and move around. Movement is rarely tolerated in board rooms, and yet many people think better when they move around (see Chapter 4).

Wall minutes

As a result of the new seating arrangement, participants' eyes are focused on the issues on the wall minutes. Wall minutes may be recorded on:

- flip chart paper;
- electronic whiteboards;
- computerized display using an overhead projector and datashow, with one person typing in data;
- computerized display with all participants keying in own ideas to networked computers in a Group Support Systems Support lab setting, and combined anonymous ideas displayed on a screen.

In West Germany, the Schnelle brothers (1979) developed 'Metaplanning' using highly visual recording of the group memory or minutes on a variety of different coloured cards. Large yellow sticky-backed pads are excellent for this purpose, as an alternative to cards described in depth in Chapter 3.

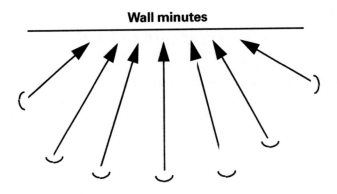

Wall minutes

Figure 8.4   Interactive meetings layout

Alternatives to wall minutes

A shorter version of minutes can be kept by everyone, and/or on an electronic whiteboard, so that everyone has a copy straight after the meeting (so that data cannot be changed).

Minutes						
Chair_____		Date_____			Next Meeting_____	
Timekeeper_____		Facilitator_____				
Scribe_____		Present_____			_____	
					_____	_____
Agenda item no	**Name**	**Agenda item**	**Time**	**Action**	**Who?**	**By when?**
1						
2						
3						

Figure 8.5   Short minutes

Electronic white boards now speed up the duplication process; however, butcher paper is still preferable since the whole group can scan all the ideas displayed round the walls at any time.

The setting is also important. Without a comfortable, non-stuffy, stimulating environment, participants cannot be expected to think creatively. Sometimes a change of venue can stimulate participants. Space is required, and participants should be encouraged to take one-minute stand and stretch breaks.

Saving time

Time can also legitimately be structured in a meeting. Doyle and Straus (1986) suggest the use of a timekeeper who informs the group of how long there is to

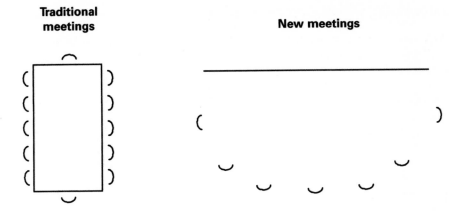

Figure 8.6   Comparison between structure of traditional and interactive meetings

go on each agenda item. This results in either a speeding-up of the group process or a renegotiation for more time.

The reader will probably have experienced long, monotonous, repetitive monologues in meetings. For some speakers, they are a way of thinking aloud or marshalling thought, and it is necessary to hear him or her to the end. On the other hand, some participants use expanded 'air space' as a way of gaining attention or trying to score points. Derschka and Gottschall (1984), suggest the '30 second rule'. This is to prevent longwinded monologues in discussions and to give others the time to express themselves. Participants agree to limit their contributions to a maximum of 30 seconds. If anyone thinks a person has been speaking too long, he/she can signal to remind the speaker to cut short the dialogue. It may be appropriate to use this method only sparingly, as it may lead to:

- some people feeling unheard;
- people whose style is more ponderous and reflective staying silent;
- people who have English as their second language staying silent.

Sharing roles and responsibilities in meetings

From the previous paragraphs, it can be seen that participants are increasingly being required to take a more responsible and active role/s in the running of the meeting, and to take responsibility for its success. In the past, this responsibility has rested solely with the chairperson, who was usually the manager and chief power holder in the group.

With this hierarchical structure, the role of chair was and still is very daunting. In a sports game we would not ask one individual to umpire, score, defend,

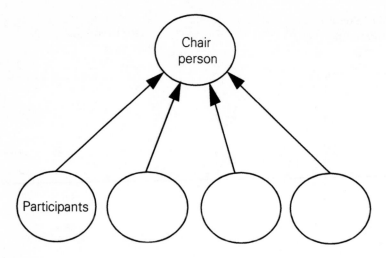

Figure 8.7   Roles in a traditional meeting

attack, yet in meetings we expect the chair to do all of these things. Doyle and Straus (1976) suggested splitting the role in half, and asking a facilitator to guard the process and stay out of content, and a chairperson (usually the manager) to be an active participant and use his/her power to remind participants of deadlines and company policy when appropriate. This molecular model is far more robust than the previous more hierarchical model of meeting structures.

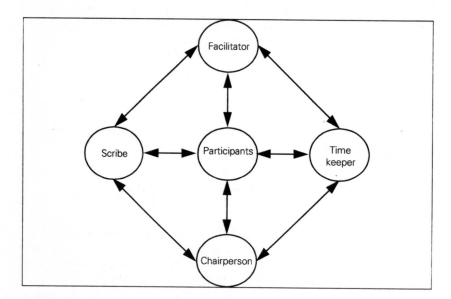

Figure 8.8   Roles in interactive meetings

Source: adapted from Doyle and Straus (1976)

I added to the Doyle and Straus model of roles in meetings the role of participants, and placed it in the centre on purpose, to try to help people think about how they can share the responsibility of making meetings successful.

Table 8.3 Comparison of roles in traditional meetings and interactive meetings

Traditional meetings (Robert's rules)	Interactive meetings (Doyle and Straus)
Chairperson Is often the manager or major power holder. Sometimes the role is rotated.	**Chairperson** Is the manager
Is responsible for the process of the meeting as well as inputting own ideas	Free to pursue own ideas as an active participant
Is frequently held responsible for the success/failure of the meeting	States organizational policy/constraints and timelines as and when necessary
Has the casting vote	Calls for votes if consensus cannot be reached
Secretary/minute taker Records his/her version of decisions, votes and pertinent points of discussion	**Scribe** Creates 'group memory' on wall minutes with flip chart paper
Confers with chairperson on points for accuracy	Checks accuracy of recording by clarifying with participants at the time
Minutes checked for accuracy at following meeting in distant future (some discussion points may be lost)	
Participants Pursue own points of view	**Participants** Take on some of the responsibility for the success of the meeting
Try by argument and persuasion to sway others to own point of view	Keep facilitator out of content
	Check that the scribe records ideas accurately
	Make process suggestions
	Timekeeper Participates in discussion
	Watches time and reminds facilitator and participants of agreed schedules
	Calls out amount of time left on an item
	Facilitator Gets agreement on processes and ground rules before beginning meeting
	Stays out of the content of the discussion
	Does not evaluate ideas
	Protects participants from attack
	Encourages the participation of quieter group members
	Helps group to reach consensus wherever possible

Table 8.3   *(continued)*

Traditional meetings (Robert's rules)	Interactive meetings (Doyle and Straus)
	Supports the scribe, chairperson and timekeeper
	Summarizes who is doing what and by when at the end
	Encourages and thanks group members for their ideas and participation in the meeting
Rules with specific terminology	**Processes**
Tied vote, casting vote, proxy, point of order, propose a motion, amendment to motion, speak for the motion, speak against the motion (win–lose), seconder, show of hands, secret ballot, motion passed	Many and varied according to the issues. Different ground rules may be generated to suit the situation Dialogue rather than debate

Derschka and Gottschall (1984) suggest the 'butler rule', that everyone should be both a thinker and a helper in the creative process. No one should feel it beneath him/her to help out with scribing, timekeeping or facilitating, or even to fetch a colleague a drink or help clearing up empty cups and glasses.

Encouraging dialogue rather than debate

Patterns of discourse and argument are frequently based on debate, where the atmosphere is competitive, win–lose, and where listening is overridden by the need to interrupt with one's own side of the argument, or rather what is perceived to be the 'correct' or 'right' side or answer.

The term 'dialogue' comes from the Greek 'dialogos' ('dia' which means 'through', 'logos' which means 'word', or rather 'the meaning of and behind the word'). Dialogue requires the use of words, moving participants to work together as a team through interaction in search of new meaning and understanding.

Facilitators can help participants to dialogue by encouraging them to:

- explore the differences between debate/discussion and dialogue (see Table 8.4);
- slow down and observe their thought processes;
- observe their patterns of thought and listening;
- explore how their thinking makes or breaks connections and meaning;
- question their 'beliefs without reason' (we don't know why we hold these beliefs but we are convinced they should be defended at all costs as we know they are true (Dick, 2002).

Bohm, Factor and Garrett (1991) propose that the dialogue stage of talk should not be concerned with trying to alter or change behaviour or ideas, though

Table 8.4 Distinguishing between debate and dialogue

Debate	Dialogue
Pre-meeting communication between sponsors and participants is minimal and largely irrelevant to what follows.	Pre-meeting contacts and preparation of participants are essential elements of the full process.
Participants tend to be leaders known for propounding a carefully crafted position. The personas displayed in the debate are usually already familiar to the public. The behaviour of the participants tends to conform to stereotypes.	Those chosen to participate are not necessarily outspoken 'leaders'. Whoever they are, they speak as individuals whose own unique experiences differ in some respect from others on their 'side'. Their behaviour is likely to vary in some degree and among some dimensions from stereotypic images others may hold of them.
The atmosphere is threatening: attacks and interruptions are expected by participants and are usually permitted by moderators.	The atmosphere is one of safety; facilitators propose, get agreement on, and enforce clear ground rules to enhance safety and promote respectful exchange.
Participants speak as representatives of groups.	Participants speak as individuals, from their own unique experience.
Participants speak to their own constituents and, perhaps, to the undecided middle.	Participants speak to each other.
Differences within 'sides' are denied or minimized.	Differences among participants on the same 'side' are revealed, as individual and personal foundations of beliefs and values are explored.
Participants express unswerving commitment to a point of view, approach, or idea.	Participants express uncertainties, as well as deeply held beliefs.
Participants listen in order to refute the other side's data and to expose faulty logic in their arguments. Questions are asked from a position of certainty. These questions are often rhetorical challenges or disguised statements.	Participants listen to understand and gain insight into the beliefs and concerns of the others. Questions are asked from a position of curiosity.
Statements are predictable and offer little new information.	New information surfaces.
Success requires simple impassioned statements.	Success requires exploration of the complexities of the issue being discussed.
Debates operate within the constraints of the dominant public discourse. (The discourse defines the problem and the options for resolution. It assumes that fundamental needs and values are already clearly understood.)	Participants are encouraged to question the dominant public discourse, that is, to express fundamental needs that may or may not be reflected in the discourse, and to explore various options for problem definition and resolution. Participants may discover inadequacies in the usual language and concepts used in the public debate.

Source: © Public Conversations Project of the Family Institute of Cambridge, 46 Kondazian Street, Watertown MA 02172 USA, e-mail: thepcpteam@aol.com, tel: (617) 923 1216, fax (617) 923 2757.

changes are unavoidable during the process. It is a chance for thoughts and feelings to play freely in a continuously engaging movement, like the ebb and flow of a river as currents and ripples intermingle in a journey of exploration and discovery.

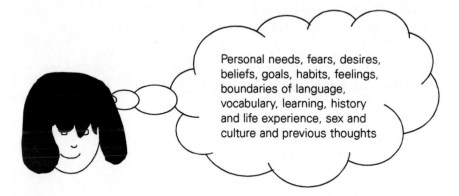

Figure 8.9   So called 'rational thought' is influenced by many things

It is suggested that participants should sit in a single circle and talk for a maximum of two hours. This should not be confused with T groups, in that the purpose of dialogues is to focus on social constructs and inhibitions that affect our communication. Feelings of frustration and dissatisfaction are normal at first, but with patience, as things develop, participants see new ideas and ways of thinking coming from their group members. There should be at least one-week breaks between dialogues, to enable participants to reflect on discussions.

Paulo Freire (1973) speaks of time that is so-called 'wasted' in dialogue as only apparently wasted. In the long run, if people have been engaged in effective dialogue they gain a greater sense of certainty, self-confidence, trust in each other; things that we can never attain when there is a lack of dialogue.

STORY: HOW CAN YOU TELL IF DIALOGUE IS OCCURRING?

On their way to a public dialogue between psychotherapist Carl Rogers and anthropologist Gregory Bateson, the moderator for the evening asked Bateson, 'How will I know whether or not we have done our job tonight?' Bateson responded, 'If either Carl or I says something that we haven't said before, we'll know that it's a success. (*Source:* Joseph Phelps Mennonite Conciliation Service.)

Clearly dialogue is a form of communication that is evolving and requires skill. See the Web sites http://www.muc.de/~heuvel/dialogue and http://www.crnhq.org.

Any other business?

In order to ensure that all agenda items are given pre-thought, it is useful to abandon 'any other business' except for items of urgency that have arisen since the agenda was drawn up. This ensures that an item is not suddenly thrust on the group when people are tired. Under this kind of pressure quick decisions are often made. This also minimizes the chance of manipulation.

Ending meetings, monkeys and delegation

At the end of meetings the job of the facilitator (or a group member) is to summarize who is going to do what, by when, and set the next meeting date. At Quaker meetings the minutes are vetted by the group members before they disband, in order to check that they are a true record of the meeting. Marie Martin (2002) suggests it would be useful to have two records drawn up, of the observed group process and key words/outcomes. Again participants can help with this.

Another useful technique is to keep a mind map of the meeting minutes. Each branch of the mind map can be devoted to one agenda item. A mind map record is useful as the technique of arrows around the edge can show the way some agenda items are interlinked. (This is not so easy in linear minutes.) Also a mind map can enable minutes on one page!

Oncken (1989) used the 'monkey' metaphor, asking, 'Who's got the monkey?' to enable groups to 'see' the weight of delegated tasks, and how much each person has to do at the end of a meeting. Some people may have ended up with small monkeys/tasks, others with large orang-utans which might require support, while others are left with nothing to do.

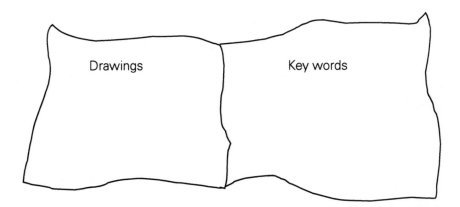

Figure 8.10 Two records of the group process

External versus internal facilitators

Some groups raise the problem of finding an external facilitator from outside their organizations. This is a valid concern and an added cost factor. However, it is easier for a good outside facilitator to confront power holders who do not listen, repeat themselves or constantly interrupt others. Internal facilitators may be caught up in the power and personality issues of their own department (see Chapter 1).

Some organizations now have a number of staff and managers who are either competent facilitators or are learning facilitation skills. If necessary, the facilitation role can be taken by a group member who is not involved in a particular item: that is, the role can rotate during a meeting.

Evaluating meetings

Meetings are rarely evaluated, yet using different techniques can provide useful data to stimulate improvements.

Participant evaluations

Suggestions can be made discreetly by using a simple participant evaluation sheet as shown in Figure 8.11. It is interesting to note that many chairpersons actually feel at times overloaded, isolated and threatened. However, frequently they welcome tactful suggestions and a sharing of the responsibility for the success of the meeting. Likewise this evaluation makes everyone think about how they can improve their contributions to meetings.

The results of these questions can be collated anonymously, distributed and discussed at the next meeting. New directions can be formulated based on this communal information. If participants choose to keep their hidden agendas hidden, then they must take responsibility for this. However, this apparently simple questionnaire is a way of enabling participants to say the unsaid.

STORY: CHANGING MEETING DYNAMICS

I first saw the use of interactive meetings at the Alcoa Refinery at Kwinana, Western Australia, where the shift workers facilitate their own monthly meetings, using the interactive meetings methods. I returned to work fired up, and asked if I could try out the new methods at our next team meeting. My colleagues readily agreed. At the end of the meeting we evaluated many aspects: the meeting; the processes used; the participants, and my role as facilitator (using the questionnaire in Figure 8.11).

At the following meeting, I fed back the collated responses anonymously to the group so they could gain a picture of what happened, including one piece of useful feedback: 'Chris, you could have been firmer with Roy (our boss).' Everyone laughed, including Roy. But it was great to have that piece of very powerful information out on the table. Indeed it helped me as every time thereafter, when Roy tried to dominate the 'air space', one of three things happened. I signalled to him with my fingers (circulating upwards to encourage him to wind up); he laughed and told himself to shut up and listen; or the group made muttering noises, that is, they co-facilitated. It is very difficult to facilitate when you are part of the power structure of the group, but by feeding back evaluations anonymously we were all able to manage upwards. I now use this strategy regularly with students and client groups to open up 360-degree feedback.

Participants' meeting evaluation sheet

1. What did you think of the meeting? Please circle a number:

A waste of time   1   2   3   4   5   6   7   Much was accomplished

2. What could have been done to help the meeting to be more effective?

   Please list suggestions.

3. What might **you** have done to help the meeting?

4. What could the chairperson have done to help the meeting?

5. What could the facilitator have done to help the meeting?

Figure 8.11 Meeting evaluation

Observer/video evaluations

Sometimes facilitators are invited to observe meetings before capacity building workshops so that they know the current meetings dynamics in an organization. Often participants in meetings are unaware of their behaviours and norms. They can be 'woken up' by use of an observer, or by someone videoing their meetings and using the observer type of questions shown below. Setting up a camera in a meeting room does impact on behaviour; however, after 15–20 minutes people usually forget that it is there.

Organization
1. Was the purpose of the meeting made clear?
2. Were agenda items clearly explained?
3. To what extent were agenda items achieved?
4. Were participants given time to consider data before the meeting?

Participation
1. Was participation invited from all?
2. What processes were used to maximize participation?
3. Did the body language of participants indicate that they were giving full attention to speakers?
4. Were some participants doing other work?
5. Did some members repeat themselves?
6. What processes were used to prevent repetition?
7. Who was listened to?
8. Who was not listened to?

Problem solving and decision making
1. Were problems analysed before solutions were generated?
2. What decision making method/s were used?
3. How were dissenters treated?
4. To what extent were decisions prevented because of lack of information?

Timing
1. Did the meeting start on time?
2. Did the meeting finish on time?
3. Were there attempts to signal use of time during the meeting?
4. Was a timekeeper appointed?

Atmosphere
1. Formal or informal?
2. Cooperative or competitive?
3. Friendly or hostile?

Room
1. Was the room temperature suitable (heating, ventilation etc)?
2. Could everyone hear what was being said?
3. Could everyone see one another?

Any other observations
1. What were the strengths of the meeting?
2. What were the weaknesses of the meeting?
3. What improvements could be made?

Source: adapted from Jenkins (1974)

Figure 8.12   Observer questionnaire

How to encourage resistant groups to use new techniques

Learning programmes are most successful if all meeting participants are present, so that there is a shared understanding of the rationale of the new ideas and processes. The traditional chairperson must attend any learning programmes and be protected from 'scapegoating', that is, being blamed for any current problems. The 'How can we do it better?' approach appears to be the most successful. I try to empathize with the difficulties faced by a chairperson, saying something like, 'In a game of football or netball you have division of labour: different people take the roles of defence, attack, goalkeeper, referee and so on. So in meetings, why do we give so many roles to a chairperson?' Interactive meetings provide a more open system for flexibility and adaptation.

In *How To Make Meetings Work*, Doyle and Straus claim, 'The divisions of some organizations have been able to increase their overall productivity by 15 percent' (Doyle and Straus, 1976: 13). However, many groups may be resistant to trying new techniques. It is useful to have a number of persuasive strategies. I use three arguments to encourage change.

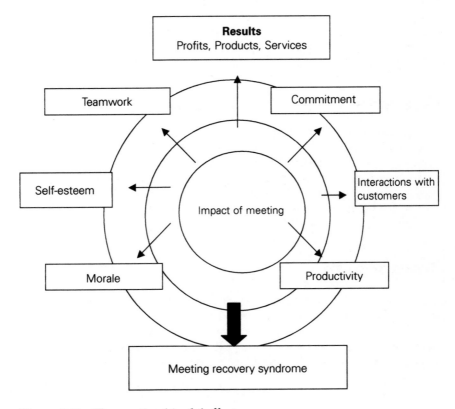

Figure 8.13   The meeting 'ripple' effect

Source: adapted from Doyle and Straus, workshop handout

Social costs of meetings

The first argument is the social cost of ineffective meetings, which can have a ripple effect across many aspects of an organization, leading to the 'meeting recovery syndrome' where some participants feel demotivated, lethargic at work (and at home). Indeed after unproductive meetings significant time may be lost because unofficial meetings carry on in wash rooms and behind closed doors.

Cost of meetings in dollar terms

The second argument is the hourly cost of the meetings: see Table 8.5.

Table 8.5   Hourly cost of a meeting

Annual salary in $	Number of participants in a meeting						
	2	4	6	8	10	15	20
$100,000	$200	$400	$600	$800	$1,000	$1,500	$2,000
$ 80,000	$160	$320	$480	$640	$ 800	$1,200	$1,600
$ 60,000	$120	$240	$360	$480	$ 600	$900	$1,200
$ 40,000	$ 80	$160	$240	$320	$ 400	$600	$ 800
$ 20,000	$ 40	$ 80	$120	$160	$ 200	$300	$ 400

Changes in the last century

The third argument is an appeal for change to a system that has been around for over 100 years: Robert's rules were published in 1876, Doyle and Straus's book was first published in 1976. When Robert's rules were published, the environment was more stable and change was slower. The perception was the need to 'control' groups and 'debates'; nowadays the feel has changed to the need to encourage the generation and pooling of creative as well as analytical thought.

Technology

Significant improvements in meeting productivity have also been made through the use of computers and group support systems software for electronic meetings in colocated groups in synchronous time (Hogan, 1994; Whiteley and Garcia, 1996); videoconference meetings (Diamond, 1996; Hogan, 1993; Justice and Jamieson, 1999). See Chapter 14 for hints on uses of technology for meetings in asynchronous time.

Conclusion

While there are many different structures and processes, there is now no one universally agreed method for running meetings. Processes need to be chosen that best match the context of the organizational culture and the issues and/or problems at hand.

Participants are now being encouraged to share the power and responsibility for the success of meetings, and to recognize that conflict and the sharing of different ideas and perspectives are needed by organizations who wish to survive in the new millennium.

With the removal of the board table, the change of layout, increased emphasis on process, and a continual search for 'How can we do things better?':

It is possible to take not only the board out of meetings, but also the bored.

9

Planning processes

If you are planning for one year
Grow rice.
If you are planning for twenty years, grow trees.
If you are planning for centuries
Grow people.

Chinese proverb

It's not the plan that's important, but the planning.

Dwight Eisenhower

Introduction

Planning in 'turbulent environments' sounds like an oxymoron. Almost as soon as plans are made they need modification.

There are many ways of planning. 'Project management' involves developing 'logical frameworks' (a term coined by the World Bank for Development projects about 30 years ago). 'Value management' is a five-stage process developed in the construction field, and now widely used for community project design to involve stakeholders in identifying creative ways to solve problems and save resources. Because of space limitations this chapter includes the following processes:

- the 'history telling process' to enable participants to acknowledge and let go of the past;
- creative visualization and the 'Fantasy Friday exercise' to enable participants to visualize desirable futures;
- the 'search conference process' to enable participants describe and plan towards desirable futures;
- the 'scenario planning process' to help participants describe and plan for desirable and plan to prevent or manage non desirable futures.

What are plans?

Plans = creative ideas to deviate from!

According to Heron (1999) there are two basic kinds of planning. Apollonian planning is called after the Greek and Roman sun god Apollo, the patron of music and poetry. He is attributed to being serene, thoughtful and self-disciplined. Apollonian planning is strict planning and adherence to those plans.

Dionysian planning is called after the Greek god of wine Dionysus, who is sensual and unrestrained. Dionysian planning involves an evolutionary approach involving improvisation and responding flexibly to the needs of the group or organization, knowing that no plan holds its strength over time.

So facilitators may work for some periods in Apollonian mode with structured topics and processes and at other times there may be a need to go totally with the flow and mood of the group.

I have noted in some communist regimes that there is a focus on Apollonian planning. The need for adaptation of plans is seen as poor planning in the first place (which may be the cause; however, nowadays few plans are set in concrete). Failure to achieve original plans is seen as failure. This mind set makes it very difficult for people to make initial decisions and later adapt plans as circumstances change. In reality such adjustment should be rewarded as illustrating adaptability. One good thing about word processors is that plans can be modified over time. However, there are limits to the frequency of change, as the following quote indicates:

> We trained hard – but it seemed that every time we were beginning to form into teams we would be reorganized. I was to learn later in life that we tend to meet any new situation by reorganizing; and a wonderful method it can be for creating the illusion of progress whilst producing confusion, inefficiency and demoralization.
>
> Petronius Arbiter (210 BC)

Letting go of the past

In some groups it is first necessary to enable participants to let go of the past before they can move on to plan for the future. This is particularly true after mergers, restructurings and so on. The following history process is particularly useful in this regard.

History telling process: looking back

Author/background

The history telling process was devised by Bob Dick in Queensland. He developed the process to aid the merging of groups or companies to develop a shared understanding of their past and contexts. He recommends that a history of each organization or group should be developed, before a vision for the future is created and strategic plans are made.

Purposes/rationale

The purposes of this process are to develop a timeline with many strands, and to compare the importance of events in the past and now.

Size of group

A maximum of 30.

Materials

Flip chart paper, pens, masking tape. You can buy uncut flip chart paper, the ends of newspaper print rolls. This is very useful for producing the timeline.

Venue/room

Large with wall space to display timelines. See below.

Table 9.1   Timeline

Year	1989	1992	2000	2002
Event	Bloggs take-over	Worker unrest due to extra pressures		
Significance then	Earthquake	Rumblings, illness		
Significance now	Major change in management style	Yes, similar problems exist today		
Bury in the past	Yes	No		
Carry into the future		Pay attention to declining morale		

Time

The time for this process will vary depending on the length and complexity of the timelines.

Stages

Stage 1: Collecting chronological history

The facilitator invites participants to think back over their time in their group/ organization, and asks a variety of trigger questions to provoke thought:

- Who has the earliest memory? Anyone before that?
- What were the corporate transitions?
- What happened before or after these transitions?
- What other major events made an impact on you?

Each person contributes a story to the group. He/she is asked to give a name to the event. These are plotted on the flip chart paper in front of the group. Gradually a story is built up to the present day.

Stage 2

The facilitator returns to the earliest event recorded and asks:

- What was its significance when it happened?
- What is its significance now?
- What parts of this event are you determined to carry into the future?
- Which parts of this event will you leave behind and bury with full celebration so you can move on?

It is important that pluralistic views of the past are heard and acknowledged.

Process adaptation

This process may be adapted for use by individuals or small groups. The results could be used for induction programmes so that new employees gain an understanding of their organization. Corporate stories are being lost as a result of so much restructuring and downsizing.

Advantages

There are many advantages to the history telling process. There are many opportunities for reality testing. Participants observe that:

- Turbulence did happen in the past.
- They have already survived and/or managed many transitions.
- There are different perspectives of the past.
- Some things should be buried and left behind.
- Individuals need to identify and reaffirm their identity through storytelling.

Disadvantages

There may be disagreement about what to leave behind, or how to leave some things behind. It may be useful for the facilitator to invite participants to co-create a ritual to let go of the past and to welcome new codes of behaviour.

Outcomes

This process engages people in storytelling, one of the most important and potent learning processes.

Planning the future in groups

People agree more on the future than they ever do on the present or the past.

Herb Shepherd

It helps people to plan if they have a common vision. So to begin with, it helps if a facilitator enables individuals to 'see' images in their minds, and then gives them an opportunity to tell each other so they can build a shared vision.

Guided visualizations and mind movies

Guided visualizations are useful to enable people to 'dream and fantasize' about ideas or the future, but especially about 'desirable futures'. The next exercise is applicable to individuals and/or groups.

Mind movies

A 'mind movie' is a positive visualization process developed by Hopson and Scally (1983), which can be remembered by the mnemonic RADAR:

Stages

1. **Relax.** Lie on the floor; breathe slowly. Focus on the ingoing and outgoing breath to relax. Allow the stresses and strains of the day to drain out of you every time you exhale.
2. **Allow the pictures to come.** In your mind visualize your future goal or dream, for example, the job interview or talk.
3. **Direct the movie.** Concentrate on positive outcomes; edit out any negative images.
4. **Act in the movie yourself.** See yourself smiling: speaking slowly, clearly and confidently.
5. **Reward yourself for being successful.** Give yourself a treat after successfully completing the movie.

Fantasy Friday exercise

Another more specific visualization process is the Fantasy Friday exercise used for life planning. This is a guided visualization to enable participants to 'see' possibilities for an ideal future, then work to make those dreams come true. It may be used for personal as well as group/organizational goal setting. I first observed the exercise as a participant in a workshop by Margery Blanchard in 1988. One difference in the wording here is that I do not include the whole day, as Margery Blanchard did: I do not include the family side in case people see a future without their partners or with different partners. The exercise requires the facilitator to 'set the scene' by providing some examples to warm up the imaginative juices of the participants:

> I want you to imagine a fantastic day five years from now. It's a day when everything goes right and you are living the life of your dreams. Perhaps you will start the day with a massage, a swim or sauna. Or a breakfast with. . . If any negative thoughts intrude, edit them out: you are in charge of this fantasy and it can only have good things.

In this context it is useful for the facilitator to prompt a little, to help people get the idea. The wording of the guided visualization might be something like this:

> Please close your eyes and relax. Take in a long deep breath. . . fill your lungs and gradually squeeze all the air out. (Repeat.) Now I want you to imagine a day five years from now in 20XX. It's going to be a wonderful day, as it will include all the things you like to do. What can you see first thing in the morning as you prepare for work? Are you working full time or part time? Do you have to travel to work or are you working from home? (And so on.)

Debriefing questions

1. What were your thoughts, feelings and reactions to doing this exercise?
2. What does the fantasy indicate about what you value, appreciate, aspire to, or want for yourself?
3. What are the differences between your fantasy and your reality?
4. How much of your fantasy is achievable at present or might be in the future? If you can't have it all, can you have some of it?
5. What are the barriers to your achieving some of your fantasy, and how might these be overcome?
6. What would be some of the consequences of your working to achieve some of the features of your fantasy for yourself or for others?
7. Would the pursuit of the features of your fantasy and their achievement be worth the possible consequences?
8. What objective/s would you like to set for yourself on the basis of this exercise tomorrow, next week, over the next six months?

The search conference process

The search conference process is robust, in that it has been used and developed over half a century.

Author/background

The search conference process is based on the original work of Professor Fred and Merrelyn Emery (Emery, 1976; Emery and Purser, 1996). Fred Emery came originally from Fremantle in Western Australia, and did much of his early work at the Tavistock Institute in London.

Purposes/rationale

Fred and Merrelyn Emery and Eric Trist realized the need for workers of all levels to be involved with managers in planning for the future. They developed the search conference process in 1959. The first workshop was called the Barford Conference (Trist and Emery, 1960), which they designed to bring together the Bristol and Siddeley aero-engine companies. The managers of the two companies mutually disliked each other, but they were about to merge. Although the process was to undergo further refinement (Emery and Purser, 1996), Trist and Emery (1960) found that certain formulae worked: for example, the facilitator eliminated the roles of visiting outside experts; kept meeting notes in an open fashion, for example on flip chart paper; focused the group on contextual issues; and focused the group on areas of agreement regarding 'desirable futures' of the organization.

Since then, many search conferences have been held for corporate planning, community development, town planning and course planning in the United Kingdom, Australia, the United States, Scandinavia and Hong Kong. The technique has been modified and refined constantly by Emery and Purser (1996) and Weisbord (1992), and will continue to change.

The process has been used in industry, government and education departments and communities, to involve, as equals, people from all levels in organizational planning modification and evaluation. The search workshop is the start of a continuous process. During the workshop, participants consider changes that are occurring in the world around them. They gradually focus their attention on desirable futures for society, and how they can take joint responsibility for project and changes based on their and the organization's present needs and problems.

The workshop is led by a facilitator who records all comments made by participants on flip chart paper. These are compiled into a workshop report which is later used as a basis for review and evaluation.

Prior planning and involvement

Involving people in the planning by having them genuinely involved is not always easy. A 'search' will only be effective if managers and/or community leaders representatives:

- want to be involved;
- acknowledge that there is a need to redesign their area/organization;
- value participation and democratic processes;
- have confidence in the people who work with them, and believe their co-workers have the capacity to both identify their present needs and make related decisions.

Initial meeting and organization

The design and sequencing of the planning session is the facilitator's responsibility. This should be done in consultation with managers, supervisors, and if possible with staff. A prior meeting, though not essential, allows the facilitator to:

- meet some participants and clarify the task of the search workshop;
- clear up misunderstandings;
- add or delete discussion items;
- encourage participants to think before the session.

Good preparation allows the workshop to flow more smoothly and efficiently.

Size of group

It has been found that about 50 people is the largest manageable group, though larger groups with co-facilitators have been successful. If there are too many people, it is desirable to take a deep slice through the hierarchy of your organization and choose representatives from each section. Keep repeating 'Who else?', 'Who else?' to ensure that all stakeholders are represented.

Venue/room

Choose a relaxed, comfortable, non-threatening environment. A live-in venue away from the normal work environment is preferable, a location where participants can form an isolated community or 'social island' away from the pressures of everyday life and interruptions, especially e-mail. Three to four small rooms are desirable for discussion groups. The ambience and size of the workshop room is important: choose a suitable room away from interruptions, with lots of suitable wall space to display flip chart paper.

Materials

Copious quantities of flip chart paper, felt-tip pens, masking tape, laptop computer (if a scribe who is not part of the workshop is available).

Length of the workshop

One to two days. Some workshops have run as long as a week. It is best to start early in the morning and have no time constraints during the day ahead.

The facilitator's role

The facilitator should:

- have experienced previous search conferences as a participant;
- be aware of the theoretical framework of the search conference process;
- be able to recognize and adapt to the emotional needs and changes within working groups;
- be familiar with the planning task and vocabulary, and have undertaken sufficient prior research to enable her/him to design an appropriate workshop plan.

It sometimes helps the pace of the session to have two facilitators, one whose major role is to encourage others to participate, guide the group, and scribe, and the other whose main function is just to scribe. In very large community groups it is useful to brief many people to act as co-facilitators in small group work.

The role of participants and department representatives

The facilitator should ensure that all participants and department representatives invited to attend a search conference are acquainted with the purpose of the workshop. The search process may create anxiety in adults who:

- find difficulty in coping with group emotional forces;
- feel uncomfortable with frank opinions, compliments and criticisms;
- are locked in to the concept of 'expert'.

To bring about a democratic learning environment it is necessary that managers and supervisors:

- function as participants' resource people, not as leaders in the traditional sense;
- do not take over small group discussion, but where necessary move between groups monitoring progress and helping when required;
- participate fully as equals.

Producing the report

The facilitator is often responsible for producing a transcript of the workshop proceedings. This document should contain an accurate record of the stages of the planning session. All participants should be given a copy, as this provides the group with a basis for conducting further action and evaluation. It is important that participants feel they can discuss and add to this document at a later date.

There are a variety of ways of producing search conference reports, and their contents will vary. This initial report should be seen as not a public document, but a confidential working report for workshop participants. Most of these reports contain the following:

- a list of participants, their departments and telephone numbers;
- the task of the search conference;
- the steps of the workshop as in Figure 9.1;
- raw data and sometimes a content analysis;
- conclusions suggested by the group.

Ongoing support

The facilitator should be available to provide ongoing support in the form of further workshops.

The stages of the planning process: external structure

The planning process is designed, first, to help a group of people form general comments about the possible future and desirable futures of their environment and society. Second, the discussion focuses down to more specific ideas about the futures (and desirable futures) of the system or institution in question. Constraints, such as lack of time, money, resources, are not discussed initially, so the values which are desired are made explicit. (See Figures 9.1 and 9.2.)

At the end of a search conference, participants sometimes indicate that time could have been saved by omitting the sections of futures and desirable futures. (I know I fell into this category at first.) It is impossible to run a search conference properly without discussing the social and economic environmental factors and forces that influence the context of the planning problem. Merrelyn Emery (1976) suggests that omitting these sections is like sailing a ship without understanding that it is a vessel designed to move through water, and without learning about the nature of the currents and the winds in order to steer the ship effectively to its destination.

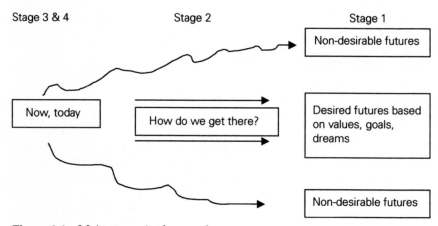

Figure 9.1   Main stages in the search process

Stage:

1.   What are your goals/values/ideals for the future?
2.   How can you get there? Initiatives and strategies to reach your desired goals.
3.   What constraints are there?
4.   Planning groups.

By homing-in on the purpose of the planning session from the widest possible perspective and by leaving the constraints to the last minute, it is possible to ensure that the values which are desired are left explicit and not easily lost. Frequently, our basic ideals are hidden when financial and technological constraints are the foremost considerations.

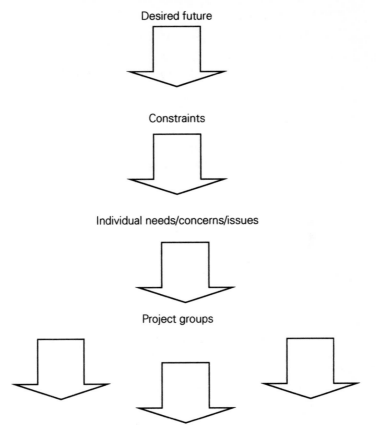

Abstract concepts: shared ideas and values

Desired future

Constraints

Individual needs/concerns/issues

Project groups

Figure 9.2   Simplified outline of a search conference workshop

Internal structure

The search process is designed to bring into being a forward thinking, learning and planning community. While the external structure is task-oriented, the internal structure is concerned with relationships between colleague and colleague, manager and manager, colleague and manager, manager and human resource consultant, support staff and manager, community and organization.

Stages

Expectations: Why are you here?

This stage gives participants an opportunity to break the ice; identify their varying needs, experience and concerns, and develop confidence and give notice to others of their presence as individuals.

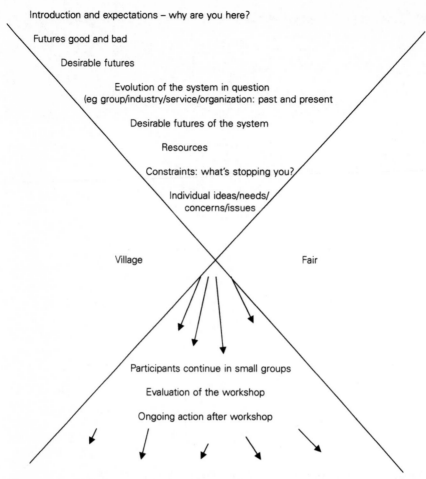

Figure 9.3   Detailed stages of a search conference workshop

Futures: your external environment

The task is to brainstorm all the possible trends and events both good and bad, significant or insignificant, that are occurring now or have occurred in the past few years. The facilitator notes all ideas on flip chart paper. She/he should make it clear that this first session is a recording one, and that discussion of right or wrong and importance or irrelevance is not allowed. Comments usually fall into the following categories:

- new technology;
- work and leisure;
- environment-energy and pollution;
- social welfare;
- politics;
- human resource development and education.

When the session is finished and all ideas have been identified, the list, complete with contradictions and inconsistencies, should remain on view so that participants can refer to it during the next session or at any time during the workshop. Participants should also be invited to add to the list at any time.

Desirable futures

Participants form small groups or syndicates. It is suggested that managers and supervisors present join different groups, but do not dominate them. (You may need to brief them beforehand.) In very hierarchical societies it may be better to place people of the same rank together in small groups.

Five to eight people per group are ideal. I have found it is useful to ask each group to nominate a facilitator and a scribe to record main points (or brief co-facilitators beforehand). Debate is encouraged, but groups are asked to achieve consensus. A participant who wishes to state a minority view may also have her/his ideas added. Suggestions are then reported back to all participants, usually by the scribe from each group (as they can read their own handwriting). In order to ensure that the writing is large enough, before the group start hold up one piece of paper with very small writing and ask the group, 'Can you read this?' The answer is usually a resounding 'No'. Then hold up larger writing: 'Can you read this?' If the answer is 'Yes', say, 'OK, please ensure your writing is this big. You want people to see and understand your ideas, don't you?'

Ask scribes to number pages and write names of group members and topic at the top. This helps when compiling reports later.

The facilitator should carefully explain the aims of this session which are to:

- work on the list of futures (good and bad) already generated and develop 'desirable futures';
- allow ideas to be discussed without constraints;
- identify a framework of shared values and beliefs which may influence how participants interact with each other and the environment;
- establish organizational and personal needs;
- identify alternative directions for the future and select desirable directions;
- develop a commitment to the desirable directions and select appropriate strategies to reach them.

Evolution of the system and desirable futures

According to the aims of the workshop, this session could focus on the system under scrutiny, such as a team, course, industry/trade/service area, organization, community. This session looks at the system in question and particularly:

- past;
- present;
- desirable futures.

This session helps the participants identify and clarify the directions in which they think the industry, trade or service should be going. Present issues and barriers that prevent the attainment of the desirable futures of the organization are identified. See the sample search conference at the end of this section, Figure 9.5.

Desirable characteristics of future plans

This session establishes overall ground rules for interpersonal relationships and desirable structuring; required flexibility; and timing.

Resources

It is desirable to start with the resources and energies within the planning room, for example people/skill/contacts, and later to broaden the session to the institution concerned, other branches, local community, town, state and so on.

Constraints: what is stopping you?

Most planning sessions start with negatives, such as we haven't enough money, time, resources. These barriers block creative thought. The search process, by leaving the constraints to the last minute, ensures that desired values and ideals are made explicit and not easily lost, as they are when economic and technological constraints are the foremost considerations. It is possible to add here compulsory aspects of the industry/service that must be included: for example legal/safety aspects of the trade area concerned, or specifics required by the industry concerned.

Individual issues, concerns, needs: What? Why? How?

The participants are asked as individuals to write down on flip chart paper (one idea per sheet) individual issues that they personally feel are important. These can be issues or concerns, or can relate to content or skills that participants would like to include in projects. Each individual is asked what the issue is, why she/he thinks something should be done about it and, if possible, how it can be incorporated into projects. Individuals are asked to put their names on their sheets.

These issues are displayed on the wall and a 'village fair' instigated. The facilitator invites participants to discuss, negotiate, lobby/barter and trade issues and ideas. Participants may polarize on certain issues and form project groups to do something about a particular issue. It may be necessary for the facilitator to undertake a quick items analysis to see if there is a clustering or grouping of needs. These project titles can be exhibited, and participants invited to add their names to first and second-choice project groups (see below). Some project groups may not get enough people, in which case there is no energy at this time for the topic. If groups are too large it may be better to divide the group, or ask some participants if they would like to work on their second choice. There is usually some trading at this stage. (See also Chapter 12, where discussion of the open space technology process begins with a generation of agenda topics like a 'Village Fair'.)

Table 9.2 Forming project groups

Project title	First choice: Names	Second choice: Names
A.		
B.		
C.		
D.		
E.		
Other		
Other		

Project groups

Ideally, project groups need from one to two hours minimum to discuss and put into writing ideas generated by the discussion sheet in Figure 9.4. It is useful if the facilitator has these questions typed and photocopied to distribute to groups to guide the discussion.

If the project group relates to a particular area, it is desirable for the manager/ supervisor of the area concerned to be present. A simple statement is required, incorporating realistic alternative strategies for the project. It is useful for participants to identify problems and resources, and to realize the importance of evaluating their projects subjectively as well as objectively. The timetable should not be inflexible, but can formalize commitment to the project. The group should also arrange a follow-up meeting, and share the responsibility for ongoing work. Each group may wish to elect a contact person to ensure ongoing commitment. A representative from each project group reports back to the whole group. Suggestions and/or help may be offered by the rest of the participants.

Evaluation of projects

It is important to raise the awareness of participants to the variety of ways available to evaluate the projects. Weekly feedback sessions may be suggested to allow a rethink of aims and project direction.

Individual commitment to the success of the projects

Participants share the responsibility for the success of their project. It is important, however, that participants write down what they personally can do to help make the project a success. It is useful if everyone reads out their comment to the whole group. This increases personal commitment to the success of the project.

Project Title:
Names:
1. Why is your project important?

_____

_____

2. What are your aims?

_____

_____

3. How will you go about your project: alternative strategies?

_____

_____

4. What problems/constraints are there?

_____

_____

5. What resources will you need? What costs do you need to find out about?

_____

_____

6. What jobs need to be done? Divide the work among your group members.

_____

_____

7. What individual goals and timelines are needed?

_____

_____

8. How can you check that your project is successful?

_____

_____

9. Timetable: when will your group meet again? Set a day and time.

_____

_____

Figure 9.4 Project group discussion sheet

Evaluation of the workshop

The facilitator can best draw the workshop to a close by asking participants what they feel they have achieved and learnt during the session. It is useful to ask participants to individually write down:

- three good things about the workshop;
- three bad things about the workshop;
- suggestions for future workshops.

People naturally feel tired at the end of a workshop, but they are usually enthusiastic and committed to the work ahead. It is important that the facilitator reinforces this optimism, congratulates the participants on their involvement during the day, and reminds them of their commitments to the work ahead.

Sample search conference agenda

In Table 9.3 is a sample workshop agenda. I have phrased the stages as questions. This means that when the agenda is distributed before the workshop, participants know what each agenda item means, and the questions automatically start them thinking about answers.

Computer technology

It is now possible to have a scribe at the back of the workshop typing the wall minutes into a laptop computer. The search process also lends itself to being used in a laboratory with networked computers for colocated groups in synchronous time. MeetingWorks software has a variety of suitable packages, and can be used in conjunction with networked compact laptop computers. Information is generated quickly, as participants can type in ideas simultaneously. Advantages are that ideas are anonymous, and the data is typed and available to everyone at the end of the workshop.

The next process (or rather groups of processes) is entitled 'scenario planning', and is different from the search process in that participants are invited to discuss and plan for both desirable and non-desirable futures.

Scenario planning

Author/background

Scenario planning has probably been used for centuries, especially in times of warfare, when people would sit around campfires trying to guess what the enemy would do next; the first stages of scenario planning are a guessing game about what the future holds. A scientific method of scenario planning was first used in the Second World War by the US Army, and the Rand Corporation furthered the development of Delphi techniques and some of the scenario

Table 9.3   Sample search conference agenda to develop a community response to domestic violence (DV)

Day 1

Content	Process	Time
Settling in	Registration. Coffee	8.15–8.30
Who is here?	Icebreaker. Introductions. Roles and responsibilities	8.30–8.45
What is the purpose of the workshop and what is a search conference?	Explanation by the facilitator. Questions from the group	8.45–8.50
Why are you here today?	Paired interviews. Scribing on wall minutes of wants and needs	8.50–9.00
How can we all get the most out of the day?	Contracting. Scribing on wall minutes of agreed ground rules	9.00–9.10
What futures do you see for the Western Australian community for next 5–10 years?	Brainstorm futures: good and bad. Whole group	9.10–9.30
What are the desirable futures for the Western Australian community?	Small group discussion and consensus decisions and feedback on areas eg health and welfare, legal, education, community attitudes Feedback to the whole group	9.30–10.00
	Morning tea	10.00–10.30
What do victims of DV and those who work with them most want/need? What do perpetrators and those who work with them most want/need?	Presentations by representatives from each group	10.30–10.45 10.45–11.00
How have our institutions responded to victims and perpetrators: a. in the past? b. currently? What are the stages of the intervention process? (Development of flow diagram)	Feedback from whole group	11.00–11.15
What are the roles/ responsibilities of each agency? (Small groups and feedback to whole group) What are the boundaries and where is there overlap?	Creative visualization of the community project in two years time	11.15–12.00

Table 9.3 *(continued)*

Day 1

Content	Process	Time
	Lunch	12.00–1.00
What are the desirable characteristics of a community intervention project? What is your mission? (What 'business' are you in?) What are your core values?	Whole group listing of ideas	1.00–2.15
What resources are there: a. in this room? b. in the community in Western Australia that could be incorporated into this project?	Whole group list ideas	2.15–3.00
	Afternoon tea	3.00–3.30
What individual issues/ concerns/needs do you have regarding this community intervention project?	Village fair: individuals list ideas on flip chart paper	3.30–4.00
Summary What did you get out of the day?	Overview of achievements. Feedback from participants	4.00–4.30
Evaluation	Questionnaire	

Day 2

Content	Process	Time
Any workshop-related thoughts, dreams and questions from yesterday?	Silence, wait for issues to emerge	8.30–9.00
What working party would you like to join?	Participants decide which group to join from issues clustered from village fair	9.00–9.30
Different topics	Group work	9.30–10.30
	Morning tea	10.30–11.00
	Group work	11.00–12.00
	Lunch	12.00–1.00
	Feedback from groups and whole group discussion	1.00–3.00
	Afternoon tea	3.00–3.30
Summary of action planning	Whole group	3.30–4.00
Closure and evaluation		4.00–4.30

methods. Through Pierre Wack, considered the father of scenario planning, Royal Dutch Shell used scenario planning in the 1970s. As a result, Shell was ready for the energy crisis in the 1970s when the APEC countries suddenly pushed up the price of oil. In the context of this book I can only give an outline of this remarkable 'disciplined method', and direct the reader to further references.

The method increased in use in the late 1980s and the 1990s, as organizations and communities struggled to cope with technological change and to plan for a rapidly changing future. As with all processes, this has evolved through time. I would like to acknowledge the process outlined here which is based on the work and advice of Professor Jo Barker (2000) and the Scenario Planning and Research Unit at Curtin University of Technology, Perth, Western Australia.

Purpose/rationale

The purpose of scenario planning is to identify possible futures (concerns and the uncertainties). It enables groups to imagine a whole range of possibilities, and compensate for mind sets like 'groupthink' (forced agreement), linear thinking ('business as usual'), or ostrich thinking ('it will never happen to us'). Scenarios are carefully crafted sets of stories, oral or written, which are built up by participants regarding possible futures for an organization, group, community, country and/or global situation/s. Scenario planning acknowledges the possibility of the impossible.

It differs from the search conference process which invites participants to focus on 'desirable futures'. Scenario planning is a management tool used as a precursor to strategic planning, working out the logistics to reach a goal by asking the following questions. What if? When? Where? Why? With what resources? How? And how do we know if we've been successful?

Scenario planning is a learning tool, and has been used by multinational businesses, small businesses, government departments, communities and the military. It has also been used to make personal decisions about life style/s, retirement, jobs, health investments and even marriage.

Archetypal scenarios

It is useful for the facilitator to know about the general types of scenarios summarized below. However, experience has shown (Barker, 2000) that it is better to let scenarios emerge from group discussion rather than impose frameworks which may stifle the thinking of the participants.

There are basically around seven archetypal scenarios or storylines:

- More of same, 'business as usual'.
- 'The transformative economy' (Schwartz, 1991): same scale, but different, shifts in values, refocusing, recreating, innovation, 'the great turning' (Macy and Brown, 1998).
- Downsizing of production, 'small is beautiful' (Schumacher ,1973).
- The 'official future' (Schwartz, 1991): growth, increasing, expanding, extending.

- The 'depression' (Schwartz, 1991): decreasing, downsizing, restructuring.
- Revolution, war, major political upheavals, physical catastrophes.
- Cycles, eg economic rationalism changing into a more humanist way of managing people; outsourcing replaced by insourcing, decay and rise of neighbourhoods, regions, and countries.

Size of group

Once the 'key issue' or focus is decided by an organization, a scenario team, comprising up to 20 people, is chosen as workshop participants. They should be articulate, good listeners who are motivated to work as part of a team. There should be a mixture of specialists and generalists, a balance of gender, age and cultural backgrounds from different levels of the organization. To prevent 'groupthink', Van der Heijden (1996) suggests that a 'freethinker' from outside the organization should be included to add additional perspectives. In addition to the workshop group, another 20 people both from within and closely allied to the organization are chosen for interview only, to gain their input into both the key issue and the organization. All participants are interviewed, and the analysis of this material into key factors or major themes forms the basis of the scenario process. This is followed by a two-day facilitated workshop, during which participants build up scenario stories from their own expert opinion and that gleaned from the interview process.

The role of the facilitator and research team

To gain maximum input from the group, it is strongly suggested that the facilitator be external to the organization and be well versed in scenario planning processes. The facilitator needs to be able to confront CEOs and their teams to challenge their own assumptions. He/she requires the backing of a skilled research team which has access to libraries, computers and electronic databases.

The most senior person in the organization should also be a part of the team. The backing of senior staff throughout the process is vital for success. The facilitator, however, may need to brief him/her on the desirable behaviours of team players; some leaders may need to suppress dominance behaviours.

Materials

Computer, data projector, sticky-backed pads and/or flip chart paper stands to display ideas for analysis. Electronic whiteboards and adhesive gum are also useful, plus handouts of the various stages of the processes to clarify thinking.

Venue/room layout

A light and airy room is required, with comfortable furniture and plain walls to display computer programs, flip charts or sticky notes. Participants sit around a table. Breakout rooms and/or garden spaces are needed for small-group discussions.

Time

Should a full scenario process be undertaken by an organization, the research team can be involved for a four-month period of interview, analysis, facilitation, research and report writing. During this time, however, the personnel chosen to participate in the process from the organization are involved in a half-hour interview followed by a two day workshop only. The skeletal or first-generation stories developed by this group are then further researched by the research team, and built up to second-generation scenarios. A further one-day workshop is run with the group, to develop strategy from the fully developed scenarios.

If the organization prefers to continue to develop the first-generation or skeletal scenarios written at the conclusion of the first workshop by itself, and develop these into fully researched stories, then approximately two months' time is required by the research team.

Pre-workshop stages

Selection of key issue

The whole management team is involved in identifying a 'key issue' based on concerns, anxieties and views on areas such as political, social or environmental change; economic change product growth or decline; market and price changes. It should:

- draw out the implications of change in the future;
- address a major element of organizational life;
- be broadly applicable within the organization.

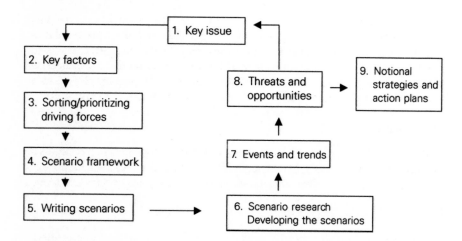

Figure 9.5   Stages of the scenario planning process

Source: Barker (2000)

Pre-workshop interviews

The workshop team are interviewed separately, face to face or via technological hook-ups. Key questions are asked in relation to the key issue (Van der Heijden, 1996; Barker, 2000: 628) such as:

- What is the future of your organization?
- What are your concerns and uncertainties about your organization's future?
- Consider the future and imagine that all goes well for your organization. Over the next five years, what would you hope to achieve?
- What past pivotal events, both positive and negative, have affected your organization's future?
- What major decisions with long-term implications is your organization facing?
- What major constraints are limiting your organization's achievements?
- What would you like to be remembered for within your organization?

A further 15–20 individuals who are allied to the organization are interviewed (suppliers, customers, board members). Recurrent themes and issues are extracted.

Environmental scanning

The researchers scan the environment for information around the key issue. Data are presented to the participants in the form of a report, to set the scene for the workshop (see the 'Hunting and gathering' section below for sources of information).

Stages: first two-day workshop

Contracting

The facilitator must involve the group at the outset in developing ground rules, roles and responsibilities that encourage 'off the wall thinking', expression of intuition and feelings, and collaborative discourse as opposed to win–lose debate. He/she should tactfully and openly describe the role of the boss as a team member (if necessary). The role of the facilitator is a 'catalyst' for a discussion and process expert, not a content expert in the subject under discussion. Under no circumstances should the facilitator ever enter into the 'content' of the workshops. Likewise when the final scenarios are delivered, the facilitator and/or researchers should never offer an opinion as to which is preferable.

Issues of confidentiality need to be discussed. The facilitator, research team and scenario planning team must keep certain data produced in workshops confidential, as future plans may impact on competitiveness.

Scenario development

The group creates up to four scenarios. They must have consistent storylines. The facilitator should encourage the group to resist labelling them as 'good' or 'bad'. Barker suggests an 'inductive approach': let the scenarios emerge by themselves, rather than attempt to impose a framework or 'deductive approach' (see 'Typical scenarios' above). The group also needs to agree on a time limit for the scenarios: 3, 5, or a maximum of 10 years.

According to Schoemaker (1995) good scenarios are:

- **relevant** to the concerns of the organization and its managers and employees;
- **archetypal** and different from one another;
- **sustainable** over the chosen length of time under discussion.

Key factors

The key factors that emerged from the environmental scan are reviewed to ensure that no ideas have been omitted. Factors that are common to all scenarios (such as demographic changes) are highlighted. The remaining factors are divided into three categories, those that:

- have global significance;
- have significance to the industry outside the organization under study;
- are internal to the organization.

Driving forces or areas of concern

The key factors are examined in the light of past and present 'driving forces' using the mnemonic STEEP, which stands for Social, Technological, Economic, Environmental and Political aspects of the environment that could impact on the organization. Participants then identify which STEEP factors are most uncertain and rank them in importance.

What ifs?

The facilitator encourages participants to think 'outside the box', about things that matter that people within the organization perhaps do not know about (Schwartz, 1991), for example:

- What if a natural disaster strikes?
- What if your product becomes redundant?
- What if robots take over the organization?

Forming scenario outlines

Participants divide into small groups to develop one scenario each. The scenarios are given boundaries such as geographic regions, projects, time frames (no longer than 10 years) to make them manageable.

Memorable names for scenarios

Each team should give their scenario a memorable name. Names of books, animals, places, events may be incorporated, such as 'leap frog', 'great glasnost', 'simple is beautiful', 'now for something completely different'. These sketched scenarios are handed over to the research team at the end of the two-day workshop.

Research phase

Scenario writing: composing a plot

A team of researchers then come together to flesh out a scenario or plot somewhat like scriptwriters (Schwartz, 1991). They develop the plot further and add qualitative and quantitative data. Where necessary they involve the team that developed the original scenario sketch. If there are four scenarios, there are four separate areas of research.

Information hunting and gathering

Hunting and gathering tactics (where to look) will vary according to the scenarios and personal choice. Schwarz (1991) suggests that six topics are worthy of special attention. I added a seventh:

- **Science and technology:** for example, the impact of the second level of the Internet.
- **Perception-shaping events** that strike a responsive chord, for example catastrophes like Chernobyl, or climatic extremes which people deem to be the result of global warming.
- **Music:** rap music themes, new types of music and its message.
- **Fringes**, 'New Age' trends, hacker activities.
- **Surprises in bookshops,** such as the impact of the Internet in societies which formerly tried to stem the flow of information, books by futurists and free thinkers (Kurzweil, 1990, 1999; Theobald, 1997: 256).
- **Filters:** for example magazines, like *Byte* (computing), *New Scientist*, consumer magazines like *Choice* (Australia) and *Which* (UK), reputable newspaper updates on IT and computing, *Guardian Weekly* (includes the best articles from the *Guardian*, UK, *Le Monde*, France and the *Washington Post*, United States). *The Whole Earth Catalogue* and *New Internationalist* describe trends in the environment and developing world which are often missed by the main media.
- **Trends:** changes in the needs and values of teenagers, baby boomers and travellers. The rise of religious fundamentalists, traditional belief systems. Anti-capitalist and anti-Western movements.
- **Electronic media**, including the Internet, discussion groups and chat rooms, databases (including full text refereed articles available through university libraries).
- **The Web**.

Second workshop

In the second workshop the facilitator enables the participants to:

- Discuss each of the scenarios in turn.
- Discuss the opportunities and threats of each scenario in relation to the organization.

- Form action plans for each scenario. The action plans are later built into the mainstream strategic planning processes of the organization.

Rehearsing the future

The last stage involves asking, 'What would we do if. . .?' Enactments of various scenarios are simulated. Strategic plans are made to align the organization towards desirable futures. Contingency plans are made to manage less welcome scenarios.

Advantages

Scenario planning invites participants to think together as a team in a variety of ways involving systematic analysis, creativity and intuition. People learn to recognize and plan for change, rather than ignore or deny it. It speeds up decision making and promotes change by allowing for opposing views to be aired rather than judged, dismissed or smothered. Managers can rehearse for the future. As a result organizations are more prepared to react quickly to change when necessary.

Scenarios allow managers and teams to think about worst-case scenarios without being labelled as pessimistic, and best-case scenarios without being labelled as dreamers. Scenarios also encourage managers to take 'the long view of decisions made today' (Schwartz, 1991:xiii).

The results are better quality decisions about the future and a quicker response time should circumstances change.

Disadvantages

The process is logical, but is more complicated than it looks. It requires experienced facilitation and research for data and information from outside the organization. The process requires commitment, time and resources from senior management over an extended period of time.

Conclusion

> The future is not some place we are going to,
> But one we are creating;
> The paths to it are not found but made,
> And the activity of making them changes
> Both the maker and the destination.
>
> Peter Ellyard

There are many different planning processes, as this chapter illustrates. Some facilitators specialize in certain processes; however it is useful to know more than one, and to choose which process or mix of processes best fits the needs of the clients.

The next chapter focuses on creativity.

10

Facilitating creativity

'There's no use trying,' said Alice. 'One can't believe impossible things.'

'I dare say you haven't had much practice,' said the Queen. 'When I was your age, I always did it for half an hour a day. Why, sometimes I've believed as many as six impossible things before breakfast.'

Lewis Carroll, *Alice in Wonderland*

Introduction

Creativity is the ability to develop original, inventive and imaginative 'things'. The things could be food, music, clothes, crafts, ideas, jokes and puns, art and design, home décor and scientific discoveries. It is part of our evolution to do new things in new ways, and it is part of problem solving (see next chapter). Creativity is an intrinsic aspect of being human; it is a process, a way of being and living.

As children we were naturally creative. But as we grew up many of us were taught to be more cautious and/or more judgmental, which may be useful as long as these perspectives do not govern our thinking processes all the time. Creative processes can be taught, and we can develop skills and use processes to enhance our creativity. But our environment or context may impact on the creation of ideas.

Children enter school as question marks and leave as full stops.

Neil Postman

Creativity is not just generating ideas; it's a process, a way of being, and a way of living. Some homes, communities and corporate systems nurture idea generation and implementation; others unfortunately stifle it. The famous quote from the television programme *Star Trek* is a 'spilt infinitive' that not only breaks traditional grammar rules (creativity breaks rules), but has also encouraged thousands of avid *Star Trek* fans:

To boldly go where no one has gone before.

Yes, creativity and implementing creative ideas requires courage.

We are normally taught to approach problems in a logical, analytical way. Creative thinking enables us to be 'legitimately illogical' through the systematic generation of ideas. There are over 50 techniques for generating ideas (Van Gundy, 1988). There are some commonalities between them (Geschka, Schaude and Schlicksupp, 1973): They are systematic: there are usually a number of stages with prompts or questions to follow, and a large number of alternative solutions are generated before evaluating and selecting the most useful ideas. Visually it looks like <>.

This chapter focuses on:

- our brains;
- prerequisites and blocks to creativity;
- levels of knowledge;
- the diamond of problem solving and the 'groan zone';
- classifications of creative processes;
- harvesting dreams;
- brainstorming;
- brainwriting;
- nominal group technique;
- comparison of brainstorming, brainwriting and nominal group technique.

Our brains

Sir Charles Skerrington who is considered to be the grandfather of neurophysiology by some commented:

> The human brain is an enchanted loom where millions of flashing shuttles weave a dissolving pattern, always a meaningful pattern, though never an abiding one, a shifting harmony of sub-patterns. It is as if the Milky Way entered upon some cosmic dance.
>
> (Quoted in Buzan and Buzan, 1993: 26]

In each human brain there is a powerhouse of an estimated one million million (1,000,000,000,000) brain cells or neurons which radiate thousands of tentacles. These can potentially make millions of connections (1 followed by 10.5 million kilometres of noughts). Hence our potential for creative thought is enormous, and we all need to be encouraged, and to encourage each other, to make use of our whole brains. Creativity is like a muscle: it needs frequent exercise.

We now know that the left and right brain theory of specialized brain functions (that the left hemisphere is responsible for logical, linear thinking and language, and the right hemisphere is responsible for creative and more holistic thought) was rather simplistic. However, the metaphor of needing to use our whole brains is still useful:

> Half a brain is useful, but a whole brain is best of all.
>
> Ned Hermann

Prerequisites for creativity

Ideally, to be creative we need:

● a stimulating rather than blocking environment; 'freeing' as opposed to 'oppressive' societies, communities, organizations and families;
● stimulating and supportive co-workers;
● supportive management who nurture creativity;
● a sense of autonomy and empowerment;
● a feeling of trust, that if things go wrong, more creative problem solving will ensue rather than blaming or scapegoating;
● to spend time in groups focusing on 'risky', 'silly', 'adventurous' or 'crazy' ideas;
● plentiful time available (time to generate ideas, time for ideas to incubate, time to re-meet and re-evaluate ideas);
● a champion/s to carry out the implementation of ideas.

This does not mean that some or all of these factors should be present. Indeed there is some truth in the saying, 'Necessity is the mother of invention'. I asked Bob Dick, a facilitator from Queensland, what triggered him to develop the 'acts of God' process for working through issues with the 'group from hell' (see Chapter 6). He replied, 'I was stuck, everything had gone wrong. . . I had to do something with the group. . . and fast'.

Blocks to creativity

> Don't refuse to go on a wild goose chase.
> That's what wild geese are for.
>
> Anon

There are many things that can block our creativity, starting within our own minds and self-talk. See Figure 10.1.

Setting the scene

If we are more creative in our 'child mode', then it helps to lighten the atmosphere of groups with some aids to encourage more playful behaviour. Some people may feel patronized and resist, so it is useful best to tell people why you have brought in some 'fun' objects (see Figure 10.2).

The Greeks knew that play was linked to learning. Plato said, 'What then is the right way of living? Life must be lived as play?'Perhaps the question should be asked, 'If these "things" and a light, colourful, well ventilated, playful environment stimulate creativity, why aren't our workplaces more like this?'

Levels of knowledge

The knowledge, intellectual and social capital of people are major sources of wealth and investment by organizations and communities. Knowledge and

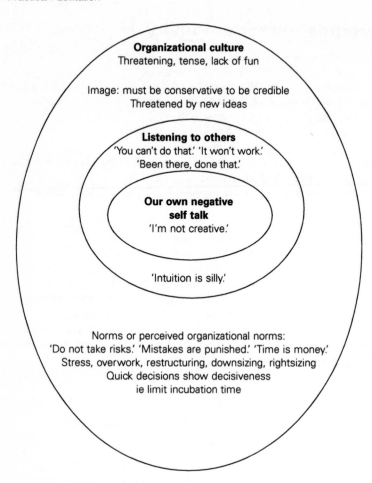

Figure 10.1   Blocks to creativity

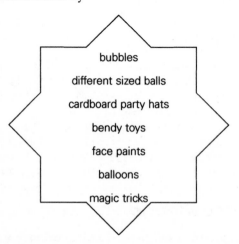

Figure 10.2   Objects to stimulate fun

ideas exchange though dialogue is one of the most important functions of groups to ensure innovation will take place (Paulus and Yang, 2000). Dualistic thinking, illustrated by phrases like, 'You are either with me or against me,' limits freedoms of speech and thought, the cornerstones of democracy.

Different levels of information may be generated or collected over different time frames: see Figure 10.3.

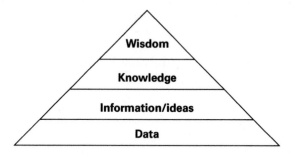

Figure 10.3　Different levels of knowledge

- **Wisdom** is accumulated information that has been applied and respected by groups and/or cultures over time, containing certain values and philosophical balances.
- **Knowledge** is information within wider frames of knowledge and/or context.
- **Information and ideas** are data that have been subjected to some interpretation, and as a result is imbued with additional meaning.
- **Data** is raw data for use in charts and so on.

Knowledge productivity is a dynamic process that involves the generation, spread and application of ideas. We all hold vast quantities of ideas and 'tacit knowledge' in our brains: 'things we just know or skills we just have' (Polanyi, 1966: 55:24). We also have the capacity to generate millions of new ideas by connecting unrelated ideas. However, it is only when these ideas are brought out into the open that others can make sense of, add to, learn from and make use of them.

Electronic searches now give us the capacity to find vast quantities of data and information. Computer programs can generate new ideas (such as names of children, businesses etc). However, they are dependent on the data that is keyed into them in the first place; our brains are not. We also then have to evaluate the quality of the data carefully to ascertain if it is data, information, knowledge and/or wisdom.

The diamond of idea generation and participatory decision making

Sam Kaner (1996) used the metaphor of a diamond to describe the structure behind idea generation and decision making, as shown in Figure 10.4. In the centre of the diamond Kaner named and legitimized a significant stage in the creative process called the 'Groan Zone': 'the struggle in the service of integration' (Kaner, 1996: 18). (Such terms are useful for facilitators so we can develop a common language to describe group behaviours.)

Struggling to understand the wide range of foreign or opposing ideas is not a pleasant experience. Group members can be repetitious, insensitive, defensive, short-tempered. When this occurs most people don't have the slightest notion what's happening to them. Sometimes the mere act of acknowledging the existence of the Groan Zone can be a significant step for a group to take. (Kaner, 1996:19).

Kaner pointed out that many groups merely list a few ideas and attempt to reach new decisions quickly (at point X in Figure 10.4) because of:

- lack of processes to break out of normal tunnel vision ideas;
- fear of branching out into uncharted territory;
- lack of time or fear of wasting time;
- self-censorship, impatience, information overload, frustration;
- fear of ambiguity and feeling out of control.

I find groups respond positively to knowing that the Groan Zone is normal, and that it is important not to seek a quick fix solution, but to try to delve into the causes of the misunderstandings or assumptions underlying problems and new ideas. Often it is useful to call a halt to discussion to allow reflection and incubation of ideas.

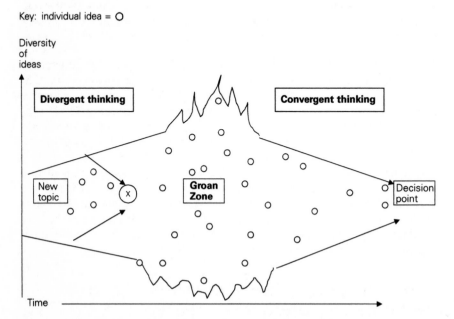

Figure 10.4   The diamond of participatory decision making

Source: adapted from Kaner (1996: 19)

The danger of premature evaluation is that nothing will ever be conceived.

Roger von Oech

It is during the Groan Zone that having co-facilitators is useful. Groups can be divided to focus on different jobs, or one facilitator can take over and give the other a break.

Table 10.1 Experiencing the Groan Zone

Common feelings	Underlying issues	Desirable behaviours	Desired state	Facilitator
Frustration	Different	Patience	Shared	Holds the
Confusion	perspectives	Perseverance	perspectives	space
Perplexity	Competing	Tolerance	Shared	Explains about
Anxious	frames of	Sense of	framework of	the Groan
Exasperation	reference	humour	understanding	Zone
	Tiredness		'Good'	Calls for
	Overload of		decision	stretch breaks
	new data		making	Encourages
				Supports

Classifications of creative processes

Kiely (1993) proposed four groups of processes designed to enhance creativity, based on the headings fluency techniques, excursion sessions, pattern breakers, and shake-up exercises. (See Table 10.2.) All classifications are limited to some degree: for example, mind mapping, brain storming and brainwriting may be used singly or in groups, *and* in synchronous or asynchronous time with the use of technology (see Chapter 14).

We need to use many different methods to stimulate our creativity. As there are many overlapping processes, I have chosen to describe dreams, then three well-known techniques, and how they compare with one another.

If your only tool is a hammer, you will begin to see everything in terms of nails.

Abraham Maslow

Harvesting dreams

Mendeleev is supposed to have awoken from dreaming with the image almost complete of the Periodic Table of Elements which we see in chemistry classes. 'Epiphanic moments' or turning points in groups (for facilitators and participants) are often reviewed and reinterpreted in our dreams. Dreams herald a change in ways of viewing the world. They may be interpreted as a kind of inner dialogue, in which the collective unconscious communicates with the unconscious and conscious mind. Dreams help us to clarify, analyse or see our

Table 10.2 Four groups of processes designed to enhance creativity

Type of process	Purpose	Name of process			
Fluency techniques	Help stimulate the generation of ideas, goal-focused, straight-line thinking.	*Brainstorming* Difficult to suspend criticism; personality differences, presence of management.	*Brainwriting* Generates social competition as individuals exchange ideas Easy to use over computer network.	*Mind mapping* Explosion diagrams using key words, colour, symbols, arrows to express and link ideas. *Mindscapes* Creative landscapes (Margulies, 1992); see Hogan's 'living frame of facilitation'.
Excursion sessions	Push the mind to grope for illuminations: wandering, unpredictable, and novel. Take the individual or group away from the problem so that the unconscious can work on it from a different perspective. Use metaphors and stories and non-sequential steps, then prompt the imagination to pull out ideas.	*Synectic questioning* (Gordon, 1961) The process makes use of absurd ideas to enable people to get out of their traditional mind sets and tunnel vision.	Focus on a *painting or word* eg 'window' or a dream, ie review your problem before you fall asleep.	*Awake dream:* imagine you are the product or are inside the product ie the process. *Mind movies.* *Creative visualization.*
Pattern breakers	Force the mind to stretch to find patterns between dissimilar concepts, in the hope of discovering unusual ideas in odd associations (a notion promulgated by surrealist poets and artists in the 1920s). Restate problems in novel ways.	*Take photos of random objects* with Polaroid or digital camera and link to goals: metaphorical exercises.	*Imagined party,* ie you are celebrating a successful innovation. Thinking about the factors that led to success.	
Shake-up exercises eg games, team activities	Help loosen up groups and make them more receptive to unusual ideas. Intended to help them relax, laugh, and fumble. Humour breaks the self-censoring mechanism and makes people less inhibited.	*Role-playing and/or games* replete with funny costumes, hats, scarves.	Different hats: Describe a new product from the view of 30 different hats eg Santa Claus. Invite primary children in to participate in business meetings. Watch kids play.	Outdoor fun activities. Humour room stacked with games, objects, juggling balls, Monty Python videos. Cartoons.

Source: adapted from Kiely (1993)

experiences from different perspectives. They can also be very confronting, but lead to reframing events. Dreams are a kind of inner dialogue. As such, they provide another perspective in which to identify significant themes and provide more material in the analysis of ideas.

Creative ideas often come to us in altered states of consciousness in dreams, half-awake states or daydreaming states: driving, in the bath or shower, swimming, playing sport. It happens less frequently at work (unless we are in a dozing state!). So it is useful if facilitators help participants to 'harvest dreams': for example, on extended workshops to describe any relevant dreams from the night before during the 'clearing session' at the beginning of the next day.

Descriptions of three processes follow: brainstorming, brainwriting and nominal group technique. Then they will be evaluated and compared.

> Nothing is more dangerous than an idea when it is the only one you have
>
> Emile Chartier

Brainstorming process

Author/background

Brainstorming was first used by Alex Osborn, an advertising executive in New York in 1938. The concepts, however, go back as far as 1926 (Wallas). The process was developed to generate a large number of ideas from a group of people in a short time. Since then the process has become popularized, but also unfortunately shortened, and used to describe a group of people throwing around ideas, or even making a simple rather unimaginative list.

It works best on open-ended issues/problems where there is no one right answer, like getting more people to use a service; finding ways of working together more productively; thinking of names for a new product. There are many variations that are useful to add into the process. Also it is useful to build in 'sleep time' for incubating ideas before making decisions.

Purpose/rationale

This exercise was written in order to help groups bring back the punch, creativity, and most of all fun, into a very useful process.

Size of group

Works best with five to nine people.

Materials

Flip chart paper, felt pens, masking tape, egg carton boxes, adhesive gum. A large blank wall and/or flip chart paper stands.

Venue layout

Participants sit in a semicircle facing the facilitator and wall.

Time

One hour minimum for the brainstorming segments. The action planning stage may take many hours.

Stages

Establish the ground rules

The role of the facilitator is to remind people of the ground rules at the beginning and to enforce them assertively during the process:

- The wilder the ideas the better.
- Suspend evaluation.
- Go for quantity of ideas.
- Piggy-back or build on ideas.
- Opposing ideas are fine too.
- No put downs.

State the problem/issue and discuss

Frequently in problem solving, people rush into finding solutions to the wrong problem!

Restate the problem/issue

Write up on flip chart paper a number of statements beginning with 'How to. . .'

Choose one problem/issue statement

Select one and involve the group in carefully rewording it: 'In how many ways can we. . .'

Warm-up

At this stage you want to get people's minds tuned in. Start off the brainstorm with a dry run, such as, 'How many uses can you think of for a paperclip? Suspend judgement and put down all the uses you can think of: good, bad, useful, useless, illegal, it doesn't matter, put them all down.' (It is useful to use two scribes.)

You may be tempted to leave out this stage. *Don't.* It is time well invested. It enables the group to switch into a creative thinking mode.

Brainstorm

Go straight into the real problem. Record every idea on flip chart paper. It's useful to use alternating coloured pens to show where one idea finishes and another begins. Keep up the tempo: there should be some joking and laughter.

Silence: one minute

When ideas slow up, encourage everyone to take one minute's silence to think about the issue. This stimulates individual thought and gives the reflectors in the group time to think. Silence is frequently used by Quakers at their meetings to gain insights and ideas. Participants can make a note of ideas if they wish.

Dictionary

Open a dictionary anywhere and without looking put your finger on a word. See if the word chosen can help generate some more ideas when linked to your problem.

Opposites

Ask the first question from the opposite angle.

Select the wildest idea

Select the wildest idea, brainstorm on it, and try to turn it into something useful.

Check understanding

Invite the group to scan the list and check call for clarification questions. Do *not* let them go into argument or debate on the issues at this stage.

Many ideas: type the ideas

Brainstorming should generate pages of data. Do not start evaluating the ideas immediately. If possible get the list typed and distributed before your next meeting.

Circulate to participants

People need time to 'mull' over ideas.

Allow sleep/dream/think time

If possible, allow 'sleep time' before evaluating. Sleep time allows the gestation of ideas and may lead to further creative thoughts and 'ahas' (see dreams above).

Dot voting

Give all participants five self-adhesive dots and ask them to place one beside each of their five preferred solutions. (This is similar to the ranking of items that Delbecq used in the nominal group process.) Or invite a series of votes with different coloured dots to highlight certain criteria, such as:

- five hardest solutions;
- five most important;
- five easiest;
- five best places to start.

Evaluation: PMI

De Bono suggests discussing the pluses, minuses and interesting points of each item (or six thinking hats on each). He maintains that we should never dismiss any idea without considering it first. This can be accomplished by the whole group or a small working party.

Remember there may be many ways of tackling the problem, not just one. Be sure to cover short-term as well as long-term solutions.

Action plans

Develop specific plans. The 5WH process will help: What? Who? When? Where? Why? How? With what resources? How do we know if you've been successful?

Evaluation of brainstorming process

Look back and analyse successes and what you would do differently next time. Discuss what was learnt along the way.

Advantages

Brainstorming can be great fun and therefore inherently a part of the team-building process. People often enjoy the interactive nature of this process. There is cognitive stimulation as ideas are shared.

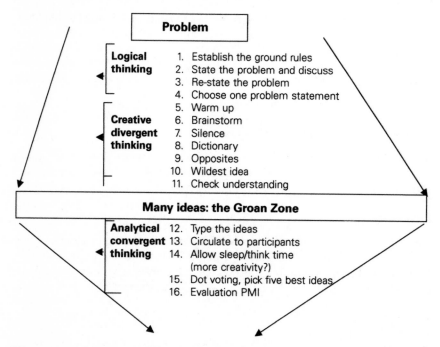

Figure 10.5   Summary of stages of brainstorming

Disadvantages

Groups using brainstorming generate fewer ideas in total than those using the so-called 'parallel' idea generation techniques like brainwriting and nominal group technique (where everyone generates ideas at the same time on paper). According to Paulus and Yang (2000), there are many possible explanations for this:

- **Evaluation apprehension:** participants may be afraid of being evaluated.
- **Social loafing or free riding:** people may feel their ideas are not needed, or they may be feeling tired or lazy.
- **Production blocking:** when one person is speaking, others need to listen.
- **Attention issues:** participants may be concentrating on what they are going to say next, rather than listening to the ideas being generated by others.
- **Interaction issues:** participants may be focusing on the timing of their interruption and contributions.

Brainstorming favours participants who are more confident, and have activist learning styles, and more extrovert personalities. In multicultural groups it favours those participants whose mother tongue is being spoken, as participants have to think very quickly. Other factors are, for example, the rapport of the facilitator with the group; the warm-up generated by the facilitator; the sense of trust and safety in the group.

There is a need for a variety of interventions during the brainstorming to trigger imaginations when ideas are flagging. Lastly there is a need for incubation of ideas. People need to be able to sleep on ideas, and dream about them consciously or subconsciously.

See the Web site http://www.mindtools.com/brainstm.html

Brainstorming depends on oral and quick thinking skills. A similar process, which was designed to overcome the shortcomings of brainstorming, is 'brainwriting'.

Brainwriting process

Author/background

Brainwriting was developed by Geschka, Schaude and Schlicksupp (1973). Variations have been developed by Goodman (1995) and Zemke (1993). It is another ideation (idea generation) technique.

Purpose/rationale

The purpose of brainwriting is to eliminate the restraints on free speaking that occur in brainstorming.

Size of group

Six to eight participants are ideal, but the process can be used with larger groups.

Materials

Cards, felt pens, adhesive gum. A large blank wall and/or flip chart paper stands to display ideas for analysis.

Venue layout

Participants sit in a circle around a table.

Time

Half an hour for idea generation.

Stages

Establish the ground rules

The role of the facilitator is to remind people of the ground rules at the beginning and to enforce them assertively during the process:

- One idea per card. (In the original process many ideas were written on a single card, but it is easier for 'piggybacking' to keep one idea per card.)
- Clear writing; do not add your name.
- When finished place card face down in the middle of the table, so others cannot see what has been written and ideas remain anonymous.

The ideas on the table form the 'brainwriting pool'. About 60–80 ideas can be generated in about 30 minutes.

State the problem/issue and discuss

Frequently in problem solving, people rush into finding solutions to the wrong problem! The facilitator discusses the phraseology of the question with the participants.

Brainwriting

Participants write one idea per card and place the cards in the middle of the table, face down. When each person runs out of ideas he/she takes a card from the central pool and starts to add his/her own ideas to piggyback (build) on the idea, or starts new cards with different ideas.

Advantages

Brainwriting avoids the 'process loss' of brainstorming: the time wasted as only one person can speak out at a time. (This can be overcome in brainstorming sessions to some extent if each participant has a card to jot down ideas whilst others are talking.) Because brainwriting is relatively anonymous, it counteracts the self-censoring by individuals who are concerned about what the boss or others will think of 'wild ideas'.

Brainwriting is an equalizing process: no one person can dominate discussions as in brainstorming. It favours people with a reflective learning style. It is useful in multicultural groups where Westerners have a tendency to dominate.

Brainwriting generates more ideas than brainstorming and nominal group technique (Van Gundy, 1995), since social competition is engendered by the exchange of cards by group members. In groups where participants were challenged to think of innovations to 'do things differently', brainstorming groups were more successful than brainwriting (Kirton, 1976).

Disadvantages

Handwriting may be identifiable. Therefore participants should be encouraged to print using large tipped felt pens. It is also useful if the facilitator keeps shuffling cards placed on the table to enhance anonymity.

Brainwriting does not have the social benefits, synergy and fun of brainstorming. It is possible, though not proven, that brainstorming aids team building and the commitment to the final outcome (Mongeau and Morr, 1999).

Nominal group technique

Author/background

The nominal group technique is a process designed to elicit ideas and opinions from a group of people. It was developed by Delbecq and Van de Ven (1971; Delbecq, Van de Ven and Gustafson, 1975) at the University of Wisconsin. The name relates to the fact that group discussion takes place at some later stages of the meeting, but at other times the participants act as individuals and are therefore only 'nominally' a group.

Purpose/rationale

The process can be used in a variety of situations:

- planning and assessing manager/staff needs;
- identifying training needs;
- identifying problems and developing innovative solutions;
- decision making;
- conflict resolution;
- evaluation of a course (Roe and McDonald, 1984).

Size of group

The method works best with 6–15 people. Larger groups need to be divided into two 'nominal groups'.

Materials

One piece of paper and a pen per participant, flip chart paper, felt pens, masking tape.

Venue layout

Ask participants to sit in a semicircle.

Time

The process takes one to two hours depending on the complexity of the question.

Stages

Pose a single question

Ask one specific question that has been carefully formulated beforehand, and invite the group to reframe it if necessary. For example:

- What ideas do you have to improve the functioning of this group/organization?
- How can a workshop be improved?
- What should be included in this training programme?
- What should be omitted from this training programme?
- What are the major problems facing your department?

Involve the group in deciding which question best fits their problem, and then brainstorm only one question.

Individuals note down responses

Distribute sheets of paper with the question printed at the top. Ask participants to note as many responses to the question as possible in silence. Up to 15 minutes may be needed. This allows individuals to reflect on their ideas in a competition-free atmosphere where premature decisions do not have to be made.

Each individual responds in turn

Ask each individual to give a single response round the group: in other words, round robin the group. As the responses are stated, write them up verbatim on flip chart paper. Go round the group several times, ensuring that you take only one response from each participant at a time. This procedure allows each individual to play a truly participatory role, but also ensures that the responses of any individual are not singled out or given undue emphasis. Do not allow any criticism or discussion regarding the form, format or meaning of the responses at this stage. Invite individuals who have 'passed' in previous rounds to add ideas, as often new ideas get triggered by ideas from others.

Clarify meaning

Ask the group members if they understand all the responses. Allow discussion of meaning of responses. Do not allow arguments or lobbying.

Clustering

Invite the group to cluster to about 12–15 items with the help of the group. Number the items.

Ranking or voting

At this stage you have a choice. You can ask participants to individually rank or vote for say seven items:

Ranking: from the total list of numbered clustered responses, ask each participant to select and rank seven. Generally people can only prioritize from five to nine items with any degree of reliability. Ask participants to write down the number of each response, starting with the most important at the top of the list, descending in rank order to the least important.

Voting: ask participants to write down the numbers of seven responses they consider to be most important. Voting is quicker and simpler than ranking and usually gives similar results. It takes the facilitator a lot longer to compute results from the ranking process.

Or try both and compare the results if you have time.

Recording

The facilitator or a participant works out the results.

Display results on flip chart paper and discussion

Discuss the various explanations of voting patterns. Discuss items with high, low and no votes. Encourage participants to reflect on their reactions. Invite people to discuss their intuitive reactions.

Ongoing action

Ongoing acting is a result of the group discussions in which all members have had a chance to participate. This helps to cultivate a feeling of responsibility in the members to be productive and achieve group goals.

Advantages

The nominal group technique:

- is non-threatening;
- encourages active participation;
- discourages competition of ideas by postponing judgement till later stages;
- prevents one person from dominating a discussion.

Disadvantages

The process is very orderly and seems to lack spontaneity at times.

Comparison of the three processes

Zemke (1993) divided up creative processes into two groups based on whether they were parallel (solitary) or interactive (group) processes. The three processes described above are compared in Table 10.3. In all three processes the quality of ideas and solutions depends partly on the selection of participants and the quality of facilitation, ie how much the facilitator engenders a sense of trust and playful creativity.

Mindbloom (http://www.mindbloom.net) is a Web site that challenges you to be creative. The site includes 'Mindxercises', and tips for bringing up creative children.

Conclusion

> The mind is like a parachute. It only works when it is open.
>
> Source unknown

Helping groups to be creative is fun. It requires us all to tap into the playful child of ourselves. There is no such thing as a 'perfect process', as this chapter illustrates. So as facilitators we need to be aware of evaluations of processes, and the merits and defects of each process. The next chapter focuses on problem solving and decision making.

Table 10.3 Comparison of the brainstorming, brainwriting and nominal group techniques

	Brainstorming *Interactive (group) processes*	Brainwriting *Parallel (part solitary, part group)*	Nominal group technique *Highly structured process (part solitary, part group)*
	Groups of individuals generate ideas verbally.	Individuals generate ideas on paper and pass around group members who read and add own ideas.	Groups of individuals who generate ideas in writing without interacting. Later their ideas are pooled verbally.
Rules/norms	Ideas expressed orally. No criticism allowed. Wilder the ideas the better. Quantity not quality. Piggybacking on ideas, ie building or combining. Two core principles: Deferred judgement. Quantity breeds quality.	Ideas are written. Ideas are anonymous after passed to second person.	Ideas are written. Ideas are not anonymous at first, but added to group memory on flip chart paper.
Claims	Oral generation of ideas stimulates creativity and synergy. Stimulates effective rivalry. Generates more ideas than individuals alone.	Generates more ideas than brainstorming.	Nominal groups created 80% more ideas than brainstorming groups (Mongeau and Morr, 1999). Useful for getting groups to make communal decisions. Produce more and better quality of ideas than brainstorming (Zemke, 1993).
Issues	Ideas are not confidential. Oral generation of ideas, only one person can speak at a time. Favours more activist type of learner. Intimidates more reflective learners. Favours many though not all Westerners who are used to voicing opinions. Best in small groups of 5–9 people where power differential is lowest. Research findings are contradictory.	Can be used in larger groups. Can be used where there is wide power differential as ideas are anonymous.	As group size increases the advantage of NGT over brainstorming increases.

11

Problem solving and decision making

> Successful problem solving requires finding the right solution to the right problem. We fail more often because we solve the wrong problem than because we get the wrong solution to the right problem.
>
> Russell L Ackoff

Introduction

From the time we are born we set out to solve problems. Babies who are hungry cry to be fed. Indeed we solve problems all the time, often subconsciously. This chapter is based on the following:

- Problems are a part of life: some are desirable, others stressful and/or unpleasant.
- Evolution and survival have meant that we are all problem solvers to some degree; we can do it automatically as well as purposefully.
- Problems require logical, creative and intuitive thinking.
- It helps to be aware of and use a variety of strategies of problem solving and decision making.
- Some participants regard problems as challenges and use a variety of strategies; others regard problems as a pain and use a limited number of methods.

Donald Woods (2000) analysed more than 150 basic strategies to solve problems in business, mathematics, engineering, design, military, music, art, psychology, history, nursing, medicine and policing, and summarized that:

- Published strategies are similar: most start with a definition stage and close with an evaluation stage.
- Stages vary between two and seven stages.
- Some link problem-solving processes with subject knowledge, past experience and past solved problems.

The chapter is divided into sections to address:

- the types of problems where facilitators are needed: 'wicked' and 'tame' problems;
- individual problem-solving styles and strategies;
- problem-solving processes: the McMaster six-stage strategy;
- strategic questioning;
- comparison of different decision making processes;
- consensus decision-making;
- the LENS process;
- group dynamics that prevent effective problem solving: group think, the Abilene paradox.

Opening up participants to their thinking about problems

A useful 'facilitative question' is to ask groups, 'What kinds of problems are there?' Once participants start thinking, the kinds of answer that come up include:

- Problems can be interconnected, complicated and complex (you solve one thing and two other problems emerge).
- Some are easy, some are hard and some are unsolvable.
- A question in need of an answer.
- Some have been described as 'soft' or people problems by information systems authors Checkland and Scholes (1990), as opposed to statistical or 'hard' problems.
- Some are pleasant, other unpleasant, some exciting, others boring.
- Problems come in assorted sizes depending on your perspective: small are big, some small.
- Any situation where we want something to be different.
- Some problems you can be in control, other problems others control.
- Some you can solve yourself, others you can solve together, others you need a facilitator.
- Different perspectives: what is a problem to one person is a challenge to someone else, 'One person's meat is another person's poison'.
- Depends on your perspective: optimism or pessimism, a glass of water can be seen as half full or half empty.
- The concept of 'crisis' in Chinese terms can represent both 'danger' and 'opportunity'.
- 'One right answer' problems (those with a single technical cause, that is, 'tame' problems – see later in chapter), 'many right answer' problems (those where there are multiple, interacting causes and solutions, that is, 'wicked' problems – see later in chapter), 'no right answer' (those which concern ethics and values where the presence of conflicting beliefs may prevent the formulation of a preventable solution) (Dick, 1984).

- Some problems emerge as time passes; this is not a reflection of poor planning or incompetence, it is caused by the type of problem being worked on.
- Some managers force dualistic solutions: 'You are either with me or against me', which is simplistic and dangerous.
- There are societal, resource, political constraints on solutions to problems and ways of generating solutions to problems (Martin, 2000).

When facilitators are needed for group problem solving

Facilitators are usually called in to help groups with problem solving when certain conditions occur:

- *Tacit knowledge* (knowledge in people's heads) needs to be elicited from individuals and groups.
- There are *wicked problems* to be solved rather than tame or one-right-answer problems.
- There is a need for a *high level of contextual information*.

These three areas were discussed by Peter Morris (2000) in his description of problems facing WWWk: 'world wide work' or work that is conducted in different locations and at different times, and often, though not always, through the use of information and communication technologies (Web sites and call centres), '7 x 24', or 7 days a week and 24 hours a day.

Morris's three classifications are rather simplistic, but they do give labels to issues that may need to be discussed when deciding what facilitation processes to use to address different types of problems.

The nature of the knowledge

The nature of the problem may require the pooling of both 'tacit' and 'codified' knowledge. 'Tacit knowledge' or 'knowledge in the head' is usually gained on the job: for example about the idiosyncrasies of certain people, or how to do things learnt by observing others. 'Codified knowledge' on the other hand is knowledge that is written down, such as standard operating procedures. See Table 11.1.

Types of problem: tame and wicked

> Some problems are so complex that you have to be highly intelligent and well informed just to be undecided about them.
>
> Laurence J Peter

Horst Rittel and Melvin Webber (1973) classified problems into two rather delightful groups: 'tame' and 'wicked' (although many problems have a

Table 11.1   The nature of knowledge

Tacit knowledge	*Codified knowledge*
Knowledge in the head: 'know how', 'tricks of the trade'	Formal information that can be 'captured', agreed upon and written down in manuals or disks: 'know what to do', 'guidelines'
May be shared or not shared with a group	Is available to the group in manuals etc
May need to be shared anonymously	Requires updating
Some may want to have their knowledge attributed to them	Requires systems for easy access
Who owns tacit knowledge?	Manuals owned by organizations
Examples: networks, knowledge of how to approach certain people, skills taught one to one or to apprentices etc	Examples: formalized procedures, specifications, manuals, legislation and formulae, modularized learning packages etc

mixture of both). Tame problems are 'easy to get a handle on': the problem and solution/s can be visualized. For example, with the problem of how to put a person on the moon, you can visualize the results. A wicked problem is more elusive: for example, where to put a bypass round a city. More and more problem solving in organizations involves wicked problems. Peter Morris makes the point that at school students are mostly taught how to solve 'tame' problems, and they hardly even know that 'wicked' problems exist. (Indeed the term 'wicked' has very different connotations for young people, as for them the word 'wicked' means 'wow'!) See Table 11.2.

The degree of context required

Context refers to the social, technical, economic and environmental background in which problems occur. The question is what amount of background inform-ation is needed. For example, knowledge of context is vital in facilitation, consulting, and the management professions, and has often been ignored by engineers and computer programmers.

Facilitators are often called upon to facilitate colocated groups when there are wicked problems, where people have to draw on tacit knowledge, and where context is important. (See Chapter 14 for descriptions of facilitating distributed groups via technology.) See Table 11.3.

Individual problem-solving styles and strategies

How we perceive problems depends on our emotional well being, hardiness (which goes up and down) and internal locus of control. ('Internal locus of control': when we feel in charge of our lives, or 'external locus of control': when

Table 11.2   Types of problem: tame and wicked

Tame problems	Wicked problems
Problem and solution can be easily defined and it is easy to imagine a solution.	Problem and solution intertwined. You have to understand both the problem and the solution.
There is a clear finish, ie when you have solved the problem.	There is no firm finish point, so a solution is considered 'good enough', eg house or office design. The problem-solving process ends when you run out of resources, time, or the group decides that the solution is 'good enough'.
Solutions are 'right' or 'wrong'.	There is no right or wrong answer. Solutions are defined subjectively as 'better' or 'worse' rather than 'right' or 'wrong'. Need to generate criteria for evaluating solutions.
Example: designing a 'widget' to a formula or pattern regarding materials, size and stress.	Example: building or designing a house, designing an information systems network for an organization, the war against terrorism. See Web site http://www.cognexus.org/id55.htm
Can be solved by groups in different locations.	Often required to be solved by colocated groups who need to share.
Problems may be repeated or appear in patterns.	Wicked problems are unique and novel, so solutions need to be custom designed and evolve, as when one stage is solved a host of new wicked subproblems are spawned.
May be solved by individuals or groups more simply according to prescribed process or learnt stages.	Require collective intelligence and tools and methods to create shared understanding and shared commitment to solving them. It is the social complexity of wicked problems rather than the technical complexity that is often overwhelming.

we believe that we have no control on what happens to us and believe in others, luck and fate (Rotter, 1975).) Some people have a propensity to see problems as challenges, actively seek out jobs as 'troubleshooters' and 'change agents', and enjoy being professional problem solvers (problem seekers). Others see problems as negative and heavy (problem worriers); others see problems as issues to be avoided, if possible at all costs (problem avoiders) (Hopson and Scally, 1986).

Perspective

All over the world, people have learnt to live with and overcome a large variety of problems. In Laos, at times, people shrug their shoulders and say, 'Bo pen

Table 11.3   Context of problems: high and low

High context	Low context
Issues that require interaction with workers, colleagues, clients, government officials	Issues that can be solved in isolation from people
Sensitivity to a culture, country, organizational and local politics	Local cultures, politics, networks irrelevant
Example: trying to assess the numbers of nurses required for different wards for different shifts	Example: accounting procedures in an ethical, static, stable environment

yang', meaning, 'Never mind'. In Nepal there is a somewhat similar phrase, 'Ke garne?' meaning 'What to do?' This may seem strange and frustrating to Westerners, but at times it is useful if you cannot cope with trying to fix everything. It is good to remember that in the West we also have a similar phrase, 'It's fate' or 'It's God's will'. In Moslem societies, the phrase, 'It's the will of Allah' may be heard. In Australia, we have similar optimistic phrases like, 'She'll be right, mate,' and 'No worries'. In many instances it is important that groups/individuals learn to 'choose their battles': which problems to tackle and in what order of importance.

How we deal with problems also varies. We may choose to deal with them, ignore them, worry about them, and delegate them. We need to know about the lifecycle of a problem. A simple exercise to help participants understand their different perspectives is to ask two people sitting opposite each other to describe the room as they see it from their perspective.

Figure 11.1   Perspective exercise

Diagrams and visual tools

In one Asian country, I facilitated a group comprising staff from six provinces and the head office team in the capital city. For the first time participants had discussed and reached consensus on their goals. In order to identify how well they were achieving these goals and where they needed help from the head office support team, each group was invited to self-rank how well they were achieving these goals at present (0–3). (See Table 11.4.)

To encourage them to be realistic we promised that when we collated the data on flip chart paper, we would give each province a number: we would not divulge the names of the provinces in public. This did, however, give head office staff useful data province by province. We hoped that the increased staff autonomy would enhance people's empowerment to state their needs, and as a result get their needs met.

Table 11.4 Self-assessment sheet given to each province and head office staff

	Not at all 0	*A little* 1	*Good* 2	*Excellent* 3
Goal 1				
Goal 2			2	
Goal 3		1		3
Goal 4			2	
Goal 5	0			

The numerical data were then collated and fed back to the whole group on flip chart paper (see Table 11.5). This helped everyone gain a pattern of areas that were ostensibly working well and goals that needed attention: in other words, the patterns of problems. It also enabled head office staff to find out privately where problems lay geographically. It also showed that in some cases head office staff were under the impression that a goal was being achieved well, but the provincial staff perceptions were less positive. In addition, head office staff perceived that the advertising goals were being achieved better than did the provincial staff. So 'perceptual gaps' were highlighted (see goal number 5 in Table 11.5). Province 5 had the least experience, and the self-rating of staff indicated this. As a result, useful data emerged regarding the identification of the location, degree and perception of problem areas.

Table 11.5 Collated data on achievement of goals by province

Location → *Goals* ↓	*Province* 1	*Province* 2	*Province* 3	*Province* 4	*Province* **5**	*Head office*	*Total*
Goal 1	3	3	3	2	3	3	17
Goal 2	3	2	3	3	1	3	15
Goal 3	2	3	2	2	2	3	14
Goal 4	1	2	2	1	1	3	10
Goal 5	0	0	1	0	1	3	5

Then each province and head office was asked to describe what help was needed to achieve each goal. See Table 11.6.

Table 11.6 Description of help needed to achieve goals

Needs ➔	Training needed	Advertising materials needed	Equipment needed	Other needs
Goal 1		Materials not reaching the provinces		Staff required for. . .
Goal 2			Amplifiers needed for village meetings	
Goal 3				
Goal 4			Motor bike to get to village meetings	
Goal 5	No training yet			

Self-assessment is of course dependent on the:

- honesty of participants;
- knowledge of participants in what skills and knowledge are required to achieve the goals effectively;
- degree of trust of participants in the facilitators;
- degree of trust of participants in the head office staff.

The saliency exercise

Another useful exercise is a 'saliency exercise' to plot the lifecycle of problems or issues. This exercise often brings out some interesting information. The question of saliency (leaping or jumping up, relevance, urgency) is extremely important, as all too often by the time we get around to making an attempt to solving problems, they have already passed the point of really mattering. The reason for including this process in a workshop is to enable the group to determine which concerns in their area are barely emergent, plateauing or on the decline. The normal path of concern can be depicted diagrammatically (see Figure 11.2). Of course some problems subside, only later to emerge in the same or mutated form (such as leprosy and malaria), or problems may be cyclical.

The group may wish to make up a list of items for consideration. Examples are given in Table 11.7, and may be added together to give an indication of the morale in the organization.

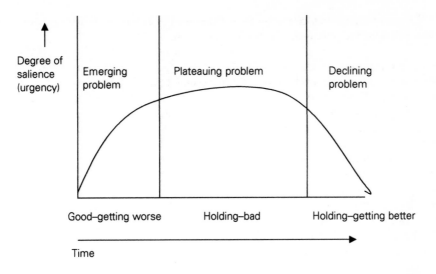

Figure 11.2   The lifecycle of problems

Table 11.7   Saliency table

Salience issue	Good–Getting worse	Holding–Bad	Holding– Getting better	Fine Leave as is/ monitor
Parking				
Library Facilities				
Physical Environment, eg air- conditioning				
Facilities for disabled				
Staff morale				

Processes for problem solving

It is useful to apply many approaches to problem solving: logic, reason, intuition and creativity. Logic and reason are not enough without listening to intuition. Using intuition is a skill. Some people feel something in their stomachs, others hear it or see it. Intuition is different from wild guessing (Goldberg, 1983).

There are many well-documented processes that can be used for problem identification and generating solutions, including:

- Mind mapping (Buzan and Buzan, 1993; Margulies 1992; Hogan 1994).
- Visualization or 'mind movies' (Hopson and Scally, 1986).
- Dreams (Jung, 1968).
- Imagine you are the problem. (Einstein used analogies and metaphors to visualize and solve problems; see also Chapter 4.)
- Force field analysis plus cyclic voting (Dick, 1984).
- SWOT analysis.
- Fishbone diagrams.
- Critical path analysis.
- Six thinking hats (de Bono, 1985).
- Brainstorming (Mongeau and Morr, 1999).
- Brainwriting (Goodman, 1995).
- Nominal group technique (Delbecq and Van de Ven, 1971; Delbecq, Van de Ven and Gustafson, 1975).
- Value management (Yeomans, 1999a, 1999b).

Whatever process/es you use, there is an underlying structure in the shape of a diamond: first defining what the problem really is, then opening up discussion about the causes, the depth and complexity of the issue (described in the previous chapter), then the Groan Zone, before bringing ideas down in order to make decisions. See Figure 11.3.

Unfortunately some groups (and facilitators) close down discussion too early (as shown by the two converging arrows at 'x' in Figure 11.3), as they do not

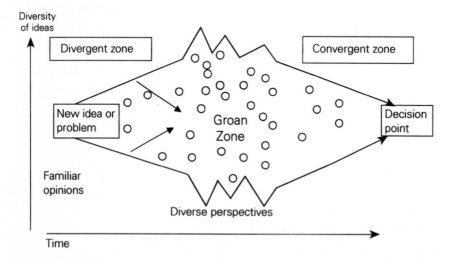

Figure 11.3 The diamond of participatory idea generation and group decision making

Source: after Kaner (1996)

want to go into what Sam Kaner (1996) called the 'Groan Zone' (Kaner 1996), described in Chapter 10. I have repeated the diagram here as the second part of the diagram is pertinent to this chapter.

It is during the Groan Zone that time gets used up, some people push for closure, and managers sometimes jump in and offer a solution. If this happens, participants come to distrust the process. The facilitator needs to hold the space and calmly let people know that the confusion and frustration are a normal part of problem solving and decision making. There is no one neat process.

Software for mapping problems includes Mind Maps Plus and Axon Idea Processor (see References).

Problem-solving strategies

Many teachers and lecturers are now using problem-based learning, an approach where the teacher in a facilitator role focuses participants on solving examples and/or real-life problems. The process works well in medical, managerial, and scientific and IT contexts. It is important first to teach participants to be aware of the stages they need to go through, and also some strategies and pitfalls to avoid.

Many authors have stressed that it is the initial steps in problem solving that are the most crucial (Doyle and Straus, 1976; Dick, 1984; Woods, 1994, 2000). Interpersonal and workplace problems are often a combination of many of the types of problem cited above.

In the West, managers often say to staff, 'Don't bother me with your problems, come to me with solutions'. This helps to develop staff autonomy, but many are not trained in problem-solving techniques, and because of work pressures people often jump to quick-fix solutions. Indeed, quick decision making is often perceived as being 'good', and yet often people solve the wrong problem.

There are also cultural differences: for example, in Japan often more time is taken getting people on side and resolving issues before solutions are implemented. As a result the implementation time is quicker. Likewise idea generation needs to precede idea evaluation. (See Chapter 10 on creative thinking.)

The next process is useful to help participants learn to be effective problem solvers.

McMaster six-stage problem-solving strategy

Author/background

Donald Woods (1994) developed a six-stage process to enable participants to:

- describe their problem-solving processes to a partner;
- monitor how long they take on each stage;
- become aware of their problem-solving strategies.

Purpose/rationale

Unsuccessful problem solvers spend most time doing something, indeed anything, to appear busy on the problem. Successful problem solvers spend more time thinking about and defining the problem, reading through the data before embarking on problem-solving strategies. Donald Woods surveyed 150 strategies as part of his research in creating the six-stage strategy, which can be applied to both tame' and 'wicked' problems (Woods, 2000).

Size of group

Any size working in pairs.

Materials

Flip-chart paper, felt pens, masking tape, pens and writing paper for each participant, adhesive gum. A large blank wall, copies of handouts of time-keeping grids and stages. Watches.

Venue/layout

Participants seated in pairs.

Time

Depends on the complexity of the problem.

Stages

The process is best used in pairs, where each person takes turns to be 'problem solver' and then 'listener'. The facilitator needs to carefully go through the six stages described below, and the roles of listener and problem solver, and provide a short written problem applicable to the group. (Sometimes it is useful to use a problem that the group does not normally face, so that it is easier to focus on the 'problem-solving process' rather than the 'content' in the debriefing session.)

Establish the roles

Role of listener

The role of the listener is to encourage the problem solver to:

- Verbalize thoughts: for example, 'What is going through your mind now?'
- Monitor the time spent at each stage on a graph: see Figure 11.4. The reason for the graph is to make patterns of behaviour visible.
- Ask the problem solver to verbalize thoughts.

The listener must not coach or make suggestions to the problem solver.

Role of the problem solver

The problem solver is required to:

- Verbalize thoughts and confusions: that is, tell the story of his/her problem solving.
- Move the coin up and down to show what stage he/she is at. (Most successful problem solvers use a strategy of some sort, but do not necessarily follow the stages in a linear fashion.)

						Time in minutes						
Start												
Minutes	**0**	**2**	**4**	**6**	**8**	**10**	**12**	**14**	**16**	**18**	**20**	**22**
Time **Stage**												
1. **Engage:** 'I want to and I can...'												
2. **Define stated problem**												
3. **Explore:** create internal idea of problem												
4. **Plan a solution**												
5. **Do it:** carry out the plan												
6. **Evaluate**												

Figure 11.4 Timekeeping grid for listener to complete

Stages

The stages of thought are not necessarily sequential, so Woods suggests using not the terms 'steps', but 'stages' or 'zones' or episodes' instead. So it is useful to show the stages as a circle. See Figure 11.5.

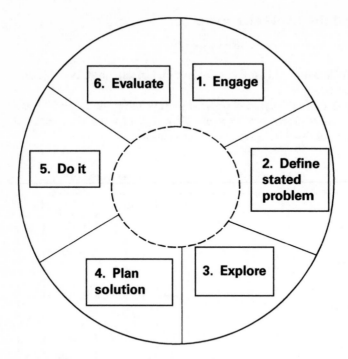

Figure 11.5   McMaster six-stage problem solving strategy

1. Engage with the problem confidently

Applying a positive and confident mind set onto a problem is powerful. If you become tense and nervous it may inhibit mental processing. The problem solver says strongly out loud a mantra, 'I want to and I can solve this problem'.

The skills involved are:

Cognitive skills: reading and listening.
Attitudinal skills: stress and anxiety management; manage motivation; confidence; fear of making mistakes.

2. Define the problem

Defining the problem may involve analysing a written or verbal statement of the problem, checking that all the words are understood, clarifying ambiguity, and finding out what you are asked to do. A strategy might be to list questions needed to elicit further information: for example, as doctors say, 'What are the presenting problems?' (the top third of the iceberg above the water line). Maybe draw a simple diagram. Underline key words. Clarify the meaning/s of key words. Identify constraints and criteria. Some participants like to draw the problem as pictures and/or symbols. The skills involved are:

Cognitive skills: analysis, reasoning, classifying, identify steps, drawing.
Attitudinal skills: attention, ability to tolerate ambiguity.

3. Explore

The 'explore stage' is an overview of the 'real problem': the two-thirds of the iceberg underneath the water level. There is a search for assumptions, seeing different points of view, broadening and narrowing points of view. The boundaries between the 'explore' and 'plan' stage are blurred at times. 'This stage is probably the most underrated, most challenging and least understood stage of all the stages' (Woods, 2000). We play around with the problem statement using our background knowledge and problem solving experience. We look for patterns and try to discover what the 'real' problem is:

- The goal: is written.
- The goal is built up incorporating the context, both general and specific.
- The goal focuses on the causes not the symptoms.
- The owner of the goal is identified.
- The stakeholders are identified.
- The goal is expressed in observable terms as results to be achieved rather than actions.

The skills involved are:

Cognitive skills: analysis, creative thinking and processes, broaden perspectives, use past experiences, structure knowledge.
Attitudinal skills: willingness to postpone judgement, open mindedness, curiosity, scepticism, honesty, stress management if get stuck, willing to guess, unafraid of making mistakes, monitor progress.

4. Plan solution/s

The 'plan solution/s stage' attends to details, for example making lists of data needed, mapping out subproblems and steps to solve them. The skills involved are:

Cognitive skills: analysis, manage resources, decision making.
Attitudinal skills: decisiveness, carefulness, persistence, tenaciousness.

5. Do it, carry out the plan

The type of problem may not lend itself to being worked out in the workshop. Mathematical problems may be calculated on the spot. However an action plan outline and timelines could be developed at this stage. The skills involved are:

Cognitive skills: analysis, organizational skills, time management, monitoring skills, attention to detail.
Attitudinal skills: carefulness, persistence, tenaciousness.

6. Look back and evaluate

This stage is often forgotten. This involves evaluating not only the solution/s but also the problem solving process/es used. What was learnt about problem solving? Maybe some strategies were used that could be useful in the future?

The skills involved are:

Cognitive skills: analysis, evaluation, generalization skills.
Attitudinal skills: intellectual honesty, manage elation, check back, persistence.

Figure 11.6 is a copy of a handout which can be given to the participants. The problem solver places a coin on the stage that he/she is working on.

Coin	Stage	Explanation
	1. Engage	'I want to and I can solve this problem.'
	2. Define stated problem	Check you understand the words. Analyse the problem. Explain what you are asked to do. Underline key words. Tolerate ambiguity and confusion.
	3. Explore	Create an internal idea of the problem. Keep an open mind. Stay curious. Play around with ideas. What factors do you need to consider?
	4. Plan solution/s	Analyse. Begin to formulate steps: I need to decide on which strategy to use first.
	5. Do it	Carry out the plan.
	6. Evaluate: check and look back	Check and double check. Evaluate the solution: Is the answer/s reasonable? Was this what you were asked to do? Evaluate the problem-solving process: What did you learn about yourself? What did you learn about your problem-solving method/s? Were the methods suitable? Could other methods have been used? If 'yes', which ones?

Figure 11.6 The McMaster six-stage problem solving strategy

Outcomes

The paired process is an equalizer in that it actively engages all participants. Participants learn from one another different approaches to problem solving.

Advantages

The process makes participants more aware of their problem-solving styles and strategies, as well as good and bad habits. Learners start to use the habit of positive mind sets before engaging in problem solving, rather than panicking or feeling stressed. Increased confidence helps people to think more clearly. The stages are the same for individuals as for groups engaged in problem solving. The stages give participants a vocabulary to work with and a flexible structure in which to move around.

Donald Woods has successfully used and develop this process over the past 20 years with students who keep diaries about their problem solving in a semester-long course.

Disadvantages

The process was designed for use with engineering problems and easily lends itself to technical problems which can be computed and checked on the spot. However, a later survey (Woods, 2000) indicated it is suitable for all disciplines.

One problem with workshop-based problem solving is that it does not allow time for incubation and 'sleep time', which is often vital to let ideas sink in and creative solutions emerge.

See the Web site http://edweb.sdsu.edu/clrit/learningtree/PBL/WhatisPBL. html. Other useful Web sites on problem-based learning are http://www.udel. edu/pbl and http://home.att.net/~nickols/tentips.htm

Strategic questioning

Another useful set of questioning skills is encompassed in the skills of strategic questioning, which enables facilitators to frame useful and thought-provoking questions to open up discussions.

Author and background

Strategic questioning is the skill of asking 'questions that will make a difference', in the emergence of new information or different ways of seeing things. It is a powerful and exciting tool for change that may involve individuals, groups, organizations or communities.

By learning how to ask 'strategic' questions, facilitators (and hopefully participants) will develop useful strategies to enhance personal and social change. These questioning strategies were developed originally by Ronald Hyman, and later published and promoted by Fran Peavey in the United States (Peavey, 2001; Shields, 1991). (See also Fran Peavey's Web site: www.crabgrass. org/article01.htm)

Purpose/rationale

The basis of all facilitation work is to ask questions rather than to tell people what they need to do. In traditional educational systems, teachers ask questions and students answer, often trying to search for the one 'right' answer. Strategic questioning is particularly useful for 'wicked' problems. Strategic questions:

- create movement in problem solving;
- create options;
- are empowering;
- ask the 'unaskable' questions like 'Why doesn't the Emperor have clothes on?' (from the 'Emperor's new clothes' story described in Chapter 4);
- are open questions (avoid closed questions and yes/no answers);
- respect the individual.

Questions to avoid are hidden suggestions:

'May I make a suggestion?' (You are not really asking permission.)
'Have you considered?' (Here's a suggestion.)
'Why don't you?' (Here's another suggestion.)

Strategic questioners avoid suggestions hiding as a question when using the question word 'Why', such as 'Why don't you move to Sydney?' This is a suggestion hidden as a question. However, 'Why is this happening?' is a valid question.

Size of group

This process may be used by individuals to question themselves, or in pairs to promote growth or change. Facilitators may use these strategies in large groups as a political process for problem solving and community change.

Materials

None. Flip chart paper is useful in a large group situation to record ideas.

Venue

Strategic questioning may be used anywhere.

Time

Variable depending on the topics. A facilitator may just use one key question in the middle of a workshop to get participants to shift their thinking.

Stages

There are no distinct stages to strategic questioning. What is required is a reframing of how we dialogue with and listen to others. For example, instead of joining in a communal gripe session, a facilitator as a strategic questioner could ask, 'I wonder what you can do to change that situation?' This shifts the situation from a passive to an active one.

First level: describing the issues or problems

1. **Focus questions:** 'What are you most concerned about in your work/ community?'
2. **Observation questions.** These questions relate to seeing and hearing, eg 'What do you see and hear?' 'What aspects of your work/community life concern you?' 'How has violence in your work/community affected you?'
3. **Feeling questions.** These questions are focused on body sensations, emotions and health, eg 'What sensations do you have in your body when you think or talk about this situation?'
4. **Analysis questions:** These questions elicit a person's understanding of a situation and its causes, eg 'What are the reasons for this?'

Second level: asking *strategic* questions

5. **Visioning questions:** identify ideals, dreams and values, eg 'What does your heart long for?' 'Practicalities aside, what wild and wonderful ideas have you had? 'How would you like it to be?' 'How would you like your workplace to be?'
6. **Change questions:** 'What would it take for things to change or X to happen?' 'What would it take for you to change on this issue?' How to move to a more ideal situation, eg 'What needs to change here?' 'Who can make a difference?'
7. **Consider all the alternatives:** 'What are all the ways you could make your desired changes happen?' 'Are there any other ways?'
8. **Consider all the consequences of the alternatives:** 'What would happen if you did. . .?' 'How would you feel if you did. . .?'
9. **Consider the obstacles:** 'How could you find out what is stopping you?' 'What do you do instead of doing what you want to do?' 'What keeps you from doing. . .?' 'What prevents you from becoming involved with. . .?'
10. **Personal support questions:** 'What support would you need?' 'What would you like to do to support these changes?'
11. **Personal action questions:** 'Who do you need to talk to?' 'How can you get others together to work on this?'

Advantages

There are many advantages to strategic questioning. It:

*   Creates motion, shifts in thinking, eg 'What would it take for you to change on this issue?' 'What would it take for you to function as a team?'
*   Creates options, eg 'What alternatives are there?'
*   Makes an individual dig deeper into problems, eg 'What is the reason underlying your stance?'

- Enables participants to realize that movement on an issue is possible, that they can make more empowered responses to their problems, eg 'What would you like to do to clean up your river?'
- Enables participants to ask the unaskable questions that challenge values and assumptions, eg 'Why hasn't the Emperor got any clothes on?', 'What keeps you from working on cleaning up your river?'

Disadvantages

None.

Outcomes

It enhances wider, deeper thinking and less adversarial (win–lose) discussions and problem solving.

Factors that prevent effective problem solving

> Remember that amateurs built the ark.
> Professionals built the Titanic.
>
> > Anon

Ways of preventing/minimizing groupthink

Groupthink occurs when groups become so cohesive that dissent is discouraged. In some groups, participants who disagree are scapegoated or even attacked by the majority. Doyle and Straus (1976) called this 'group rape'. The theoretical background and causes of groupthink are discussed in detail in *Understanding Facilitation* Chapter 8. However, in practice managers and facilitators need to be aware of the problems of groupthink, and have a range of strategies to prevent it and/or bring it to the attention of a group. For example:

- Include the 'right to say no' and 'It's OK to disagree' in workshop ground rules and meetings. Tell the group, 'Sometimes it takes more courage to say "No" than to go along with the group'.
- Establish trust and openness. Thank participants for being open and raising concerns/issues.
- Encourage participants to 'rock the boat', knowing that 'no decision is perfect'. Promote the devil's advocate role by using processes like pluses, minuses and interesting points' (PMI) or six thinking hats (which include a black hat for negative thinking) (de Bono, 1985).
- Use card sorts for anonymous stocktaking of 'real' opinions, to ensure that participants are not swayed by the ideas of the boss or a persuasive or threatening group member.

- Use separate small group discussions and then feed back ideas anonymously to the whole group.
- Allow participants to sleep on a decision and hold 'second-chance meetings' to re-evaluate recent decisions.
- Arrange for the group to meet occasionally without the manager/leader present, as frequently that person is listened to most.
- Invite in outsiders to add different information and perspectives to group discussions.
- Encourage managers to not recruit and surround themselves with 'yes' people.
- Encourage the formation of heterogeneous teams (Belbin, 1993).
- Examine all warning signals of groupthink and take them seriously.
- Encourage dialogue rather than win–lose debating of ideas.

Taking a trip to Abilene

The Abilene paradox, a true story described by Jerry Harvey (1974), is useful for illustrating the problem of managing agreement and the danger of not checking out the 'perceived collective reality' versus the reality of individuals.

STORY: THE ABILENE PARADOX

One afternoon in Coleman, a small town in Texas, Jerry, his wife, and his parents in law were playing dominoes on the back porch under a fan, sipping cold lemonade. It was 104 degrees Fahrenheit, with the wind blowing topsoil, but things were tolerable in the shade and shelter of the porch. Then Jerry's father in law suggested, 'Let's drive to Abilene for dinner.' Jerry didn't want to go in the dust in an un-air-conditioned 1958 car, but his wife said, 'Sounds like a great idea', her mother agreed, so Jerry kept his misgivings to himself.

As a result they made the hot, sticky and dusty 100-mile round trip, and four hours later returned tired and irritable. It then materialized that none of them had really wanted to go. 'I didn't want to go, I just suggested it in case you were bored,' said the father in law. As a group these four people were at the 'norming' stage of group development (described in *Understanding Facilitation*, Chapter 8) where they did not feel they could openly disagree or 'rock the boat'.

For family members read 'organizational members':

- As individuals, they were enjoying themselves: in other words, 'individually in private' they agreed they were enjoying themselves.
- As individuals, they would have preferred to stay put in the shade: that is, 'individually in private' they agreed that was the best solution to how to spend a hot day.
- They failed to communicate their true feelings and desires, leading to a misperceived 'collective reality', when each said, 'Yes, let's go'.
- They made a decision based on inaccurate and invalid information.
- As a result they were frustrated, angry, irritated, and blamed one another for a poor decision.

- They failed to manage agreement, through inability to manage conflicting ideas in an open way.

In 1988, Harvey revisited the issues raised in the Abilene paradox. Although he admitted that terms like 'group tyranny' (that is, group pressure) and the fear of individuals being separated from the group (separation anxiety) did influence the tendency of individuals to conform to the group norm, he delved more deeply. He agreed that individuals in groups do sometimes behave the same, but for different reasons. He proposed that people sometimes think or perceive that there is agreement, when in fact there is not. He believed that if facilitators could encourage participants to explain the thinking behind their suggestions, better group decisions would be made. (This of course goes against the pressure for speedy decisions and action in many workplaces today.)

Harvey tried to show that reality was often different to individuals' perceptions of reality, therefore facilitators must make frequent 'reality checks'. He suggests the following questions which the reader may like to apply to the family in the Abilene story above:

- What action would you really like to take; that is, what feels sensible to you?
- What keeps you from taking such action; that is, what negative fantasies prevent you from doing what you think is sensible?
- What are the best and worst possible outcomes if the desired solution were to be attempted? Or conversely, what are the best or worst possible outcomes if the desired solution is not attempted?

Now these questions presuppose an environment where participants feel safe and there is mutual trust. Consider a round robin where safety and trust are lacking and there are major power differentials. Also consider the work by Moscovici, Mugny and Avermaet (1985) that showed that any behaviour by a minority that conveys self-confidence tends to raise self-doubts amongst the majority, who doubt the so-called 'majority wisdom'. This is especially so if doubts are repeated over time and in a confident manner.

So facilitators in these situations may have to think of ways of ensuring that individuals can put forward responses to the above questions anonymously and synonymously. For example, individuals could respond to the questions posed above on cards, so that all ideas are placed on the table at once. Then participants can speak about the ideas mooted in more detail.

> It is my contention that the inability to cope with (manage) agreement, rather than the inability to cope with (manage) conflict, is the single most pressing issue of modern organizations.
>
> (Harvey, 1988)

Two stories to confront stuck thinking

Stories can be a useful tool to make a point to shift or confront stuck thinking and assumptions.

STORY: POWER AND ASSUMPTIONS

It was a very foggy night in the middle of the ocean. The captain of a ship saw lights ahead and radioed, 'We are heading straight towards you. Pull over.' The reply came, 'No, you pull over.' The captain was irritated. 'I am the captain of a battle-ship. Pull over.'

'Pull over or you will be sorry. I am a lighthouse.'

STORY: POWER OF SYSTEMS THINKING

A battleship needed repair and a specialist plumber was flown in by helicopter to fix the problem. He walked around checking equipment, talking and listening to the crew and the captain about the leak. Then he went over to a pipe, tapped it, and this fixed the problem. He wrote out an invoice for $1,000.

The captain was appalled, and said, 'That's far too much for tapping a pipe.'

The plumber replied, 'Yes. Tapping the pipe cost $5, and the $995 was for know-ing where to tap.'

Decision-making processes

In workshops everyone has to know how decisions are going to be made and why. There is no such thing as one perfect decision-making process. Decision making is about how power will be used and/or shared with the group. Remember Arstein's ladder of participation, described earlier: if decision-making power is not going to be shared, then participants need to know, otherwise trust is lost.

One of the legacies of the scientific revolution is the emphasis on so-called logical, linear, rational thinking. However, creative and intuitive thinking are just as necessary, and what may be considered logical and rational on the surface often is not. In recent years it has been reported that some organizations have contacted clairvoyants to aid decision making.

For centuries, the ancient Chinese art of feng shui (pronounced 'foong-shway') has been used to alter people's environment, homes, offices and hearts, to align them with the universe and to instigate changes in their tides of fortune. International organizations in Hong Kong, Taiwan and Singapore often bring in feng shui experts to decide on 'good' office locations, design workspaces to minimize conflict, and so on. Western entrepreneurs like Richard Branson also utilize feng shui (Skinner, 2001).

Consensus is often mooted as being the best decision making process. However, facilitators who strive for this need to negotiate alternative decision-making strategies at the outset of workshops, should a consensus be impossible. When individuals are weary they often resort to voting, but is a 51 per cent to 49 per cent vote enough to ensure that all will support a proposed solution? Some groups agree that a super-majority of 75 per cent of votes is necessary to pass a motion. If there is not a substantial majority, perhaps it is better to wait until time clarifies the issue.

Facilitators need to help the participants listen to the voice of minorities, as these people's ideas may be ahead of their time. The film *Twelve Angry Men* is a very interesting depiction of a jury where one person eventually sways the whole group.

Some participants are just not aware of the variety of decision-making methods possible, so Table 11.8 may be useful.

Table 11.8   Advantages and disadvantages of decision-making methods

Methods of decision making	Advantages	Disadvantages
Authority rule without discussion	Applies more to administrative needs. Useful for simple, routine decisions. Should be used when very little time is available to make the decision, when group members expect the designated leader to make the decision, and when there is a lack of skills and information among group members to make the decision in any other way.	One person is not a good resource for every decision. . . Advantages of group interaction are lost. No commitment is developed for implementing the decision by other group members. Resentment and disagreement may result in sabotage and deterioration of group effectiveness. Resources of other members are not used.
Expert	Useful when the expertise of one person is so far superior to that of all other group members that little is to be gained by discussion; should be used when the need for membership action in implementing the decision is slight.	It may be difficult to determine who the expert is. No commitment is built for implementing the decision. Advantages of group interaction are lost. Resentment and disagreement may result in sabotage and deterioration of group effectiveness. Resources of other members are not used.
Average of members' opinions	Useful in a situation where it is difficult to get group members together to talk, when the decision is so urgent that there is no time for group discussion, when member commitment is not necessary for implementing the decision, and when a lack of skills and information exists among group members to make the decision any other way. Applicable to simple, routine decisions.	There is not enough interaction among group members for them to gain from each other's resources and to get the benefits of group discussion. No commitment is built for implementing the decision. Unresolved conflict and controversy may damage future group effectiveness.
Authority rule after discussion ie consultation	Uses the resources of the group more than previous methods; gains some of the benefits of group discussion.	Does not develop commitment for implementing the decision. Does not resolve the controversies and conflicts among group members. Tends to create situations in which group members either compete to impress the designated leader or tell the leader what they think he/she wants to hear.
Majority vote	Can be used when sufficient time is lacking for decision by consensus or when the	Usually leaves an alienated minority, which damages future group effectiveness.

Table 11.8   *(continued)*

Methods of decision making	Advantages	Disadvantages
	decision is not so important that consensus needs to be used, and when complete member commitment is not necessary for implementing the decision. Closes discussion on issues that are not highly important for the group.	Relevant resources of many group members may be lost. Commitment for implementing the decision is not totally present. Full benefit of group interaction is not obtained. May need to determine what level constitutes majority, ie 51% or 70%.
Straw vote	A straw vote can be used to assist consensus decision making to test the lie of the land. A variation is to ask participants to show degrees of agreement or disagreement by holding a hand in one of four different positions. In one group I noted that some members were upset as when everyone agreed, it looked like the Nazi salute. As a result participants agreed to vote with the palm upwards.	Not anonymous.
Dot vote	Must discuss and cluster before voting otherwise similar ideas spread the votes. Everyone is given a number of sticky dots to place beside items of their choice, one dot per item. Useful for finding groups of ideas, eg top A, middle B and last C grouping. Useful for straw poll at beginning to see what major agreements are already reached, followed by dialogue, questioning, clarifying. Number of dots determined by agreement with group, or number of items divided by 3–5. Visual and energizing technique, gets dialogue going.	Not anonymous unless items are numbered, participants write the numbers of their choice on the dots, and the dots are mixed up so people do not place their own dots. It is still voting, ie winners and losers. May be very frustrating for a participant who has an idea ahead of its time which only receives his/her vote (see multi-voting).
Multi vote	Rounds of voting. Different coloured dots for each round representing different criteria, eg: ● the most important; ● commitment and energy: I'll volunteer; ● sounds intriguing, need more discussion; ● the most difficult place to start; ● the easiest place to start; ● the best place to start.	Not anonymous unless items are numbered, participants write the numbers of their choice on the dots and the dots are mixed up so people do not place their own dots. It is still voting, ie winners and losers. May be very frustrating for a participant who has an idea ahead of its time which only receives his/her vote.

Table 11.8 *(continued)*

Methods of decision making	Advantages	Disadvantages
	Participants decide to start on things that are both most important and easy.	
Decision by minority	Can be used when everyone cannot meet to make a decision; when the group is under such time pressure that it must delegate responsibility to a committee; when only a few members have any relevant resources; when broad member commitment is not needed to implement the decision. Useful for simple routine decisions.	Does not utilize the resources of many group members. Does not establish widespread commitment for implementing the decision. Unresolved conflict and controversy may damage future group effectiveness. Not much benefit from group interaction.
Consensus	Produces an innovative, creative and high-quality decision; elicits commitment by all members to implement the decision; uses the resources of all members; the future decision-making ability of the group is enhanced; useful in making serious, important and complex decisions to which all members are to be committed.	Takes a great deal of time and psychological energy and a high level of communication skills. Time pressure must be minimal and no emergency in progress. Win–win.
Compromise	Participants attempt to 'split the difference' or to say, 'I'll give in to you this time, but you owe me one'.	Differences suppressed. Mediocre decisions, lose–lose. No synergy. Lack of understanding of how people really think.
Spontaneous agreement	Fast, easy. Unites participants. Feeling of accomplishment. Look for symptoms of the 'Abilene paradox' and 'groupthink' and reality versus 'perceived reality'.	Too fast. Lack of discussion. Quick gut reaction. Lemmings: 'Let's do it'.
Multi-criteria decision making or decision grids	Very useful to systematically analyse and compare the pluses, minuses, costs and other criteria of different options. Useful in complex and controversial situations. Sometimes aided by software packages: www.logicaldecisions.com	'Weightings' of criteria may adversely affect decisions. Using numbers to express subjective values may not be possible.
Feng shui, fortune telling, stars	Leaves decision making to someone gifted or skilled in these arts	May be regarded as invalid by some people

Source: adapted from Johnson (1997: 245–46)

For an in-depth discussion on 'Voting with dots' see the summary compiled by Mike Dennison (2000) from an electronic discussion on group facilitation.

> After your group votes (dots etc) run the result by your brains. Even though you have been 'objective', the result may not make any sense.
>
> Anon

As is shown above, there is no one perfect mode of decision making, and all the various forms of voting have their limitations. Next I will outline two processes to help groups come to consensus.

Consensus process

Definitions

Consensus is 'A state of mutual agreement among members of a group where all legitimate concerns of individuals have been addressed to the satisfaction of the group (Saint and Lawson, 1994: 21).

A consensus meeting has more to do with intent and spirit. Participants do not have to think the same way, but must be willing to try to see issues from someone else's perspective. The following stages are adapted from the work of Saint and Lawson (1994).

Stage 1: Understand the proposal

- Clarify the proposal (which should have been circulated well beforehand).
- Ask participants to state legitimate concerns, ie those that may adversely affect the organization or common good.
- If no concerns: **first call for consensus**. If concerns are raised, move to stage 2.

Stage 2: Resolve concerns

- List all concerns on wall minutes; avoid repetition.
- Resolve concerns by thinking cooperatively to integrate concerns into the proposal. Or explain why the proposal as stated is not in conflict with the group's values. See if those with concerns will 'stand aside': have concerns, feel heard, but can live with it. The concerns must be noted in the minutes.
- **Second call for consensus.**
- Evaluate group purpose and values (if no consensus and concerned members are unwilling to stand aside). Check how unresolved concerns fit with the group's purpose and values.
- **Third call for consensus.**
- Facilitator identifies one of the following:
  - person unwilling to withdraw concern or stand aside;
  - concerned member withdraws the concern or stands aside;
  - member withdraws the concern based on group purpose evaluation.

- Evaluate individual motives. Any further impasse may be caused by ego or vested interests regarding authority, rights, personality conflicts, competition or lack of trust. If these occur the group cannot proceed with the consensus process, as trust is a prerequisite to the consensus process.
- **Final call for consensus.**

Stage 3: Closing options are examined

- Contract for more time.
- Presenter withdraws proposal.
- Concerned member withdraws or stands aside and allows the proposal to pass.
- Conduct a non-binding straw poll.
- Send proposal to a subgroup to modify proposal.
- Create community building if there have been personality clashes, or even use formal mediation.
- Conduct a supermajority vote, ie to avoid 'the tyranny of the majority' and the 'tyranny of the minority': a vote requires, for example, over 65 per cent majority for passage.

LENS process

A deceptively simple, but clever, visual process for consensus decision making is the Lens process.

Author/background

The acronym 'LENS' stands for Leadership Effectiveness in New Strategies. The process was developed by the Institute of Cultural Affairs (ICA) in the United States, and documented by Laura Spencer (1989). It is also known as the ToP workshop method (ToP = technology of participation). (See also the ORID process which was also developed by this group in Chapter 3). The aim of the ICA is to involve all levels of workers in participatory consensus decision making.

Purpose/rationale

The LENS process is most suited to issues that have many answers, decisions or options. It is designed to enable consensus decision making using visual techniques in the form of cards. The card process has similar elements to the Metaplanning card sorts developed in West Germany by the Schnelle brothers (1979) after the Second World War. The LENS technique may be used for strategic planning, team building, mission planning, or for teaching a new concept using the experience of the group members. The facilitator needs the help of a scribe who can write quickly and clearly on the cards.

Size of group

This technique may be used with groups of up to 40 participants. Larger groups are possible with support facilitators and modifications to the process.

Materials

About 40 index coloured cards at least 210 mm x 150 mm. About 10 cards of a different colour for headings. Alternatively use A4 paper cut in half or large sticky-backed notes. Felt pens. Masking tape. Adhesive gum. Flip chart paper. A large blank wall.

Venue/layout

Participants sit in a semicircle facing the facilitator and the wall. The scribe sits at the side and numbers all cards clearly before the start of the workshop.

Time

The time is dependent on the complexity of the issue and the levels of cooperation of the participants to reach consensus.

Stages

To illustrate this process I will give an example where the LENS process was being used as a teaching tool to enable group facilitators to draw up a code of key elements to remember when consulting with internal or external clients.

1 Context

The facilitator introduces the workshop by explaining the context, purpose and proposed length of the workshop, the LENS process and consensus decision making: that is, reaching a decision that everyone can live and work with.

Formulate the focus question

The facilitator asks participants to phrase the question or purpose of the meeting. All questions are recorded on flip chart paper, for example:

- What are the attributes of a consultant?
- What are the skills, knowledge and values needed for effective consultant?
- What are the desirable elements in the consulting process?
- If you saw effective consulting happening, what would be going on?

The participants discuss and choose the question that most fits their purpose. This question is clearly displayed on flip chart paper and should be visible at all times.

2   Individual brainstorming

The facilitator explains the rules of brainstorming:

- Generate as many ideas as possible.
- Include wild and imaginative ideas.
- No discussion or evaluation.
- Go for quantity not quality of ideas (see Brainstorming section for more information).

The facilitator invites participants individually to list responses to the focus question on paper on their own. The facilitator invites each person in turn to contribute one idea, choosing the best ideas first. Explanation may be called for, but no evaluation is allowed. The idea is captured by the scribe on card and displayed on the wall in sequence. No discussion is allowed. When between 20 and 30 ideas have been collected, the facilitator stops the process. This should allow at least two ideas per person.

3   Organize: cluster the ideas

Participants group the ideas first into pairs and then into bigger clusters. As the cards have been numbered, this process is speeded up, as cards are quickly identified by their number. The facilitator holds the two cards together and 'listens to the energy' of the group: positive 'ums' or 'yes' versus 'groans', 'no' or silence that may indicate thoughtfulness, confusion and/or disagreement. Probing is necessary to get individuals to explain why they see connections between ideas. Be prepared to move ideas to other clusters or to form new clusters.

4   Name the new clusters

The group chooses a heading and the scribe writes this on the other coloured card.

5   Reflect and rank the categories

During this ranking process ideas are evaluated for their importance or worth. This stage is optional but is especially useful if the group is working on missions and plans.

6 Create an image

This stage is optional. It is, however, useful as an aide memoire to construct a diagrammatic representation of the key ideas. These visuals may then be later displayed in the workplace. These may be represented as a 'rocket' shape or a mandala or circular diagram. The first item at the front of the rocket shape or at the centre of the mandala is the most important. See Figure 11.7.

Rocket shape

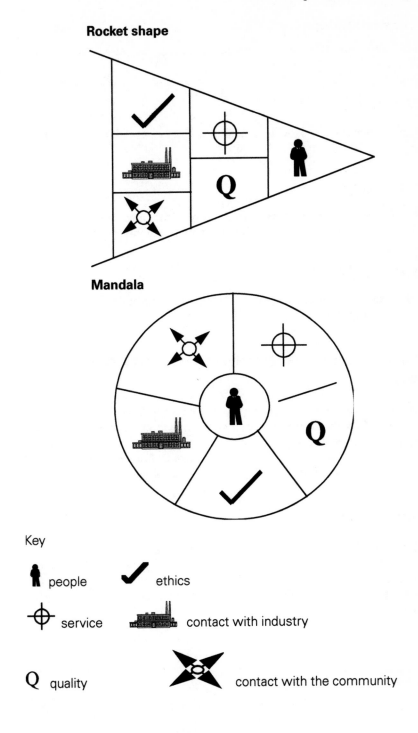

Mandala

Key

† people   **✔ ethics**

⊕ service   **▄▄▄ contact with industry**

Q quality   **✦ contact with the community**

Figure 11.7 Visual techniques

Discuss next steps

The facilitator asks, 'What struck you during the process?' and 'Where to from here?'

Outcomes

Participants feel a sense of achievement in that they have all contributed to a plan.

Advantages

As this process focuses on consensus decision making at all stages, there is usually commitment from the participants to implementing the agreed plans.

Disadvantages

Consensus decision making takes time. Participants who have a predominantly 'activist' learning style may wish to work faster.

Evaluation of solutions and processes used

At the end of workshop it is always necessary to build in time to reflect and evaluate not only the solutions, but also the processes used to reach those solutions. If participants complain that time plans were not adhered to, you may need to remind them that time spent in the Groan Zone was in actual fact productive, even though it may have felt uncomfortable.

Conclusion

The purpose of this chapter was to give an overview of a wide variety of structures and processes to enable individuals and groups to learn about problem-solving and decision-making processes. In the next chapter the problem-solving theme continues with a focus on processes for developing workable relationships.

12

Developing workable relationships

> A community is like an orchestra: each instrument is beautiful when it plays alone, but when they all play together, each given its own weight in turn, the result is even more beautiful. A community is like a garden full of flowers, shrubs and trees, each helps to give life to the other.
>
> Vanier (1979)

Introduction

We live in extraordinary times. The advances in human genome research tells us that out of the 30,000 known genes in the human body we are similar to other races across the planet in 99 per cent of these; we have so much in common. However, despite our similarities we cannot prevent conflict: it is part of life, caused by our colourful diversity of values, ideas, motives, personalities and also by the inequities of wealth, power and resources. It is how we manage to build societal systems to prevent and manage conflict that is important.

Facilitation is really about peace building, peacemaking and helping to develop 'workable relationships'. The topic of conflict resolution has been covered extremely well by various authors. My favourites include:

- *Everyone Can Win*, a simple easy to read text (Cornelius and Faire, 1989).
- *The Mediator's Handbook*, an easy how-to-do-it introduction to mediation (Beer and Stief, 1997).
- *Non-Violent Communication: A language of compassion* (Rosenberg, 1999).
- *Conflict Resolution Trainers' Manual* is full of activities for facilitators (Hollier, Murray and Cornelius, 1993). This comprehensive file of resources was developed by the Conflict Resolution Network in New South Wales, which also has a useful newsletter, and Web site: http://www.crnhq.org

The focus of this chapter is on:

- principles for developing workable relationships;
- community participation (terms, frameworks, choosing processes);

- community processes and models;
- restorative justice;
- open space technology;
- stories of social change.

Principles for developing workable relationships

Here are some suggestions for building the foundations of workable relationships in group work and communities. I am sure you will be able to add more:

- Collaboratively set, refer to and develop ground rules.
- Attend to process, make the process visible, have metaprocess discussions.
- Make needs and concerns explicit (see conflict mapping process in Hollier, Murray and Cornelius, 1993).
- Make roles and responsibilities and boundaries explicit.
- Have fun and celebrate achievements.
- Use 'principled negotiation' (see Chapter 1 and also Web site: http://www.colorado.edu/conflict/peace/treatment/pricneg.htm).
- Use processes that seek win–win solutions and healing rather than hurting.
- Each person takes responsibility for his or her own actions.
- Each person finds ways to use his/her powers in a way that helps the group and/or community to develop and grow.
- Recognize each other's right to see the world differently.
- Have a variety of methods for resolving conflict.
- Recognize points of discomfort early and invest time in communicating with each other.
- Utilize appreciative inquiry, a strengths-based approach to help people look at what is working, rather than focus always on negatives (Hammond, 1996).

Community participation: how we do it

Community participation has been occurring, in various forms, since people started to live and hunt together in groups. The social upheavals in the 1960s led to a rise in expectations and demands for involvement in decision making in universities, bureaucracies, and communities in many Western countries.

'Co-operacy' is a word that Hunter, Bailey and Taylor (1997) coined to describe the technology of collective or consensus decision making as distinct from democracy (decisions by the majority) and autocracy (decisions by one leader). They see co-operacy as being represented by networks, teams, cooperative organizations (as opposed to hierarchical organizations), communities and virtual communities, and juries using collective decision making. They see this as a developing trend in certain areas:

> Co-operacy is not yet an integrated system of thought or a coherent phil-
> osophy. It may be this in the future but so far we have only some pieces of the
> jigsaw. . . What we do know is that the old ways of doing things are breaking
> down or, in some cases, no longer relevant. New ways that honour rather than
> debase humanity need to be found.
>
> (Hunter, Bailey and Taylor 1997)

One method to develop co-operacy is for facilitators to help participants to
engage in 'dialogue' rather than in 'debate' (see Chapter 8).

Whose knowledge/opinions count?

There is now an inherent tension in contemporary society between using
'experts' and community/decision making. Constructive community participation is based on the philosophy that:

- citizens have the right to be informed early about a policy/programme/
  project that will affect them;
- those interested and affected have a right to be consulted, heard and
  responded to by the proponent and where possible involve din decisions
  that affect them;
- all people are intrinsically of equal worth;
- difference is normal and should be valued, honoured and celebrated;
- resolution of public concern will require a mutual education process and
  joint problem-solving or conflict resolution activities;
- while some participation is advisory, recommendations cannot be disreg-
  arded lightly;
- public participation contributes to social justice objectives, 'accountability'
  and 'responsible government' to create a more inclusive and equitable
  society;
- open participation builds citizen capacity, and learning about responsible
  citizenship and strengthens democratic institutions;
- open participation builds trust between communities and government;
- communities have a right to be involved in resolving and preventing crime;
- communities have a right to be involved in setting up learning centres so
  that learning is not confined to formal institutions which may be too
  expensive or intimidating for some people;
- transparency and accountability are worthwhile contributors to 'civil
  society'.

Participation is an integral part of many projects in both the public and private
sectors. Engineers, planners and environmental scientists now have little choice,
as communities have the power to stall and even sink programmes. It is not a
question of whether to involve the public, but really to question:

- 'To what extent should the public be involved?'
- 'Who decides to what extent?'
- 'How will the public be involved?'

For managers and government officials need to behave more as 'facilitators' than as 'experts', and government departments and organizations need to hire non-aligned process facilitators to implement a variety of techniques to enable productive interaction.

In the West, public participation strategies tend to cater for the English-speaking white middle classes. We need to be creative to ensure that everyone has a voice. There is no one process or recipe for success. Triangulation is necessary to gain all perspectives and to ensure that the 'silent majority' has a voice.

> The idea of citizen participation is a little like eating spinach: no one is against it in principle because it is good for you. Participation of the governed in their government is, in theory, the cornerstone of democracy: a revered idea that is vigorously applauded by virtually everyone. The applause is reduced to polite handclaps, however, when this principle is advocated by the have-not blacks, Mexican-Americans, Puerto Ricans, Indians, Eskimos and whites. And when the have-nots define participation as redistribution of power, the American consensus on the fundamental principle explodes into many shades of outright racial, ethnic, ideological, and political opposition (Arnstein, 1969:176).

The e-divide (electronic divide) is again giving some sectors of society a voice, but restricted access and lack of resources and skills limit the chance for others to be heard through these media. In a pluralistic society it is important to remember that it is unrealistic to think that a project will gain the full acceptance of all the groups involved, but provided people are involved in a process that is open and transparent, they are more likely to feel there has been 'fair play' for the community as a whole, even if they do not achieve their own personal goals.

Terms

Words like 'community', 'participation', and 'power holders' mean many different things to different people. As such these concepts can become the source of misunderstandings, so I will first expand on these terms.

Community

The word 'community' includes the word 'unity', and yet in one small community there may be people with many different values and interests. Definitions and examples of 'community' vary. A community may be regarded as a group of people or 'stakeholders' with similar interests: perhaps a group who live with or near one another, have similar interests/beliefs/values, work or play together, are of similar gender or age, or have similar services provided, used or needed. Some strive to 'build community', and question whether many of us in the Western world really know what it means to be part of a really interconnected community. In urban areas, communities are sometimes very difficult to identify. One person may belong to many overlapping communities with competing and/or conflicting interests. There are 'multistakeholders'.

Questions that might be asked by facilitators include:

- Who decides what the community needs? What does the community want?
- What are the boundaries of the community? Does everyone agree on those boundaries, or are they imposed by part of that community or a group from outside?
- Whose knowledge counts (Chambers, 1983)?

Power holders

Power holders, like community members, are not a homogeneous group. Representatives of government hold 'legitimate' or position power. This gives them access to and power over the use of resources (money, skills, equipment and so on). Community members also hold power, including the power of passive resistance and non-compliance, and the power of passion in their cause. See *Facilitating Empowerment* (Hogan, 2000) for exercises and a detailed description of 60 power bases.

Community discernment

> Community discernment is essentially a way of enabling people to overcome their own passions and ideas, and so to understand as clearly as possible the advantages and disadvantages of a particular project or situations.
>
> (Vanier, 1979)

We achieve 'community discernment' by asking everyone to look at the positives, negatives and shades of grey about proposed ideas, using processes to aid presentations, listening and analysis. Indeed, individuals do change their opinions, as citizens' juries have shown.

Participation

In *Understanding Facilitation* Chapter 4, I introduced Sherry Arnstein's ladder of participation (1969). Arnstein's seminal work has been translated into several languages. Arnstein showed that participation is not a neutral process. Her 'ladder' may be applied to bureaucracies, government departments, universities and religious organizations.

Participation has at least two meanings (Bohm, Factor and Garrett, 1991): to take part in (speaking, joining in physically) and to partake of (listening, joining in mentally). Unfortunately to many people, participation implies speaking only.

Limitation of the Arnstein ladder of participation

The metaphor of a ladder implies that 'higher is better', and that the more participation is involved, the more power citizens have. However, this may not be the case. Projects may require a number of different methods at different stages. The ladder assumes that there are two distinct groups, 'haves' and 'have nots', whereas in reality there are many groups. The ladder could create unrealistic expectations; it is not possible for everyone to participate in every-thing. Arnstein cautions that in the real world there may be 150 levels with blurred boundaries, rather than rungs of a ladder. Participation can be obtained in many ways. However, Arnstein was aware of the possibilities of corruption by power holders, who have in the past delegated the responsibility of a project to the lowest levels of participation, but without the requisite resources.

A–Z process

We need to teach young people how to participate in their families, schools and communities. It does not come naturally. I developed an A–Z questioning exercise when working with long-term unemployed young adults (Hogan, 1988b). The exercise was developed in response to the need to initiate discourse on the meaning of 'participation'. The exercise encourages individuals to open up the meaning of a concept in a quick and non-threatening way. The process starts with an open question: 'What does "participation" mean and involve?'

I wrote the letters of the alphabet in order down the left-hand side of sheets of flip chart paper, and left people to add words that were triggered. (X,Y and Z triggered some interesting words). Students used the letters of the alphabet to trigger any words that came into their heads. For example, if exploring the concept of 'participation', the letter 'A' might trigger words like: authority, anger, anxiety and altogether.

The outcomes of this process are increased interaction between students and lecturers about concepts. I also noted a 'perceptual gap' in many areas (see Table 12.1).

Table 12.1   Perceptions of participation

Young adults' perceptions	Lecturers' perceptions
Being there	Empowerment
Joining in	Learning to learn
Answering questions	Setting own goals

The exercise opened up useful discussions, including exploring the issues of 'silent participation'. One quiet student who participated in the vocal sense very little wrote to the course coordinator later, voicing how much she had learnt from the course and how much more confident she felt as a result and the activities she was now engaged in. This is why I get very frustrated with lecturers who insist on giving marks for 'participation' in class.

Questions that might be asked include:

- What does participation mean and involve?
- What are the blocks to participation?
- What level of participation is required, and by whom, at what stage of a project?

A useful Web site is 'A–Z of effective participation': http://www.partnerships. org.uk/guide/AZpartic.html#Community

Blocks to participation

There are many blocks to achieving genuinely high levels of participation. First of all the 'isms' like racism, sexism, ageism, and paternalism have tried to silence large sectors of the community. Second, participation requires enormous resources like time, money, energy and commitment from both the power holders and community members (the latter are frequently unpaid for their time and inputs). Third, it requires patience and communication skills: active listening, empathy and understanding on all sides.

There is often resistance by some community leaders to sharing power, and some community members feel reluctance, distrust and alienation in taking on the responsibility of being involved in decision making: 'How come you are asking me to give up my time to come and talk today when I voted for politicians and they get paid for doing this?' The majority of schools still do not teach students how to participate in decision making because it is time-consuming, muddy, and perhaps because some would not know how to go about it (Hammond, 1996). At times residents may be 'co-opted' to a committee, but the implications are, 'You were there, you participated in the meeting, therefore you agree with the outcomes'.

Issues

There are many issues in community participation:

- Problems change, grow or decline and new ones arise during the project.
- It should not be assumed that representatives of lobby groups and/or communities fully represent their community or fully inform their community.
- There is great potential for filtering and massaging information by the media. So fully inform and involve the media and if necessary write press releases rather than asking a reporter to write stories for you.
- Language: voice, writing and presentation skills.
- Technology: access and skills.
- Public involvement does not ensure public support.
- It is almost impossible to please everyone. Sometimes some people lose out.

Wealth in the community

How can we measure community wealth? The King of Bhutan suggested some years ago that we should measure 'gross national happiness'. There are many ways of measuring community wealth; unfortunately, however, it is the financial aspects that are given undue emphasis. 'Unpaid aspects of work in society such as the work of volunteers, homemakers, parents and carers do not "count"' (Cox, 1995). Yet remove them and society as we know it would collapse. 'Social capital refers to the processes between people which establish networks, norms and social trust and facilitate coordination and cooperation for mutual benefit'

(Cox, 1995) and effective community participation processes help to build social capital. But first it is important to build trust.

Table 12.2   Ways of measuring wealth and capital

Capital	Description
Financial	Profit, growth, gross national product, money markets etc
Physical	Trees: native forest and plantation forests, clean fresh and sea water, clean air, energy etc
Human	Skills, knowledge, creativity, learning and research
Social	Trust, networks, cooperation, time together, healthy risk-taking and reciprocity, civic virtues

Source: adapted from Cox (1995)

Trust is a fragile commodity which takes a long time to nurture and grow, but can be destroyed in an instant. Trust and commitment are part of the development of social capital. In Western countries, people tend to regard participation in decision making as part of their democratic rights as citizens. They are more highly educated than ever before, and are often sceptical of what politicians at all levels do and do not do. They may not want or be available to put in the time and energy needed, but they get very upset if something happens without their being at the very minimum informed 'what' is happening and 'why' it is happening.

Choosing the level of community participation in decision making

Facilitators and community planners are faced with a number of decisions regarding which process/es to use with communities. First, who chooses the facilitators and community planners, and what criteria are used? Second, the choice of process/s depends on the:

- purpose and/or problem, its size, complexity and urgency;
- amount and type of information required;
- stakeholders and their location;
- context, including the history of the problem (ie what has been used before);
- resources available: time, people, money, venues etc.

It is useful to work as a team, including people who have lived or have experience with the community (ie people who have access to the unwritten stories/information from the past).

The public participation matrix

Les Robinson (2002) developed an assessment questionnaire inspired by a similar tool developed by the International Association for Public Participation.

According to Robinson, the choice of a community involvement process depends on your assessment of two factors: first, the risk inherent in the situation (such as the potential for negative environmental or social impact, or the risk of community conflict); and second, the complexity of the information that needs to be digested before informed participation is possible. Here are some questions to help you evaluate these factors.

Inherent risk

How do you rate the potential for conflict with the community over this decision?
Low   Medium   High

How do you rate the potential for social, environmental, or financial damage if the wrong decision is made?
Low   Medium   High

How many unknowns are there in the current decision-making equation?
None   A few   Many

Complexity of information

How much information needs to be communicated to the community for them to participate?
A few simple facts   A detailed proposal   A significant amount of
                                             technical data

How much learning is required by the participants before they can be expected to make an informed decision?
Low   Medium   High

How many abstract or technical concepts need to be digested before an informed decision can be made?
None   A few   Many

Interpretation

If most of your answers are in the left hand boxes, then *consult* methods may be sufficient.

If your answers are scattered between the left, centre and right-hand boxes, then *involve* methods may be sufficient.

If most of your answers are in the right-hand boxes, then you should consider using *partner* techniques to minimize your risk and maximize the amount of knowledge and perspectives brought into the decision-making process.

The matrix in Figure 12.1 is a guide to particular community involvement methods which may be suited to the risk and complexity of your situation.

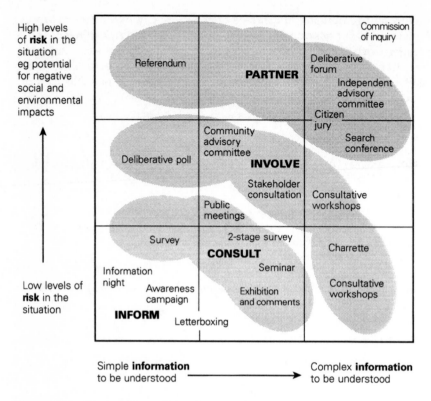

Figure 12.1   The public participation matrix

The facilitator

As a facilitator you need to be clear about the roles you are engaged to perform, which might be:

- facilitator;
- cultural interpreter (between groups);
- advocate;
- mentor;
- mediator;
- liaison person;
- shuttle negotiator;
- change agent;
- conveyor of information;
- other?

You need to be clear about your own stance:

- Do you believe in the philosophy of public participation?
- Where do you stand (values, beliefs, motives)? No facilitators can pretend to be totally bias-free.

- Are there any areas/issues that you cannot be involved in?
- What do you want to achieve by working in a participatory way?
- Who will have the final say over decisions?
- How ready/able are people, organizations, and communities to work in a participatory way? Will their rhetoric be matched by their actions?
- Is training needed?

Facilitating community participation in contentious issues is exhilarating and complex. First I will describe some research on how facilitators can best open community meetings to get participants on side. Second, I will describe the open space technology process.

Building trust and rapport

> People everywhere need to be treated as 'people of account'.
>
> Dr John von Sturmer

Community meetings are not easy, and facilitators need to build and maintain empathy, rapport and connectedness with participants *and*, over a period of time, trust. We all build empathy in different ways, there are no hard and fast rules. Community meetings require a tremendous amount of prior preparation and planning. The more people you have met beforehand, the better. People need to be informed about proposed community changes early on, so that when a community meeting is announced it does not come as a shock.

Communicate, communicate, communicate

> The two words 'information' and 'communication' are often used inter-changeably, but they signify quite different things. Information is giving out; communication is getting through.
>
> Sydney J Harris

See the 'Coke' model in Chapter 2.

Layout of meetings

I have often noticed the way in which organizers hide behind desks (often placed strategically on platforms above participants) at community meetings. One of the best meetings, I attended was where chairs were set out in a con-centric hexagon, and microphones were set up at each corner so that people could easily reach a microphone and speak when the need arose. At times it is useful to 'turn the table' on the usual process of community meetings by disseminating information beforehand, then inviting participants to bring along questions. Have a panel ready and well briefed to answer them.

Community meetings may release old hurts and frustrations, as illustrated in the following story.

STORY: A COMMUNITY PARK

In 1994 I was invited to facilitate a community meeting for the City of Murray. It would involve local residents and councillors in the development of Green Park. The small 'park' was at the time an area of sand with some tall Norfolk Island pine trees and a primary school on one end. The school principal was openly rigid in his vision: he wanted the park made into an asphalt running track for his school. The planning meetings were called by the City of Murray community officer, Janet. The principal and interested teachers came. I was at once impressed by Janet's communication skills. Outside, she spent seemingly ages just talking to the principal about nothing in particular. Then I saw the rapport building. I realized how skilful she was. She found out that the principal's daughter was a drama student. We wanted to involve the primary school children in the planning process, and Janet immediately invited the principal's daughter to undertake drama sessions with the children in the space. Next the art teacher took over, using multimedia-modelling resources with the children to enable them to build images of what they wanted in their park.

A week before the community meeting, the schoolteachers focused their curricula on the park. I visited the art class and saw primary school children absorbed in building small scenes, rock pools and 'little areas where we can have secrets'.

The Saturday community meeting day arrived. Local families filed into the school library that had been specially set up with chairs for the meeting. The children's models were displayed around the edge. An artist was on hand to draw the images that came out of the visualization session. People arrived slowly, and I had time to talk to the kids. They seemed so small (after university students), so I crouched down to talk to them, and made a point of giving them nametags and shaking their hands in welcome.

I planned to start the workshop by a short, relaxing sensory walk around the park. So, after the official welcome and introductions, we all went outside. I thought the walk would be an appropriate warm-up and said, 'Use all your senses. Close your eyes. Listen. What do you hear? What would you like to hear? What do you see? What textures, colours, smells would be appropriate for your park?'

We passed a small green electricity substation that I had not noticed before. Suddenly a man loudly roared, 'When are *they* going to do something about that thing? It's an eyesore. I've been to these kind of bloody meetings before.' This man was storming against the council, but transferred his anger on to me. I was taken aback by the outburst. The spell was broken completely. I asked him to explain. He continued, 'Nothing ever gets done. I don't know why my wife and I bother. This local council is a complete waste of time.'

I inwardly cursed the councillors for not briefing me in previous meetings about this issue. I invited the man to have his say, and we all had a look around the space and, rather more quickly than I anticipated, retreated to the school library for the workshop. My mind was racing.

Inside, the tirade against the council and me continued. I wrote up the issues onto flip chart paper. My inner voice kept saying, 'They are angry at the council, not at you. Now get the issues onto the flip chart paper.' I then acted as mediator and asked for the council members present to give their point of view. Ralph, a council employee, was professionally unruffled and explained it was not within the council's power to remove a substation; they had to negotiate with the Electricity Commission.

Eventually the steam was released and the anger started to dissipate. I realized it was time to revert to the planning meeting. But how could I get the audience into a brainstorming mood for creative suggestions? You could have cut the atmosphere with a knife. I started to explain the idea of having an artist to add to the wonderful models the children had already exhibited. I went through the rules of brainstorming, then asked the question, 'Can you think of as many different ideas as possible for Green Park?' I waited and waited. Silence. I prayed. Suddenly a small child in the front row piped up, 'Some rocks'. I thanked her and the artist started to draw. We were off. The mood changed and the children took the lead.

To this day, I am grateful that I had met the children during the week while they built their models, and greeted and gave them all nametags. The latter was not planned, but it reminded me that everyone in a community meeting counts, no matter how young they are. After the meeting I spoke to the council members, who apologized for not briefing me about the lack of action resulting from previous community meetings before their time. The principal did not get his running track, but he was happy with the results. In time the park was landscaped with native trees and bushes. Large, interesting rocks and boulders formed interesting nooks and crannies just like the children had modelled, that is, places to sit and share secrets.

Community participatory processes/models

There are now a plethora of processes that have been developed for community participation. See Wates (2000) and the Web sites listed on page 473. Community facilitators require a wide variety of processes in their toolkit.

Restorative justice

Forms of conflict resolution in which a third party helps disputants resolve their conflicts and come to their own decisions have probably been practised since the existence of three or more people on earth (Folberg and Taylor, 1984). A restorative justice conference is an interactive, structured meeting between victims, offenders, their families and friends, and other community members directly affected by the offence. Conferencing is a straightforward, practical, problem-solving process. It enables people to resolve their own problems, by giving them a guided, emotionally sensitive forum and process.

Terms

First of all, the type of conferencing described in general terms here appears under a number of different names around the world and in different contexts, including 'transformative justice', 'real justice', 'community conferencing' and 'family group conferencing'. Also the facilitator is sometimes referred to as a 'convenor'. For the purpose of this chapter the term 'restorative justice' is used.

For a detailed comparison of different restorative justice models, see McCold and Wachtel (1998).

One issue with merely restoring a community to how it was before the crime is that society remains the same. The theory behind 'transformative justice' is to find ways of developing the community to make it safe for all, and to address the underlying injustices which often create ideal conditions for crime: that is, to work towards wider societal change and to prevent crime in the first place, as well as to minimize reoffending.

Background and rationale

Restorative justice is about restorative processes and restorative values. It has its roots in the peacemaking processes and healing circles of North America indigenous peoples, the Maori marae justice systems, South African traditional systems and Celtic Brehon Laws (Consedine, 1995; Strang and Braithwaite, 2001). Communities used to take responsibility for keeping the peace, bringing together offenders and victims, and administering penalties when the well being of the community was been threatened by antisocial behaviour. The purpose of the meeting is to discuss the offence, decide how best to repair the harm, and 'combine the achievement of some degree of emotional restoration for victims, often some form of reparation for the community and also a more positive and constructive means of dealing with offenders' (Booth, 2002).

As a process it brings together stakeholders affected by some harm that has been done (offenders, their families; victims and their families; affected communities and stage agencies such as the police). After much groundwork by the convenor/facilitator, the stakeholders voluntarily meet in a circle to discuss how they have been affected by the harm, and work out what should be done to right any wrongs committed.

What is truth?

In a meeting people have a number of options (with various shades of grey). In summary they can:

- speak their perspective of the truth, ie what they can remember and from their perspective;
- speak the embellished truth, ie truth partly linked to what they have heard since the incident (sometimes it becomes hard to distinguish your own memories from the stories built up around an incident);
- lie.

In a restorative justice meeting, participants are invited to speak their story into the circle. As a result all the stories come into the circle, to become collective stories and different perspectives on the truth. The more honest people are, the more honest is the collective truth. It is a truth-seeking meeting.

See the poem 'Six blind men and the elephant' in Chapter 4, a traditional story which evolved from Persia, and is useful for illustrating the issues of perception and perceptual gaps based on personal experience. The story has an excellent moral. It supports conflict resolution sessions and discussions on points of view.

According to McCold and Wachtel (1998), there are four steps in the restorative justice process:

- Acknowledging the wrong (truth discussed).
- Developing shared understanding of the harmful effects (feelings expressed).
- Agreeing on terms of reparation (reparation determined).
- Reaching an understanding about future behaviour (reform implemented).

Uses

Conferences may be used:

- in the criminal justice system;
- in the community;
- within organizations;
- within schools.

When children are involved, it is important that they have supportive peers present, otherwise it may feel like too many adults 'ganging up' on a smaller person. In schools, teachers, year advisors and counsellors are often present. It is important that counsellors do not take a moralistic view if they feel their work with the children has been unsuccessful.

Adversarial and restorative justice systems

Our society is based on the adversarial justice system, in which crimes are punished by fines and imprisonment, and occasionally community service. Prisons have been called 'universities of crime' in that people who are incarcerated often reoffend, as a result of the hardships caused by being imprisoned, feelings of resentment rather than remorse, and the increased skills and knowledge in methods of committing crime learnt in jail.

Restorative justice seeks healing and reparation for victims and the affected community through a process of 'reintegrative' (Braithwaite, 1989) rather than 'stigmatic' shaming of offenders. It encourages offenders to take responsibility for their actions, and see and hear the impact on others. When offenders are required to face their victims, it becomes more difficult for them to depersonalize their crimes and ignore the harm they have done. Through the restorative process, offenders are obliged to listen to their victims' stories, and to acknowledge the pain and hurt that their actions have caused. See the comparison between adversarial and restorative justice systems in Table 12.3).

Table 12.3   Differences between adversarial and restorative justice systems

Adversarial/retributive justice	Restorative justice
Key questions	
Who is to blame?	What happened?
Who is guilty?	Who has been harmed/affected in the community?
What rule was broken against the system?	Whose obligation is it to shift and/or change?
What is the punishment?	What different ways are there to punish?
	Eg financial reparation, community service, apologies and other obligations to the victims
How shall we punish the offender?	How can we repair the damaged relationships?
Characteristics	
Crime seen as an offence against the state/crown	Crime seen primarily as a fracture in relationships – only secondarily as law-breaking
Crime is dealt with by the state	Crime is dealt with by the state and community
Lawyers do all of the questioning (often leading and closed questions) on the victim's behalf	No lawyers present
Victims and their families and friends have no voice, are marginalized, ignored, and often feel like powerless onlookers, treated as a source of evidence	The victim is central to the process and has considerable power within it
Victims, if called, only speak in answer to questions	Victims and their families and friends speak and can ask questions like, 'Why did you do it?'
Offenders speak only in answer to questions	Offenders speak and are encouraged to take responsibility for actions to apologize and show remorse
Sentencing by a magistrate/judge	Outcomes decided by the group (may need to be ratified by magistrate)
Strictly rational process, showing emotions frowned upon	Feelings are vented legitimately, movement between communicating from the head and heart
Justice seen as dispassionate and bureaucratic	
Accountability defined by length and type of punishment	Accountability defined as showing empathy, remorse and eagerness to repair harm
Involves stigmatic shaming	Involves reintegrative shaming
	Everyone has ownership of the outcomes
	The aim is to heal, repair and restore relationships
	Provides opportunity for the offenders to apologize
	Provides opportunity for victims to forgive and move on with their lives

Source: adapted from Mitchell (2002)

Roles of victims

Victims have different circumstances and different reasons for attending a conference. Some want to feel safe again; for others it is restitution and the need for an apology; for others it is a chance to ask questions so that they can move on from their fantasies and fears. I heard of one conference where the 'victims' could not attend because they were 1,000 kilometres away. A 'stand-in' victim was briefed and told the story, and at the end the offender apologized to the proxy.

Roles of offenders

The role of offenders is to listen to the stories about the impact of their actions. They are invited to give their story too. They often apologize, although there is no obligation.

Roles of accused

John Button, who was wrongly jailed for an offence, attended a conference in 2002 (see page 334). Likewise in the community an accused person may benefit from attending a conference to try to get to the bottom of the accusations.

The difference between mediation and restorative justice

Restorative justice differs from mediation in many ways, which are summarized in Table 12.4.

The fundamental structures of mediation and restorative justice are different. Mediation involves usually (but not always) only three people (though there may be co-mediators and more than two 'parties'). It often occurs in a triangle layout, whereas restorative justice is organized in a circle (see Figures 12.2 and 12.3).

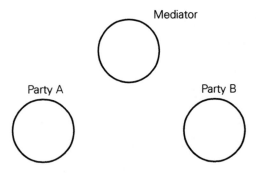

Figure 12.2 Mediation seating plan

Table 12.4   Comparison of mediation and restorative justice

	Mediation	*Restorative justice*
Different	Brings together individuals in conflict with one another with a mediator. Generally only three people	Brings together 'victims' and 'offenders' or in some cases 'accused' as well as families and local officials eg teachers, police
	Language: mediator or co-mediators, party A and party B, reconciliation, issue, disagreement	Language: convenor/facilitator, victim, offender, accused (these terms not used directly to these people in the conference), bullying, restitution, incident, offence, accountability, community safety
	Focus on disputes and conflict	Focus breaking of ground rules of the community, crime
	The parties are facilitated to develop win–win solutions	Outcomes may need to be ratified by court of law
		Involves reintegrative shaming
Same	Involve parties in settling disputes together	
	Both enable people to display emotions connected to their issues	
	Stories, interests and feelings are acknowledged and shared	
	Voluntary attendance	
	Can choose to stop process at any time and revert to formal systems	
	Goal to restore harmony in society	
	Develop solutions collaboratively	

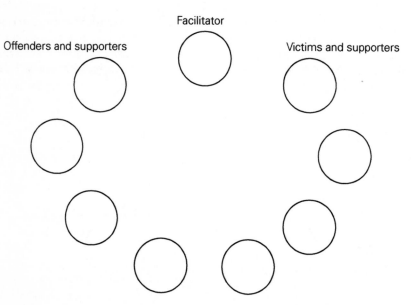

Figure 12.3   Conference seating plan

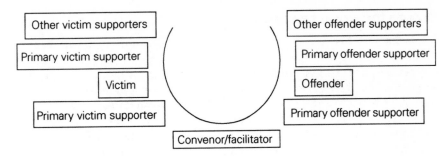

Figure 12.4 Seating plan

Restorative justice process

The summary below is adapted from O'Connell, Wachtel and Wachtel (1999: 55–70) and Blood and Korner (2001).

Roles of the convenor/facilitator

A trained convenor/facilitator has responsibility for:

- determining who should participate;
- meeting with and preparing the parties beforehand;
- guiding the group through the process.

It is the group who decides the outcomes.

In restorative justice the facilitator is called a 'convenor', who takes responsibility for working separately with all parties before the conference, in some cases for months or even a year. He/she must remain neutral at all times, use personal names, and never use terms/labels like 'offender' or 'victim' (although for convenience these terms are used below). The facilitator needs to be as invisible as possible and:

- stays with the script as far as possible in some models, eg the Wagga Wagga approach described in O'Connell, Wachtel and Wachtel (1999);
- does not answer questions (except process questions);
- does not ask 'Why' questions (however, some facilitators do allow this question from victims as many need to know 'Why did you do it?');
- 'holds the space' including periods of silence to give people time to reflect.

Some facilitators work in pairs or teams rather than as individuals.

Givens

The victim/s and offender/s must be willing to attend. There must be an admission of guilt on the part of the offender, or at least an acknowledgment that he/she was part of or involved in the problem.

Before the conference

The facilitator must be motivated, but patient. He/she must be unattached to the outcome and must not coerce people to attend. However, it is useful to tell prospective participants about the history of restorative justice and the potential outcomes. The process is time-consuming, and the facilitator must be prepared at times to bear the brunt of individuals who need to vent their anger. The job of the facilitator is to build trust and rapport between him/herself and the participants. He/she must check that all necessary stakeholders have been invited to attend and are free on the date selected. There must be a contingency plan if things do not go as intended.

Participants/size of group

The size of group in a conference is usually up to about 12 people. Some conferences have involved up to 30 people.

Materials

Boxes of tissues, script for facilitator (if required). Seating labels indicating where each person should sit. Agreement forms. Refreshments ready in an adjoining room.

Venue/room layout

The conference should be held in a quiet, private room. Place a 'Do not disturb' sign on the door. Chairs should be placed in a circle. The circle is a shape that has had significance for human communication across the globe and throughout time: 'The circle, an age-old symbol of wholeness, helps to emphasize unity and equality' ((Tyson, 1998). The facilitator and participants have equal space and height.

The seating plan should be prepared carefully beforehand. There should be no tables, as they form barriers and can obscure body language.

Time

The meeting may take several hours. Generally there are no breaks so as not to interrupt the ambience and continuity of the meeting.

Variations of process

As with any human endeavour, some facilitators advocate that a particular process be enacted in a set way, while others promote more flexibility. Terry O'Connell (O'Connell, Wachtel and Wachtel, 1999) suggests sticking to a convenors' script. This can be useful for both new and experienced convenors.

There are facilitators in Western Australia who work with a much freer, almost unobtrusive facilitative style, starting by addressing the 'victim' by name, then letting the discussion flow from there, only intervening and redirecting the flow of discussion where necessary based on information gained by pre-meeting interviews with participants. Dr Dorothy Goulding and Brian Steels commented that they found a certain restriction and 'sameness' in the scripted process, and individualized their approach on a case-by-case basis. They work in pairs or teams of facilitators, and use the pre-conference issues to guide their questions to help get their needs met: 'for some it's an issue of feeling safe again, for others it's restitution and apology' (Goulding, 2002b).

Stages

Establish the ground rules

The facilitator discusses ground rules with the participants beforehand, and sets the tone at the beginning of the conference. If there is fear of violence, there may be a need to state clearly what is and is not permissible. Experienced restorative justice facilitators I have spoken to comment that even if a participant crosses the circle physically to speak to an individual, no violence has broken out. However, participants need to be reassured that they will be protected. During the conference, however, people will change levels of communication frequently, sometimes communicating from the head and at other times from the heart.

Attendance must be non-compulsory: in other words participants need to be reminded that they are free to leave at any time, and that the issue will be decided by whatever authority is in charge of the dispute, for instance the court, manager, organization and/or school principal.

During the conference

The facilitator welcomes participants and shows them to their designated seats calmly and confidently. Participants should not mingle before the conference is declared open. Mingling is encouraged at the end, when drinks and biscuits are served, and participants continue to find out about one another as people. The convenor/facilitator focuses the discussion on addressing the act or behaviour, without condemning the character of the person.

If the victims and their supporters have indicated fear of violence, then the facilitator needs to lay down clear ground rules at the beginning of the conference.

The following script is adapted from O'Connell (1999: 55–70) and Blood and Korner (2001). This script has been tried and tested. It is useful especially for facilitators who are new to restorative justice.

1. Welcoming preamble.
   - 'Thank you all for attending. As you know my name is. . . and I will be facilitating this conference. I know this is difficult for all of you, but your presence will help us deal with the matter that has brought us together. This is an opportunity for all of you to be involved in repairing the harm that has been done.

- This conference will focus on an incident that happened (briefly state the date, place and nature of the offence). It is important to understand that we will focus on what (offender name/s) did and how that unacceptable behaviour has affected others. We are not here to decide whether [offenders name/s]is/are good or bad. We want to explore in what way people have been affected, and hopefully work toward repairing the harm that has resulted. Does everyone understand this?' (Look around for reactions.)
- '[Offender name/s] has/have admitted his/her/their part in the incident.' (In some community conferences the so-called 'offender' may not have admitted guilt, and the meeting may be called to try to find out more about what happened and why a person has been accused.)
- To offenders: 'I must tell you that you do not have to participate in this conference and you are free to leave at any time, as is anyone else. If you do leave, the matter may be referred to court or handled by the school disciplinary policy/work grievance officer/or other way. This matter may ,however, be finalized if you participate in a positive manner and comply with the conference agreement. Do you understand?'

2. Offender/s. 'We'll start with [state one of the offender's names].' If there is more than one offender, ask each to respond to all of the questions before you move to the next person.
   - 'What happened?' 'What were you thinking about at the time?'
   - 'What have you thought about since the incident/s?'
   - 'Who do you think has been affected by your actions?'
   - 'How have you been affected?'

   Do not bring in the offenders' supporters before the victim and his/her/their supporters have spoken, otherwise they understandably get very frustrated.

3. Victims. If there is more than one victim, have each respond to all of the following questions:
   - 'What was your reaction at the time of the incident?'
   - 'What did you think about what happened?'
   - 'What has been the hardest for you?'
   - 'How did your family and friends react when they heard about the incident?'

4. Victim's supporters:
   - 'What did you think when you heard about the incident?'
   - 'What did you think about what happened?'
   - 'What has been the hardest thing for you?'
   - 'What do you think are the main issues?'

5. Offender supporters. To the parent/caregiver say, 'This has been difficult for you, hasn't it? Would you like to tell us about it?' Then ask each supporter:
    - 'What did you think when you heard about the incident?'
    - 'What did you think about what happened?'
    - 'What has been the hardest thing for you?'
    - 'What do you think are the main issues?

6. Offender/s. Ask the offender/s, 'Is there anything you want to say at this time?'

7. Reaching agreement. Ask the victim, 'What would you like from today's conference?' Ask the offender/s to respond.

Involve participants in discussion. Ask the offender/s to respond to each suggestion, and before the group moves to the next suggestion ask, 'What do you think about that?' Confirm that the offender agrees before moving on. Allow for negotiation.

Clarify and summarize each item, and make a written note of specific details, deadlines and follow-up arrangement.

Summarize: 'Before I prepare the written agreement, I'd like to make sure that I have accurately recorded what has been decided.' Read out agreement and check body language for acknowledgement. Make alterations where necessary.

Closing the conference

'Before I formally close the conference, I would like to provide everyone with a final opportunity to speak. Is there anything anyone wants to say?' Allow think time. When all comments cease, say, 'Thank you for your contributions in dealing with this difficult matter. Congratulations on the way you have worked through the issues. Please help yourselves to some refreshments while I prepare the agreement.'

Refreshment time

Allow participants and facilitator time to have refreshments and interact. The informal period after the formal conference is very important to allow feelings of relief and reintegration. Everyone should be given copies of agreements before they leave.

Outcomes

In Canada, studies of 'sentencing circles' and different systems more suited to the worldview of First Nation Peoples are to be found on the Correctional Services Canada Web site: scc.gc.ca/text/prgrm/rjstc/award/info_e.shtml
www.real.justice.org

Advantages

Effective restorative justice sessions:

- foster awareness in offenders of the outcomes of their misdemeanours;
- avoid scolding or lecturing;
- involve participants actively;
- accept ambiguity;
- focus on addressing the behaviour, not the personhood of the offender;
- see every instance of wrongdoing and conflict as an opportunity for learning and healing.

Paul McCold's PhD research on restorative policing in the United States, using the New South Wales 'Wagga Wagga' process (McCold, 1993), concluded that:

- Police officers were quite capable of facilitating conferences according to restorative justice principles.
- The use of conferencing resulted in a cultural shift in the police officers involved, from a punitive, legalistic approach to a more problem-solving restorative approach to their work.
- Victims, offenders and parents reported high rates of satisfaction with the process and experiences of fairness.
- The process appeared to motivate offenders to almost universally complete financial reparation, community service, apologies and other obligations to the victims.
- As the process was used only on certain crimes and was on a self-select basis, the study could not confirm that it reduced recidivism (that is, that people who volunteer to undergo the process may be less likely to reoffend).

Dr Dorothy Goulding's more recent PhD research in Perth, Western Australia (Goulding, 2002a) concluded that the basic principles of restorative justice could be adapted successfully for use within the prison setting, and while this would help victims, communities and offenders, she called on the need for trans-formative justice to address the problem of high reoffending rates. She cited the success of the combination of both approaches in six prisons in Belgium, which let the Minister for Justice to introduce restorative justice practices to all 30 prisons in Belgium. All prison staff are trained in generic skills, to facilitate restorative and transformative processes in diverse situations. These skills are also transferred to managing situations of conflict among prisoners, and between prisoners and prison staff. This is clearly another area in which the facilitation profession can play an active role.

Magic moments

Sometimes there is an irreversible 'switch' or 'magic moment', you can actually see a change in the ways in which people perceive themselves and others. A victim sees that the offender has been a victim too or the offender sees the victim has been hurt in deep and long lasting ways.

(Mitchell, 2002)

Even if a restorative justice session does not eventuate, there are often significant shifts in thinking and behaviour. I heard a story recounting Terry O'Connell's experience in a jail where he was setting up a role play with inmates to show them how a restorative justice meeting worked. When he called for people to take on roles, he invited one man to play the role of the victim's father. The inmate looked visibly stunned for a few moments: 'Do you mean to say what I've done has hurt my parents?' One of those magic moments ensured as the light dawned. The inmate asked the prison authorities for a special meeting with his parents the following week.

Disadvantages

Setting up a conference takes time, and some conferences never happen, as participants have the right to pull out. Where this occurs, a lot of useful things may have already happened, and considerable change and healing may have taken place as described above. However, when compared with the cost of incarceration and the dismal statistics on reoffenders, the evidence indicates that this is a viable and worthwhile system. Add to this the impact on health systems when victims remain 'stuck' in the anger and/or grieving stages after a crime, then restorative justice would appear to be a worthwhile alternative justice system for some crimes.

Application of the restorative justice process in the workplace

There are many occasions when restorative justice may be used in the workplace, for instances of bullying and/or occasions when there are no clear-cut offenders and victims. A conference might be convened using the following restorative questions for the workplace:

● What happened?
● What were you thinking about at the time?
● Who has been harmed/affected? How?
● What needs to happen to repair the harm/make things right (Blood and Korner, 2001)?

Administration of restorative justice systems

There is a burgeoning debate as to who should 'control' restorative justice systems: state systems, or non-government groups working to create a civil society such as schools, churches and private workplaces (Strang and Braithwaite, 2001).

Resources

The Conferencing Handbook (O'Connell, Wachtel and Wachtel 1999) is an outstanding, easy to read text on this area.

A Web site of resources: http://www.realjustice.org/Pages/booksvideos.html

Australian Institute of Criminology RJ site: http://www.aic.gov.au/rjustice/australia.html

The work of Terry O'Connell who pioneered the process with the New South Wales police is documented at: http://www.smh.com.au/news/0006/13/pageone/pageone03.html

The International Institute for Restorative Practices (Bethlehem, PA, USA) is contactable by e-mail on info@restorativepractices.org

Real Justice is an international non-profit provider of conferencing, training, books and videos: Web site: www.realjustice.org. E-mail: Australia@realjustice.org (e-mails for the UK and United States, place the initials before @; Canada, Hungary, New Zealand, type whole name before @). Netherlands: oks@wxs.nl

For the RJWA Schools Project contact www.transformingconflict.org (Belinda Hopkins); www.thorsborne.com.au (Margaret Thorsborne) or Circlespeak (CircleSpeak@aol.com)

Videos

The two Australian Story videos, *Murder She Wrote* Parts 1 and 2 (2002) tell the story of John Button, who was wrongly convicted and imprisoned for murder in Perth, Western Australia. They describe the miscarriage of justice, and the devastating consequences still being played out in the lives of three families nearly 40 years after the event. The three families are eventually brought together to meet each other through the restorative justice process for the first time in four decades, and confront 40 years of grief, guilt and anger.

Facing the Demons is an hour-long documentary video about the journey of the family and friends of murder victim Michael Marslew, confronting face to face in a restorative justice conference two of the offenders responsible for Michael's death.

For reports on restorative justice trials check: www.aic.gov.au/rjustice/rise.html

Open space technology

> The wise person looks into space,
> and does not regard
> the small as too little,
> nor the great as too big,
> for she knows that
> there is no limit to dimensions.
> Lao-tse

Next, I will outline a process that seems to accommodate many of the requirements for active participation in complex situations. It has elements of the search conference described in Chapter 9 in that it starts at the 'village fair' stage, yet it has a different feel and quality, partly I sense because of the introduction and use of the circle, and a more spiritual dimension to facilitation. It is almost as if the facilitator is calling the group members to go forth on a quest to be greater than they normally are, a call like the hero/heroine's journey described earlier.

Author/background

Harrison Owen attributes the basic ideas of open space to a small West African village, the Native American tradition, and the wisdom of the East. Indeed Owen said he was inspired to develop the process after having watched the way things happen in African markets and communities. He developed open space technology in 1992 (Owen, 1992; 1997; Owen and Stadler, 1999). Like many creative ideas he said, 'It began out of frustration, almost as a joke.' He cites a two-day meeting of over 200 people (Native Americans, federal and local government bureaucrats) in 1992, whose focus was to develop effective expenditure of 1.5 billion dollars designated for a highway across tribal and public lands in the United States. 'On the face of it, the prospects for a peaceful, let alone productive meeting seemed less than bright' (Owen, 1992: 1). The agenda comprised 52 different task groups and was generated in less than one hour with one facilitator. The meeting resulted in 150 pages of proceedings which were input to computers and printed for all participants on the third day.

The method's current popularity may be explained by its enabling people to focus immediately on issues of concern to them, and on complex issues where the outcomes and/or answers are unknown and there is a great deal of uncertainty and need for new ideas. It appears to be a mix of chaos and order: what Dee Hock (the banker who reorganized Visa International, or Visa card) calls a 'chaordic' organization.

Owen had noticed that after a conference he had organized, participants had commented that the coffee and lunch breaks were the most useful sessions, when real issues of personal interest were aired. The problem at conferences, however, is how to make contact with people who are concerned about the same issues.

As a result, Owen created a process that mimicked the relaxed nature of coffee breaks, where people are free to join and leave groups as they please. He incorporated ideas from indigenous peoples in West Africa, North America and Asia who have met in circles as 'a fundamental geometry of open human communication' for centuries (Owen and Stadler, 1999:11). The process has been used successfully in the United States, Latin America, South East Asia, Australia, New Zealand and the EEC.

Purpose/rationale

The purpose of open space is to enable individuals to generate their own agendas, and to recruit people to join with them in discussing areas of mutual interest. Ownership for the outcomes is firmly placed with the participants. It

is most suitable 'in situations where a major issue must be resolved, charac-
terized by high levels of complexity, high levels of diversity (in terms of people
involved), the presence of potential or actual conflict, and with a decision time
of yesterday' (Owen and Stadler, 1999:10). It is not suitable if management and
sponsors are not willing to share power.

Open Space operates on:

- the motivation and passion of people working on issues that concern them;
- the personal autonomy and responsibility of participants;
- the confidence of sponsors/management and/or conference planning
  committees to let go of control and support the outcomes.

Size of group

From 5 to 500, seated at the outset in circles or concentric circles. Invitations are
sent to everyone who might care about the question/s and solution/s. If the
group would be overly large, representatives can be invited to form different
groups. Participants are expected to attend on a voluntary basis and:

- be themselves;
- participate with whatever energy they have (enthusiasm, frustration,
  creativity etc);
- be open to outcomes;
- take responsibility for making 'things' happen after the workshop.

> May the space be vast enough to give rise to all thoughts.
>
> Gabrielle Roth

Duration

Less than one day gives people a taste of the possibilities of open space. One
day is intense. If action planning is required, then two or three days are needed.

Materials

Sticky-backed notes, flip chart paper, computers/lap tops, printers, photocopying facilities. A white board performs the function of a bulletin board.

Venue

The venue should have large blank walls. Space is required for the whole group
to sit in circles or concentric circles. There should be several 'break-out' spaces,
not necessarily rooms: they could be areas of large rooms, verandas, under trees
or pergolas. If you are convening in a hotel, the facilitator may need to warn
staff in advance.

Tea/coffee should be available at all times. Likewise meals should be
provided in smorgasbord format so that groups can eat when, and if, they like.

Room layout

Participants' chairs are arranged in a circle. If there are more than around 18 people it may be better to have concentric circles; however, people on the outer circle are likely to feel slightly cut off.

Role of the facilitator

The roles of the facilitator are to create and hold the space in which people can work, then to get out of the way and trust the group and the process (Owen and Stadler, 1999). According to the purists, a facilitator should not intervene in any of the groups or with the group as a whole unless 'space invaders' take it upon themselves to try to influence specific outcomes. The facilitator maintains the space, keeps it tidy, safe, collects dirty cups, and talks to those who wish to talk.

Facilitators of open space have to be able to live with ambiguity, and to instil confidence in managers and organizers to do the same, as they will all be working directly in Heron's 'autonomous mode', which is uncomfortable for some.

Harrison Owen suggests that during the hierarchical introduction the facilitator does not stop to invite questions. The underlying message is, 'This is how it will happen, and then this will happen, then people follow'. If you ask for questions, the 'spell' is broken. There are four stages that the facilitator needs to cover in the opening:

- State the purpose of the open space conference.
- Describe the process.
- Create the community bulletin board.
- Open the market place.

Stages

The shaman's walk

The facilitator's key task is to open the space at the beginning. He/she sits in the circle. The facilitator must be calm and centred when establishing the 'four principles' noted above and opening the space for the meeting. This usually takes about 15–20 minutes. Some facilitators prefer to meditate beforehand to put themselves into a calm and centred frame of mind (see the discussion of charisma in Chapter 4).

Owen suggests the facilitator stand at the edge of the circle, say, 'Welcome to open space', then walk slowly around the inside boundaries of the circle, describing the story of open space, and invoking the archetypal power of the circle and the feminine. He calls this the 'shaman's walk' (Owen, 1997). The facilitator should look at as many people as possible to include them and affirm trust in the process, as there is often a high degree of anxiety. To allay fears the facilitator is implicitly communicating, 'This is how it works. Trust me, you won't fall off the edge.' Then he/she stands in the centre to invoke male energy:

that is, to balance the male energy for confrontation and truth telling, and the female for inclusion, community and mutual support.

Purpose/rationale

The facilitator describes the focus or question that has brought people together as succinctly as possible.

Principles

Next the facilitator describes the four principles of open space:

- **Whenever it starts is the right time;** the facilitator and participants begin when it feels right to begin.
- **Whoever comes is (sic) the right people.** This emphasizes the quality of interaction between those who chose to attend.
- **Whatever happens is the only thing that could have:** in other words, there will be a minimum of invention by the facilitator.
- **Whenever it is over it is over:** if the whole group finishes early the group disbands, or perhaps some or all might decide to carry on longer than the original plan (Owen, 1992 :70).

I feel that 'Whatever happens is the only thing that could have' is perhaps too simplistic, and that there are groups where some intervention by the facilitator may be necessary, as illustrated by the story later in this section.

Ground rules

The '*law of two feet*' (or law of personal initiative) may be applied by anyone who is bored, not comfortable to contribute, or not learning in a particular group. This person may withdraw and either join another group, or sit and thinks alone (a luxury we do not often get at work). Participation in groups is voluntary. If someone dominates and individuals are not happy, they can move on if they wish. Individuals are held responsible for how they wish to spend their time.

Owen describes two possible behaviours that can contribute positively to open space discussions. '*Bumble bees*' take the law of two feet very seriously, and constantly flit from one small group to the next; they cross-pollinate ideas and give variety to discussions. '*Butterflies*' choose not to go to some meetings, but create areas of non-action and silence. Often 'butterflies' are visited by others, and significant conversations begin.

Opening the market place

Every time a person speaks with passion he/she is the leader.

The facilitator opens the 'market place', a place where individuals generate ideas for discussion. (The analogy with a market is most apt, as in a market people exchange goods as well as ideas.) Sticky-backed notes are distributed.

Participants are invited to identify their own ideas, issues, opportunities and problems that relate to the main theme of the workshop. The facilitator emphasizes that one idea only is to be written on each sticky-backed note, and asks everyone to sign their names to their ideas.

Members usually busily start writing. When energies diminish, the facilitator invites participants one at a time, to announce their name and one idea to the group, then to 'post' the idea by placing it on the bulletin board. Some facilitators invite the speakers to stand in the centre of the circle; to take the centre energy to proclaim their issues strongly.

Even with 300 people, about 70 appears to be the maximum number of cards that get posted. If there are not enough rooms, create meeting 'spaces' in corridors.

The bulletin board

When everyone has finished posting all their ideas, the facilitator helps the group to cluster ideas and work out sequencing of discussions according to the number of time slots available. Then participants sign up for the groups they feel passionate about. As a result the participants have selected their agenda and their groups.

Table 12.5   Sample community bulletin board layout

Day 1

	Time	Room a	Room b	Room c	Room d
Registration	08.30–09.00				
Opening circle: Introduction to open space and market place	09.00–10.00				
Session 1	10.00–11.00				
Session 2	11.00–12.00				
Session 3	12.00–01.00				
Session 4	01.00–02.00				
Session 5	02.00–03.00				
Session 6	03.00–04.00				
Closing circle	04.00–05.00				

Time conflicts

If one person wishes to attend two sessions that are scheduled for the same time, he/she finds the convenors and asks them to change time slots, or combine sessions if the topics are similar.

Combining sessions

There may be several topics on the same issues, but it is better to have three groups of 10 rather than one group of 30.

Helping one another

If a group runs over time it should finish in a different room so as not to hold up the next group. Or if the next group decides to meet somewhere else, it should post a notice on the door.

Small group sessions

The person who posted the item convenes the group and takes notes or minutes. Each group decides how to make the best use of its time. After the session is over, the convenor 'publishes' the notes on the bulletin board (and/or prints out a summary using a laptop). It is useful to distribute handouts to ensure that everyone follows the same basic format (see Figure 12.5).

The role of the facilitator is to 'hold the space'. According to Owen, the groups should self-regulate themselves: if an individual dominates a group, individuals who feel unheard should withdraw. I believe that the convenor of small groups should take on the role of facilitator, and bring quieter participants into the discussion. Or the workshop facilitator can remind all the participants of their facilitator roles.

End of the day

For meetings of more than one day, there are morning announcement and evening news sessions to discuss changes in meetings, and a chance to share anecdotes and so on.

Session Report

Topic

Facilitator

Full names of participants

Main points of the discussion
–
–
–
–

Figure 12.5   Small group discussions minutes format

The role of technology

At a conference of 350 people we hired six laptops. These were set up around the main room. Not only is it important to print out and display findings, it is also important to get participants to take responsibility to ensure that all data is saved to the hard disk as well as a floppy disc for back-up.

Convergence stage

If there is a need for communal action planning, the facilitator can call the group together in a circle after everyone has read the posted group minutes. First, give everyone six dots to stick on those topics that they think are most important. Pick out the five or six with the most dots. Then ask participants to cluster the remaining sheets under those five main headings. Key suggested recommendations can then be read out, and the five WH action planning questions applied (what, when, where, how, and with what resources?).

Endings

There is no plenary or report-back session in the conventional sense. Owen (1992: 102–06) suggests using an adaptation of the Native American talking stick ceremony for the grand finale (if the group is not too large). A talking stick is a decorated piece of wood which was passed around a circle of people gathered together for a particular purpose, for example to speak from the heart. The ground rules are whoever has the stick talks, while everybody else actively listens. There is no time limit, no interruption allowed, and no discussion. Nowadays, in large groups, the microphone is often a psuedo-talking stick. Each person is asked to share briefly what the event may have meant for him or her, and what he/she proposes to do in the future; or individuals may choose to stay silent and pass the mike on to another person. This is not a traditional summary session. Owen suggests that the talking stick elicits deeper sharing and understanding:

One might question the appropriateness of such intimacy in a 'business setting', but I think we may be achieving a level of maturity which understands that feeling, passions, spirit and sharing not only have a place in business, they are the very wellsprings from which business and all other human activities emerge (Owen, 1992:102).

The proceedings from each group are on the bulletin board and in the computers ready to be e-mailed to all. At the end Owen says:

I ask the group to stand and allow their eyes to move around the circle to acknowledge each other in silence, what they have accomplished, and what they hope to do... So after a few moments, I ask each person to turn completely around in their place, face outwards, and imagine what they are going to be doing in the days immediately ahead... And then it is over.

(Owen, 1992: 106)

Having multiple laptops available means that proceedings, in the form of raw data, should be available to participants quickly and easily at the end of the forum.

Outcomes

Open space workshops often have surprising outcomes. (See the description of open space combined with playback theatre in Chapter 4.)

Advantages

In open space workshops, participants are given a large amount of autonomy. Responsibility for timekeeping and being in the right place at the right time is placed on the shoulders of the participants, not the facilitator. The technique is simple and easy to learn, and therefore enables 'developmental facilitation' in that participants can learn and use the process later to follow up on ideas (Schwarz, 1994).

Participants are also invited to move from one group to another. So often at conferences people feel embarrassed to withdraw from a group that is not meeting their needs.

There are two levels of leadership in open space conferences: the facilitator, and the people who post their ideas and become 'emergent leaders': that is, they lead with their ideas. The process gives permission to lead with ideas rather than rank or longevity in a company or community. At the end of the workshop, issues should have been tabled (unless people were fearful of being identified with a particularly contentious issue).

As people should only attend voluntarily, facilitators usually do not have to cope with disgruntled attendees (see Chapter 6). The process is flexible and adaptable to different organizations, communities, cultures, issues and needs.

Disadvantages

According to Owen, the small groups do not need facilitation and 'whatever happens is the only thing that could have'. I feel this is too much at times towards laissez-faire. If a person feels that he/she is not heard, there is the choice to withdraw and join another group, or sit alone. I feel that this is an issue, since useful ideas may be lost and/or some individuals could feel unheard.

STORY: OPEN SPACE

I attended an 'open space conference on open space' in Adelaide, attended by facilitators, a couple of years ago. One participant had called a meeting on 'Ways to advertise open space'. I suggested that she could contact the HR people in organizations rather than CEOs, since the HR people would be more likely to know about open space. Plus she could contact the HR course co-ordinators in universities and offer to visit postgraduate classes to promote open space. A male participant immediately jumped down my throat, and basically said that HR people and academics were useless and a waste of time. In one sentence he had managed to put down my profession, my work in a university at that time, and my contribution to the discussion. I wondered how less 'hardy' participants would have handled this affront to their being. And this was an open space about open space!

As a result of this experience, in large groups I have facilitated, I ask the convenor of each small group to take on a facilitator role and be responsible for including quieter members into the discussion. However, I have found that convenors often do not easily take on the facilitation role, as by convening a meeting they often have a lot to say and are committed to 'content' rather than 'process'. I am still pondering this issue. The lack of facilitation in small groups presupposes high levels of communication skills and a willingness to share air-time. I would love to hear the opinions of readers on this issue.

When not to use open space

Facilitators should not attempt open space if:

- participants are being coerced to attend;
- the CEO's mind is already made up;
- the CEOs are not ready to let go of power and structure;
- participants are afraid of retribution later if they raise contentious issues.

Open space purists maintain that mainstream conferences should be either all open space or not at all. In Chapter 4 I described a conference which opened with playback theatre followed by one open space session. It was a risk for the organizers to abandon traditional conference mores; however, it went so well that it was a useful comparison for participants who the following day had to listen to keynote speakers, then attend workshops. As such, I observed it was a useful introduction to the area and left people wanting more.

For other processes which may be used with large groups see Bunker and Alban (1997).

Stories of social change

Social change takes time: takes time, time and more time. So I have added the story of the 'hundredth monkey' as a way of stimulating hope and encouragement for facilitators who are working as social change agents.

At the beginning of the book I mentioned my plea for peace. I believe this is possible, and in terms of developing workable relationships we can do it, as this change story in the animal kingdom illustrates:

Hope: The Story of the Hundredth Monkey

The Japanese monkey, *Macaca fuscata*, has been observed in the wild for a period of over 30 years. In 1952 on the island of Koshima, scientists were providing monkeys with sweet potatoes dropped in the sand. The monkeys liked the taste of the sweet potatoes, but they found the dirt unpleasant.

An 18-month-old female named Imo found she could solve the problem by washing the potatoes in a nearby stream. She taught this trick to her mother. Her playmates also learnt this new way, and they taught their mothers too. This cultural innovation was gradually picked up by various monkeys before the eyes of the scientist.

Between 1952 and 1958, all the young monkeys learnt to wash the sandy sweet potatoes to make them more palatable. Only the adults who imitated their children learnt this social improvement. Other adults kept eating the dirty sweet potatoes.

Then something startling took place. In the autumn of 1958, a certain number of Koshima monkeys were washing sweet potatoes; the exact number is not known. Let us suppose that when the sun rose one morning there were 99 monkeys on Koshima island who had learnt how to wash their sweet potatoes. Let's further suppose that later that morning, the hundredth monkey learnt also to wash potatoes.

Then it happened! By that evening almost everyone in the tribe was washing sweet potatoes before eating them. The added energy of this hundredth monkey somehow created an ideological breakthrough!

But notice, a most surprising thing observed by these scientists was that the habit of washing sweet potatoes then 'jumped' over the sea. Colonies of monkeys on other islands and the mainland troop of monkeys at Takaskiyama began washing their sweet potatoes!

Thus, when a certain crucial number achieves an awareness, this new awareness may be communicated from mind to mind. Although the exact number may vary, the 'hundredth monkey phenomenon' means that when only a limited number of people know of a new way, it may remain the consciousness property of these people. But there is a point at which if only one more person tunes in to a new awareness, a field is strengthened so that this awareness is picked up by almost everyone. (Source: adapted from Watson, 1980:147–48.)

Incidents like this do not just happen to monkeys as the following true story from my friends illustrates.

A True Human Story

A friend recently told me the story about the founding of the Gaia Foundation in Perth, Western Australia. Vivienne and her partner John both had a dream on the same night, that they should establish a Gaia Foundation in Perth. This they did. They now have a substantial library of resources, a bookshop, a wide network of activist friends, and they facilitate workshops and so on. But there is an interesting twist to the story. When they went overseas they found other Gaia organizations set up in other countries unbeknown to them. Convergent evolution is wonderful! It can happen to monkeys and it can happen to humans too!

Conclusion

This chapter has aimed to give an overview of methods to create workable relationships. Clearly this is a complex area of human endeavour, brought about via a wide range of strategies and processes.

13

Facilitating outdoor learning

Introduction

Outdoor learning, or adventure training, involves integrated programmes of carefully planned activities and debriefings linked to individual and/or group development. It is not adventure *per se*, though for some it holds elements of adventure, as people are often undertaking unfamiliar activities or visiting areas for the first time. It involves learning to learn by doing, with and from others. It is only 50 per cent action learning and 50 per cent reflection and analysis of events. The outdoors is a metaphor for our own lives, but as we all know we are better able to reflect about our beliefs, values and ways of doing things when we are away from our normal work/home environments. It is holistic learning, involving real tasks and problems, real people in real time with real emotions and real constraints (Bank, 1994).

This chapter includes:

- types of outdoor activities;
- the origins of outdoor learning;
- choosing outdoor companies;
- division of labour;
- risk and trust;
- insurance and safety;
- debriefing and learning transference;
- equity issues: gender and cross-cultural issues;
- teamwork: the spotto process;
- using journals;
- impact of outdoor learning programmes;
- videos about outdoor learning.

Types of outdoor activity

There are different ways of classifying outdoor activity. One way divides the types of activities within a programme. The first type is 'individual challenge' using team support, which includes a wide range of activities, for example trust falls, abseiling, flying foxes, and low and high ropes courses. The second is 'group problem solving', including orienteering, sailing, raft building, and simulated problem solving, for example, 'the alligator crossing', where teams are given planks of wood to get across an imaginary river filled with imaginary alligators.

Programmes may be organized 'in-house' for managers and teams, cross-sections of organizations, or as a 'stand alone' programme for people from different organizations. The advantage of in-company programmes is that a team gain a shared experience, which adds to the communal stories of an organization. These stories are important, especially when during times of restructuring the lives and stories of teams are being lost.

There is another distinction between the characteristics of locations, for example camping wilderness programmes, say to the Kimberly area of north-west Australia, and residential outdoor centres with high–low rope courses and nearby quarries used for abseiling. In wilderness training participants engage in sailing, climbing, caving and white-water rafting activities. In outdoor centres participants live and eat indoors, but most training occurs in the outdoors.

The origins of outdoor learning

Outdoor learning draws from many different fields:

- school/university journeys/camps and outdoor sports;
- military training;
- the Outward Bound movement;
- the Scouts/Girl Guides, school cadet and Duke of Edinburgh Award schemes;
- adventure activities (Bank, 1994).

Why use outdoor training?

The Institute of Personnel and Development guide (Adams and Balfour, 1998) suggests that clients should ask themselves the following before embarking on outdoor training:

- Why use outdoor training to meet the training need?
- What do you want to achieve through outdoor training and how will it fit in with your business strategy?
- How will outdoor training fit in with your other development activities?
- Can the learning be achieved in any other way – is outdoor training the most appropriate tool?
- What are the specific, and where possible measurable, objectives?
- How can you reinforce the learning that has taken place when participants return to the workplace?
- How is the outdoor training to be evaluated?

Some clients ask if the outdoor training can be used as part of an assessment procedure. I find this request unfair, as the outdoor environment and associated activities are so alien for some.

Essential criteria for outdoor programmes

There are a number of assumptions regarding attendance on outdoor programmes:

- Adults attend voluntarily.
- People are medically fit.
- Physical activities must be suited to desired outcomes.
- Part of the ground rules includes the right to say 'no' and the right to change your mind. The learning must be 'challenge by choice', and many other activities need to be offered, eg observational roles and photographic roles.

Goals of outdoor development

The goals of outdoor learning may include activities that enable participants to:

- get to know one another out of the work situation;
- extend their perceived limits and develop calculated risk management skills;
- open up communication about goals, leadership etc;
- disclose their needs and support one another;
- build trust between individuals at similar and different levels in the organization;
- plan risk taking and perceived risk;
- develop self-confidence;
- delegate/share/rotate tasks;
- take responsibility;
- learn to be ready to act or not act;
- learn how to resolve conflict in an open and positive way;
- reflect and learn from direct experience;
- develop teamwork and group problem-solving skills and decision making.

People are often different outdoors away from their normal work environments. They often look and behave differently, in their own clothes, away from the trappings of rank and office. Many people rarely spend extended periods of time out of doors. Our lives are extremely sheltered from the elements as we go to and from work in air-conditioned/heated cars to air-conditioned/heated offices. Nature is a great equalizer. If people get caught in a storm, they all have to take shelter; they all get wet. Of course people have different tolerances to extremes of the elements, but then as a team they are encouraged to make their needs known, and to accommodate and help one another.

There are, however, potential conflicts between the norms of cooperation and competition which need to be addressed before a programme begins and during

Cooperation  Competition

Figure 13.1

a programme. Norms of individual advancement through workplace agreements and the like in the workplace may be contrary to the desired norms of cooperation in an outdoor programme, where information sharing is vital and where individuals have to look out for and help one another.

There is an urban legend that knowledge and data apparently double every 18 months (I'm not sure by whom or how this is measured). But the metaphor is useful. In the outdoors, participants are in a different environment from their work places. They don't know what they don't know. The activities help them to surface assumptions about what is held to be true. They may have to unlearn. For example, most people are taught not to go over cliffs backwards, and in abseiling they learn to do something that they may have considered impossible before.

Choosing outdoor training companies

There are many outdoor training companies; however, they vary tremendously in their approaches. At one time I interviewed all the companies in my home city to gain an overview of the people available. Ex-army personnel set up some companies. These people have many training and outdoor activities: some show photo albums, others bring brochures. But the thing is to look beyond these products and ask many questions. Some ex-army personnel have to lose some of their prior conditioning to:

- be action oriented;
- achieve goals no matter what (at the expense of debriefing time);
- make sexist comments;
- be autocratic leaders.

I have worked with ex SAS personnel who have been wonderful, gentle, giants who have the maturity not to be 'gung ho' or to show off their physical prowess. Conversely, I have met some education officers who have been so immature that they were positively dangerous with a group, as they constantly need to prove themselves physically or by telling the group of their prior exploits.

Questions to ask yourself about outdoor companies

The following questions are adapted from a list drawn up in the *Institute of Personal Development Guide on Outdoor Training* (IPD, 1998):

- What training qualifications do they have?
- What outdoor training skills/training/experience do they have?

- What is their industrial/commercial/educational background?
- What is the length and type of experience?
- What are their abilities in terms of review or facilitation skills?
- What is their knowledge of management theories and processes and their ability to handle any management issues that may arise?
- What is the safety policy? What first aid training have instructors had? What are the dates/updates of this?
- How often does the company conduct its own staff development and safety training activities?
- How do their outdoor specialists handle problems related to peer pressure, conflict etc?
- How will their outdoor specialists work with your facilitators?
- Can the company provide you with the phone numbers of previous clients so you can gain first-hand evaluation of their services?
- What is the company policy and values?
- What accreditation do they have from local training bodies?
- What training have they provided for their staff regarding the coordination of safety procedures?
- What first aid and safety equipment do the instructors carry with them?
- What wet weather options have they got in place?

Roles, risks, reality and responsibility

In the outdoors, people can see the direct results of their actions. For example, when I took a group of management undergraduate students for a day to a quarry, a couple of the more laid-back students did not bother to bring/borrow wet weather clothing, and assumed they could buy take-away food nearby. This was despite the verbal briefing and a written list of requirements. The onset of a cold front gave them immediate feedback about their lack of preparation and forethought, and during the debriefing the group took this to its conclusion: that the lack of forethought of two people in an outdoor or work situation could have jeopardized the rest of the group.

In other words, outdoor programmes involve people with real roles (which can be rotated); various levels of risk; and real experiences whereby they experience the results of their actions or inactions, planning or lack thereof. The three Rs (role, risk and reality) were highlighted by Colin Ball in talks on the prerequisites for courses for long-term unemployed youth (Ball, 1984). In this programme the need for youth to be able to 'hunt bears' was addressed: young people in many non-Western societies have by their teenage years been given large amounts of responsibility, for example to go to work, care for siblings, hunt or gather for food. This energy is sometimes diverted in our society to antisocial activity, in order to get adrenalin pumping or to work off excess energy and stretch limits and boundaries. Outdoor learning provides activities for people to try out new roles and/or new behaviours, but at the same time take responsibility for themselves and for each other's emotional and physical well being.

Division of labour: roles and responsibilities

It is important to understand the interlinking network of roles and responsibilities involved in outdoor development programmes, and to negotiate roles before and sometimes during a workshop. Frequently, though not always, the roles of outdoor skill instructors and learning facilitators overlap, and they work as co-facilitators since they observe different things about behaviours.

The roles and responsibilities of learning facilitators

Responsibilities to the participants

The learning facilitators have responsibility to:

- help participants to contract mutually acceptable group norms and to renegotiate these when and where necessary;
- help participants find a safe balance between self-examination and self-disclosure, and between encouragement and group pressure;
- encourage learning about self and others;
- respect the feelings of others and everyone's right to say 'no' to some activities;
- encourage active listening and questioning;
- reflect individual/group behaviours;
- give feedback to participants either individually, or in small-group or whole-group contexts;
- act as mediator if necessary;
- encourage reflection;
- act as a catalyst;

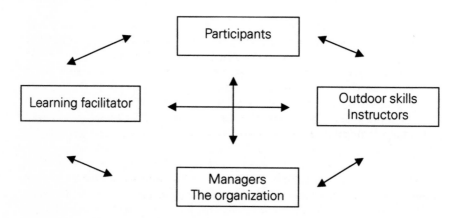

Figure 13.2   Roles and responsibilities

- promote creative problem solving;
- structure problem-solving exercises;
- debrief all activities;
- promote transfer of learning back to workplace.

Responsibilities to the client organization

The learning facilitators have responsibility to:

- liaise with organizations to ensure that learning contributes to the achievement of the organization's objectives;
- promote horizontal and vertical transfer of participants' learning back to the workplace.

Responsibilities to the outdoor skills instructors

The learning facilitators have responsibility to:

- ensure that participants give full attention to instructions for activities;
- adhere to group's safety ground rules;
- promote physical safety of all involved;
- ask questions;
- involve outdoor skills instructors in debriefing discussions;
- give feedback to outdoor skills instructors.

The roles and responsibilities of the outdoor specialists

Responsibilities to the client organization

The outdoor specialists have responsibility to:

- ensure that the programme is structured to meet the objectives of the client.

Responsibilities to the participants

The outdoor specialists have responsibility to:

- ensure that everyone understands instructions.
- ensure by personal example and instruction that all safety standards are maintained (eg wearing of safety helmets).
- respect the feelings of others and everyone's right to say 'no'.
- organize physical activities and simulations.
- check and maintain equipment.

Responsibilities to the learning skills facilitators

The outdoor specialists have responsibility to:

- liaise regarding the development of learning activities.
- share observations of useful and non-useful behaviours.

Roles and responsibilities of management and the client organization

Responsibilities to the participants

The client organization has responsibility to:

- ensure that participates know why they are going on this type of course.
- inform participants about insurance cover.
- discuss and support changes as a result of the course.
- conduct post-course evaluation and follow-up activities.
- arrange for work to be covered to ensure that participants are not interrupted during the course.

Responsibilities to the outdoor skills instructors

The client organization has responsibility to:

- ensure that participants reveal any major physical/emotional limitations before booking on a course.
- ensure that workers are properly covered by the organization's workers compensation insurance.

Responsibilities to the learning facilitators

The client organization has responsibility to:

- liaise to ensure that the course meets the organization's desired outcomes.
- reveal any hidden agendas (if they know them).

Roles and responsibilities of the participants

Responsibilities to the client organization

The client organization has responsibility to:

- discuss group and individual goals before departure.
- reveal any physical/emotional limitations when nominating for the course.
- ensure that all safety standards are maintained.

Responsibilities to fellow participants

The client organization has responsibility to:

- respect feelings of others and everyone's right to say 'no'.
- be aware of the difference between encouragement and coercion for different individuals.
- promote physical and emotional safety of all.

Responsibilities to the outdoor skills instructors

The client organization has responsibility to:

- listen to instructions.
- ask questions.
- reveal needs.

Responsibilities to the learning facilitators

Participants have responsibility to:

- attend pre-course briefing and post-course debriefings.
- be open to learn, unlearn, question, problem solve.
- listen to instructions.
- ask questions.
- reveal needs.

Risk and trust

> The art of living is nothing. . . if not a leap into the dark; a finding of alternatives to what commonsense holds to be inevitable. Those who look before they leap seldom leap.
>
> Laurens Van Der Post, *A Story like the Wind*

'"Risk" refers to physical and emotional vulnerability, including self-disclosure and awkwardness' (Long, 1987: 35). I am not advocating that you should not look before you leap. A wide variety of risk taking occurs on outdoor programmes, and participants have very varied perceptions of those risks. But what is quickly evident is the perceived psychological risk as opposed to physical risk. Some can, and need to be, meticulously planned, but there are others where participants may need to just go with the 'flow' (for example, letting the rope out slowly, going over the edge of a cliff). There is a fine dividing line between creating a 'safe' learning environment and giving people experiences in which to stretch their comfort zones to create space for new learning to occur.

The perception of what constitutes a 'risk' varies from one person to another. Examples include:

- asking for help;
- stating needs, limitations;
- looking down from a height;
- talking about feelings;
- going into water;
- taking the hand of a member of the opposite sex.

Children are often warned against doing things differently by phrases like:

- Get it right.
- Don't make a mistake.
- There is only one right answer.
- There is only one way to do this.

Boys are often limited by:

- Don't cry.
- Be a man.
- Be strong.

Girls tend to be limited even further:

- Be careful.
- Don't go too far.
- Stay in the garden to play.

Abseiling if carefully managed is a 'high bluff' activity, in that the perceived risk is far greater than the actual risk (which is the same in many work situations). The real risk is very low provided that:

- experienced outdoor instructors and learning facilitators are used;
- everyone follows standard safety procedures and wears correctly fastened safety helmets and harnesses;
- equipment is of the highest quality and regularly maintained;
- brake persons are properly briefed.

I have incorporated a one-day outdoor learning component in a five-day 'Train the Trainer' course. The outdoor component especially appears to become etched on people's minds, as this long-term evaluation feedback illustrates:

> Six months later it is the outdoor learning experience that remains most vivid. Learning to deal with fear was very important as it helped me deal with my fear of making presentations in front of people.

> Peter McCann, Train the Trainer course

Figure 13.3

Trust activities

At the outset of a course participants are encouraged to develop trust in themselves, the instructors, the equipment, and in their fellow participants. However, this needs to be accompanied by the encouragement of healthy questioning from participants, for example, 'How deep is this stake in the ground which is anchoring these ropes?'

Figure 13.4

There are a wide variety of short so-called 'trust activities' that can be used at the beginning of an outdoor programme. Three are described below, but I always add 'the right to say "no"' to the list of ground rules, and emphasize the need for individual responsibility regarding 'saying no' on health grounds. There is another delicate balance between encouragement and coercion.

STORY

On one course we had an afternoon of abseiling. Next day, a participant hobbled into class in obvious agony. 'What on earth happened?' I asked. 'Oh, I overdid it yesterday.' 'Why didn't you stop?' I asked. 'My knee was hurting. It's an old problem, but I was enjoying myself so much I didn't want to stop.'

During contracting with participants I now spend some time on the meaning of the ground rule concerning the right and personal responsibility at times to 'say no' versus support, encouragement and coercion.

Blade of grass

The 'blade of grass' activity involves one individual at a time standing in the middle of a circle with arms folded across the chest and with a rigid body. The person closes his/her eyes and rocks forwards and backwards, but is always supported by the raised palms of team members.

Trust fall

A 'trust fall' is where a person falls backwards slowly into the waiting arms of the team, who are carefully arranged facing inwards according to strength to break the fall in their arms. All glasses need to be removed, and there must be careful sending and receiving of messages before a person falls. If participants get over-excited and rowdy it is the responsibility of the facilitator to stop proceedings and remind them of the goal of the activity.

Blind walk

A 'blind walk' occurs where participants in pairs take turns to be either blindfolded or to keep eyes closed. The idea is to place the responsibility for safety in the hands of the sighted person. The person who is not sighted has to learn to trust the other. There is another version where the person is not blindfolded. A continuing choice has to be made to keep eyes closed.

Storytelling to teach safety

There is an inherent friction between the need for learners to experience life for themselves and the need to learn some things from a body of knowledge. For example, there is an ancient Chinese story of 'the woodcutter' which I use each time I take a group abseiling.

STORY: THE WOODCUTTER

Once upon a time there was a revered teacher in Ancient China. He was famous as he taught all the youth in his village how to chop branches from the highest of pine trees without accidents. His fame spread far and wide. One day a young man paid him a visit, as he too wanted to become a great teacher. He asked if he could watch him teach. The next day at dawn they went out with the youth of the village into the silent pine forest, which was covered with a carpet of snow. The sage instructed the learners and sent them up to the very tops of the trees, then he withdrew and lay under a nearby tree, closed his eyes, and promptly went to sleep. The young teacher watched in amazement but said nothing.

Gradually the apprentices cut the upper branches, and as they came lower down the trunks the sage awoke, ran up close, and called out, 'Be careful now, watch where you put your feet. Look out, go slowly.'

That night as they warmed themselves beside a glowing, roaring log fire, the young teacher said, 'Master, may I have permission to ask you questions about today?'

'Of course,' said the master.

'Well, today I saw you giving careful instructions before the apprentices went high into the pine trees, but then I watched in amazement as you slept under the trees and only awoke when they were 20 feet from the ground. Why did you not watch them the whole time?'

'It's like this. When they are high up in the trees their fear keeps them alert and high in concentration, but my experience has taught me that when they think they are close to the ground their concentration wanes. This is when the accidents most often occur.'

Once novice abseilers have heard the story, the participants who are acting as 'break persons' at the bottom of the cliff only have to call out, 'remember the woodcutter,' and everyone is reminded of the learning point.

Insurance and safety

Questioning exercise

Before I take any participants out of their normal work/learning environment, I invite a representative of the outdoor company to come and meet the group. This has an obvious advantage in the beginnings of building trust and rapport. I introduce the person (let's call him John), then ask the group to brainstorm all the questions they need to ask John before agreeing to venture into any activities with his company. I display all the questions, and do not allow the group to stop until someone has voiced questions about safety and insurance, and questions about the training and safety plans of the outdoor instructors. I will not venture out of an organization until all aspects of insurance, health and safety are covered. Outdoor companies have 'medical declaration' forms that are required to be completed prior to a programme by all participants, and that include questions on health, medication, allergies, level of fitness and so on. However, even though they are marked 'confidential' they should not be taken at face value, as some participants may not wish an organization to know about certain ailments. This also has insurance implications. So it is useful to ask everyone:

> What can everyone do to ensure the safety of everyone so that we all look out for ourselves and one another?

It may be useful to discuss the issues and dangers that may arise from not making needs known.

Debriefing and learning transference

> Experience is not what happens to you, but what you make of what happens to you.
>
> Aldous Huxley

The concept of debriefing comes from the military and emergency services, who routinely have 'briefings' at the beginning of an activity and 'debriefings' afterwards. During an activity participants become engrossed in the content. It is very hard for them to perform the roles of both participant and observer. As a result, periods assigned for 'structured reflection' are necessary; debriefing usually takes as long as, or longer than, the activity itself.

During an activity, a facilitator is trying to watch many behaviours at once. It is useful to keep a small journal unobtrusively (like the participants) to record observations, hunches and ideas to be debriefed.

During debriefing, the facilitator is trying to get different perspectives on an event. There is no one reality. The social construction of reality was well illustrated by the Japanese film director, Kurosawa, in his film *Rashomon* in which there are four main characters: a woodcutter, a bandit, a man and a woman. The story is observed by a storyteller and a listener. The drama is replayed four times over, from the perspective of each of the characters. The storyteller and the listener are left to draw their own conclusions on what 'really' happened. The beginnings of the English novel in the eighteenth century started with letters from people of different status depicting the same events from different viewpoints, for example, *Pamela* by Samuel Richardson published in 1739 (Richardson, 1974) and *Humphry Clinker* by Tobias Smollett published in 1766 (Smollett, 1983). The point is that 'pure facts' and 'true reality' are elusive beasts that resist capture. Indeed we never quite manage to trap the 'whole truth' in the absolute sense, even in courts of law.

STORY: ASKING FOR DIRECTIONS

In an outdoor programme a group of managers were map reading in the Kimberleys, a stunningly beautiful remote area in the north of Western Australia. The group's goal was to rendezvous with others at the northern edge of a gorge. They met an Aboriginal man under a tree, and after some chatting asked his advice on how to get to the gorge. Of course he gave them directions and the shortest route. When they arrived they were elated, thinking they were the first to arrive, but they were at the southern end of a steeply-sided gorge, and their instructions were to rendezvous at the northern end. Such 'process blunders' often produce initial mirth, but also memorable or 'epiphanic moments' (Denzin and Lincoln, 1994). The learning on giving explicit requests and crosschecking responses was well learnt that day.

Learning from experience

All learning is experiential. Even listening to a lecture is an experience, albeit a rather passive one. Kolb (1984) developed an easy model based on the work of John Dewey, cited already in Chapter 3 (page 73), which is a useful tool to help us learn from experience.

Kolb's model does not mean that we should get stuck in this circle; in fact it is more like an upward spiral, as next time we come to a similar experience we will be older (hopefully wiser) and the people and the situation may be different. So we should learn from the past, but not condemn ourselves to repeat it. Also note we do not necessarily go around the stages of this model sequentially. We miss stages: for example, we may jump from an experience to applying new learning without reflecting on it. However, this simple model does help us to analyse our actions and see if we miss out any of the stages. The model is very easy to remember (and therefore apply at any time) through the mnemonic ERGA, from the first letter of each stage.

Experiential learning involves trial and error, and enables you to modify your behaviour in different situations. It is a very personal way of learning. People may experience the same activity, but learn very different things from it.

Debriefing should occur as soon as possible after an activity, and if possible close to where the activity took place. It can occur as a:

- solo reflection (contemplation and journal writing);
- dyad or paired interviews;
- small group discussion;
- whole group discussion.

I find a mixture of the above is useful. Basically debriefing is composed of three questions, 'What happened?', 'So what?' and 'Now what?'

Debriefing tends to be verbal, thus less easy for participants (and facilitators) whose preferred learning style includes 'seeing' the results and summaries of a discussion. Flip chart paper is surprisingly versatile, and I have managed to use masking tape to attach it to trees and Land Rovers when needed.

It is best to start with non-threatening issues: 'What did you see, hear, do, during the last exercise?' 'What went well?' Facilitators should avoid dominating a discussion with their own observations, unless dysfunctional behaviour is noticed and not raised and/or noticed by participants. It is beneficial to end up on a positive note, perhaps with the facilitator summarizing positive behaviours observed, otherwise participants see the debriefing sessions as a time for 'kicking butts'.

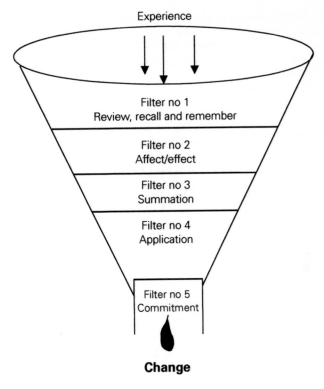

Figure 13.5 The debriefing funnel

Source: Priest and Naismith (1993: 21)

Simon Priest and Mindee Naismith (1993) use the metaphor of a funnel to illustrate how experiences can be channelled into change. It basically follows the same stages as the ORID process (see Chapter 3) but adds a fifth stage, 'commitment', as illustrated in their dialogue (Figure 13.5).

Some facilitators (usually the more experienced) like to use unstructured open questions to see what arises from the group; others prefer a more structured approach like the ORID process as a questioning framework.

However, it is useful to use the ORID questioning process which basically follows the Kolb model (see Chapter 3). Better still it is useful for facilitators to teach participants how to use the ORID method individually or in groups, so that they learn how to learn, and can transfer this debriefing process to incidents in their work and home lives.

The facilitator has to tread a fine line: it should not become an inquisition of what went wrong, rather a celebration of what went well and a determined diagnosis of what could be done better in the future. Ideally, the programme should build in opportunities to practise these new and/or modified behaviours. Ideally there should be a mix of light humour and thoughtful analysis. (This process works best in cooperative rather than competitive, and participatory rather than hierarchical, work cultures.)

Table 13.1   Sample dialogue

Facilitator:	Can you relate an instance where communication was poor?	Filter no 1
Participant:	Yes, when everyone seemed to be talking at once and no one was listening.	
Facilitator:	How did that impact on the group?	Filter no 2
Participant:	We were totally confused and were getting nowhere with the problem.	
Facilitator:	Can you cite an example of how communication improved?	Filter no 1
Participant:	Yes, when one person took control and began channelling our ideas. We all had a chance to take turn to speak.	
Facilitator:	How did you feel about that?	Filter no 2
Participant:	Great, I felt like I was going to be heard and we were bound to work it out.	
Facilitator:	What do you know now about effective communication?	Filter no 3
Participant:	Without it we are a dysfunctional lot: we need it in order to be successful.	
Facilitator:	Ever need it at work?	Filter no 4
Participant:	Yes, all the time. Without it we act the same way as we did just now.	
Facilitator:	How are you going to change at work?	Filter no 5
Participant:	I believe I will make an effort to listen to other people's ideas more.	
Another participant	I think it would be useful if we tell each other when we are not communicating well, like just now, so we don't slip back into our old habits.	

Source: adapted from Priest and Naismith (1993: 22)

Problem-solving activities

A variety of consecutive problem-solving activities enable group members to observe their 'good' and 'bad' habits and to set revised goals for the next problem. Behaviours are 'seen' and discussed openly during debriefing activities, but there is a chance to try out improved behaviours in the next activity, or at times it may be useful to repeat an activity.

In the workplace managers often deal with known problems and methods of dealing with them. However, increasingly they are being faced with new problems for which there are no well-established solutions. Outdoor training

Table 13.2   Types of problem

	Solution known	*Solution unknown*
Problem clear	1	2
Problem unclear	3	4

Source: adapted from Cacioppe (Barnhart, 1988)

is particularly useful for dealing with problems in the 2 and 4 boxes, where solutions are unknown.

Uses of outdoor programmes

I first became involved with outdoor programmes in the 1980s, and have used them with: managers and teams; mature students in a human resource development course; women as part of an assertiveness course; disabled and unemployed people.

Learning transfer

Learning transfer is the process of integrating learning and applying it to another environment. If there is a permanent change of behaviour, then learning is successful. 'Specific transfer' is where the skills/knowledge are similar, for example a computing course. 'Non-specific transfer' is the transfer of non-specific skills, such as problem-solving behaviours. 'Metaphoric transfer' is a subset of non-specific transfer. For example, standing on the edge of a cliff is similar to taking the first step to jump out of an organization to go for a new job; or managing the fear of heights during abseiling is similar to managing the fear of speaking in front of large groups.

Equity and gender issues

A number of equity issues need to be considered before embarking on outdoor programmes. I have been involved in outdoor programmes that were totally designed to cater for people with disabilities. Watching the faces of people abseiling from within their wheelchairs was an incredible experience. There are a number of roles that can be performed in outdoor learning. As mentioned before, not everyone has to do every activity; the element of 'choice' is so important.

Gender issues

A number of issues will impact on women who participate on outdoor programmes:

- prior physical experience;
- prior risk-taking experience;
- technical/practical activities as opposed to intellectual problem solving;
- physical strength and size;
- being in the minority (if the group comprises predominantly males);
- different perceptions of reality from males (Belenky *et al*, 1997);
- hygiene factors: periods and sanitary requirements;
- impact of menopause for some.

Even in Western society, there is a tendency for males to have had more prior experiences of physical risk-taking, rope use and knotting techniques (through sailing, or Boy Scouts), four-wheel driving, caving and so on.

STORY: WHEN THINGS GO WRONG

On one occasion, we were with a group of 'macho' men from a mineral sands company. By the third day everyone was quite relaxed, having achieved a variety of abseils, including at night into a very deep cave. Our last major activity was in Brides Cave, a huge sinkhole open to the sky, with majestic vertical drops and overhangs of about 100 metres. As per usual, I had my hair tied back in bunches and was wearing a helmet. I waited until everyone had gone over the edge. You could hear the rope sing as people disappeared over the edge, and with their increased confidence sped down the descent. There were odd 'Yahoos' of excitement.

My turn came, and I decided also to 'let rip' and loosened my right braking hand. As I descended, there was a sudden, sharp jolt on the rope. I turned my neck to the right and downwards quickly to see what was happening, and my hair went straight up the 'figure of eight' and was immediately twisted into the metal and rope. I clenched my right hand to brake myself immediately, then called to one of the instructors below: 'David, please take over the brake. I won't be coming down for a while.' He quickly realized what had happened, secured the rope at ground level, and called to Stephen, an instructor who was at the top of the cliff. They then set about a rescue activity whereby they could winch me up to get my body weight off my rope, so that I could disengage my hair.

Meanwhile I was chatting to the men below, who seemed far more worried than I was. As I had heard about such operations before I wasn't unduly worried; all I wanted was to make sure I didn't lose my hair. I had learnt enough about the equipment to know I wasn't going anywhere, just dangling. (I was slightly concerned, though, as Stephen was the least experienced of the instructors, and was being 'talked through' the rescue operation by David.)

A good 20 minutes went by before I was unthreaded and descended. The man who had acted as my brake rushed up to me, obviously very distraught. 'Are you OK?' Puzzled, I asked him, 'I'm fine, but what happened?' 'I was frightened, you were coming down so fast!' I replied, 'But so was everyone else', to which he responded, 'But you're small and female, I was scared for you.'

Stephen also descended from his rescue rope smiling, very pleased with himself. He gave me a hug. 'You kept your cool well.' 'Thanks. What would you have done if I hadn't?' Seriously he replied, 'If you had gone hysterical I would have cut your hair off.' Proudly he took out his shining bush knife. 'Terrific,' I thought. I've noticed before and since that some men (and women) cannot handle people showing distress, and will take prompt and often inappropriate action to stop distressed behaviour and tears. In this instance, attempting to cut my long hair would have led to far more distress.

Women-only programmes

Many outdoor programmes are 'male only' or 'male dominated', as the norm is that often only senior managers are sent on these types of programmes. Women-only programmes are criticized as being:

- unrelated to the male-dominated business world;
- artificial and less likely to transfer to reality, as women tend to be more cooperative and collaborative;
- trivial and artificial, as women do not mix mainly with women in the workplace.

I see the need for both single-sex and co-ed courses. 'Women-only' programmes do give women opportunities to break away from their traditional roles. For example, on one programme I met a female participant getting out of a car. She looked around and said, 'I need a big strong man to help me with my bags.' I replied, 'Well there's you and me. How about you take one handle and I'll take the other?'

Outdoor education should give everyone an opportunity to break out of gender-defined roles. In mixed groups, men tend to dominate, giving opinions and seeking support, while women tend to listen and praise others more. Men tend to interrupt more and state their feelings less. Women tend to express feeling more openly in single-sex groups.

Women-only programmes may be part of a company's affirmative action policies: in women-only courses women feel freer to talk about the issues they face. They can openly discuss the power imbalances at work. They have to negotiate unknown situations themselves. Women can practise assertiveness skills they might use with males, and obtain support and feedback from female co-participants who can empathize with their experiences.

STORY: ROLE MODELS

I built in a one-day outdoor component into a three-day assertiveness for women course in a management institute I once worked at. After initial resistance, the groups found the activity was beneficial, especially as it did not require muscle power. It was an activity that required listening; clear, loud verbal communication and feedback; and most of all, mind control over fear. After a number of courses, I noted the feedback from the women given to the male instructors: 'You were terrific', 'I couldn't have done it without you', 'You were so calm.' The next time I watched more closely and recalled my own first reactions. I too had attributed my success to the one strong male who helped me go over the edge. Indeed, I then saw this quiet, attractive male almost seducing women over the edge.

I made a vow to find female instructors after that: all female instructors for women's courses, and a mix of male and female for mixed programmes. The participants must 'own' their success, not attribute their success or failure to someone else (attribution theory).

Cross-cultural issues

There are many cross-cultural issues with outdoor programmes, although I notice that this method of learning is now used in Singapore, Indonesia and Malaysia. In one group we were on a short hike and I noticed one Indian gentleman looking rather puffed. We chatted and he said, 'You know, I don't think I've ever walked a whole mile in my life. Back home in Southern India, middle-class people just did not walk as a form of exercise because of the heat.'

The Australian bush is an alien environment for many Australian city dwellers, let alone visiting managers. On one outdoor programme I noticed a Mauritian woman who was distinctly scared of meeting a snake. She needed to go to the toilet, so I suggested that we go together. As we walked through the bush she shrank with horror when she spotted an object on a rock. It turned out to be a child's doll, but she thought it was some kind of spirit statue.

Many outdoor activities involve touch, which may be an issue. Some individuals in all cultures do not like to be touched; 'male to female' touch may be an issue and in some instances so is 'male to male'. Therefore these issues should be discussed when ground rules are set. One facilitator I spoke to in Malaysia said she often set up all-male circles and all-female circles where touch was involved, so as not to embarrass anyone. She also commented that she used strong tarp for the 'trust fall' exercise.

Staff at the University of Singapore cited the following potential issues (Tseng, 1991: 702). Some Asian participants may be less forthcoming in expressing feelings and emotions, and may feel uncomfortable during debriefing in which issues are openly confronted. They believe in maintaining group harmony, and 'giving face' to others. Bodily contact during the blade of grass activity, or activities which include touching the head of another person, could be very offensive for participants from Thailand, Laos and Cambodia. Likewise the positioning of people is a concern; being above someone else's head occurs frequently during abseiling activities, and yet this is again culturally inappropriate for people from Thailand. The timing of activities is also important, as the more superstitious Chinese will not participate in any outdoor activities during the seventh month of the lunar calendar, or the fasting months of Ramadan for Muslims. Likewise if training occurs on a Friday, time will need to be built in for Muslim participants to pray.

Likewise there may be conflict between the trainers' values and the culture. Anthony Tseng (1991) cited an example of a course for Japanese managers (both male and female). The Japanese client specifically stated that in Japanese culture the norm was that men are expected to take leadership roles and the women follow. In the programme the facilitators felt it was necessary to involve the women more, to enhance group cohesion. They took a calculated risk, and gradually encouraged the women to take more leadership roles. Luckily for the facilitators the transition was accepted by the men and welcomed by the client. A difficult dilemma.

In summary, issues such as food (halal, koshes, vegetarian etc), time for prayer, clothing and touch need to be addressed.

What to wear/bring

The needs of participants will vary according to the climate, season and types of activities. Comfort is important. Old loose comfortable clothing is best. I always ask participants not buy anything new for outdoor learning. I ask everyone to bring along a small pocket-sized notebook and half pencil for capturing ideas in the field. (See Chapter 7 on journal writing.)

Depending on the duration and types of activities, the following are useful items to add to a check list: hat, insect repellent, sunscreen, loose trousers or track suit pants, long-sleeved shirt, lace-up non-slip joggers or sneakers with rubber soles, jumpers, bathers, towel, washing implements, sunglasses, lip salve, weatherproof jacket. Band to tie up long hair in a ponytail! Cameras are useful to record people and aid the group memory/story back at work (and help people to see what happened if they could not attend). Digital cameras are useful, as copies can be e-mailed to all participants and used in in-house journals and reports.

Drinks

It is important for everyone to carry a (full) water bottle and have reserve stacks in vehicles. It is advisable to ban and/or limit alcohol except on the last night. Alcohol stays in the bloodstream and may impair judgement.

Sleep outs under the stars

In Australia in summer we often sleep outdoors during these programmes. There is a useful exercise where everyone has a night alone. People are dropped off at no great distance from each other, but out of eye contact so they feel alone. For safety reasons they must be in earshot as the story below illustrates. This is a super experience to give everyone quiet reflective space away from participants for one evening.

STORY: A NIGHT ALONE

At dusk one day we were given surprise orders, 'Collect your sleeping bag, journals, water, torch and so on.' We were dropped off by our facilitator alone in the bush for a night.

I checked out the ground and avoided putting my sleeping bag near a large crack in the ground, which I suspected might have been a cosy home for snakes. For once, I actually enjoyed being alone. I climbed a sparse acacia tree and watched the sun set, and listened to the sounds of the bush. I sorted out my belongings as dusk fell quickly, and wrote in my journal by torchlight.

Then my new water-resistant caving torch started to splutter and suddenly exploded. The battery acid quickly burnt holes in my sleeping bag, and I doused my hands with my drinking water, breathing deeply, feeling lucky I had not been badly burned. I was so tired that night I slept soundly, and got a shock next morning when the Land Rover arrived to pick me up and I was unprepared.

I learnt a lot about myself and being alone, independent and isolated. I could handle it all and emergencies without panicking.

Teamwork

There are many ways of measuring teamwork:

- self-reporting questionnaires;
- time taken to complete a task successfully (but, the interpersonal dimension is also vital);
- observation of positive teamwork behaviours by facilitator or designated observer.

It is useful to conduct a team inventory questionnaire at the beginning and end of an outdoor programme. Or create your own based on the dilemmas of teamwork that management have highlighted they wish to develop during the course. Conversely, at the briefing session use the 'Spotto' process to enable team members to identify the items they think need to be developed.

Spotto team building process

Author/background

This process was developed by David Napoli at Alcoa, Perth, Western Australia (unpublished). David developed this process to enable teams to work on their own issues as opposed to simulated team-building activities that sometimes allow team members to ignore their own problems.

Purpose/rationale

The purpose of the process is to enable teams who interact regularly to identify and prioritize desirable team-building behaviours, and to plan and monitor ways of achieving them.

Size of group

Up to 30 people.

Materials

Butcher paper, pens, masking tape.

Venue/layout

Semicircle of chairs and/or tables. Shady spot under a tree. It is useful if the team can work on issues away from the normal work venue.

Stages

If the participants have little or no background knowledge about effective team behaviours, it is useful to give prior reading and/or background information on what criteria enable a team to be effective and efficient.

Purpose

The facilitator outlines the purpose of the session. It is important to ensure that there is agreement that everyone wishes to be involved on an ongoing basis in improving the team's behaviour, to enhance the equality of work output and the quality of work life.

Creative visualization

Participants are asked through a creative visualization process to individually recall a team they have been part of at work, home or in the community that was particularly effective and efficient to work in. Individuals write down their own ideas.

Round robin

The facilitator 'round robins' the group and asks each individual to read out one example in turn, until all ideas are collected on flip chart paper. Repetitive items are ignored and/or clustered.

Discussion

The group members identify the top four items and discuss and clarify the meaning of each. Broad headings like 'communication' should be discussed so that participants can identify exactly what aspect of communication they wish to improve.

Dot voting

Each participant is given four dots and asked to place them on four separate elements that he/she thinks the current team needs to improve.

Visual display

The facilitator draws on flip chart paper horizontal lines representing each dimension.

Openness/trust 0 100
Cooperation   0 100
Fun/enjoyment   0 100
0   =   low performance
100 =   excellent performance

Action planning

The group members then discuss specific ways of improving each dimension over the next three months.

Long-term review

After three months the group reconvene and dot vote again to plot the new behaviours. The old flip chart record is compared with the new. Reasons for no change or declines are discussed, and new action plans formulated.

Celebration

Improvements are celebrated.

Outcomes

The team members have a shared vision for improving elements of teamwork.

Advantages

Everyone is involved and is hopefully supportive of the proposed changes. The team members confront their own behaviours in a constructive rather than destructive way.

Disadvantages

This process may be very time-consuming if clarification is needed.

It is important to conduct a number of trust and team-building exercises before venturing into the more complex, such as the spider's web exercise, or the more demanding, such as a high ropes course. Otherwise the activities may quickly develop individualistic, macho, competitive norms. The 3Rs of adventure training, 'ropes, rocks and rafting', may sound 'sexy' (and be suitable goals in themselves for adventure training), but the goals of the workshop must be clear and paramount at all times.

In a team activity it is not necessary for every member of a team to do everything. In fact, it is not always an effective or efficient way of achieving goals. Division of labour, help and support are required. Outdoor programmes ask individuals to make an effort to stretch their perceived limits. The amount of stretching will vary from individual to individual.

STORY: SAYING 'NO'

On one occasion we took a group comprised predominantly of young male managers to the quarry. The agreement was to finish around teatime before it got dark. The group was particularly enthusiastic and became very confident during the abseiling. The outdoor instructors responded, and after the successful completion of the group problem-solving activities allowed the keen individuals back on the main face for 'one last abseil'. Dusk falls quickly in Perth, and I noted the changing light conditions, quickly made worse by gathering clouds. I called a halt. One of the participants came striding up to me. 'Look, Chris, we don't have to finish yet. I want at least three more abseils to catch up with Sam.' 'Maybe another time, it's getting dark.' 'Hang on a minute,' he replied angrily, and some of the others supported him. I insisted: 'No, we are packing up now. It takes at least 20 minutes to pack up all the gear, and very soon you won't be able to see.' The man was about to explode. 'And anyway', I continued, 'you came here today for team building, not just abseiling, and packing up and getting everyone out of here safely is part of it.' He stopped in his tracks, and muttering, went off to join the others.

It was an interesting example of 'groupthink': that is, many of the team started to think they were invincible and were stopping dissent. Maybe I was a 'killjoy', but we had not prepared them for night work physically or mentally. We often built in night stalks at full moon or a night alone in the bush during longer courses, but on this occasion there was no prior planning, nor agreement for this kind of activity. I learnt that in the pre-briefing I had to spell out to participants the full context of the activity: that is, the journey to and from the quarry, learning about safety, use and care of equipment, abseiling and packing up activities were all part of the teambuilding process.

Using journals in outdoor programmes

Journals are a very useful tool for individual and group reflection, and a chance to monitor self-development and change on outdoor programmes. I ask participants to bring a pocket notebook.

If you are going to incorporate journal writing you also need to build in time for individual reflection and writing. Some people will enjoy the space to do this. Others who dislike writing may prefer to talk into dictaphones or small tape recorders.

During the risk management abseiling activity, participants were asked to monitor their thoughts and feelings before, during and after. Two 'thermometer gauges' were used so that they could record how their stress and confidence levels varied before, during and after each activity. A number scale is used to monitor changes, for example, 1 = before the first descent, 2 = after the first descent, before the second descent, and so on.

Figure 13.6 Graph to monitor personal risk management

Learning any new skill frequently involves some levels of stress for adult learners. In this activity, participants learn that fluctuations in stress and confidence levels will occur as they practise the skill and/or move on to harder aspects of the skill: for example, steeper and higher cliffs.

The journal is also used by participants to reflect on their role/s and those of others in problem-solving activities, aspects of teamwork and communications. The graph in Figure 13.7 is used to evaluate each problem-solving activity in terms of what the individual put into it and got out of it, and how the individual thought the group managed the task and process.

0 = low, 10 = high

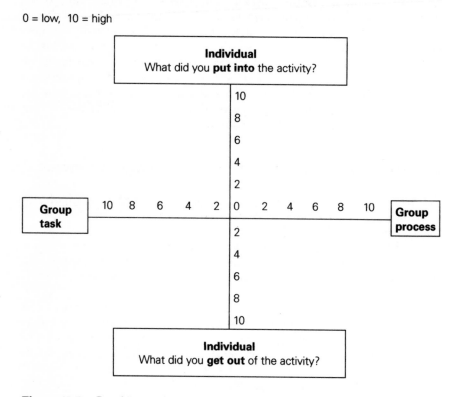

Figure 13.7   Graph to evaluate problem solving

Individuals can monitor what they put into the activity, such as thought and contribution to task/group maintenance, and what they got out of the activity, such as satisfaction and learning, and analyse the group's handling of the task and the process to achieve the task. As a result learning is enhanced. If time permits, you can repeat the activity so that everyone can practise the desired behaviours and strategies discussed in the first debriefing, then evaluate performance on the graph again.

Dialoguing may be between the writer and another person (living or dead), a piece of work (eg assignment or text), his/her body, events, institutions, animals, a problem or fear, religious, racial or cultural heritage. For example, a participant who was in touch with her fear when contemplating abseiling for the first time decided to confront the cliff:

Diana: Hello, cliff.
Cliff: Hi, there are a lot of people here today.
Diana: Yes. I wish I wasn't here.
Cliff: Why?
Diana: Because I'm scared stiff.
Cliff: What of?
Diana: You, of course! You're horrible, I hate heights.
Cliff: Why are you afraid of me? I'm just part of nature.
Diana: But I've got to confront you and get over you.
Cliff: You can always say 'no'.
Diana: True, but that's not my way. I hate giving in.
Cliff: OK, take a good look at me.
Diana: I'm not sure my stomach can handle it.
Cliff: Go on. Look at all the strong footholds and that strong rope and your gear. Are you afraid of heights or depths?
Diana: Both. No, depths, falling.
Cliff: Well, don't look down, as you go over the edge.
Diana: That's easy for you to say.
Cliff: Sure, but give it a try.

One participant wrote the following poem in her journal. Note the interesting change of writing perspective, ending with herself:

> We create our own
> structure of meaning
> And we are free to change
> we can choose.
>
> You can't always change
> what happens to you
> But you can always change
> how you feel about it.
>
> I can change.
>
> Rae Peverett

Impact of outdoor learning

As with many forms of personal development training, it is not easy to evaluate the effects of outdoor learning through a conventional questionnaire. As Mossman (in Bank, 1994) points out, ideally you need to compare four groups:

- one group that experiences an outdoor programme;
- one group that experiences a conventional short course;
- one group that receives some kind of extra attention;
- one group that receives neither course nor attention.

Even then it would be impossible to match groups of similar people, as there are just too many variables.

I believe an important evaluation question to ask participants is, 'Would you recommend this for the next group? If "yes", why, and what changes would you make?' Invariably I get an overwhelming 'yes'. Outdoor learning, when handled well, provides long-term joint memorable experiences.

As with any training activity, we cannot assume that people on outdoor programmes who learn to take risks by abseiling down a cliff will apply the same techniques in daily life, but as Conger states, 'What the experience does give me, however, is a sense of mastery and a metaphor for risk taking in other areas of my life' (Conger in Banks, 1994: 79).

Environmental and resource issues

I have observed a variety of behaviours in outdoor programmes. People become more aware of their use and/or abuse of resources, for example when water, food or equipment are scarce. As a result of being short of water in the Kimberley Ranges in northwest Australia, we all admitted later that as a result we use water far more sparingly. I have observed rather pampered managers from a mining company discard good food, throw down equipment without care (and lose it. . . temporarily), and suffer the consequences in such outdoor programmes.

Ending an outdoor course

The last debrief is important, to enable groups to re-enter their home and work lives. Participants often feel rather 'gung ho' at the end, and highs are wonderful to observe. See Chapter 15 on endings.

How outdoor learning differs from indoor training programmes

Training programmes are simulated learning environments, in that there is a kind of theatre and ritual. Trainers/facilitators design a number of interactive processes, but it is possible for participants to 'sit on the fence' for a few days. Analysis of case studies generally does not involve the feelings of the individual, and nothing is at risk when pronouncing answers to the problems of others in a story. In the outdoors it is very hard not to be involved physically, emotionally and mentally, even if an individual chooses legitimately to say 'no' to participation in some activities.

What is unique about outdoor learning

There are many distinctive features about outdoor learning:

● It is dramatic. Participants need to stay focused and attentive, and as a result they remember more.

- The activities are novel for most people, and therefore to some extent it is an equalizer (see also equity issues cited above).
- It is consequential: the results of mistakes are visual (people get wet, get lost, get hungry/thirsty), and they can be debriefed immediately so that learning is made apparent.
- It lends itself to the use of metaphors. The exercises are used as metaphors for work situations, and participants are encouraged to make up their own metaphors.
- Learning is transferable to work and home lives.

Videos about outdoor learning

She'll Be Wearing Pink Pyjamas was filmed in the Lake District in the UK, and stars Julie Walters. This video provides insights into women-only outdoor training programmes.

The Cutting Edge: Exposure is a Channel 4 documentary of an outdoor programme facilitated by John Ridgeway, with a group of managers from Rockwell, an international engineering company. The six-day course was conducted in Scotland, and the hardships experienced led the group to mutiny against the facilitator. The editors did not show the debriefing meetings, and the video damaged the outdoor learning industry. It is a good example to show facilitators and companies what not to do.

Conclusion

There is no doubt that outdoor learning programmes can be fun and give people long-term memorable experiences. The costs are greater than in-house workshops, but participants usually develop strong bonds as a result of being together over an extended period of time.

14

Facilitating distributed teams using technology

Introduction

This chapter was written by Sue Jefferies, a friend and colleague whose facilitation work I greatly admire. She has kindly summarized below some of the results of her current work using technology with distributed teams. I am indebted to her for writing this chapter and her contributions to this book.

This chapter outlines the particular issues that arise when using technology to enable a meeting or exchange of knowledge to take place. The issues are considered from the point of view of facilitating an online interaction of some type. This chapter is not intended to explain or describe all the technologies that are available in the market; they are too numerous.

This chapter includes:

- how and why modes of work are changing;
- what types of communication can be facilitated by technology;
- the difference between distributed and colocated groups;
- roles of e-facilitators;
- the role of trust in building distributed teams;
- the role of silence;
- the advantages and disadvantages of using photos;
- the role of humour;
- the role of feelings;
- ground rules for distributed groups;
- the future;
- description of tools.

Modes of work are changing

The proportion of work that is undertaken with groups of people that are geographically separated is increasing significantly. As Figure 14.1 illustrates, estimates are increasing of the proportion of work that will be performed by

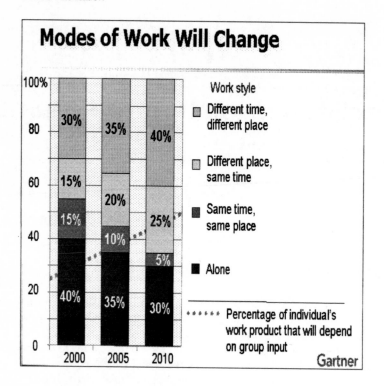

Figure 14.1   How modes of work will change

Source: Bell, Hayward and Morello (2000)

groups or teams with members in different time zones and different geographical locations, such that working together in the same time zone and same geography is actually 'unusual'.

There are several key drivers working together to push this increase in working together while being 'apart', chronologically and geographically. These drivers include:

- the increasing dominance of multinational corporations, spanning countries, means that intra-firm teams and groups must work across time zones, cultures and distance;
- advances in information and communications technologies (ICT), to enable distributed conversations and work to occur;
- increasing connections via technologies such as the Internet, between individuals and groups, that spawn distributed conversations and drive the further uptake of distributed technologies.

Communication technologies and tools to facilitate conversations offer the participants in that conversation, and the facilitator of the conversation, significant opportunities or 'advantages' over face to face conversations and workshops. But they also carry significant challenges. Being aware of the differences will assist facilitators, in that they can be as prepared as possible to leverage from the opportunities and prepare for the challenges.

Some of the opportunities and challenges of facilitating technology mediated conversations are listed in Table 14.1. Some can 'balance' each other out: challenges presented by e-meetings can be counterbalanced by the opportunities they present.

Table 14.1   Challenges and opportunities of technology mediated facilitation

Challenges	Opportunities
Reduced body language signals for participants to read and interpret.	Removes need to travel: fatigue and expense are removed or reduced. Less fatigued participants in group discussions.
Facilitator must develop different listening skills, being able to read 'e-body language'.	With no need to travel in order to meet, conversations can happen more frequently and be of shorter duration.
Participants may actually 'prepare' more for an e-meeting than they would for a traditional meeting. For example, apprehension and nervousness about appearing on a videoconference may prompt someone to prepare more ahead of time, since they may feel that there is more focus on them or that because they are 'being recorded', they don't want to make a mistake.	There may be reduced physical 'nervousness', as participants are not confronted by body language and physical presence. Note that participants may be nervous about the technology or tools – that is, self-consciousness about their physical presence may be replaced by self-consciousness about their technical awkwardness.
Participants may not 'say' (write) something, as they may fear being quoted on it at a later date, given that they often assume that conversations are being recorded.	May be more inclined to 'say' (ie write) something because they are not intimidated by the hierarchy or the physical presence of others.
Conversations can be slower, if they comprise typed text. Fear of making spelling errors can inhibit the speed even more. Dynamics change to the person who types fastest saying the most, rather than the person who talks the loudest in a colocated situation.	Participants sometimes 'come out' when not confronted by the physical presence of others. People are often self-conscious of their own physical presence, to the point where they speak or move less, for fear of making a fool of themselves or looking silly.
The lack of physical body language signals reduces the feedback available, and new skills must be learnt in how to read e-body language.	The conversation can be more focused, as participants are not distracted by the physical messages. Possibility of removing hierarchies: physical presence replaced by e-presence means that the existing hierarchy is not 'present' when people meet. This may encourage more dialogue. Obviously, participants will eventually reveal 'who' they are, by what they say.

STORY: THE CAMERA MADE ME DO IT

When I was talking to clients about the pros and cons of interviewing job applicants via videoconference, the clients mentioned that they had really noticed a
significant difference between those interviewed face to face (colocated) and
those interviewed via videoconference. They noted that the applicants on
videoconference had clearly spent more time preparing themselves than those
interviewed face to face. It seemed that the thought of being in front of a camera
was more stressful than the thought of being interviewed by a person, therefore
they became more nervous with the former – and prepared more.

Types of communication that can be facilitated via technology

Table 14.2 illustrates the different types of communication or interaction that
can occur, mediated by technology. There is a plethora of technologies (tools),
available in the market that allow groups to work together and exchange
knowledge. Facilitators working in technology-mediated conversations should
become familiar with a range of tools, in order to understand how the medium
affects the message. Examples of such tools are provided at the end of the
chapter.

Each of the factors in Table 14.2 will have implications in terms of the tasks
for facilitators and the skills required of them to complete these tasks. In a
traditional face to face facilitation, the facilitator coordinates a conversation that
is moving along at speed, can see all the participants, and is moving the
conversation along in a defined, set period of time. By contrast, in a distributed,
asynchronous conversation, the facilitator may not be able to see all the
participants, will be coordinating a conversation that will move along at a
different pace because of the tools being used, and the conversation may be
extended over many months, or be open-ended.

The classification system in Table 14.3 may be useful in thinking about the
different types of interaction that are available. Examples of factors for the
facilitator to consider are provided for each category of interaction.

These factors occur in a multitude of different combinations when working
with groups mediated by technology. The effects of these factors need to be
taken into account when designing technology-facilitated communication.

Different facilitator-mediated scenarios

A facilitator in a technology-mediated conversation or session can be required
to facilitate in a wide range of situations: a broader variety of settings than for
facilitation in colocated settings. The following are just some examples of
possible scenarios for e-facilitators.

Table 14.2   Types of distributed work

Interaction type	Sample tool	Example/comments
Same time, same place *Participants are in the same geographic location, at the same time.*	Traditional whiteboards Group decision support	F2F team meeting, facilitated session. There is no time delay between the message being sent and it being received. Sender and receiver are in the same geography.
Same time, different place *Participants are all logged in at the same time but they are in different geographies.*	Telephone Web whiteboarding Internet relay chat ('chat') Videoconferencing Teleconferencing	You are chatting to a group of people using Internet chat: real time, synchronous communication. There is no time lag between the message being sent and it being received.
Different time, same place *Participants are all in the same geography but they log in at different times.*	E-mail Shared file storage	You send e-mails to colleagues who are in the same geography. They respond. There is a time lag between you sending and them receiving (and then replying). You are working on a joint document with colleagues. Each of you accesses the document at a different time, retrieving a copy of it from a central, shared repository. There is a time lag between the message being sent and it being received.
Different time, different place *Participants are in different geographies and they log in at different times.*	E-mail Bulletin boards Threaded discussions Shared document repositories	Several people working together to produce a book store their materials at a specific location on the Web. There is a time lag between the message being sent and it being received. The sender and receiver are in different geographies.

Table 14.3   Comparison between meetings in different times and locations

Same time *Synchronous (S)*	Same place *Colocated (C)*	Different time *Asynchronous (A)*	Different place *Distributed (D)*
Synchronous Conversation speed is relatively high. Reactions are instant. Conversation usually within a restricted time period.		**Asynchronous** Conversation can move slowly. Reactions are delayed. Conversation can be over an extended time period.	
Colocated Facilitator may not be able to see all of the participants: they may be in the same city but communicating via technology. Facilitator will have a better idea of the physical context of the participants.		**Distributed** Facilitator may not be able to see all the participants. Facilitator has less idea of the physical context of the participants. There may be language or cultural differences to take into account.	

Synchronous distributed

You are asked to facilitate a group discussion that will occur via 'Webinar' (electronic conference). There are six groups of participants, in six different locations. Each group has between one and four members, with a total of 14 participants in the group you are facilitating. The session is three hours, and you are to guide the group to identify solutions for a series of issues that the organization is facing. The Webinar will consist of a central presentation, followed by a facilitated discussion of issues, questions and ideas generation.

Synchronous distributed is perhaps the most challenging for the facilitator in terms of managing the dynamics of the conversation/session. The conversation can move quickly, and the facilitator must be very alert in order to stay in touch with each of the participants, monitor and feed the conversation as it moves, and maintain momentum.

Synchronous colocated

You are asked to facilitate a group discussion that will occur via a group decision support system. In this scenario, all participants are in the same location (generally in the same room), with all having access to a computer that is linked to a central group decision software system. The software allows the facilitator to pose questions that will appear on the screens of all participants, as well as being projected onto a large screen that all can see. Participants can type their answers to the question(s) from their own computers; all answers can be seen on the larger screen.

You are facilitating a 'brainstorming' session, in which participants are seeking to identify creative solutions to a series of problems facing their group and the organization.

Synchronous colocated (technology-mediated) facilitation is the most similar to a colocated (non-technology mediated) facilitation (Hogan, 1994).

Asynchronous colocated

A large organization has created a number of internal communities of practice (CoP) that communicate via threaded discussion software within the company intranet. The CoPs need a facilitator, to drive the discussions forward, moderate the content and encourage the expansion of CoPs within the organization. The participants in the CoPs are located in the same geography, but the conversations occur via the intranet. Some of the participants sometimes meet face to face.

Asynchronous colocated communication can be skewed by the fact that some participants may have met, or will meet, some or all of the other participants – but they may not. The facilitator should make a decision whether to organize such a meeting for all or some of the participants, and think carefully about the impact of such a face-to-face meeting on the dynamics of the group.

Asynchronous distributed

You have been asked to facilitate the use of an extranet to plan, build and test new product prototypes, in a collaborative exercise that will occur between designers in three countries and customers in six countries. The collaboration will utilize virtual office software: an intranet with document sharing, whiteboarding, online polling, synchronous chat, video and voiceover IP, and threaded discussion facilities. As facilitator, you must establish the ground rules for the collaboration, establish team roles and responsibilities, coordinate online meetings, moderate discussions, assist participants to understand the technologies, and lead brainstorming processes.

Asynchronous distributed is perhaps the most difficult in terms of getting momentum of the conversation going and sustaining it.

The differences between distributed groups and colocated groups

In order to understand what types of skills and behaviours are required when facilitating distributed groups, it is useful to identify what is 'different' between distributed groups and colocated groups, in terms of the dynamics of the conversations. There are several major differentiating factors for facilitating distributed groups, the three most significant being the:

- absence, or reduction of, body language that is available in a colocated facilitation;
- time dimension: groups can converse over an extended period of time;
- ability to record the conversation.

Table 14.4 lists the key factors that are different in a distributed conversation to a colocated conversation, together with some possible implications of these differentiating factors.

Table 14.4   Differences between distributed and colocated groups

Differentiating factor	Comments and examples of implications
Time delays (for asynchronous conversations)	Allows participants time to think, as they can read and reflect upon what has been said so far. Possibility for several subconversations to occur over a period of time, as participants have time to read the threads of several conversations.
Conversation can be recorded	Participants can go back to reread and understand items. Points that might have been lost in a non-recorded situation can be picked up later. The amount of information to be absorbed is higher; in a non-recorded situation, participants would skim over such material, not able to read it later. It is more obvious who is commenting, who is talking, who is and is not participating actively.
A tool is used to transfer the message (rather than simply speaking)	This is a new behaviour for some participants. Techno-awkwardness must be taken into account, whereas most people are familiar with working in colocated groups. The dynamics of the conversation or interaction can be affected by the medium itself, as the tool can shape the message.
Removal of body language	By far the biggest impact. Participants and facilitators must learn to listen to new types of communication signals, when body language cannot be seen. The concept of listening to the 'feeling' or 'mood' of the room is entirely different. The intangible 'something' that is transmitted between people when they are in the same room is not, for the most part, transmitted in electronic rooms.
The medium influences the message	In terms of how simple or sophisticated the tools are: whether you have voice, video, data transfer or a combination of these, will affect the message. In a colocated situation, the facilitation is affected by the room layout or set-up. You are more reliant on the medium to work. Technology can fail.
Much wider range of situations than colocated	The wide variety of technology and tools available for distributed groups means that there is a much wider variety of situations for the facilitator to learn to handle and respond to.
Time required	The time required to have an e-conversation is generally longer than in a colocated situation. In particular, text-based conversations are significantly slower. This affects the dynamics of the conversation and the ebb and flow of emotions. Reactions would be different in an instant signal send/receive colocated situation.
Multiple conversations can occur	Generally this is not possible in a colocated situation. Many people speaking at once results in chaos. With distributed group tools, many conversations can happen at the same time. Even in synchronous interactions, the tools can allow several conversations to be 'watched' at the same time.

Roles for e-facilitators

In an electronic conversation, the facilitator wears several 'hats': he or she takes on several roles, or functions, just as in a colocated facilitation. For example, a facilitator can be leader, negotiator, conversation stimulator, pseudo psychologist and counsellor, depending on the situation. In an e-conversation, the facilitator is required to pay more attention to listening to the e-signals from participants and prompting further discussion, as required by the mood of the group.

Note that several of the 'roles' listed in Table 14.5 are 'titles' in their own right for specific work that occurs in specific electronic situations. For example, the term 'moderator' is most often used to describe a person who checks electronic conversations as they are happening, to ensure that participants are keeping to the ground rules and ejecting material that is not acceptable, or if necessary, ejecting participants from the conversation. An e-facilitator will take on this role at some stage, in many different situations.

> You are the leader, every time you speak.
>
> Anon

Trust: the key element for e-groups

Trust is fundamental to human relationships. When a team is working towards a goal, or a group of people is exchanging information, participants will do so more effectively and efficiently when they know how much they can 'trust' the people with whom they are interacting.

Trust is a value-laden concept, in that it may have a specific denotation but will have a variety of connotations, dependent on the background, world experiences and context of the person interpreting the term. Ask a group of people what they think 'trust' means and you will receive a variety of responses.

In a colocated team or group situation, trust is built up over time, through a series of interactions, including but not limited to:

- Seeing people (face to face). People tend to use their 'gut feel' about another person, to make an assessment of them, often (sometimes unfortunately!) during their first or initial meeting. 'Eyeballing' someone is about listening to all of his or her body language.
- Professional 'events' that occur on a daily basis, such as meetings, specific tasks being undertaken with other people, gatherings for social occasions, chats in the coffee room, etc.
- Ad hoc meetings. Seeing people in the corridor, bumping into them in the tearoom, a brief chat while waiting for the lift. All these interactions add up in the minds of those who are interacting, building a picture of the other person(s).

In a colocated situation, the group or team expects there to be a future association with the other members.

Table 14.5   The many roles of e-facilitators

Role	Description
Moderator	Frequently required in threaded discussions and asynchronous communities of practice.
	A moderator 'listens' to the conversation, reading contributions and checking whether the contributor(s) have adhered to the standards and rules for content. For example, a moderator may be empowered to remove or prohibit posting of material that is of a commercial or marketing nature, or that includes profanity or otherwise offensive material.
	In an asynchronous conversation, a moderator may be empowered to read all contributions, deciding whether the material will be posted at all. In a synchronous conversation, where there is no delay between speaking (or typing) and the material being visible to other listeners, the moderator may be empowered to eject the contributor from the conversation. (Similar to a colocated moderator.)
Conversation stimulator	Particularly in asynchronous group conversations, the facilitator may be required to plant seeds to keep the conversation going, or to pose questions in order to encourage continuous contribution to the ongoing conversation.
Listener: e-body language	When members of the group cannot see the other contributors, the facilitator must be proactive in listening for e-body language, in order to monitor the mood of the group and react accordingly. Just as a facilitator in a colocated situation must listen to the mood of the group and respond, so must an e-facilitator listen and react. The key difference, of course, is that the e-facilitator generally cannot see the participants and often may not hear their voices.
Coordinator	Passes the 'talking stick', allocating the right to speak to the next appropriate person.
Chairperson	Less 'participative', in that the chairperson listens to the debate or conversation and is deferred to when there is a ruling to be made. The chairperson does not take such an active role in prompting discussions and guiding the conversation; he or she spends more time listening.
Concierge	Shows participants how the tools work, where 'things' are, how to find their way around.
	Note that the term 'concierge' is also used to describe a specific function taken on by the person leading the use of a group decision support tool.
Counsellor	Listening to the emotions of the participants, offers a listening role and emotional support and guidance. This can be particularly challenging in a distributed conversation.
Conference Leader	In a Webinar or online conference, the conference leader guides the session, coordinating speakers and session progress.
Gatekeeper	Opens up technology to luddites. Controls access to the technology – and hence the conversation.

Trust is built slowly, but lost quickly.
Trust is hard won, but easily lost.

Why trust is important

When you trust someone, you tend to:

- forgive their mistakes more easily;
- assume that they have good intentions, when they do something that would otherwise be taken to be an act of poor or incorrect intention(s);
- help them;
- share information with them more readily;
- reveal something of yourself to them, eg snippets of information about who you 'are', as a person.

Trust is even more important for distributed teams, as their 'normal' or 'traditional' means of communicating are removed or reduced. (Note that 'normal' refers to same time, same place meetings, but this increasingly will not be 'the norm' in the future, so perhaps 'normal' should be replaced with the word 'traditional').

Distributed groups have a reduced set of interpersonal 'signals' to read. When something goes wrong, participants cannot see the person involved, to make a 'gut feeling' assessment of what the intent was. Trust can be and must be built, to provide a cushion in such situations.

The impact of being recorded

An interesting issue for e-facilitated meetings is the fact that there is often the option (perhaps by default) to record the session. When participants are aware of this, it can impact levels of trust and the level of 'openness' considerably. It may arise that participants feel uneasy about being recorded. They may hesitate to say or type something, for fear of it being used at a later date, perhaps taken out of context. They may also not wish their 'knowledge' to be 'captured', for fear of losing their status of being important or even irreplaceable. How often have you hesitated to put something down in an e-mail, that you might be brave enough to say in a non-recorded conversation?

How to build trust in distributed teams

Trust is built in colocated teams over a period of time. There is an expectation that you will see the other people in your group or team again and repeatedly. You build trust by sharing common experiences over a period of time. According to Sitkin and Roth (1993), there are several factors that tend to contribute toward trust:

- personal relationships with frequent face-to-face interactions;
- shared social or demographic characteristics or affiliations;
- expected future association;
- cooperative behaviour.

In situations where communication is mediated by information and communications technology, as it often is with distributed teams, the 'face to face' interactions often do not occur. That is, of course, if we use the traditional definition of face to face; where the interaction occurs between participants who are in the same geographic location at the same time.

We can, however, create similar trust-enhancing factors for distributed groups, if we are proactive about creating 'electronic relationships'. Table 14.6 gives some examples of activities that can contribute to the building of trust within distributed groups.

Table 14.6   Trust factors

Trust contributing factor	Distributed group activity
Personal relationships with frequent face-to-face interactions	Create frequent electronic interactions: voice, video, text, and combinations of these.
Shared social or demographic characteristics or affiliations	Allocate and spend time on sharing information about such similarities; proactively make the connections between group members. A strong common goal draws the group together with a sense of purpose.
Expected future association	Create a vision of what the group is doing, what is its purpose, what are the expected outcomes, talk about future events. Talk about time and how long the group is expected to be working together.
Cooperative behaviour	Encourage and support collaborative behaviours, such as participants helping each other, sharing knowledge and information. Create and enforce group ground rules.

Source: adapted from Sitkin and Roth (1993)

Generally speaking, activities that will contribute to the building of trust within distributed groups include the following:

- Set ground rules for and with the team behaviours.
- When someone breaks the ground rules, follow through on the consequences : do what you said you would do when someone breaks the rules.
- Log in to e-meetings on time. Just as it is rude to walk into a physical meeting late, it is also rude to do this electronically. Some types of software will announce your late arrival to everybody, causing a distraction to them all.

- Take the time to learn how to use the tools well. Don't expect your colleagues to put up with your lack of knowledge about your basic working tools.
- Actively participate in e-conversations, don't just 'listen in'. Silence can be misinterpreted. (More on silence in a later section.)
- Do what you said you would do – get that document out, send that e-mail, organize that event, make that telephone call – on time. Remember, following through on actions builds trust.
- Proactively offer at least a little 'personal' information about yourself. Find ways to let your personality show through the e-communication tools.
- Proactively participate in some 'self-disclosure': letting people get to know you, as a person. The facilitator should ensure that time is actually allocated to socializing. Using a tool to mediate a conversation can place a level of 'formality' on the interaction. The facilitator should work proactively to encourage informal, socialization interactions, to balance this formality.
- Spend time on team building, just as you would (should) for a colocated team.

This last point, spending time on team building, is important. Managers increasingly accept that they should spend time team building for 'colocated' teams: identifying strengths and weaknesses, allocating roles and responsibilities accordingly, introducing group members to each other, allowing time for human relationships to form, articulating and encouraging desired behaviours, monitoring activities and providing follow-up support. Distributed groups also need similar team-building activities, adjusted to account for the differences that occur when working in distributed mode.

Do what you said you would do

The fastest way to build trust is to do what you say you will do. That of course means that you don't make promises unless you are fairly sure you will be able to keep them; and if for whatever reason it looks as if you will not be able to do so, you contact your other team members as soon as possible to let them know and work to find alternatives.

The role of silence

Remaining silent will reduce trust.

Team members do not have the ability to 'meet each other or the facilitator in the corridor', or to 'see body language'. If a person is electronically silent, team members will not know what he/she is doing, what he/she is thinking, or what is going on. Often, they will assume the worst: that he/she is not working on what he/she said would be done, that he/she is are not contributing to the team, and so on. It is important for facilitators and team members to take time to not be silent.

E-loafers and e-lurkers

In a distributed group, an issue that quite frequently arises is that of e-loafers and e-lurkers. This is particularly so in distributed collaborations, where the knowledge being shared and created is dependent on the contributions of the participants as a whole.

E-loafer

An e-loafer is a person who does not do the work that is required in an e-conversation or e-group. An e-group or e-conversation requires more proactive behaviours, to avoid being labelled an e-loafer.

E-lurker

An e-lurker is a person who 'hovers' around an e-group or e-team, without making a contribution or saying anything. A lurker may not want to be 'seen' or even recognized; he or she may be lurking in order just to listen, in case something interesting or of use to them happens. E-lurkers can cause resentment among other members of the group or conversation, as they may be seen as 'free-riders' or even 'peeping Toms'. Frequent comments about e-lurkers are that other group members do not trust them, as they do not know why these people are 'hanging around', and therefore assume the worst. (See the comments on silence and trust.)

As an e-facilitator, it is important that you 'listen' for e-lurkers and e-loafers, identify why they are exhibiting this behaviour, what impact it is having on the group and, if appropriate, encourage the e-lurkers and e-loafers to be more active in their contributions. You may wish to have an open conversation with the group about how they each feel about e-lurkers and e-loafers.

Photos: to see or not to see

Knowing what people look like (their bodily appearance) can have an interesting impact on how we communicate with them.

A picture is worth a thousand words

What a difference a photo can make. When you are interacting with someone electronically, someone you have never met face to face, a photo can really make a difference to how the other person interacts with you. We tend to use the way a person looks on the outside to 'add' to our picture of who they are. When you are trying to build trust in a distributed group, try providing photos of the members, as well as some brief details of 'who they are'. The participants will feel more at ease, and will feel that they 'know' the others better, when they have photos available. For example, when we converse with people over a period of time, we begin to assume things about them, such as their race, colour and voice. Seeing a photo of them can sometimes change the way we feel about them. Try this with an e-group. Establish the conversation for a while, without sharing photographs, then ask participants to share their assumptions about each other. Then ask them to provide photos, and review the assumptions they had made.

Table 14.7   Pros and cons of using photos

Advantages	Disadvantages
Participants may feel that they 'know' each other better.	Judgements may be made, based on what a person looks like.
May 'break the ice' a little faster: participants may feel closer to each other in a shorter period of time.	Participants may feel more vulnerable or exposed, if others know what they look like (depending on the subject matter for the group interaction).
In group conversations, it is slightly easier to keep track of who is speaking when you have photographs to mentally attach to them.	Two-dimensional photographs are rarely reflective of what a person 'really' looks like when animated, but there is still a tendency to make assumptions based on the photograph.
If the team does eventually meet, they will feel more comfortable and familiar if they have seen photographs. If they have not, they will have formed mental pictures of the other participants, and will be working to reconcile the difference with what the person actually looks like.	

The role of humour

Humour can be used very effectively to build rapport in teams, to 'break the ice' and to contribute to the culture of the group. You can use humour, carefully, in e-groups but there are some traps. For example:

- Be careful. You can't see reactions, so you have no cues as to whether humour is going well. In particular, people cannot see that you are 'kidding' or 'joking'. They cannot hear tone in your voice or see your facial expressions of caricature. Adding smiley faces in text messages is an indication of 'I'm joking' – but there is a fine line between a smile and a smirk.
- Distributed group work means that you are more likely to be working with groups that cross cultures, hence a reasonable proportion of the humour that you might want to use is unlikely to be universally acceptable to all participants.
- Cartoons attached to e-mails and pasted in bulletin boards can be fun, but be sure you are not breaching copyright laws by use of such material.
- You cannot retract anything that is typed, so be careful with online joke telling.

How to use humour in distributed groups

Some very simple advice with regard to the use of humour in distributed groups:

- Wait until you get to know participants a little, before testing out humour.
- Take very small risks with humour; be sure to get feedback as to how it was received.
- Start with humour that is least likely to be offensive to the group, according to what you know about them.
- Ask others in the group to share their ideas on humour, fun, etc, to assist in gauging the opinion of whether and how it could be used.
- Consider the use of a ground rule for the group that cartoons, jokes and so on cannot be used by participants unless seen by the facilitator first.
- Consider establishing ground rules with the group as to what is and is not appropriate with regard to humour, similar to EEO guidelines for colocated groups.

STORY: THE ROLE OF THE RITUAL; FACILITATING IN A DRESSING GOWN

Facilitating from home via technology means I have to get into the role of facilitator differently. The ceremony or ritual of putting on that smart suit, make up (if applicable!) and travelling to a physical venue gets the nerves ready, the adrenalin pumping, the mind into formal mode.

Zipping downstairs to the home office, in the middle of the night, still with warm socks and track pants on, creates a somewhat less formal mental mode. The session feels different, in that I do not have that edge that comes from the nervous build-up occurring during the dressing and travelling ritual.

The role of feelings and intuition

Expressing our feelings and listening to the feelings of others is a key contributor to successful groups. In colocated groups, 'listening' to the feelings of others includes watching their body language, reading their facial expressions, and being in the same physical room, to absorb the 'atmosphere', or 'room vibes'.

In a distributed group, these types of signal are not available, hence feelings must be both expressed and 'heard' via different methods. Facilitators need to learn to listen to 'e-room vibes'. E-intuition must be sharpened, just as colocated facilitation requires attention to intuition. Just as a blind person must learn to use senses other than sight, so must distributed groups learn to listen for and express their feelings via different methods. Technology is improving rapidly and will continue to advance, improving the ability to mimic physical presence. Rich context interactions are facilitated by technology that transports voice, video and text simultaneously. In particular, video has improved extensively, enabling smoother transport of images and synchronous voice.

We can add expression of feelings to electronically mediated conversations by tools such as the use of:

- emoticons (see below); the most commonly used is a smiley face ';-)';
- bolding, italics, underlining, exclamation and question marks;
- colour, larger fonts;
- avatars or 'caricatures' or 'pictures' that denote each person in an e-conversation.

At the contracting stage find out what tools people are working with

Note that people may not always be able to see extra formatting and special characters that you are using to add emotions. You should check to find out what they can and cannot see. Obviously, if you think recipients can see your use of colour and highlighting to express yourself and they actually cannot, there could easily be misunderstandings along the track. That is, in the contracting stage of the communication, find out what tools are being used and what is available.

Emoticons

Sometimes called 'smileys', emoticons are symbols and characters used to add expressions of emotion and feeling to what is said in plain text. So, for example, a colon, ':' is placed next to a hyphen '-' and a close bracket ')'. Together, they look like a smiling face (tilt your head on the side if you can't see it). Note: emoticons will appear on the page differently, according to the font being used.

Table 14.8   Examples of emoticons

Emoticon	Approximate meaning
☺	Smiling face; happy, laugh, 'I'm joking' = colon plus hyphen plus close bracket
☹	Sad = colon plus hyphen plus open bracket
;-)	Wink, 'nudge nudge, wink, wink', or 'secret between you and me' = semicolon + hyphen + bracket
!-)	Black eye; you knocked me out = exclamation mark + hyphen + close bracket
#:-o	Shocked; 'oh no!', = hash sign + colon + hyphen + lower case letter o
:-P	Sticking tongue out = colon + hyphen + lower case p (or upper case for emphasis)
:-X	Kiss, or my lips are sealed = colon + hyphen + lower case x (or upper case for emphasis)

There are dozens of these emoticons in circulation. If you wish to explore more of these, simply enter 'emoticon' or 'smiley' into a search engine and you will rapidly find pages that are compiled by enthusiasts. Remember, there is no strict definition for each of these: they have a general use and generally accepted meanings.

People who spend a lot of time in Internet chat often build up a vocabulary of at least 20 or 30 of these, sometimes more. For general users the 'happy' and 'sad' faces are common, as is the 'wink'. As always, if you are going to use such symbols, check to see that they are within the vocabulary of your participants. Similarly, be sensible in your use of these. Too many can annoy your readers, and some are open to interpretation, so may be taken in a way you had not intended. For example, the 'wink' can have many connotations, depending on the topic of discussion. Be particularly careful in cross-cultural (cross-nationality) exchanges.

E-shorthand

An extension of the concept of the emoticon is the use of abbreviations in the form of acronyms. These are used to speed the process of getting meaning across in a text-based conversation. Many add 'emotions' or 'inferred meaning' to the words being typed.

As with emoticons, there are many of these acronyms in circulation, but only a short list that is used and understood widely. Those that are generally well understood are 'LOL', 'IMHO' and 'WDYT' (refer to Table 14.9 for translation). If you are holding an e-conversation about a specific topic or a technical issue, you may see a number of others entering the conversation, that is, created for just that topic or speciality.

As an e-facilitator, use these shorthand items to save time in an e-conversation, particularly in a typed (text-based) synchronous conversation. You can also use them to 'bind' the group together, in that the language that the group uses becomes part of their culture. Of course, you should ensure that all the acronyms used are familiar to and understood by everyone in the group. If not, they can exclude members of the group.

Language is culture

As with most forms of language, you must understand the meaning of the 'words', in order to be a part of the group that is communicating. Just as teenagers and children create new words or new meanings for existing words, in order to create their own culture (and perhaps to 'lock out' adults!), so can the words and symbols of e-communication create new cultures and lock out those who do not understand the words. Sometimes, as with the teenagers, this esotericism is intentional. For example, in some frequently used Internet chat room situations, circles or cliques can form, and those who are new ('newbies'), show themselves up by not knowing the 'lingo' or 'in phrases'.

An example of this is 'AWGTHTGTATA', which means 'Are we going to have to go through all this again?' Clearly, most people would find it hard to guess what that acronym means. It is so long that it is almost 'ridiculous', in that you almost may as well type all the words, rather than try to remember the acronym.

Table 14.9   Examples of e-shorthand acronyms

Acronym	Translation
LOL	Laugh out loud
ROFL	Rolling on the floor laughing
BRB	Be right back
WDYT	What do you think?
IMHO	In my humble opinion
LTHTT	Laughing too hard to type
TTYL	Talk to you later
<g> or ***grin***	Grin You can put multiple '<>', or more '*' on either side of the 'g' to mean more emphasis
<G> ***Grin***	Big grin
AISI	As I see it.
ANFAWFOS	And now for a word from our sponsor
AWGTHTGTATA	Are we going to have to go through all this again?
BAK	Back at keyboard
PMFJI	Pardon me for jumping in
PTMM	Please tell me more
GTSY	Great to see you.
IBTD	I beg to differ
YMMV	Your mileage may vary (or your experience could be different)
IYSWIM	If you see what I mean

However, it is used by 'hard core' Internet chat room users, as an expression of exasperation toward those who don't 'get it' (whatever is being discussed) quickly.

Ground rules for distributed groups

Just as colocated groups work better with clearly articulated, fully accepted ground rules that are adhered to, so do distributed groups. In reality, distributed groups need clearly articulated ground rules more than do colocated groups, since as a generalization, colocated groups can more easily discuss issues as they come up and can of course see each other, so are likely to be able to have an idea of why someone is behaving in a certain way.

Distributed groups are generally in need of more discussions and help regarding 'How do we work effectively?', in that the participants may not have worked in a distributed setting before. Even those that have done so before may have found that the group process suffered because of its being geographically or chronologically distributed, without specific ground rules.

Ground rules can help

Generally, people do not yet know how to behave effectively in distributed teams, and will therefore need specific guidance in what is acceptable and/or not acceptable. E-mail is a good example. A surprisingly high proportion of e-mail users have not taken the time to learn how to use this medium well. It can become the source of great frustration and misunderstanding.

Table 14.10 gives some examples of ground rules for distributed groups.

Table 14.10 Sample ground rules for distributed groups

Example ground rule	Explanation
Acknowledge receipt of e-mails within 24 hours	The sender then knows that the e-mail has reached its destination. Never assume that it has! Remember that a 'receipt' only indicates that an e-mail has been displayed on the computer of the recipient; it does not mean that he or she has read it or understood it.
Don't demand an immediate response to an e-mail	Technology has bred impatience! Don't accost a person over the phone with 'Why haven't you responded? I know you have received it.'
Make an effort to say something occasionally in an e-meeting	Respect the time of your colleagues and that they are likely to have many other e-mails to answer, just as you do. Remember, the others generally cannot 'see' you, so it is important to participate proactively, letting others know that you are present and you are contributing.
Do what you say you will do	If you state that you will return a phone call within 24 hours, do so, even if you have to just call to say, 'Can I talk with you later?', or you have to get someone else to call for you to explain the delay. Do not just leave the other party wondering. Silence is an easy way to break down trust.
Use the telephone	If your distributed group uses e-mail or other tools a lot, ensure that some time is spent talking with each other, when possible, either group teleconference or one to one.
Turn up on time	Log in to e-meetings on time. Give notice if you are going to be late or unable to attend.

Electronic etiquette

The use of electronic tools for communication has seen the creation of some interesting behaviours, particularly in the area of patience. People are apparently becoming more impatient, in that they are demanding instant responses to messages and making assumptions that messages sent will instantly be received, read, understood and acted upon. For example, e-mail is now an almost ubiquitous tool. Its misuse is the source of much interpersonal friction, communication breakdown, misunderstanding and escalation of issues that would not have become issues, had the sender and receiver taken the time to establish ground rules for its use, learn good e-mail etiquette and use the tool responsibly.

Setting ground rules for the use of electronic tools will assist in reducing the possibility of misunderstandings and communication breakdowns. Table 14.11 gives just a sample of possible ground rules for a selection of electronic tools. Take the time to articulate your ground rules with your group, for the tools that they are using. This list is not intended to be exhaustive, these are merely examples of the types of ground rules that can apply to the various tools.

Table 14.11   Ground rules for technology tools

Tool	Comments
E-mail etiquette	Acknowledge receipt of e-mail! You can simply replace the subject line with the word 'received' and send it back, or if the sender requests a received receipt, send one. You may wish to add a 'disclaimer' to the receipt, indicating that receipt does not imply that the receiver has read or understood the message; it has simply reached its target.
	Agree as a group that acknowledging receipt of e-mail does not mean that the recipient must then immediately respond to it, or that the sender can in fact demand an immediate answer.
	Do *not* assume that the e-mail has reached its destination. It sometimes does not.
	Do not assume that because you have sent an e-mail, the intended recipient has been able to read it instantly.
	Do not use e-mail to advise of urgent matters, such as last-minute changes to appointments, unless you are absolutely sure that the target will be able to receive, open and read the e-mail immediately.
Voicemail etiquette	Don't play voicemail tennis. Leave a useful message: clearly state your name, the time you called, the reason for your call, the specific information you are providing or requesting, a number (or medium) on which you can be reached, and importantly, some suggestions to the recipient about times that you are likely to be available.
	State numbers slowly and clearly, repeat them.
	Always leave your return number, for the convenience of the recipient.
Videoconference etiquette	Place name cards in front of participants, as well as location name.
	As in a teleconference, the moderator should be checking continuously for participation, seeking confirmation that messages are being heard and understood.
	Depending on the quality of the video, be wary of making rapid or expansive movements, but don't sit 'stone still' either.
Teleconference etiquette	Trust in a teleconference can be greatly improved by a good conference moderator, who ensures that all participants are being paid attention to. Ensure everyone has a list of all attendees, and if possible a photo of them as well. The moderator should check

Table 14.11   *(continued)*

Tool	Comments
	continuously to see that everyone has heard the conversation, and that all are logged in and actively participating.
	State your name before speaking, unless you are very sure that everyone can recognize your voice (Hogan, 1993a, 1993b).
Web conference etiquette	If you arrive late, remember that your late arrival will be announced to everyone who is logged in. Depending on the technology, this announcement may be a loud 'Joe Smith has entered the conference', broadcast to everyone.
	Don't be late. Aim to login a couple of minutes before planned commencement time.
	Consider not logging in if you are late.
	Remember to find out from the e-facilitator what the protocol is for entering the web conference late. He or she may be able to mute your arrival so that it doesn't disturb others.
	If you do arrive late, don't demand that you be provided with details of what has happened so far. This is frustrating and rude to others in the conference, just as it is in a colocated meeting.
E-conferencing etiquette	Ensure that you spend your time before the e-meeting learning how the technology works, what is expected of you, which buttons you should press, etc. Do not enter an e-conference, and then expect other participants to wait while you catch up with 'how does this technology work'?

The future

As the level of technology-mediated group communication increases in the future, the demand for e-facilitators is likely to increase. As technology advances and improves, the types of interaction that are possible using technology are expected to broaden: the complexity of conversations and interactions that can occur will increase, as tools become more convergent. As access to these tools and technologies increases and broadens, groups are more likely to have high-context, high-complexity conversations.

Interestingly, tools being developed tend to mimic existing methods of group interaction, perhaps because it is easier to change the technology than to change the human behaviour. For example, Web-based software tools that enable Web-based presentations to occur, start from a base of mimicking the current presentation process: a speaker (or speakers) on a stage or podium, with the audience sitting in rows in front of the speaker.

The increasing use of distributed teams and ever-shrinking budgets mean that there is less likelihood that such teams will be able to travel in order to establish initial relationships. This means that increased skills will be needed to establish and build distributed groups to effectiveness and efficiency. Facilitators will increasingly be called upon to manage e-facilitation scenarios.

Description of tools

Please note that Table 14.12 is not intended to be an exhaustive list, but only a sample of the types of tools that are available. New tools are continuously being developed. Similarly, the facilitator issues and example applications are not comprehensive, they are indications only.

Useful Web sites

www.collaborate.com: this site is titled 'Strategies for collaboration and knowledge management'. It contains useful information about online collaboration, creating, developing and transferring knowledge among team members. There is a useful list of tools and software technologies for enabling online collaboration.

www.collaboration-tools.com: contains a handy list of tools that enable and support online collaboration. The list is not exhaustive and does contain vendor-specific information.

www.3m.com/meetingnetwork: 3M Meeting Network. Contains a range of resources about meetings: tools, tips and techniques. This site is about meetings in general but also contains useful resources for online meetings.

www.emoderator.com: 'This page is a growing set of resources for moderators and moderators-to-be of online discussion in both academic and non-academic settings' (quote from Web site)/

www.iaf-world.org/: International Association of Facilitators

www.whatis.com: a good source of reference for definitions for thousands of information technology terms.

Conclusion

E-moderating is an exciting and challenging branch of facilitation. As this chapter illustrates, e-moderators require technical as well as people skills. The area is constantly changing, and facilitators need to work with programmers to devise new ways of making technology serve human communication.

Table 14.12 Sample of e-conversation tools

Tool	What it does	Example applications	Facilitator issues
Bulletin board	A Web site where topics of discussion are 'posted'. That is, messages are typed in plain text and 'pasted' or 'pinned' to an e-bulletin board. Other visitors to the site can post messages next to previous messages, or start new conversations (topics), etc. Depending on the sophistication of the software, visitors can search through messages, access them chronologically, or in reverse or randomly.	Asynchronous colocated or distributed. Special interest groups (SIG). Communities of practice (CoP).	Maintaining momentum of the conversation, maintaining interest of the participants to continue to contribute to the ongoing conversation. Needs attention to introduce socialization elements.
E-mail	Send messages to a recipient. Can attach documents, pictures, sound files.	Asynchronous colocated or distributed. Ubiquitous communication tool.	Asynchronous problems: delay, possible misinterpretation, multiple answers interleaved. E-mail is notorious for creating friction and interpersonal issues because of misinterpretations.
Chat (or Internet relay chat, IRC)	Software that allows two or more participants to send typed (text) messages to each other. Participants are in a 'room' in which the text of conversations appears as text scrolling up on the screen. Participants type text, 'send' it to the room, and it appears on screen so that all participants can see what has been said.	Synchronous colocated or distributed. Real time, or synchronous conversations, one to one, one to many or many to many.	Speed of the conversation: intervening and guiding the conversation when many participants are contributing at once. Subconversations can occur as the 'main' conversation is progressing. In a colocated situation, this is easily controllable.

Tool	What it does	Example applications	Facilitator issues
	More sophisticated software allows voice and video to be added to the conversations.		
Document sharing	Generally refers to software that enables a specific location on the Web to become a central document repository for a group or team. Documents are stored on a Web server, and participants log on to that site in order to view, upload or download documents.	Asynchronous or synchronous, colocated or distributed. Groups can access documents via a more secure method than attaching and sending them via e-mail.	Grouping, ordering or categorizing documents in a manner that is most acceptable and logical to the group. Maintaining document order and managing versions.
Guided surfing	Software that allows participant A to take 'control' of the computer of participant B, in order to 'show' him or her any site on the Internet. That is, participant A types in the address of a particular Web site and the screens of both participant A and B show the contents of it.	Asynchronous or synchronous, colocated or distributed. Useful for showing participants particular content, as a group.	Few issues. Perhaps need to be wary of the speed at which surfing is done.
Instant	Software allows users to communicate via the Internet 'instantly' with others who are also online (connected to the Internet). When someone logs on that you want to talk to, the software will 'page' you to let you know that the person is online and whether	Betty wants to talk to Joe. Betty sets up her IM software to page her when Joe logs on. Betty waits, going about other work, with her IM sitting in the background, listening for Joe.	Side conversations that can occur at the same time as the main conversation; possible distractions. Agreeing on ground rules for when participants will/will not be able to present themselves as 'available' or 'not available'.

Table 14.12 (*continued*)

Tool	What it does	Example applications	Facilitator issues
	they are possibly available to talk. Users can choose to make themselves 'visible' or 'invisible', according to whether they wish it to be known that they are online, or not.	Joe logs on. Betty is sent a message that Joe has logged on. Betty can then click on Joe's name to send Joe an 'instant' message that she wants to communicate with him. Betty can open up a chat conversation (text and/or voice and/or video), with Joe. Joe must accept the call for this to happen. If the call is accepted, Joe and Betty are connected and any messages they send are 'instantly' received by the other. This software is very useful if you wish to 'catch' someone to exchange information.	
Newsgroup	A conversation, or discussion about a particular topic. Participants in the discussion write comments or materials about the topic. These are sent to a specific server (storage device) on the Internet, and then the material is redistributed by Usenet, to all participants who are listening in to the conversation.	Asynchronous colocated or distributed.	Ensuring subscriptions to the lists are up to date. Controlling frequency of messages sent and quality of materials being sent.

Tool	What it does	Example applications	Facilitator issues
	Usenet participants can subscribe to an e-mail list, in order to receive updates of what is new to the newsgroup.		
Paging	When participants are logged on, a message can be sent to them to respond to a specific request, such as to enter into a conversation with other participant(s).		Possible distractions to the main conversation.
Polling	A method of taking a vote on an issue. Software allows a question to be posed and participants can then respond with their answers, or votes. The software can automatically count responses and display them graphically, updating 'on the fly', as further votes are received and counted.	Useful to gauge the mood of the group, reach decisions, take consensus, etc. Tools are available with a variety of functions, such as blind voting, open voting, multiple choice, open ended answers, etc.	Being wary of how the results can be 'manipulated' or skewed by the software functionality or behaviour of the voters.
Smart boards	An interactive whiteboard. A physical board (imagine a whiteboard), on which person A writes. Person B, who is located geographically separate, also has a smart board in front of him or her. Whatever person A is writing on the board, appears on the (separate) board in front of person	Very useful when there are two (or more) groups, in different locations, who wish to brainstorm something together. Group A can use one smartboard, all being able to watch and contribute to what is being written. Similarly, group B	Few significant issues are specific to this tool.

Table 14.12 (continued)

Tool	What it does	Example applications	Facilitator issues
	B. In this way, persons A and B appear to be looking at the same board. Similarly, the information can appear on a computer screen in front of person B. This can be extended to any number of receiving locations. Person B can also write on his or her smartboard and it will be mimicked back on the smart board of Person A.	can join in, adding to the content that is appearing on both boards. Each group can be, and usually is, of course, also connected to other groups, with voice conferencing, so that they can discuss what is being composed on the 'common' smartboard.	
SMS (short message service)	Method of sending text-based messages from one mobile phone to another mobile phone(s). Participants use the telephone keypad to type letters and numbers, usually up to 160 characters in length. This is then sent via the mobile system and received as a text message that can be displayed on the recipient's mobile. Sometimes called text messaging, or other similar label, according to the mobile operator.	Participants in an e-group can be notified of the next meeting via mobile phone messaging. E-mails can be sent to mobile phones. Groups can have (limited) conversations via mobile, such as voting on an issue.	Limited number of characters per message limits the functionality.
Teleconferencing	Users are connected via voice. That is, all are using a telephone of some	Frequently used in business situations to hold	Adherence to 'teleconference rules' helps these conversations considerably. For example, state your

Tool	What it does	Example applications	Facilitator issues
	description, to have a conversation with one or more people. Typically, this refers to a group of people, all listening to and contributing to the same conversation, via telephone. 'Bridging' software is used to enable participants to dial into the same conversation and all be heard.	group conversations. Often, there will be a group of people sitting around a speaker phone, holding a conversation with another group of people sitting around a speakerphone at another location.	name each time before you talk, unless your voice is very well known by the listeners.
Threaded discussion	Sometimes referred to as message board (or bulletin board). A threaded discussion has the facility to enable conversations to be categorized into 'threads' or topics of discussion, so that a reader can see all the comments and contributions toward a topic to date, when he or she arrives at the site.	Ongoing conversations abut a variety of topics. Special interest groups (SIG). Communities of practice (CoP).	Prompting or maintaining the momentum of the conversation. Enabling methods of socialization: threaded topics do not naturally provide space for socialization to occur. Smoothing the disjointed nature of the discussions.
Voicemail	Allows participants to leave verbal messages for recipients. Generally attached to either a landline or a mobile telephone, but increasingly used in Web-based applications such as chat and instant messaging.	Can be an effective adjunct to development of a culture for a group, maintaining contact and coordination of schedules for events.	Encouraging participants to use voicemail effectively, particularly for groups in several time zones.
Web conferencing	Software that allows conferences to be 'broadcast' via the Internet (the 'Web').	A conference, or convention, or exhibition can be held on the Web. That is, participants	Complexity of managing a conference online. A range of skills is needed, in a dynamic situation.

Table 14.12 *(continued)*

Tool	What it does	Example applications	Facilitator issues
		can log in, move around the exhibitions, listen to speakers, download conference papers, ask questions, interact with other conference participants, and attend 'live' seminars.	
Web whiteboarding	Users sit in front of their PC screens. Software allows them to turn the PC screen into a 'whiteboard'. That is, whatever they 'draw' on their screen, can be seen (instantly) by others in the conversation. 'Drawing' (freehand lines, curves, shapes, etc), can be done with the mouse, or with a drawing tablet, that is, a pressure-sensitive pad on which the user draws with a 'pen' or stylus. The pen and drawing tablet bring the user much closer to a paper and pen scenario, just like standing before a physical whiteboard with a texta.	Very useful for 'freehand sketching', such as drawing a quick diagram, that you want others in the conversation to see. Very useful to 'mimic' the whiteboard style of capturing thoughts and ideas from a group of people, much as you would do so in a face-to-face situation with a physical whiteboard (or butcher's paper).	None significant or particular to this tool.

15

Facilitating endings

Paul Simon (1981) once sang, 'There are fifty ways to leave your lover'. There are probably more ways to enable participants and the facilitator to leave a workshop productively.

The purpose of this chapter is to address the much neglected subject of how to end workshops using processes that are both empowering and ethical for facilitators and participants. This chapter focuses on the planned dissolution of a group, as opposed to the spontaneous dissolution that occurs when a group disbands because the members no longer feel a need for the group to exist.

I was motivated to write this chapter when I read a paper by Keleman, Egri and Frost (1992), and while incorporating some of their ideas, I wish to pursue the area further by reflecting on the exercises I have used with groups from government departments, industry and universities in the past. I call these endings 'now what' sessions.

The chapter is divided into a number of sections:

- definition of terms;
- the importance of endings;
- factors that need to be considered when planning a 'now what' session;
- the components of a 'now what' session;
- ending rituals.

Definition of terms

At this stage it is appropriate to define terms used.

Endings

I often call endings the 'now what?' session. Endings refers to the dissolution stage of a group; mourning, terminating (Sarri and Galinsky, 1967) or closure (Heron, 1992). In the 1950s work had already started on analysing the ways in which groups change over time (Bales, 1950; Bennis and Shepard, 1956). By 1973, Hill and Gruner had collected 100 theories concerning developmental stages in groups. Perhaps one of the best known is that by Tuckman (1965), who described the possible stages in a group's development as forming, storming, norming and performing. It was 12 years later that attention was drawn to the final stage, and Tuckman and Jensen (1977) called this the adjourning stage. This last stage is the focus of this chapter.

This stage may be best visualized by observing the painting entitled *The Gleaners* by Jean-François Millet (Louvre, Paris). In this picture, gleaners are picking up pieces of corn left by the harvesters. Nothing is wasted. The work is tedious, challenging and back-breaking. Asking participants to translate and transfer what they have learnt to their workplaces often has similar elements. Heron takes this autumnal pastoral image further:

> As the group draws to a close, the members gather in and review the fruit of their learning, and prepare to transfer it to life in the wider world outside. At some point in this process separation anxiety will loom up – the distress at parting after such trust and depth of interaction. It can slip the group back into defensiveness (ie forming) unless dealt with awarely – firstly by accepting that the end is nigh, secondly by dealing with any unfinished business, thirdly by celebrating each other and what has one on, fourthly by saying a warm, friendly farewell in the group and one-to-one. Autumn: the fruit is harvested and stored, the harvesters give thanks and go their way.
>
> (Heron, 1989: 27)

Empowering

Endings, where possible, should be empowering. I believe that facilitators should be ethical and ensure that participants know that in almost all cases they have the right to choose what they will or will not adopt and implement from a workshop or course. Hopson and Scally define empowerment as 'A process by which one increasingly takes greater charge of oneself and one's life. . . There is always an alternative and we can choose. None of these alternatives in some situations may be desirable, but it is the knowledge that there is always a choice that heralds the beginning of self-empowered thinking' (1981: 57). For further explanation of the 'empowerment' concept see Hogan (2000).

Ethical

The term 'ethics' is defined in the *Concise Oxford Dictionary* as 'relating to morals, morally correct, honourable' (*COD*, 1982: 331). The concept is open to many interpretations. However, all facilitators need to consider every proposed activity in the light of this definition. Useful questions to ask are 'Why am I using this activity?' and 'What are the potential outcomes/consequences of using this activity?'

Examples of unethical endings I have observed include, 'To really appreciate this workshop/course to the fullest you must attend a follow-up programme', and 'You can do anything you want to. Go for it.' Facilitators who orchestrate hyped endings in order to achieve high ratings in the evaluation 'happy sheet' are, I believe, unethical.

The importance of endings

Endings are important for many reasons. Each reason will be discussed in turn.

Transition rituals

Considerable time and attention has been given to icebreaker activities (Dick, 1987; Watson, Vallee and Mulford, 1981) and contracting for content and desirable group norms (Dick, 1987): activities that attempt to enable individuals to make a positive transition from the outside world into the workshop group. Very little attention has been given to planning an effective transition back to home and work life. Kubler-Ross (1975) and Parkes (1977) have documented rituals and responses to deal with death and dying; Sheehy (1977), Bridges (1991), Adams, Hayes and Hopson (1977) and Hopson and Scally (1983) have described stages and methods for dealing with transitions.

Human memory

The human brain remembers beginnings and endings more than the middles, hence the importance given to the preparation of beginnings and endings by public speakers (Pike, 1993, 1994). If the workshop/course has been more than one day in duration, it is useful to build in many 'endings', for example at the end of each day or main topic. For example a facilitator may ask participants to note down answers to the following:

Ideas: What are the most important things you have learnt?
Action: What are you going to do about them?

The affective domain

Considerable conflicting emotions may be experienced by participants and the facilitator at the end of a programme. For example, if the group has formed a strong bond and individuals have formed close attachments, there may be considerable feelings of loss, sadness and 'mourning'. Some participants may not feel ready for parting, and may initiate the ideas of regular reunions. On the other hand, some may be merely confused by the sheer bulk of material delivered (consider the amount of material covered in one to two-week workshops/ courses). Others may be pleased that the end is nigh, as they have experienced considerable discomfort because of the level of difficulty of the workshop/ course, or because their own ideas and beliefs have been challenged. A person may have had interpersonal problems with other group members and may be relieved to be leaving.

The workshop/course may have made some issues surface for a participant. In that case it may be necessary to talk to the individual quietly. Suggestions of contacts for ongoing counselling and/or guidance may sometimes be necessary.

Some members may experience grieving and loss, and may exhibit avoidance behaviour. They may fail to turn up for a last session, complaining of important matters elsewhere. This may be the case; however, all participants should be encouraged to attend their last session together. Members of a group may feel very vulnerable and wish the group to continue. If the group has reached the performing stage, frequently networking groups form.

A facilitator may be experiencing mixed emotions also: a sense of loss at the termination of an exciting group, or a feeling of 'burn out' at having been emotionally and physically drained through over-exposure to groups. It is the facilitator's job to enable participants to deal with this 'emotional baggage' as positively and effectively as possible. The needs of facilitator will be considered in the 'post-termination' section later. See the post-termination stage described in Chapter 17.

Celebration of individual and group achievement

Endings are important in that participants need to be able to celebrate their individual and group achievements and learning. They need to feel good about themselves in order to return to the workplace with a positive outlook to try out new ideas and skills.

Linking elements of the workshop/course together

It is important that participants should have an opportunity to see how elements of the workshop/course link together. The human brain likes patterns. Many learners remember the whole picture, or gestalt, better than a string of unrelated parts. People frequently feel more satisfied when there is a sense of completion of the whole task.

Converting ideas into actions

Participants need quality time for action planning. It is impossible and frequently undesirable for participants to incorporate everything that is covered in a workshop/course into their work lives. Some processes and skills may be unsuitable and/or undesirable. It is empowering for participants to know that they have a choice (except in workplace laws and regulations) to adopt aspects that suit their needs or style, or those of their organization.

Ideas and new skills do not become reality unless they are translated by individuals into their own words and own work context. Writing down thoughts helps to clarify ideas and turn them into action. Too often many new ideas and skills are introduced in workshops/courses but few are transferred into the workplace. For learning to be complete there has to be some resulting change in behaviour.

Factors that need to be considered when planning a 'now what' session

According to Keleman, Egri and Frost (1992), a number of factors need to be considered when planning your ending session. These are described below.

The age, maturity of the participants

Was the group composed of young undergraduates, postgraduates, managers or executives, or a mixture?

The classroom/training room culture and climate

Was the primary mode of learning lecture-based, experiential, group discussion, individual reflection, or a mixture of the above?

The level of intimacy of the group

Had the group been together for a matter of days, weeks or months? How big/ small was the group?

The developmental level of the group

What was the stage of group development? Was the group still at the 'storming' stage or had it developed to the 'norming' or to the 'performing' level? (Tuckman, 1965; Tuckman and Jensen, 1977).

Nature of the content

Was the content restricted to abstract theory or did it include self-development and self-disclosure to the group?

The power dimension

Who should organize the end sessions: the facilitator alone; the facilitator and the participants together, or the participants alone?

The cultural background of the participants

What is the background of the participants? Is the nature of the exercises such that they would be comfortable for people of white Angle-Saxon descent, but may embarrass people of Aboriginal or southeast Asian descent?

The style of the facilitator

What exercises do you feel comfortable with? The exercises chosen frequently are based on the comfort zone of the facilitator. It may be necessary for the facilitator to stretch his/her comfort zone to encompass a variety of activities.

Music to accompany the ending session

What music would be appropriate? Music immediately invokes the affective domain. Many songs and tunes could be used to set the scene. To elaborate on the pastoral scene described earlier, the last section of *The Four Seasons* by Vivaldi or the last movement of Beethoven's *Pastoral Symphony* could be appropriate. On a lighter note, songs that could be used to lift the emotional tone of the group include 'Breaking up is hard to do' by Neil Sedaka, and the theme from *Mahogany*, 'Do you know where you're going to?' sung by Diana Ross. For further music ideas see Keleman *et al* (1992).

The length of the ending session

Basically the longer the workshop/course, the longer the ending session will usually need to be. A one-day workshop/course may require up to an hour; a one-week workshop/course two hours; a semester (13 weeks) a whole three-hour session. It all depends on the other factors described above. The important point is to plan for the ending and not to just run out of time.

The components of a 'now what' session

There are many phases of an ending session. Not all are applicable to every group.

Summary of content

At the end of a course it is normal for some participants to feel somewhat overwhelmed. They realize how much there is to learn, often more than they realized at the outset; perhaps some 'cannot see the wood for the trees'. A summary of the content of a workshop/course is a useful tool to enhance memory, and may be achieved in a number of ways. The facilitator may choose to go through a long workshop/course using a 'mind movie' (Hopson and Scally, 1986) or creative visualization (Fanning, 1988). This is achieved by asking participants to lie on the floor or relax in their seats. I always give participants the choice. There is usually resistance to lying on the floor; however, when participants really relax in this way they always respond positively afterwards.

Many people find visualization difficult, because of distractions. I explain that if they hear the air conditioner or some other noise that they should name it and let it go: 'Oh, that's the window rattling, that's all.' It is normal for a noise to trigger out brain patterns to identify potential danger, so instead of 'beating ourselves up when we get distracted, it is more beneficial to allow sounds to come in, name them, and let them flow out of consciousness again.

To explain the movie I introduce the group to the mnemonic RADAR (Hopson and Scally, 1986) which helps them generate the visualization (see Chapter 9). A simple breathing and/or muscle relaxation exercise (see Chapter 17) may be followed by the following type of script:

> Remember Monday morning when you arrived for this workshop/course?. . . What went through your mind when you came through the door?. . . How did you feel?. . . Remember the introduction when we contracted. . .? What were you looking for? Did you get what you wanted? If not, why not? Remember session one on motivation? . . . What are the main things you remember from this session?. . .

Please note that the pauses (indicated by ellipses) are very important in this exercise.

Mind movies are very relaxing, and enable participants to reduce some of the stress related to information overload. At the end of this exercise participants may be asked to summarize their main points in pairs or small groups, and given time to write down key points.

Building up confidence

Visualization exercises may also be used to help participants build up confidence to use new skills. For example:

> See yourself standing in front of your next group. . . feeling confident and at ease with yourself and the world. Feel your shoulders back, breathing is relaxed. . . you feel centred and confident.

Participants frequently arrive at workshops/courses feeling confused about their level of skill development. During the contracting phase they often indicate that they wish to feel more confident in the topic of the workshop/course. When learners realize how much they do not know, they frequently become demoralized and/or demotivated. It is productive therefore for the facilitator to review the stages of skill acquisition, so they will be encouraged to try and retry new skills until they are perfected.

Stages of skill acquisition

If skills training was part of the workshop I show participants an adapted version of the 'stages of skills development' (see Figure 15.1). Pike and Howell developed the first four stages. I added the fifth and sixth stages. The model is simplistic; learning is not sequential or even; there are steep learning curves, progressions and regressions, plateaus, overcoming blocks and prejudices and the unlearning of old ideas and skills.

Also many participants have tacit knowledge and skills: they 'just know' or 'just know how' to do something (Polanyi, 1966; 1969). Learners may have been 'unconscious of their incompetence' at the beginning of the workshop, and becoming 'conscious of their incompetence' may have made them feel inadequate, challenged or whatever. Trying out new skills in role play or real life may have felt aware or awkward: they felt 'consciously competent'. I reassure them that if they practise they will become 'unconsciously competent': they will internalize the skill, as most have with driving. They need to then be 'conscious of their unconscious competence', not become cocky or overconfident, and be aware that overconfidence may lead to a return to the stage of 'unconscious incompetence'. The latter stage occurs to some trainers/facilitators, who become so familiar with their materials that they no longer explain them simply and clearly for new learners.

Figure 15.1 enables learners to understand that they may have been unaware of the intricacies involved in learning certain skills. The awareness of how much they do not know may be deflating for some. However, if learners persevere they can become consciously competent, and later unconsciously competent.

Re-entry issues

It is important to give participants a moment to imagine how they will re-enter both their home and work-life environments. Learning frequently makes an impact on both work and home life, so the following questions are useful:

> Remember that your partners and family may have had a very busy day. What are you going to say to them when you get home? What are you going to tell them about the workshop/course?

> Remember that your work colleagues may have had extra duties to perform in your absence, or may be curious about what you have learnt. What are the key things you will tell them about the workshop/course? How will you introduce them to any changes you may like to make?

A useful strategy is to ask participants to state what they will say in 'lift time': the two minutes you might share with a colleague in the lift when you get back.

Short-term action planning

Action planning helps to turn ideas into reality, and is necessary to assure transference of learning back to the workplace. It may be long or short term.

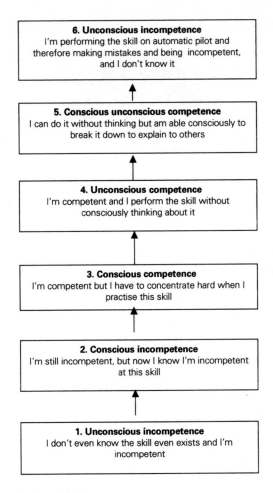

Figure 15.1 Levels of skill development

Source: adapted from the work of Pike and Jones (1994), who used ideas from Howell, with stages 5–6 added by the author.

First of all, it is productive to commit participants to doing something as a result of the workshop/course within one week. A practical exercise is to ask participants to draw a television screen (about 5 inches x 2 inches) in the middle of a sheet of A4 paper. In it they draw themselves 'looking smiling and confidently out into the world'. They should draw lines radiating from the four corners of the television box, and add up to four short goals (like a mind map). These are to be started, if not fully achieved, within a week of the end of the workshop/ course. One example is reading through the workshop/course notes and writing key points as reminders in diaries. Another example may be arranging a time with the boss and/or work team to give feedback about the workshop/ course.

Figure 15.2   Short-term action planning

To ensure these goals are carried out, I ask participants to exchange phone numbers with a partner, and to arrange to ring each other in one week's time to check out how they have progressed. This may appear somewhat manipulatory, but I contend to them that this is done with the best of intentions.

Forming buddy pairs for future support can be a very empowering way for individuals to work on changes: buddies formed in workshops can support one another after the workshop. They do not have to be from the same workplace (Hogan, 1991).

Long-term action planning

As Figure 15.3 shows, action planning which involves huge goals, beyond the sphere of influence of participants, frequently fails because they fall into the 'swamp'. This does not mean that such changes should not be attempted, but that they should be broken down into smaller goals, starting with the participants themselves and people around them. Action plans can get lost in the swamps of the future and tasks that are too big to handle.

Goals should be specific, stretching, but not impossible, and should be accompanied by answers to the 5WHA formula, which ensures that action plans start on firm ground:

Why?

Who?

What?

When?

Where?

How?

And with what resources?

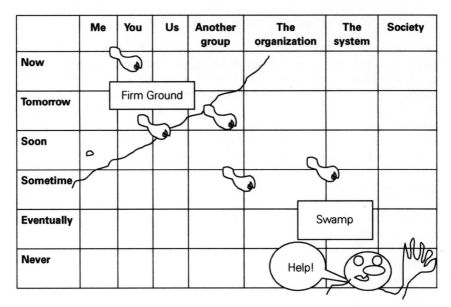

Figure 15.3 Appropriate action planning

Source: Hopson and Scally (1984)

Final ending rituals

Human beings have developed elaborate rituals in every society for dealing with the emotional loss of death and parting. In groups that have developed to the 'performing' stage (Tuckman, 1965; Tuckman and Jensen, 1977) a ritual may be a productive means for the discharge of emotions.

Summary ritual using photos

Sometimes participants find it hard to summarize what they got out of a workshop/course. Photos stimulate thinking, and give shy people something to hold and talk to in front of the whole group. Cooney and Burton (1986) produced a set of 120 black and white photos which can be used in many different ways. To use these photos in an ending ritual, spread them around the floor and invite participants to choose one or two which summarize the meaning of the workshop/course to them. In a circle, each person is given two minutes to explain. No discussion is allowed at this stage. Individuals speak when they are ready, holding up the photo for everyone to see. When the person has finished, the photo is placed on the ground facing into the group.

The set of pictures by Cooney and Burton has the advantage that the pictures have been tested across different ethnic and age groups in Australia. Alternatively you can make up your own sets of photos with the use of a digital camera, or collect postcards.

Goal setting and letting go ritual

Bringing balloons into a room immediately changes the ambience to one of playfulness and celebration. Helium balloons are easily purchased from party goods wholesalers. Ask participants to draw with felt pens on one side of the balloon symbols that represent anything they wish to let go of: maybe negative feelings, old skills, old ideas. On the other side they should draw new ideas, ways of doing things, goals that they want to launch. If there is time it may be appropriate to give opportunity for discussion of these goals.

Take participants into the open air and ask them to form a circle. You can invite them to decide how the launch should take place. It is interesting to note how long participants stay looking at their balloons as they rise high and higher in the atmosphere. It is a very uplifting feeling, and brings something of the 'creative child' back into the seriousness of a workshop/course. According to air traffic controllers, balloons are not dangerous to light aircraft. However, there is some concern about the environment, in that animals may get entangled in the long synthetic tape, which also takes some time to biodegrade. Alternatively, balloons may be launched indoors or taken home.

Eye ritual

Another way of saying 'goodbye' is to ask participants to form a tight circle, shoulders touching, facing inwards. Invite them to silently say 'goodbye' to everyone in the group with their eyes. When this has finished, ask them to all turn to the right and outwards.

Individual ritual

Heron (1993) demonstrated what he called a 'holonomic exercise' in which participants and facilitator formed a circle, holding hands:

- Participants move into the centre saying, 'I am'.
- Participants hold hands and move inwards with a big 'whoosh', saying, 'We are'.
- Participants move back to the edge of the original circle, drop hands and cross arms across the chest, saying, 'This is me'.

Exhortation for future learning ritual

Heron (1993) suggested a circle ritual which could be used at the beginning or end of a workshop/course. He asks a participant to bring in a small branch of a bush (about a foot long). Holding it, the bringer turns to the first person in the circle, and lightly brushes the individual with the branch on the stomach, the chest and the head, saying simultaneously, 'May you continue to learn with your stomach, your heart and your head.' That person takes the branch, turns to the next person and repeats the words and actions, and so on until everyone has had a turn.

During these rituals, Heron modelled 'emotional switching': if the atmosphere became too heavy he would lighten the mood with a jovial, though not belittling, remark.

The cauldron: Putting in and getting out

Three postgraduate students devised a very interesting ritual for a facilitation class. They asked everyone to bring in a tub of biodegradable 'things' that represented what they put into the workshop/course. The facilitator had to provide a large pot or cauldron, and another student brought along a thick stick as a stirrer. We all sat on the floor around the pot at the start of class, and one of the students explained that we should explain the reason for the choice of ingredients. 'What did you bring to the workshop/course, and how did you feel at the beginning?' As each person spoke, norms developed, and each had to stir the 'brew' after speaking and adding to it. There was much laughter. A wide variety of ingredients appeared: coloured rose petals, soil, pebbles, lavender flowers and dried flowers. One student added some perfume, another some hand-made paper torn into pieces, each with an individual's name on it. The creativity and symbolism was delightful.

The cauldron stayed in the middle of the room during the class. At the end the group returned to their seated position and the facilitator asked, 'What have you gained from the workshop/course, and what major goals do you have as a result?' There were some tears of sadness as well as joy. The students' idea was that we should all take home the 'brew' and bury it in a favourite space (Elanta, Hancock and Williams, 2001). It was a very moving experience.

Conclusion

This chapter has covered a wide variety of techniques for use in ending workshops. Adequate time needs to be built into workshops for endings, as was stated above. The next chapter focuses on evaluation, which is also a most valuable part of workshops.

16

Evaluation

There are those who know the cost of everything, but the value of nothing.

Source unknown

Introduction

Evaluation is an attempt to find out the value, merit or worth of something (however that might be defined). Evaluation is something we all do to a greater or lesser extent, in many situations from simple choices in the supermarket to serious life situations. Unfortunately, although we do it every day, evaluation is often the poor relation in the planning of workshops (or for that matter in the planning of research projects, workplace change implementations and so on). It is often 'tacked on' as an afterthought at the end of a process, rather than being considered from the beginning of the process or project, at the contracting stage. Often consultants say, 'If I get repeat business I know the workshop must have been OK.' But this is not enough. This chapter is designed to demystify evaluation, and includes:

- questions to ask yourself;
- a four-level evaluation model;
- a personal model of evaluation: formative, summative and long-term evaluation;
- use of computers for evaluation;
- long-term goal setting and long-term evaluation;
- what to do with the data;
- whose opinion counts?

Questions to ask yourself

Why should you evaluate? There may be many reasons. One is to find out if the money spent was worthwhile (however this is defined). Another is to assess a process to see if you can improve on it (however you choose to define that). It may be that you want to know if an outcome has been achieved: either what you set out to achieve, or perhaps something different, or even better (whether by your own definition, or that of your clients, and again, there are many issues of definition).

However, I will concentrate here on the evaluation of facilitated and planned workshops designed to achieve some specified outcomes of interest to the participants, their employers, their partners, or themselves. Facilitators need to evaluate according to what they and the group set out to do. It is useful to ask yourself:

- What am I really trying to evaluate? How will I know if I have succeeded, in terms of what I set out to do? Is this an evaluation of process only, or of outcomes or both? What resources do I have? (Evaluations cost time, energy and money, but reward you with new insights.)
- What don't I want to evaluate? That is, do not try to evaluate everything.
- What will I do as a result of the information obtained?
- Whose feedback/perspectives do I need?
- Whose perspective counts?

> We should measure gross national happiness rather than gross national product.
>
> King of Bhutan

Why evaluate a workshop? Some responses might include to:

- find out if the workshop was effective in meeting the planned goals of the organization (the problem is that these often change as you progress through a workshop);
- find out if the workshop met the expectations and needs of participants;
- find out if there were any serendipities (good unexpected outcomes);
- find out if there were any unexpected negative outcomes;
- decide whether to repeat a particular workshop and/or process;
- improve workshops and processes in the future;
- appraise your worth as a professional facilitator and highlight areas for further learning;
- find out if the workshop met your personal goals as a facilitator.

Remember as a facilitator you will make some judgements of 'how it went', and your participants will also do so. So may the people who asked you to conduct the workshops, and each may have different ideas of what constituted a successful process and/or outcome.

Many facilitators evaluate, but do not change their behaviours or workshop designs. You have a choice. There may be aspects of your facilitation style/s that you wish to keep but that do not suit some people. On the other hand, if you do not internalize and/or use some of the information you gather, why evaluate? Are you doing it just to be seen to be 'going through the motions?' Some useful self-evaluation questions include:

- Did the group achieve goals I negotiated with the organization?
- Did I achieve my personal goals?

- Did the goals/activities change as the workshop progressed? If so, why?
- What did I learn as a facilitator?

Workshop plans often change, and may need to be renegotiated with the group. Hidden agendas may be revealed, and need attention before the group can concentrate on the original purpose of the workshop. There is a tension between at least three elements, as shown in Figure 16.1.

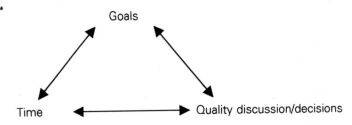

Figure 16.1 Tensions

If achieving the goal is the most important factor, then extra time for quality discussion and decision making may be important. If time is limited, goals may need to be ranked and less important ones discarded to allow for quality discussion and decisions. There is no point in racing to achieve goals if there are 'people casualties' as a result of rushing insensitively through an agenda.

Kirkpatrick's four-level evaluation model

One of the most influential models of evaluation is the outcome 'four-level evaluation model' designed by Donald Kirkpatrick in 1959 (1994: 643; 1996; Gordon, 1997: 642). It is simple, practical and has stood the test of time.

Level 1   Reaction or short-term evaluation

Reaction is a way of gaining information on participants' feelings and degrees of satisfaction or discontent. Ask yourself 'What do I want to eveluate?'

At the end of the programme, ask participants if the workshop met their expectations. Hint: always keep the flip chart paper from the beginning of the workshop, where you contracted with the actual members of the group a response to 'What do you want to get out of this workshop?' or 'Why are you here?', and use this sheet as a basis for discussion. If you asked participants to place dots on their most wanted items (having marked the dots with their initials or symbols), you can ask them to remove their dots if they have had those needs met. I had one workshop where all were removed, and figured I should retire while I was ahead.

The evaluation sheet given on the last day of a course is sometimes sarcastically called the 'happy sheet'. An entertaining presentation may gain very high

Table 16.1   Possible evaluation items

Content	Process/es	Facilitator	Accommodation
Subject matter: depth	Suitability of processes for the content	Contracting skills	Support staff (if outside venue)
Subject matter: breadth	Variety of processes used	Interpersonal skills	Room ambiance, shape, lighting
Length and pace of workshop	Appropriateness of processes for the group/time available	Confronting skills	Food
Relevance/ appropriateness		Questioning skills	Ventilation, air quality
Objectives met?		Responsiveness to individual and/or group needs	Heating-cooling system
Omissions		Cross-cultural skills	Furniture: seating comfort
Quality of handouts			Efficiency of equipment
Quality of learning aids			

Source: adapted from Rae (1986: 644)

ratings, but does not necessarily ensure learning. However, immediate reactions can give some useful data, and enjoyment can relate to learning and motivate ongoing learning. An end-of-course discussion can elaborate on written answers and gives the facilitator a chance to clarify responses where necessary. There are many different evaluation methods available. See Table 16.2.

If you have built up trust in the group, it is often very useful to initiate a relaxed, open discussion by introducing open ended questions, like: 'What would you do to improve this course for future participants, and why?'

These questions invite participants to make constructive suggestions for improvement. In order to enable participants to build on ideas, it is appropriate for the facilitator to note down suggestions, and ask for elaboration or explanation where necessary. It is important not to go into defensive mode, as this will militate against further suggestions.

I believe that the Kirkpatrick model is lacking, in that leaving evaluation to the end of a programme is too late (see formative evaluation below).

Level 2   Learning

Ask yourself, 'What am I really trying to measure/assess?' Testing or assessing the learning – that is, the conceptual understanding, skills or attitudes of

Table 16.2 Evaluation methods

Method	Advantages	Disadvantages
Questionnaires eg combine Likert scales with space for explanations. Use open-ended questions	Quick to administer. Anonymous. Individual ideas. Invites quiet reflection	Lack of discussion, as facilitator cannot get a chance to clarify. Sometimes rushed because little time. Framing of questions may lead to omissions of vital data.
Focus groups eg facilitated by someone else, or leave a group alone with a tape recorder	Unstructured discussion	Some may feel inhibited to give real opinions. Some may dominate discussion.
Nominal group technique eg what did you get out of the workshop? How could the workshop be improved?	Anonymous at first during writing stage. Open thinking. Ranking of ideas enables facilitator to see weighting.	
Six thinking hats (white = facts, yellow = positives, red = feelings, black = negatives, green = creative ideas for improvement, blue = facilitator's hat)	The five hats helps to structure discussion. Who should wear the blue facilitator's hat, ie should a participant take that role so that the facilitator can listen and reflect?	Discussion may be dominated by a few people. Some may feel inhibited from giving real opinions.

participants – can be achieved by quizzes, videoed role plays, assignments, tests and exams. In cross-cultural and diversity workshops the aim may be to change attitudes, which is very difficult to assess.

Who assesses? And who decides who will assess? Assessment may be conducted according to Heron's (1999) power modes:

- hierarchically ie by the facilitator or an external body;
- cooperatively ie between the facilitator and participant;
- autonomously, ie participants may self-assess and/or peers assess one another's work;
- combinations of the above.

Level 3   Behaviour

Behaviour refers to 'learning transfer': has the workshop resulted in some new or different behaviours of participants afterwards, either back at work or in the community? Changed behaviours may be practised in the training room via role plays, but the question is, 'Is the person willing and/or able to transfer this behaviour to the outside world?' Remember the workplace and/or community may not be conducive to supporting new behaviours, so part of a facilitator's job is to help participants think ahead to how they might handle resistance to their trying out new skills and knowledge.

In some organizations people keep journals about the changes in their behaviour, a form of self-assessment. Team members, peers and supervisors can be asked to contribute to 360-degree feedback, which is also useful if it is well introduced. Giving and receiving constructive feedback requires skilful handling.

Level 4   Results

Organizations usually want to find out if the money invested in workshops has been well spent. Costs include:

- facilitator's fees;
- venue and hire of equipment fees;
- costs of replacement staff;
- loss of production;
- travel and accommodation costs.

Questions to assess benefits include:

- Is conflict handled better?
- Is there greater job satisfaction?
- Has morale improved?
- Are people talking more openly to one another?
- Is production more efficient?
- Is there saving of resources?
- Have productivity/profits increased?
- Has quality improved?
- Have complaints decreased?
- Have accidents decreased
- Has absenteeism decreased?

Human behaviour is so complex, and even with the use of control groups it is often difficult or impossible to separate the variables in a change process. In many instances the use of a control group raises ethical problems, as in measures to improve occupational health and safety.

Three-stage evaluation

I use a continuous approach to evaluation which involves formative, summative, and long-term evaluation strategies to obtain feedback from participants. I also use a personal computerized journal of my own reflections, observations, hunches and so on. This enables me to make linkages from issues raised in previous workshops.

Stage 1　Formative evaluation

Formative evaluation means evaluating as you go along. The methods are endless, and may include questionnaires, maintenance sessions, and informal chats at breaks with participants to monitor feelings, reactions and needs (Scriven, 1967). Even discussions that you overhear in the toilets can give you some interesting insights.

A simple formative evaluation at the end of day one of a two-day course might resemble Figure 16.2.

Evaluation and feedback

1. What were the **most useful** things today?

2. What were the **least useful** things today?

3. If you found it difficult to participate today, please give your reasons and suggestions on how the situation could be improved.

4. Tomorrow I want more of. . .

5. Tomorrow I want less of. . .

6. Any feedback and/or suggestions regarding my facilitation please?

Please add any other comments you would like to make.

Thank you

Figure 16.2　Sample formative evaluation

The feedback loop

I also feed back to participants a summary of the results of formative evaluation, to keep communication channels open (and show that their responses are collated and given thoughtful consideration). I then discuss and negotiate changes to content or ground rules with participants. Some people are understandably becoming very sceptical of repeatedly being asked their opinions, and then never seeing any changes or hearing reasons for how things do not change.

Stage 2   Summative evaluation

The summative evaluation is the same as the 'reaction' level of Kirkpatrick's model. Evaluations conducted on the result of a workshop are called summative evaluation (Scriven, 1967). The sample in Figure 16.3 includes far more items than are needed. Note that a space for 'comments' is included. Likert scales alone only give feedback on trends; you will need to know *why* a person thinks in a particular way.

There are many items in the sample. Not all are necessary: it depends on your focus. See also 'creative and visual evaluations' below.

Stage 3   Long-term goal-setting incorporated into long-term evaluation

Depending on the nature of the workshop, I send a short questionnaire to participants three months later. At the end of workshops I ask participants to set short and long-term goals (related to the workshop) and include then in a letter to themselves. Then I ask them to address two envelopes: one to themselves (at home) and one to me, and place a long-term evaluation sheet (Figure 16.3), letter to themselves, and envelope addressed to me inside the envelope addressed to them.

I ask them to put their names and phone number on the sheets (unless it prevents them from giving honest feedback) as it helps me to understand the context of their feedback. Also sometimes people ask me for more information and forget to let me know how I can contact them.

I make a note in my diary to post the letters three months from the workshop date. Because participants receive a reminder letter, I find the response rate is quite high.

Use of computers for evaluation

New methods include the use of computers in decision support laboratories for speed and anonymity. For example, MeetingWorks software can be used by participants in synchronous time. Computers need to be arranged in a semi-circle, preferably with lowered monitors so that at times participants can talk to each other 'off the record'. MeetingWorks software is programmed to keep information anonymous: you cannot go into the data later and find out which data was generated by which computer station (Whiteley and Garcia, 1996). Other packages include Plexus and Grouputer.

Evaluations may also be completed after a workshop in asynchronous time via e-mail feedback.

Title of workshop_____

Location_____

Date_____

Facilitator/s_____

Please take time to complete this evaluation as fully as possible. Your effort will help to assist in developing future workshops and provide useful feedback to the facilitator/s.

1. What part/s of the workshop did you find **most valuable** and why?
   Please comment

   _____
   _____
   _____
   _____

2. What part/s of the workshop did you find **least valuable** and why?
   Please comment

   _____
   _____
   _____
   _____

3. Were your expectations/needs met? Yes/No
   Please comment

   _____

4. Listed below are the **objectives for the workshop**. Please indicate the extent to which these objectives have been met.

	Poor	Fair	Good	Excellent
List objective 1 *Comment:*				
List objective 2 *Comment:*				
List objective 3 *Comment:*				
List objective 4 *Comment:*				

5. How would you rate the **workshop facilitation** overall?

Beginning	**Poor**	**Fair**	**Good**	**Excellent**
Introduction of the workshop *Comment:*				
Objectives were well written *Comment:*				
Explanation of roles and responsibilities *Comment:*				

Contracting for individual/group needs *Comment:*				
Contracting for ground rules *Comment:*				
Middle				
Appropriate confronting if ground rules broken *Comment:*				
Knowledge of subject matter (if appropriate) *Comment:*				
Appropriate processes were used to engage participants actively *Comment:*				
Clear facilitator questioning *Comment:*				
Encouragement of participants' questions *Comment:*				
Responsiveness to participants' questions *Comment:*				
Adaptability of facilitator/s *Comment:*				
Instructions to participants regarding activities *Comment:*				
Your personal learning needs were met *Comment:*				
Ending				
Outcomes summarized *Comment:*				
Ending ritual/event *Comment:*				

6. How would you rate the **workshop aids/materials** (handouts, flip chart paper, white board, props etc)?

Visual aids *Comment:*				
Handouts *Comment:*				

7. How would you rate the **quality of group interaction**?

You were encouraged to participate *Comment:*				

You were encouraged to ask questions *Comment:*				
Facilitator/s responded well to participants' questions				

8. How would you rate the **organization** of the workshop?

The amount of content for the time available was about right *Comment:*				
The stages of the workshop were coordinated *Comment:*				

9. If you found it **difficult to participate**, please give your reasons.

_____
_____
_____
_____

10. The facilitator/s
    Please practise your feedback skills. What did he/she/they do well?

_____
_____
_____

Suggestions for improvement

_____
_____
_____

11. Are there any comments you would like make about the room, refreshments etc?

_____
_____

12. Would you recommend this workshop to your colleagues? Yes/No
Reasons_____
_____
_____

13. Is there anything else you would like to add?

_____
_____

Name (optional) _____ Date _____

Thank you for completing this evaluation.

Figure 16.3 Sample end of workshop evaluation

Creative and visual evaluation

I once read a very a provocative article (alas since lost) entitled something like, 'Who reads evaluations anyway?' The author suggested that participants should bring in items or pictures and create a 'museum of exhibits' to illustrate their evaluation of the course. Each participant in turn verbally explains the meaning of his/her exhibit, which is photographed. Later each person completes an open page of a scrapbook of photos, pictures and a page of written evaluation. This process is now made easier with the use of Polaroid and digital cameras. It's great fun and 'yes' people do need this kind of evaluation.

Long-term goal setting incorporated with long-term evaluation

Materials needed for this exercise include two envelopes, a sheet of coloured paper to write a letter, and a long-term evaluation sheet (see Figure 16.4) per participant. This exercise involves asking participants to write a letter to themselves, including long-term goals for the next three months. Explain to participants that they should follow the following directions carefully:

- Address one envelope to themselves at home.
- Address one envelope to you, the facilitator.
- Write a letter to themselves describing long-term goals.
- Place the letter, envelope addressed to the facilitator, and the long-term evaluation sheet in the envelope addressed to themselves.
- Seal the envelope and give to the facilitator.

I usually display these instructions on an overhead transparency. The advantage of this exercise is that participants are reminded about the course in three months' time. This sometimes gives them an extra reminder/motivator to achieve their goals. Also the response rate to the long-term evaluation questionnaire is very high, and this provides valuable data for the facilitator.

Pike (1993) suggests that participants should use a postcard and include:

- something they are going to start;
- something they are going to stop;
- something they are going to continue;
- a compliment to themselves.

In my opinion a postcard is too public. Participants feel more secure writing personal goals knowing that their letters will be sealed.

What to do with the evaluation data

A key question which is often overlooked is, 'What are you going to do with the data you collect?' Many people conduct evaluations, but programmes never

---

Long-term evaluation: participants' feedback

It is three months since you attended this course. It would be very helpful for me if you would answer the following questions and return this sheet in the mail.
Thanks
Chris Hogan

Your name
Contact address
Course   Date

1. What do you do differently now at work/home as a result of attending this course?

2. What were the most important things you learnt on this course?

3. Is there anything I should know? (Do you have any suggestions for planning future courses?)

Figure 16.4   Long-term evaluation

change. Indeed many participants become cynical of procedures with reason. It is helpful if you tell group members, 'This part of the course is done in this way because of feedback I got from the last group. I would be interested to hear what you think of this approach.'

Whose opinions count?

The last question you need to ask yourself before making changes is, 'Whose opinion counts?' You may receive negative feedback about specific content, or a particular exercise, but in your opinion (or company regulations or the laws of the land) it is vital that participants learn about 'x' or try out new behaviours in role play so that you can observe that they have learnt skills they are required to exhibit by law.

Formative evaluation on long-term courses

When I am teaching long-term courses I add to forms like the above a summary of ways in which participants may contact me for help. This enables me to gauge if participants have had trouble contacting me and if they need help. It helps to keep the lines of communication open. (See Figure 16.5.)

There are now many ways in which you can communicate with me and the class participants and the rest of the world to help your learning. Indicate below what you have used.

Method	Used: yes or no?	Any problems?	Solutions?	Your needs re using this technology
1. Telephone leave message on aspen				
2. Retrieve message from Chris (electronic message retrieval system)				
3. E-mail to Chris				
4. General HR discussion group via e-mail				
5. Class discussion group via e-mail				
6. Internet				
7. Chris, before, during or after class				
8. Chris's office				

Figure 16.5 Communication feedback from participants

Conclusion

The aim of this chapter was to elaborate on processes used by the author in order to stimulate discourse amongst facilitators about endings that are empowering and ethical for facilitators and participants alike. The importance of endings has been highlighted, and a variety of factors that need to be taken into account when planning have been described. Many different types of processes and activities have been described. It is necessary for the facilitator to choose suitable activities with care and forethought, always taking into account the aims of the session and the needs of the participants.

Whatever may emerge there needs to be a consistency, a sense of being true to yourself and to the group experience (Keleman *et al*, 1992: 3).

17

Ongoing learning and maintenance

We are human be-ings
Not human do-ings

Loretta Do Rozario

Introduction

Working as a facilitator is both rewarding and tiring. There are times when facilitators are busy 'doing', but there is equal need for time for reflecting and just 'being'. There are a number of different ways in which you can attend to your well being in order to maintain a balance in your life. We are all different in our needs and what works for us as individuals, but here are some ideas:

- learning from positive experiences, mistakes and/or negative feedback;
- learning about facilitation by observing our own practice;
- developing your own 'frame of facilitation';
- use of self-assessment tools for facilitators;
- learning about facilitation from others;
- courses, accreditation, participant observation, shadowing, researching;
- self maintenance and stress management.

Post-termination stage of group development

The 'post-termination' stage of group development was identified by Hartford (1972). A professional facilitator needs to step back and reflect as objectively as possible on a workshop/course. It may be that a facilitator wishes to work in private on some personal learning, celebration of success, issues, hurt or distress. In this case some creative and reflective journal processes may be useful (see Chapter 7), or it may be more appropriate to work through these issues with a mentor or critical friend (Jeruchim and Shapiro, 1992; Shea, 1992; Collins, 1983). As facilitative work is very complex, it is most important that facilitators support each other in many different ways.

When things go wrong: learning from experience

> If God has sent me so many good things then I shouldn't grumble if he sends
> me a few bad.
>
>   Robert Browning, 'The melon seller'

Facilitation is at times stressful. There is a need for facilitators to build in strategies for their maintenance and recovery, since frequently they are bought into organizations when the environment has become 'toxic' (Frost. 2002; Frost and Robinson, 1999). I have walked away from a workshop stressed with the toxicity of the group, almost like the black goat in the Bible going out into the wilderness carrying the sins of the community. In facilitation classes, I talk of the 'Colgate ring of confidence' (an imaginary ring shown on television advertisements for Colgate toothpaste). I explain that a facilitator can take in the toxicity through the ears, and then transmit it through a pen onto the flip chart paper so he/she does not take it in.

When things go well we move quickly on to our next experiences. When things do not go so well we are stopped short. We often learn more from when things go wrong than from when things go 'right'.

Professor Chakraborty, lecturer in Human Values in Management Workshop, Calcutta, January 1998. 'One day I received my mail as usual. The fourth letter was from a management expert who had read my article on human values. He critically wrote, "Even a child would have known this. . ." I felt my face go hot as I read.

'The next letter was about the same article. Another person wrote, "I was so impressed by your article. Please will you come and visit my organization? I would like you to facilitate a workshop for us."'

Chakraborty suggests, 'If you are given praise you must have criticism too. Do not become attached to praise. Do not just seek good feedback; feeding your ego will become too stressful and eventually will distort your facilitative interventions.' Why? We need to discipline ourselves to reduce the enjoyment of positive feedback, and reduce the negativity of constructive/change feedback.

We often learn far more from mistakes and/or negative experiences than from positive experiences. What are you going to do if you receive positive, praise feedback? What are you going to do if you receive constructive, challenging, change feedback?

Learning from mistakes process

> One should never be sorry one has attempted something new –
> Never, never, never.
>
>   Sybil Thorndike

Planning ahead is one way of preparing for the unknown, but we need to spend time reviewing. The process entitled 'Learning from your mistakes' by Ross Colliver (1988) is useful in this regard. First of all settle down and make some time to review a workshop or incident.

- **Reconstruct the situation.** Reconstruct it in your mind by seeing it happen the way you saw it, hear yourself talking the way you did, feel what happened physically.
- **Review positives.** Review what you did well. It is essential that you review the positives as well as the negatives.
- **Review and assess negatives.** Now assess your thoughts, feelings and actions.
- **Stop criticizing yourself.** Now stop criticizing yourself, and say things like, 'Making mistakes is the only way to learn.' 'It will only make matters worse if you keep beating yourself up.' If you need to keep talking to yourself, use positive self-talk.
- **Shape a positive outcome.** Reframe what is happened; ask, 'What outcome do I really want here?' 'What do I want to hear, see and feel myself doing here?' 'What do I want from others?'
- **Give the positive a home.** Now imagine the complete positive outcome. Be specific. For example, what exactly do you want when you say you want more understating? Imagine using the new behaviour. Ask yourself, 'What outcome do I really want here?' 'What effect do I want to have on others?' Then review what you have imagined and edit or improve it where necessary. See yourself enacting the new behaviour really well.

Remember:

> No matter how well the facilitator does, she can never satisfy all the expectations of group members.
>
> Adapted from McClure (1998)

This process is a useful tool, with a mentor or critical friend asking the questions. The process of speaking out the issues can be very cathartic.

Learning about facilitation: observing your own practice

> A good facilitator never stops learning.
>
> Phil Bartle

Individual reflection

There are times when you may just have to 'pull up the drawbridge' and quietly reflect at home or in a quiet space, as the following poem illustrates.

Poem
Without going out of my door
I can know all things on earth.
Without looking out of my window
I can know the ways of heaven.
For the further one travels

The less one sees
The sage therefore
Arrives without travelling
Sees all without looking
Does all without doing.

Lao Tzu

Developing your own 'frame of facilitation'

In *Understanding Facilitation* I described a 'living frame of facilitation'. It was a mindscape or picture of how I saw facilitation at this stage of my work. As it is constantly changing, it is called a 'living frame', as opposed to a model set in concrete. I have included it here as it may be useful as part of your professional development and observation of your practice to develop your own frame or model of facilitation. (See Figure 17.1.)

The facilitator is in the boat, fishing. There is another person in the boat, representing a co-facilitator, mentor, critical friend or supervisor. External influences may be positive and/or negative. They may come from the past or from the immediate context, or be worldwide trends or a mix of all of these. The lightning of serendipity, that is, positive unusual combination or unexpected events (and negative surprises) indicates the need for facilitators to be able to utilize such comets positively.

The sea of context may be calm and positive, or rough and negative, representing the cultural, societal and organizational contexts in which the facilitation takes place. The waters may contain fish, mermaids and sea horses, which represent the varieties of friendly supports, critical friends and mentors. But there also may be snakes, crocodiles and sharks to watch out for. There are islands of different shapes, climates and cultures that the facilitator may visit in order to work with the inhabitants. They are in different climates, latitudes, longitudes, elevations and depths. Some islands have welcoming harbours, others do not. Before docking at each, the facilitator needs to investigate the environment carefully, and on arrival needs to listen and to watch carefully.

The design of the ark/houseboat will vary according to the facilitator's current culture and/or cultural background, gender and experiences. The foundations of the ark represent the facilitator's 'higher purpose', his/her deep-seated rationale for facilitating (Hunter, Bailey and Taylor, 1999). The more aware he/she is of these, the deeper the hull and the more stable the boat. The houseboat itself includes the facilitator's 'espoused theories' or values (Argyris, 1990; Argyris and Schön, 1994). These may differ from one facilitator to another according to his/her facilitation styles (but there are some 'common values' as exemplified in the Declaration of Human Rights). These 'espoused theories'/values should be made explicit for clients when they are deciding whether or not to recruit the services of the facilitator and when evaluating services.

The roof of the houseboat represents the facilitator's 'theory in action', that is, how the facilitator behaves under pressure, and the gaps between what he/she espouses and what happens in practice. The aerial protruding from the roof of the ark represents the many applications of technology for facilitators. The

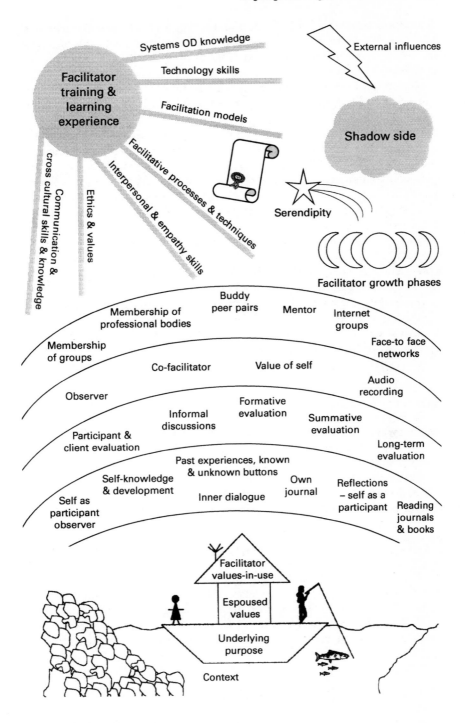

Figure 17.1 A living frame of facilitation

facilitator is holding a fishing line, representing ways of gaining nurturance from the seas around, and the occasional recreational breaks when the facilitator needs to put up a metaphorical sign 'Gone Fishing'. Facilitators, like counsellors, need a variety of activities outside their work to enable them to maintain equilibrium and recharge energies. There is a certificate which represents formal course learning and/or accreditation, that is, symbols of the professionalization of facilitation.

The rainbow represents the need for lifelong reflexivity. The layers of the rainbow are like different coloured mirrors that are held up in front of us: self-knowledge and development and ways of monitoring our learning; participation and client evaluations; co-facilitator and/or observers (not acolytes), and lastly feedback from facilitator groups: buddies, mentors, face-to-face support groups, Internet groups and professional bodies. All these contribute to our work as facilitators.

The sun and its rays represent lifelong learning about facilitation: awareness of ethics and values, communication and cross-cultural skills and knowledge; interpersonal and empathy skills; facilitative processes and techniques; models; knowledge of organizational systems, development and change.

The facilitator growth phases are represented by the cycles of the moon, though they are more erratic than the regular waxing and waning of the moon. The cloud represents our shadow side. The cloud can grow and cover the sun if we are not careful. It links to the bottom band of the rainbow and continuing self-development.

Journal writing

Another way of self-assessing your facilitation practice is to keep a self-reflective journal about your own development and observations of group behaviours. This allows you to see your development over time, and identify patterns in your behaviour. (See Chapter 7.)

For further detailed discussion on researching your own practice, see Radnor (2001); Stewart, McGoldrick and Watson (2001); and Coghlan (2001).

Self-assessment tools for facilitators

What factors contribute to the makings of an excellent facilitator? There are many self-assessment tools on facilitation. Some lists are overwhelming, and not all the skills and knowledge may be required by facilitators in different contexts and cultures. Plus there is the added factor of how the skills and knowledge of a facilitator are used. (See the discussion on ethics in *Understanding Facilitation* Chapter 11.)

IAF competency model

Since 1990, the International Association of Facilitators (IAF), in conjunction with the Institute of Cultural Affairs (ICA), has orchestrated discussion across the world on facilitator competencies. The resulting model published by Pierce, Cheesebrow and Braun (2000) is the result of discussions at the IAF and ICA conferences in the United States and Canada, e-mail discussions and literature reviews. See *Understanding Facilitation* Chapter 6 for a discussion of the IAF competency model, and Pierce, Cheesebrow and Braun (2000) or the IAF Web site.

Criteria of excellence

Heron (1989, 1999) has developed seven 'criteria of excellence' by which the competency of a facilitator may be judged:

1. **Authority.** Facilitators should be able to use 'distress-free authority' when making group interventions, without displacing their own pathology on the individual or group.
2. **Confrontation.** Facilitators can supportively confront individuals and/or the group when necessary about defensive or rigid behaviour.
3. **Orientation.** Orientation means the ability to give a clear conceptual orientation to experiential work when appropriate.
4. **Care.** Having a caring, empathetic, genuine manner is important for facilitators.
5. **Range of methods.** Heron suggests that facilitators should be able to handle deep regression and catharsis and transpersonal work. He adds that a repertoire of techniques and exercises is also desirable.
6. **Respect for persons.** Facilitators must respect 'the autonomy of the individual and the right of the individual to choose when to change and grow' (Heron, 1999: 340).
7. **Flexibility of intervention.** Facilitators need to be able to move within the modes and dimensions described in Heron's model (described in *Understanding Facilitation* Chapter 6).

I would add to this list:

8. **Knowledge of and respect for cultural differences.** Facilitators need skills and knowledge to accommodate the differing needs of people from cultures other than their own.
9. **Knowledge of technology.** Increasingly facilitators need to be able to use effectively varying complexities of technology, from simple flip chart paper to technology-mediated discussion groups.

What are your criteria for excellence in facilitation in your field/s of work? What would you add or subtract from the list above?

Some other examples of self-assessment questionnaires are to be found in Bens (1997, 1999); Kiser (1998) (a 'masterful facilitation skills assessment' self-scoring questionnaire which can also be used for 360 degree feedback); Glaser (1991, 1997); University Associates (1980); and Bostrom and Associates *The Facilitator Role Shuffle* (http://www.negia.net/~bostrom/bahome.htm).

Learning about facilitation: from and with others

Courses

An easy way to get your 'foot in the door' of facilitation is to join a course. Check that there is a strong percentage of practical work. There are a variety of levels of courses:

- community-based short courses;
- accredited tertiary courses;
- IAF accreditation.

These types of programme will help you to learn the basics of group dynamics, and should give you experience in facilitating groups within your own learning situation. You will be able to learn by observing others in action. Usually there is some form of supervision and guidance by a facilitator/lecturer. You will receive feedback (from the facilitator and participants).

An advantage of accredited university units in facilitation is that they are part of a wider programme which gives students qualifications for their CVs. Plus there is access to library and technological resources. One drawback of accredited university courses is that the assessment procedure gives the facilitator extra power. As a result participants might be inhibited in challenging the ideas of that person, unless this dynamic is addressed early on in the contracting stage. This may also be partly overcome if the facilitator shares power by incorporating negotiated learner contracts (to make marking criteria clear), self-assessment and peer assessment.

Facilitator accreditation

The IAF model of facilitator competencies was described in *Understanding Facilitation* Chapter 6. Information about the Facilitator Accreditation Board and Accreditation Guidelines for Candidates can be found at http://www.iaf-world.org

Learning by doing

You can also practise basic facilitation skills at home and with your friends. (Parents are often in facilitation and mediation roles with children and family members and some children practise mediation between their parents.) For example, if you are in a group where a couple of people are dominating the conversation, you can practise the roles of 'gatekeeper' and 'equalizer'. Wait for a pause and then (using an open-ended question rather than a closed question) invite a quieter group member to talk in a non-threatening way: for example, 'Thelma, what do you think about this issue?'

Participant observation

You can also learn a great deal by watching other facilitators at work as a 'participant observer' when you attend workshops. You have to keep yourself firmly focused on the process at hand rather than get involved in the content.

You can also try observing different kinds of meetings. Watch the chairperson and the participants. Who speaks and when? What happens when someone speaks and no one takes any notice? A few years ago I visited a number of different kinds of meetings: Quaker meetings, Alcoholics Anonymous (in Australia visitors are welcomed, but regulations vary from one country to another) and various community meetings. It helps to keep your mind focused if you keep a journal and stay in the role of 'participant observer'.

Shadowing

Another way to learn is to 'shadow' an experienced facilitator. Some groups do not mind having a learner present. For example, when I facilitated some workshops in a teaching hospital the participants were quite happy to have one of my students shadow me, as training 'on the job' was part of their work culture. But the openness of groups to strangers depends often on the intensity of the workshop topic, and maybe also the confidentiality and sensitivity of issues involved. Alternatively, you could take the role of scribe or co-facilitator.

Reading and researching

It is important to get a theoretical background to what happens in groups. There is now a vast array of books on facilitation, and certain publishers focus on participatory work, including New Society Publishers, and University Associates in North America. Go to Amazon.com and type in the word 'facilitation' for the latest publications.

Journals

Journals provide the most up-to-date information on new developments in the field. Useful examples include:

- *Group Facilitation*: http://www.thefacilitator.com/
- *The Learning Organization*
- *The Facilitator*: a research and applications journal
- http://iaf-world.org
- *Leadership and Organisation Development Journal*
- *Small Group Behaviour*
- *Training and Management Development Methods*
- *Journal of Management Education*
- *Organizational Dynamics*

- *Participation and Empowerment*
- *Conflict Resolution Network News*
- *Empowerment in Organisations*
- *Management Development Review*
- *Fast Company*

Full text electronic databases

There are a number of electronic databases available via university libraries, where you can type in keywords and download the full text of articles including diagrams and pictures. Some examples include:

- ABI/Inform Global Proquest Direct (includes a list of latest books);
- Science Direct;
- Social Science Plus;
- SwetsNet.

Networking groups

> You need lots of ropes.
> An expression from Papua New Guinea for needing lots of networks

Make sure you have someone you can debrief with: buddies, mentors, networks. There are many varieties of networking group. Often it is best to form your own. I belong to one which has few rules. We meet regularly at a different café every first Monday of the month, and have a very flexible agenda. We always start with a round robin to find out what people have been doing, then move on to address issues arising for group members.

Internet sites and discussion groups

There are a number of discussion groups on the Internet where you can:

- post facilitation issues/problems;
- look at previous discussion of issues;
- find out about short courses and resources.

There are many electronic discussion groups. Here is a selection. (See also *Understanding Facilitation*, Appendix 1.)

- International Association of Facilitators: www.iaf-world.org
- Latin American Association of Facilitators: e-mail: mbr@amauta.org
- Facilitators' newsgroup/discussion group: send a message to: listserv@cnsibm.albany.edu then, in the body of the text type: subscribe Grp–Facl YOUR NAME;
- 3M Meeting Network Web site: http://www.3m.com/meetingnetwork

Self-maintenance

Sitting at a computer

If you are spending long periods of time writing proposals, typing up sheets of flip chart paper or reports, you may be spending surprisingly large amounts of time at the computer. It is useful to have an exercise package on your computer to remind you to take breaks. There are many available, and as companies come and go I suggest you search the Net using linked keywords like 'break', 'ergonomic' and 'computer'. Trade names like 'stretch break' and 'break reminder' or 'gym break' will appear. Some companies allow you to download packages like Stretchware from the Web for trial periods.

It is a useful investment to ensure that your work area is set up ergonomically. As I am only 5 foot tall I use a sloping footrest to ensure that I keep my back upright and supported by my chair back. A slope board to hold notes and papers is useful between the keyboard and the computer screen, to ensure that you keep your head straight. Do not keep a clipboard on one side, otherwise you will over-extend one side of your neck continually.

Sleep deficit

Consulting and facilitation work is demanding. It is not evenly distributed: usually there is a 'feast' of overwork, followed by 'famine' of underwork. Facilitators often work late, and think and reflect 'off the job'. I have met many who have trouble sleeping (myself included). According to Stanley Coren (1996), there are many 'sleep thieves', and sleep deficit is a major problem for many professional people. I sometimes wake up and realize my mind is processing what happened in the group the previous day. Dreams can be useful, and I keep some sticky-backed notes by the bed so I can record any ideas, as I usually find I forget them the next day if I don't.

As more and more facilitators start to use technology with groups in different time zones, they will be facilitating online at odd hours of the night (see Chapter 14). As a result they may suffer from some of the same stresses as shift workers, when body clocks become maladjusted.

Stress management

> Take time to smell the roses.

We need to take time out to 'smell the roses', from 'doing' to 'being' and relaxing. Below are a couple of suggestions which are also useful in group work.

Progressive muscular relaxation (PMR)

Progressive muscular relaxation is a physical technique for relaxing your body when muscles are tense. The idea behind PMR is that you tense up groups of muscles in turn, so that they are as tightly contracted as possible. You then hold them in a state of extreme tension for a few seconds. Then relax the muscles to their previous state. Finally you consciously relax them again as much as you can. You can apply PMR to any or all of the muscle groups in your body, depending on whether you want to relax just a single area or your whole body.

For maximum relaxation you can use PMR in conjunction with breathing techniques and visual imagery or mind movies of relaxing scenes.

It can also be effective to link the exercise of PMR to a keyword or mantra that you can say to yourself. Associating the feeling of relaxation with the keyword means that in a moment of tension you can bring the feeling of relaxation purely by repeating that word.

Breathing control

Deep breathing is a very effective method of relaxation and centring. It is a core component of everything from the 'take 10 deep breaths' approach to calming down, right through to yoga, relaxation and meditation. It works well in conjunction with other relaxation techniques such as progressive muscular relaxation, relaxation imagery and meditation to reduce stress. See the Web sites http://www.mindtools.com/page2.html and http://www.mindtools.com/pages/main/newMN_TCS.htm

Punch bags, sport and walks

Sometimes it is best to 'let out' our stress in more active ways: walking, jogging, aerobics, swimming, squash, and even the Japanese version of punch bags are ways of generating endorphins. It appears that 30 minutes of walking a day can make all the difference to our overall health.

Relaxing baths, saunas, massage and pets

One of the many advantages of living and working in Lao PDR is the cheap availability of Lao massage and saunas. Money and time spent on our own maintenance is investment in our own health and well being.

What are the best methods for you?

Conclusion

'Who are you?' said the Caterpillar.
. . . Alice replied, rather shyly, 'I – I hardly know, sir, just at present – at least I know who I was when I got up this morning, but I think I must have been changed several times since then.'

Lewis Carroll, *Alice in Wonderland*

Just like Alice in Wonderland, facilitators take on many different roles and change their personas as they develop and grow. This chapter has focused on how we can learn from mistakes when things do not go as well as anticipated, and processes to help us learn by observing our own practice and that of others. Finally, some ideas for self-maintenance were discussed.

Appendix 1: Community consultation and participatory processes/models

Adapted from Citizens and Civics Unit (2002) and Hartz-Karp, Dudley and Chambers (2002)

Methods are in alphabetical order for easy reference

Methods	Things to consider	Advantages	Disadvantages
Advisory committees A group of representative stakeholders is invited to sit on planning committees to make input into planning process.	Define roles, responsibilities and levels of power up front. Be forthcoming with information. Use a consistently credible process. Interview potential committee members before selection. Use third-party facilitation. Ensure that members communicate with their constituencies.	Provides detailed analyses for project issues. Participants gain understanding of other perspectives, leading toward compromise.	Very hard for a minority of '1' person to sway a committee. Inexperienced community representative may feel intimidated by language and processes used in a committee. May require mentors. Committee members may not reach consensus. Time and labour-intensive. Constituencies of rep may feel let down by him/her.
Citizens advisory committees Intended to represent broader public views.	Benefits from balanced committee. Can be made up of variety of organizations from government and public. Advice of committee should influence decision making.	Informs public, aids trust in government, reduced conflict	Not always representative group. If advice not taken without adequate reason given, trust is quickly lost.
Citizens panels and summits Made up of people with particular interest in the idea. Contact may be through forums or discussion groups.	Find relevant groups, what they do and who they represent. Determine best contact method.	Access the body of research and make it digestible for the panel. Consultation with knowledgeable experts. Allows in-depth discussion. Relatively inexpensive.	Opportunity for representative to capture discussion. Not necessarily representative. Can be time-consuming.
Citizens' juries 12–16 representative citizens called to sit on a 'jury' to learn about an issue, cross-examine	Requires skilled facilitator for the full session. The jury is also facilitated. Commissioning body must follow	Great opportunity to develop deep understanding of an issue. Jury given pre-reading which should be balanced and neutral.	Resource-intensive. Expensive. Not suitable for all issues. Extensive preparatory work.

Methods	Things to consider	Advantages	Disadvantages
witnesses, and make recommendation/s. Always non-binding without legal standing.	recommendations or explain why (trust can be lost easily). Be clear about how results will be used. Consensus sought, but may need to vote. Advisory committee selects 'expert witnesses' (reps of local, state government, professionals, scientists, pressure groups and individuals with (concerns, social or ethical views).	Jury can ask questions and for extra information and/or call in extra technical people if required. Provides informed feedback. Public can identify with representative citizens. Lobby groups have to present issues coherently to the jury. May result in shift in thinking by 'Nimbys' (not in my backyard) people.	May not be representative.
Citizens' panels Comprise between 500–2500 citizens who are representative of population. Used as sounding board to test, assess and develop proposals over an extended period of time.	The roles of panel members need to be made clear. Can be conducted in partnership with other connected organizations/agencies.	Useful to track views over time. Can be directed towards particular targets. Access to wide range of population including minority groups.	Resource-intensive in initial stages. Maintaining interest for panel members hard over time. Difficult to replace panel members throughout process.
Community learning centres Set up by and for communities. Staffed often by volunteers who gain funding from a variety of sources.	Provide a wide variety of informal courses based on local demand. Teachers and facilitators often give their time voluntarily or gain credits to attend other courses free of charge. Safety issues, cost of insurance etc.	Freedom to experiment and promote unusual or one-off programmes. Non-threatening. Very cheap to attend.	May become dependent on the enthusiasm of a few people

Methods	Things to consider	Advantages	Disadvantages
Consensus conference 10–16 panel members come together to research a complex issue and then question expert witnesses before reaching a consensus decision. Open to the public.	Requires high level of commitment from panel members. Requires compilation of complex material for preparatory days. Make available expert witnesses as determined by panel. Requires skilled and independent facilitator.	Panel determine questions to ask witnesses, leading to greater impartiality. Open to public, transparent. Provides informed deliberation.	High level of commitment from panel. Resource-intensive. Costly. Extensive preparatory work. Not representative. May be difficulty in reaching consensus.
Deliberative opinion polls Measures informed opinion on an issue during a 2–3 day meeting.	Does not expect or encourage participants to develop a shared view. Requires skilled facilitator.	Polling of an informed group. Exposure to different backgrounds, arguments and views.	Resource-intensive. Can be costly to set up and pay expenses of those attending. Not statistically representative.
E-democracy Using technology, eg e-mail and Internet for democratic processes to enable two-way communication between government and citizens.	Fast and cost-effective transfer of information documents, news, online surveys, televotes and telesurveys. Important to identify respondents and use high security to stop double voting, but also to maintain anonymity of voters. Web sites, e-mails, for political parties and politicians. Prompt online discussion of 'hot' news topics. Networked NGOs. Networked interest/lobbying/minority groups. Requires an e-moderator to stop abusive material without stifling	Cost-effective after initial outlay. Quick response rate. Easy to keep information current. Can incorporate large amount of data.	Monitoring and maintaining the systems. Keeping information up to date. Coping with sheer mass of data generated. Access to computers may be limited. Skills to use computers may be limited. Won't reach everyone. Technical problems. Requires expert IT staff to work closely with expert 'people facilitators'. Result may be unrepresentative.

Methods	Things to consider	Advantages	Disadvantages
	open debate. Requires careful archive of all materials.		Scheduling multiple interviews can be time-consuming and expensive. Interviews must engender trust or risk negative response. Not necessarily representative.
Face to face interviews One to one meetings with stakeholders to gain information on public concerns and perspectives.	Where feasible, interview should be conducted in person, particularly when considering candidates for citizens' committees. Take advantage of opportunity for citizens to input on how they participate. Use trained researchers/interviewers.	Provides opportunities to understand public concerns and issues. Provides opportunity to learn how to communicate best with public. Can be used to evaluate potential citizens' committee members.	
Focus groups 8–10 people led by trained facilitator in 'one-off' discussion on a particular topic.	Selection of group is of primary importance. May need to have several groups to investigate views from different perspectives. Value the input and commitment of group members. Requires skilled facilitator. Rewards/incentives may be offered to attend.	Allows for brainstorming of ideas. Can include those who may usually be excluded, eg culturally and linguistically diverse groups, elderly, disabled. Allows in-depth discussion.	May be costly. Lack of confidentiality. Qualitative information only. Difficulty of prioritizing issues. Does not lend itself easily to discussing sensitive issues.
Future search conferences Consider multiple future scenarios and ways to influence outcomes in uncertain situations.	Independent and skilled facilitator. No pre-set proposals. Who to invite: deep slice of representatives from different parts of community together in a 'social island'. How to document findings (now quick if have access to lap tops).	Allows an exchange of information about desirable futures. Many viewpoints can be heard.	Resource-intensive. Could be captured by large interest groups. Difficulty in reaching consensus.

Methods	Things to consider	Advantages	Disadvantages
	Participants should leave with whole minutes of meeting.		
Open days and community exhibitions Informal events to inform citizens about an organization and/or issue.	Locate suitable venue. Publicize events widely. Provide information displays. Opening times/days important for access.	Gives public flexibility to attend. Allows contact with public and can provide ad hoc feedback. Publicizes organization and/or issue.	May not be representative. Feedback may be limited. Difficulty in recording responses.
Open public meetings Formal meeting with scheduled agenda.	Accessible and convenient public location. Widespread publicity. Timing so that maximum number of people can attend (plus opportunity for absentees to send in ideas via phone, fax, letter, e-mail). Clearly defined objective. Defined meeting structure. Good amplification accessible by public, ie radio mikes.	Opportunity to provide information and obtain feedback. Demonstrates commitment to public consultation. Builds up relationships with local community. Relatively inexpensive.	Not representative. Localized knowledge only. May need to bring in more than one 'expert', eg to gain different perspectives on danger of trees overhanging road. Difficult for non-English speakers to participate. People who attend and speak out tend to be extrovert and articulate.
Open space technology workshops	Independent and skilled facilitator. No pre-set proposals. Open invitation to all.	Many issues can be heard concurrently. Flexible size 5–500.	Participants are responsible for setting the agenda in front of the whole group.
Public hearings Formal meetings with scheduled presentation offered.	Try to use informal meetings immediately before to build knowledge base.	Provides opportunity for public to speak without rebuttal. Meets some legal requirements. Puts comments on record.	Does not foster dialogue or trust. Creates 'us' versus 'them' feeling. Minority groups not easily included.

Methods	Things to consider	Advantages	Disadvantages
Referenda Issue put to popular vote.	Initiated by government. Issue should stand on its own (ie closed question requiring simple 'yes' or 'no' answer, not complex question). Result usually binding for some years.	Incites discussion. All voters have equal influence. Results cannot be ignored.	Expensive. Potential for undue influence by organizations/groups with greater resources, eg for media coverage of views. Limited use.
Representative groups Made up of people with particular in the issue. Contact via forums or discussion groups.	Find relevant groups, what they do and who they represent. Determine best contact method.	Access to body of research. Consultation with knowledgeable group. Allows in-depth discussion. Relatively inexpensive.	Opportunities for individuals to capture and dominate discussion. Not necessarily statistically representative. Can be time-consuming. Large group format may prevent some from attending and /or speaking.
Restorative justice conferences Used in the criminal justice system, community, organizations and schools.	Focuses on healing and repairing damage to relationships and the community. Brings together victims' families and friends and organizations. Viable and worthwhile system increasing in use around the world.	Feelings are vented legitimately. Provides opportunity for offenders to apologize and for victims to forgive and move on. Provides a more balanced approach to problems than the adversarial approach to justice.	Some conferences do not take place as attendance of all parties must be voluntary.
Scenario planning	Independent and skilled facilitator and research team. Requires access to electronic databases for comprehensive research.	Allows an exchange of information about desirable and non-desirable futures. Many viewpoints can be heard. Enables contingency plans to be made.	Time-consuming and expensive.

Methods	Things to consider	Advantages	Disadvantages
Small neighbourhood meetings Small meetings in a person's home.	Issue relevant to a neighbourhood. Staff should be polite and appreciative. May need to be aware of other neighbourhood issues.	Relaxed setting conducive to effective dialogue. Maximizes two-way communication.	Requires a lot of labour to reach many people, through repeated small meetings.
Staff feedback and suggestions Encourage feedback and suggestions from frontline staff who interact with the public.	Establish a system for obtaining feedback.	Shows you value staff and are open to suggestions. Valuable source of information on service use and users. Gives staff a chance to put ideas forward anonymously.	Relies on staff taking time to give feedback. Doesn't necessarily represent all staff views.
Surveys and questionnaires Inquiries mailed randomly to sample population to gain specific information for statistical analysis.	Ensure statistically valid results before making investment. Survey/questionnaire should be professionally developed and administered to avoid bias. Most suitable for general attitudinal surveys.	Provides input from individuals who possibly would not attend meetings. Provides input from cross-section of public, not just activists. Statically tested results are more persuasive with political bodies and public.	Response rate is generally low for statistically valid results. Can be labour-intensive and expensive. Level of detail may be limited. May be regarded as a public relations tool. Often do not ask the 'right' questions. You only get answers to the questions you ask. Assume that people spend time to answer conscientiously.
User comment and complaints box Encourages feedback from users through use of comment cards.	Make feedback forms available. Ensure comments are posted on a board with replies.	Provides input from those using the services. Easy and cheap to set up. Provides information about service's weaknesses and strengths. Anonymous.	Not representative. Basically reactive to existing systems rather than generating new ideas/systems.

Methods	Things to consider	Advantages	Disadvantages
User ideas box Encourages constructive suggestions for improving the status quo.	Useful to post ideas publicly. Acknowledge inputs so that people know they are taken seriously.	Provides opportunity for constructive suggestions from those using the services. Easy and cheap to set up. Anonymous or may wish to provide small rewards for 'good ideas'.	May provoke unwanted media attention. Can polarize issues if not conceived and facilitated well. Users can become too closely linked to organization. Often excludes minority groups.
User panels A small group regularly assembled to debate or provide input on specific issues over a long period of time.	Small size no more than 12. Have clear objective and time frame.	Useful sounding board. Relatively quick feedback. Continuing dialogue. Can build credibility if all sides are represented. May provoke media attention. Gives user perspective.	
Written consultation exercises Inviting public submissions for written comments on specific proposals.	Provide full details of issue for which views are sought. Publicize event. May need multiple format for documents. Allow ample time to respond.	Provides detailed information on the issue for those interested. Elicits a considered view. Favours those who can express themselves well in writing.	Response rate is generally low for statistically valid results. Lengthy process.

Contacts and references

Professional organizations for facilitators and consultants

International Institute of Management Consultants

Based in the United Kingdom, this organization has many interesting job opportunities and references.
Web site: http://www.mcgl.co.uk/

International Council of Management Consulting Institutes

Web site: http://www.icmci.com

Institute of Management Consultants: Western Australia

Web site: www.wa.imc.org.au

Nonprofit Managers Library

Web site: http://www.mapnp.org/library/

International Association of Facilitators

760 West 145th St, Suite 202
St Paul MN 55124
USA
E-mail: office@iaf-world.org
Web site: www.iaf-world.org

Latin American Association of Facilitators

Coordinación Latinoamericana
Apartado Aéreo 50717
Santafé de Bogotá, Colombia
E-mail: mbr@amauta.org

Facilitator Accreditation Services Ltd

Jo Harrison, Administrator
Tel: + 44 (0)1233 500839
Fax: + 44 (0)1233 500838
E-mail: jo@facilitator-accreditation.com
Web site: www.facilitator-accreditation.com
Mailgroup: facilitator-accreditation-subscribe@egroups.com

H H Owen and Co

E-mail: owen@tmn.com
Web site: www.tmn.com/~owen

Open Space Institute

E-mail: osi@tmn.com
Web site: www.tmn.com/openspace
Provides education, publishing information, research by members.

References

Abdullah, A (2001a) *Solution Engineering: Ten tips for beefing up your problem solving toolbox* [Online] http://home.att.net/~nickols/tentips.htm (accessed June 2002)

Abdullah, A (2001b) *The Influence of Values on Management in Malaysia*, PhD Thesis, Universiti Kebangsaan, Bangi, Malaysia

Abdullah, A and Shephard, P (2000) *The Cross Cultural Game*, Brain Dominance Technologies, Kuala Lumpur, Malaysia [Online] http://asma.braindominance.com/game.htm (accessed June 2002)

Adams, G B and Balfour, D L (1998) *Unmasking Administrative Evil*, Sage, Thousand Oaks, CA

Adams, J, Hayes, J and Hopson, B (1977) *Transition: Understanding and managing personal change*, Martin Robertson, London

Adams, S (1996) *The Dilbert Principle: A cubicle's eye view of meetings, management fads and other workplace afflictions*, Harper Business, New York

Adams, S (1997) *The Dilbert Future: Thriving on stupidity in the 21st century*, Harper Business, New York

Akin, G and Palmer, I (2000) Putting metaphors to work for change in organisations, *Organizational Dynamics* (Winter), pp 67–79

Argyris, C (1990) *Overcoming Organizational Defences: Facilitating organisational learning*, Prentice Hall, Englewood Cliffs, NJ

Argyris, C and Schön, D (1994) *Theory in Practice: Increasing organizational effectiveness*, Jossey-Bass, San Francisco

Arnstein, S R (1969) A ladder of citizen participation in the USA, *Journal of the American Institute of Planners*, **35** (4) (July) pp 216–24

Bales, R F (1950) *Interaction Process Analysis: A method for the study of groups*, Addison-Wesley, Cambridge, MA

Ball, C (1984) *Role, Risk and Reality in Courses For Unemployed Youth*, talk given to the Participation and Equity Programme Team, Technical and Further Education Division, Perth, Western Australia

Bank, J (1994) *Outdoor Development for Managers*, 2nd edn, Gower, Aldershot, UK

Bankston, C L (1995) Who are the Laotian Americans? in *The Asian American Almanac*, Gale Research, Washington, DC

Barbalet, J M (1998) *Emotion, Social Theory and Social Structure*, Cambridge University Press, Cambridge, UK

Barca, M and Cobb, K (1993) *Beginnings and Endings*, Connaught Training, Aldershot, UK

Barker, J (2000) *What is Scenario Planning?* Scenario Planning and Research Unit, Curtin University of Technology, Perth, Western Australia

Barnhart, R B (ed) (1988) *The Barnhart Dictionary of Etymology*, HW Wilson, New York

Beck, R and Metrick, S B (1990) *A Guide to Creating and Performing Your Own Rituals for Growth and Change*, Celestial Arts, Berkeley, CA

Becker, B (1988) *Art of Communicating*, Crisp, Los Angeles, CA

Beer, J E and Stief, E (1997) *The Mediator's Handbook*, New Society, Gabriola Island, Canada

Belbin, E, Downs, S and Perry, P (1981) *How Do I Learn? An experimental programme to introduce young people and their teachers to the many ways of learning*, Further Education Curriculum Review and Development Unit, London, UK

Belbin, R M (1993) *Team Roles At Work*, Butterworth-Heinemann, Oxford, UK

Belenky, M F, Clinchy, B M, Goldberger, N R and Tarule, J M (1997) *Women's Ways of Knowing: The development of self, voice and mind*, 10th edn, Basic Books, New York

Bell, M, Hayward, S and Morello, T (2000) *The New Synergy: People, systems, settings*, paper presented at the Gartner US Symposium

Bennett, B and Richardson, J (1984) Applying learning techniques to on-the-job development, *Journal of European and Industrial Training*, **8** (1), pp 35–44

Bennis, W G and Shepard, H A (1956) A theory of group development, *Human Relations*, **9**, pp 415–37

Bens, I (1997) Facilitation skills self assessment, in *Facilitating with Ease! A comprehensive guide to the practice of facilitation*, Participative Dynamics, Sarasota, FL

Bens, I (1999) Facilitation core practices observation sheet, in *Facilitation at a Glance*, Association for Quality and Participation Cincinnati, OH

Biggs, J B and Telfer, R (1987) *The Process of Learning*, 2nd edn, Prentice Hall, Sydney

Block, C H (1999) *Flawless Consulting: A guide to getting your expertise used*, 2nd edn, Jossey-Bass/Pfeiffer, San Francisco

Block, P (ed) (2001) *The Flawless Consulting Fieldbook and Companion: A guide to understanding your expertise*, Jossey-Bass/Pfeiffer, San Francisco

Blood, P and Korner, J (2001) *Training in Restorative Practices*, Workshop 22–23 November, Fremantle, Western Australia

Boal, A (1992) *Games for Actors and Non-Actors*, Routledge, London

Bohm, D, Factor, D and Garrett, P (1991) *Dialogue: A proposal* (from Richard Burg [Online] raburg@well.com) (accessed 2 April 1995)

Boje, D M (1991) Learning storytelling: storytelling to learn management skills, *Journal of Management Education*, 5 (3), pp 279–94

Bolman, L G and Deal, T E (1995) *Leading With Soul: An uncommon journey of spirit*, Jossey-Bass, San Francisco

Bolman, L G and Deal, T E (1997) *Reframing Organisations: Artistry, choice and leadership*, Jossey-Bass, San Francisco

Bolton, R (1987a) *New Circus*, Calouste Gulbenkein Foundation, London

Bolton, R (1987b) *People Skills: How to assert yourself, listen to others, and resolve conflicts*, Simon and Schuster, Brookvale, NSW

Bolton, R (1998) *Showtime! Over 75 ways to put on a show*, Dorling Kindersley, London

Booth, C (2002) To restore justice to the law, *The Tablet* (20 July), pp 6–7

Bostrom and Associates (undated) *The Facilitator Role Shuffle: Assessing critical facilitation behaviors*, Bostrom and Associates, Columbia, USA [Online] (http://www.negia.net/~bostrom/bahome.htm) (accessed April 2001)

Boud, D, Keogh, R and Walker, D (eds) (1985) *Reflection: Turning experience into learning*, Kogan Page, London

Braithwaite, J (1989) *Crime, Shame and Reintegration*, Cambridge University Press, New York

Brant, L and Harvey, T (2001) *Choosing and Using Music in Training*, Gower, Aldershot, UK

Bridges, W (1991) *Managing Transitions*, Addison-Wesley, Reading, MA

Bunker, B B and Alban, B T (1997) *Large Group Interventions: Engaging the whole system for rapid change*, Jossey-Bass, San Francisco

Buzan, T and Buzan, B (1993) *The Mind Map Book: Radiant thinking: the major evolution in human thought*, BBC Books, London

Campbell, J (1973) *The Hero with a Thousand Faces*, Princeton University Press, Princeton, NJ

Capacchione, L (1979) *The Creative Journal: The art of finding yourself*, Swallow Press/Ohio Press, OH

Carhoon, A R (1993) The search conference technique: an organisational development tool for strategic planning, in *Handbook of Organisational Consultation*, ed R T Golembiewski, Marcel Dekker, New York

Castro, E (2000) *HTML for the World Wide Web: Visual quickstart guide*, 4th edn, Peachpit Press, Berkeley, CA

Chambers, R (1983) *Rural Development: Putting the last first*, Longman Scientific and Technical, Harlow, UK

Chan Kim, W and Mauborgne, R A (1992) Parables of leadership, *Harvard Business Review* (Jul–Aug), pp 123–28

Chauderi, U S (1975) Questioning and creative thinking: a research perspective, *Journal of Creative Behavior*, **9** (1), pp 30–34

Checkland, P B and Scholes, J (1990) *Soft Systems Methodology in Action*, Wiley, Chichester, UK

Cherniss, C and Adler, M (2000) *Promoting Emotional Intelligence in Organizations: Make training in emotional intelligence effective*, American Society of Training and Development, Alexandria, VA

Citizens and Civics Unit (2002) *Consulting Citizens: A resource guide*, Department of Premier and Cabinet, Perth, Western Australia [Online] www.ccu.dpc.wa.gov.au

Coghlan, D (2001) *Doing Action Research in Your Own Organisation*, Sage, Thousand Oaks, CA

Collins, N (1983) *Professional Women and Their Mentors*, Prentice-Hall, Englewood Cliffs, NJ

Colliver, R (1988) Learning from your mistakes, *Business Directions*, **1** (April 5), p 9

Concise Oxford Dictionary (1982) 7th edn, Oxford University Press, UK

Conger, J A (1989) *The Charismatic Leader: The art of transforming managers into leaders*, Jossey-Bass, San Francisco

Consedine, J (1995) *Restorative Justice: Healing the effects of crime*, Ploughshares, Lyttleton, New Zealand

Cooney, J and Burton, K (1986) *Photolanguage Australia: Human values A and B*, Catholic Education Office, Leichhardt, NSW (black and white study prints)

Coren, S (1996) *Sleep Thieves: An eye-opening exploration into the science and mysteries of sleep*, Free Press, New York

Cornelius, H and Faire, S (1989) *Everyone Can Win: How to resolve conflict*, Simon and Schuster, East Roseville, NSW

Covello, V (1992) Trust and credibility in risk communication, *Health and Environment Digest*, **6** (1), pp 1–5

Cox, E (1995) *A Truly Civil Society*, Boyer lectures, Australian Broadcasting Corporation, Sydney

Crawford, F (1999) *Autoethnography and Connecting to Working with Context and Culture*, School of Sociology, Curtin University of Technology, Perth, Western Australia, unpublished handout

Crombie, A (1985) The nature and types of search conferences, *International Journal of Lifelong Education*, **4** (1), pp 3–33

Crum, T F (1987) *The Magic of Conflict: Turning a life of work into a work of art*, Simon and Schuster, New York

Dahmer, B (1992) Kinder, gentler icebreakers, *Training and Development* (Aug), pp 47–49

Dart, B C and Clarke, J A (1991) Helping students become better learners: a case study in teacher education, *Higher Education*, **222**, pp 317–35

De Bono, E (1985) *Six Thinking Hats*, Penguin, London

Deal, R (1999) *Strengths in Teams: 28 qualities of successful teamwork*, card pack, St Luke's Innovative Resources, Bendigo, Australia

Deal, R and Veeken, J (1992) *Strength Cards*, St Luke's Innovative Resources, Bendigo, Australia

Deal, R and Veeken, J (1997) *The Bears*, St Luke's Innovative Resources, Bendigo, Australia

Delbecq, A and Van de Ven, A H (1971) A group process model for problem identification and programme planning, *Journal of Applied Behavioural Science*, 7, pp 466–91

Delbecq, A L, Van de Ven, A H and Gustafson, D H (1975) *Group Techniques for Program Planning: A guide to nominal group and Delphi processes*, Scott Foresman, IL

Dennison, M (2000) *Voting With Dots*, [Online] Grp-Facl@listservalbanyedu http://wwwalbanyedu/cpr/gf/ (summary of electronic discussion on group facilitation) Accessed 20/3/2002

Denzin, N K and Lincoln, Y S (eds) (1994) *A Handbook of Naturalistic Research Methods*, Sage, Thousand Oaks, CA

Diamond, L (1996) *Effective Videoconferencing: Techniques for better business meetings*, Crisp, Menlo Park, CA

Dick, B (1984, 1987) *Helping Groups to Be Effective: Skills, processes and concepts for group facilitation*, 2nd edn, Interchange, Chapel Hill, Australia

Dick, B (2002) *Beliefs Without Reason* [Online] www.scu.edu.au/schools/gcm/ar/arp/bwr.html (accessed July 2002)

Dick, C F (1984) *Search Workbook*, University of Queensland, Brisbane

Distefano, J J and Maznevski, M L (2000) Creating value with diverse teams in global management, *Organizational Dynamics*, 29 (1), pp 45–63

Downs, S (1981) *How Do I Learn?*, Further Education and Curriculum Review and Development Unit, London, England

Doyle, M and Straus, D (1976) *How to Make Meetings Work: The new interaction method*, Jove, New York

Duarte, D and Snyder, N (1999) *Mastering Virtual Teams*, Jossey-Bass, San Francisco

Edwards, B (1988) *Drawing on the Artist Within: How to release your hidden creativity*, Fontana, London

Egri, C P and Frost, P J (1991) Shamanism and change: bringing back the magic in organizational transformation, *Organizational Change and Development*, 5, pp 175–221

Elanta, V, Hancock, F and Williams, R (2001) *The Cauldron Ritual*, Curtin University of Technology, Perth, Western Australia

Ellis, A (1987) The use of rational humorous songs in psychotherapy, in *Handbook of Humor and Psychotherapy: Advances in the clinical uses of humor*, ed W F Fry and W A Salameh, Professional Resource Exchange, New York

Emery, F and Emery, M (1975) *Participative Design: Work and community life*, Occasional Papers in Continuing Education 4, Australian National University

Emery, M (1976) *Searching: For New Directions – In New Ways – For New Times*, Occasional Papers in Continuing Education 12, Australian National University

Emery, M and Purser, R E (1996) *The Search Conference: A powerful method for planning organisational change and community action*, Jossey-Bass, San Francisco

Estes, C P (1992) *Women Who Run With The Wolves*, Rider, London

Fanning, P (1988) *Visualisation for Change*, New Harbinger, Oakland, CA

Fisher, R and Ury, W (1981) *Getting to Yes: Negotiating agreement without giving in*, Business Books, London

Folberg, J and Taylor, A (1984) *Mediation: A comprehensive guide to resolving conflicts without litigation*, Jossey-Bass, San Francisco

Forbes-Greene, S (1980) *The Encyclopedia of Icebreakers: Structured activities that warm up, motivate, challenge, acquaint*, Applied Skills Press, St Louis, MO

Foreman, K and Clem, M (1995) *Something Like A Drug: An unauthorised oral history of theatresports*, Red Deer College Press, Red Deer, Alberta, Canada

Forsyth, D R (1993) *Group Dynamics*, 2nd edn, Brooks/Cole, CA

Frank, A (1945) *The Diary of Anne Frank*, Pan, London

Franklin, M (1901) *My Brilliant Career*, Georgian House, Melbourne

Franklin, M (1946) *My Career Goes Bung*, Georgian House, Melbourne

Freire, P (1972) *Pedagogy of the Oppressed*, Penguin, Harmondsworth, UK

Freire, P (1973) *Education for a Critical Consciousness*, Seabury Press, New York

Frost, P J (2002) *Toxic Emotions at Work: How compassionate managers handle pain and conflict*, Harvard Business School Press, Cambridge, MA

Frost, P J and Robinson, S L (1999) The toxic handler: organizational hero and casualty, *Harvard Business Review* (Jul–Aug), pp 96–106

Frost, R (1969) *The Poetry of Robert Frost*, ed E C Lathem, Jonathan Cape, London

Gardner, H (1993) *Multiple Intelligences: The theory in practice*, Basic Books, New York

Garmston, R J (1994) The persuasive art of presenting: what's a meta-phor? *Journal of Staff Development*, **15** (2), pp 60–61

Geschka, H, Schaude, G R and Schlicksupp, H (1973) Modern techniques for solving problems, *Chemical Engineering*, **6** (80), pp 91–97

Ghaye, T, Gillespie, D and Lillyman, S (2000) *Empowerment Through Reflection: The narratives of healthcare professionals*, Mark Allen, Dinton, UK

Gilligan, C (1982) *In a Different Voice: Psychological theory and women's development*, Harvard University Press, Cambridge, MA

Glaser, R (1991) *Facilitator Behavior Questionnaire: Helping teams become empowered*, HRDQ, Organization Design and Development, King of Prussia, PA

Glaser, R (1997) *Facilitator Behavior Questionnaire: Facilitator guide*, HRDQ, Organization Design and Development, King of Prussia, PA

Goldberg, P (1983) *The Intuitive Edge*, Jeremy Tarcher, Los Angeles

Goleman, D (1996) *Emotional Intelligence: Why it can matter more than IQ*, Bloomsbury, London

Goleman, D (1998) *Working with Emotional Intelligence*, Bloomsbury, London

Goodman, G (1995) Brainwriting: what to do when there's not a cloud in the brainstorming sky, in *Marketing Encyclopedia: Issues and trends shaping the future*, ed J Heilbrunn, NTC Business Books, Lincolnwood, IL

Gordon, J (1997) The HRD hall of fame, *Training*, **34** (2), pp 45–50

Gordon, W (1961) *Synectics*, Harper, New York

Goulding, D (2002a) *Recapturing Freedom: Issues related to the release of long-term prisoners into the community*, PhD thesis, Murdoch University, Perth, Western Australia

Goulding, D (2002b) Restorative justice processes (e-mail received Jan 16)

Grindler, J and Bandler, R (1979) *Frogs into Princes*, Real People Press, Moab, UT

Hall, E T (1990) *Understanding Cultural Differences*, Intercultural Press, Yarmouth, ME

Hammerskjold, D (1964) *Markings*, Faber and Faber, London

Hammond, S A (1996) *The Thin Book of Appreciative Inquiry*, 2nd edn, Thin Book Publishing, Plano, USA

Hanson, M (1997) Facilitating civil society, in *Beyond Prince and Merchant: Citizen participation and the rise of civil society*, ed J Burbidge, pp 234–47, ICA International, New York

Harris, C (1991) Using short stories to teach international management, *Journal of Management Education*, **15** (3), pp 374–78

Hartford, M E (1972) *Groups in Social Work*, Columbia University Press, New York

Hartz-Karp, J, Dudley, J and Chambers, L (2002) *New Ideas in Community Consultation*, Institute of Public Administration Australia and Department of Premier and Cabinet, Perth, Western Australia

Harvey, J B (1988) *The Abilene Paradox and Other Meditations on Management*, Jossey-Bass, San Francisco

Heron, J (1987) *Confessions of a Janus Brain*, Endymion Press, London

Heron, J (1989) *The Facilitator's Handbook*, Kogan Page, London

Heron, J (1992) *Feeling and Personhood: Psychology in another key*, Sage, London

Heron, J (1993a) *Group Facilitation: Theories and models for practice*, Kogan Page, London

Heron, J (1993b) *Advanced Facilitator's Course Notes*, sponsored by the School of Management, Curtin University, Perth, Western Australia

Heron, J (1999) *The Complete Facilitator's Handbook*, Kogan Page, London

Hill, W F and Gruner, L (1973) A study of development in open and closed groups, *Small Group Behavior*, **4**, pp 355–81

Hillman, J (1996) *The Soul's Code: In search of character and calling*, Random House, Milsom's Point, NSW

Hofstede, G (1980), *Culture's Consequences: International differences in world-related values*, Sage, Beverly Hills, CA

Holden, C (1994) Random samples: smart music, *Science*, 266, pp 968–69

Hogan, C F (1981) *Education: What for?* Search Conference, Hong Kong Polytechnic

Hogan, C F (1982) *Education: What for?* Report on a search conference, Education Technology Unit, Hong Kong Polytechnic, Hong Kong

Hogan, C F (1988) *Student Participation in the Planning, Implementation and Evaluation of a Participation and Equity Programme*, Masters thesis, Curtin University of Technology, Perth, Western Australia

Hogan, C F (1989) Developing personal risk management skills in Hong Kong and in Australia: four experience-based approaches, in *Proceedings of the 2nd International Conference on Personnel and Human Resource Management*, ed J B Shaw, City Polytechnic of Hong Kong

Hogan, C F (1990) *Taking the Board out of Board Meetings*, Western Australian Department for the Arts Occasional Papers: The Effective Board

Hogan, C F (1991) Strategies for enhancing empowerment, in *Training and Development Methods*, MCB University Press, Vol 6, pp 325–42

Hogan, C F (1993a) How to get more out of video conference meetings, *Training and Management Development Methods*, 7, pp 5.01–5.16

Hogan, C F (1993b) Simultaneously teaching facilitation skills to students at separate locations using interactive videoconferencing, *Training and Management Development Methods*, 7, pp 517–532

Hogan, C (1993c) *Creative and Reflective Journal Writing Processes*, paper presented at the 20th Annual Organisational Behaviour Teaching Conference, Bucknell University, Pennsylvania

Hogan, C F (1994a) Mind mapping: some practical applications, *Training and Management Development Methods*, 8 (1), pp 301–18

Hogan, C F (1994b) Course design in half the time: how to generate ideas using a network of computers, *Training and Management Development Methods*, 8 (2), pp 5.01–5.14

Hogan, C F (1996) Cross-cultural communication workshop, *Training and Management Development Methods*, 10 (2), pp 801–16

Hogan, C F (1997) The study buddy system: you are not studying alone, *Training and Management Development Methods*, 11 (3)

Hogan, C F (1999) *Facilitating Learning: Practical strategies for college and university*, Eruditions, Melbourne

Hogan, C F (2000) *Facilitating Empowerment: A handbook for facilitators, trainers and individuals*, Kogan Page, London

Hollier, F, Murray, K and Cornelius, H (1993) *Conflict Resolution Trainers Manual*, Conflict Resolution Network, Chatswood, Australia

Holly, M L (1984) *Keeping a Personal-Professional Journal*, Deakin University, Victoria, Australia

Honey, P (1986) Learning from outdoor activities: getting the balance right, *Industrial and Commercial Training* (Nov/Dec)

Honey, P (1989) *Peter Honey's Manual of Management Workshops*, Peter Honey, Maidenhead, UK

Honey, P (2002) *Songs of Life And Learning*, Peter Honey, Maidenhead, UK

Honey, P and Mumford, A (1986) *Using your Learning Styles*, Peter Honey, Maidenhead, England

Honey, P and Mumford, A (1992) *The Manual of Learning Styles*, 3rd edn, Peter Honey, Maidenhead, UK

Hopson, B and Scally, M (1981) *Lifeskills Teaching*, McGraw Hill, Maidenhead, UK

Hopson, B and Scally M (1982) *Lifeskills No 2*, Lifeskills Associates, Leeds, UK

Hopson, B and Scally, M (1983) *Lifeskills Teaching Programmes No 1*, Lifeskills Associates, Leeds, UK

Hopson, B and Scally, M (1984) *Build Your Own Rainbow: A workbook for career and life management*, Lifeskills Associates, Leeds, UK

Hopson, B and Scally, M (1986) *Lifeskills Teaching Programmes No 3*, Lifeskills Associates, Leeds, UK

Horn, R E (1998) *Visual Language*, MacroVU Press, Washington, USA

Hunter, D, Bailey, A and Taylor, B (1997) *Co-operacy: A new way of being at work*, Tandem Press, Birkenhead, New Zealand

Hunter, D, Bailey, A and Taylor, B (1999) *The Essence of Facilitation: Being in action in groups*, Tandem Press, Auckland, New Zealand

James, R (2000) *The Transitional Learning Model: A handbook for training design with special application to cross cultural training*, eworks, Wangara, Australia

Jenkins, D H (1974) Feedback and group self-evaluation, in *Group Development*, ed L P Bradford, University Associates, La Jolla, CA, pp 81–89

Jeruchim, J and Shapiro, P (1992) *Women, Mentors and Success*, Fawcett, Columbine, New York

Johnson, D J F (1997) *Joining Together: Group theory and group skills*, 6th edn, Allyn and Bacon, Needham Heights, USA

Jones, K (1995) *Ice Breakers: A sourcebook of games, exercises and simulations*, Kogan Page, London

Jung, C (1968) *The Collected Works of C G Jung*, 2nd edn, Routledge and Kegan Paul, London

Justice, T and Jamieson, D W (1999) *The Facilitator's Fieldbook*, American Management Association, New York

Kaner, S (1996) *Facilitator's Guide to Participatory Decision-Making*, New Society Publishers, Gabriola Island, Canada

Kaye, M (1996) *Myth-Makers and Story-Tellers: How to unleash the power of myths, stories and metaphors to understand the past, envisage the future and create lasting and positive cultural change in your organisation*, Business and Professional Publishing, Sydney

Keating, C (2002) *So You Want and/or Need to Work with Groups: A guide to some techniques and tools for facilitation*, Perth, Western Australia

Keleman, K S, Egri, C P and Frost, P J (1992) *Breaking Up is Hard to Do: Building separation and transitions at the end of the course*, paper presented at the 2nd International Organisational Behaviour Teaching Conference, Curtin University of Technology (December)

Keller, E F (1983) *A Feeling For The Organism: The life and times of Barbara McClintock*, W H Freeman, San Francisco,

Kember, D and Kelly, M (1993) *Improving Teaching Through Action Research*, Herdsa Green Guide, Higher Education Research and Development Society of Australia, Campbelltown, NSW

Kemmis, S and McTaggart, R (eds) (1988) *The Action Research Planner*, Deakin University Press, Geelong, Australia

Kiely, T (1993) The idea makers: the importance of creativity training in business, *Technology Review*, **96** (1), pp 32–41

Kipling, R (1908) *Kim*, Pocket edn, Macmillan, Basingstoke, UK

Kirby, A (1993) *Icebreakers*, Gower, Aldershot, UK

Kirkpatrick, D (1994) *Evaluating Training Programs: The four levels*, Berrett-Koehler, San Francisco, CA

Kirkpatrick, D (1996) Great ideas revisited, *Training and Development* (Jan), pp 54–59

Kirton, M (1976) Adaptors and innovators: a description and measure, *Journal of Applied Psychology*, **61**, pp 622–29

Kiser, A G (1998) *Masterful Facilitation: Becoming a catalyst for meaningful change*, American Management Association, New York

Kliewer, G (1999) The Mozart effect, *New Scientist*, 6 (November), pp 35–37

Knowles, M S (1984) *The Adult Learner: The neglected species*, Gulf, Houston, TX

Knowles, M S (1986) *Using Learning Contracts*, Jossey-Bass, San Francisco

Knowles, M (1989) *The Adult Learner: A neglected species*, 2nd edn, Gulf, Houston, TX

Kolb, D A (1984) *Experiential Learning: Experience as the source of learning and development*, Prentice-Hall, Englewood Cliffs, NJ

Kornfield, J (1994) *A Path With Heart: A guide through the perils and promises of spiritual life*, Random House, Sydney

Kubler-Ross, E (ed) (1975) *Death: The final stage of growth*, Prentice-Hall, Englewood Cliffs, NJ

Kurzweil, R (1990) *The Age of Intelligent Machines*, MIT Press, Cambridge, MA

Kurzweil, R (1999) *The Age of Spiritual Machines: When computers exceed intelligence*, Allen and Unwin, St Leonards, NSW

Laker, D R (1989–1990) Management class journals, *Organizational Behavior Teaching Review*, **14** (3), pp 72–78

Lane, D (1988) Using learning contracts – pitfalls and benefits for adult learners, *Training and Development in Australia*, **15** (1), (March) pp 23–25

Lewin, K (1946) Action research in retrospect and minority problems, *Journal of Social Issues*, **2** (4), pp 34–46; reprinted in Deakin University (1988) *The Action Research Reader*, Deakin University, Geelong, Australia

Long, J W (1987) The wilderness lab comes of age, *Training and Development Journal* (March), pp 30–39

Macy, J (1991) *World as Lover, World as Self*, Parallax Press, Berkeley, CA

Macy, J and Brown, M Y (1998) *Coming Back To Life: Practices to reconnect our lives, our world*, New Society, Gabriola Island, Canada

Margulies, N (1992) *Mapping Inner Space: Learning and teaching mind mapping*, Hawker Brownlow Education, Cheltenham, Australia

Martin, J N T (2000) *Managing Problems Creatively*, 2nd edn, Open University Business School, Milton Keynes, UK

Martin, M (2002) Discussions with author, Perth, Western Australia

Martin, M (work in progress) *Understanding Co-Facilitation*, PhD thesis, School of Management, Curtin University of Technology, Perth, Western Australia

Marx, R D, Frost, P J and Jick, T D (1991) *Management Live! The video book*, Prentice Hall, Englewood Cliffs, NJ

Martini, C and Foreman, K (eds) (1995) *Something Like A Drug: An unauthorized oral history of theatresports*, Red Deer College Press, Canada

McCann, D and Stewart, J (1997) *Aesop's Management Fables: The wombat manager and other cautionary tales*, Butterworth Heinemann, Oxford, UK

McCarthy, B (1980) *The 4-Mat System: Teaching to learning styles with right/left mode techniques*, Excell, IL

McClure, B A (1998,) *Putting a New Spin on Groups: The science of chaos*, Lawrence Erlbaum, Mahwah, NJ

McCold, P (1993) *Restorative Policing Experiment*, PhD in Criminal Justice, University at Albany SUNY, Community Service Foundation, Pipersville, PA

McCold, P and Wachtel, B (1998) *Restorative Policing Experiment: The Bethlehem Pennsylvania Police Family Conferencing Project, A report to the National Institute of Justice*, US Department of Justice, Washington, DC

Mitchell, R (2002) Discussions with the author on restorative justice, Perth, Western Australia

Mongeau, P A and Morr, M C (1999) Considering brainstorming, *Group Facilitation*, 1 (Winter), pp 14–21

Morgan, G (1986) *Images of Organisation*, Sage, Beverly Hills, CA

Morris, P (2000) *World Wide Work: Globally distributed expert business services*, Emerging Industries Section, Department of Industry Science and Resources, Canberra

Moscovici, S, Mugny, G and Avermaet, E V (eds) (1985) *Perspectives on Minority Influence*, Cambridge University Press, Cambridge, UK

Muller, W (1997) *How, Then, Shall We Live? Four simple questions that reveal the beauty and meaning of our lives*, Bantam, New York

Mumford, A (1980) *Making Experience Pay*, McGraw-Hill, Berkshire, UK

Mumford, A (1987) Using a learning log, *Training and Management Development Methods*, 1, pp 101–103

Mumford, A (1999) *How to Choose The Right Development Method*, Peter Honey, Maidenhead, UK

Myers, I B with Myers, P B (1980) *Gifts Differing*, Consulting Psychologists Press Palo Alto, CA

Neal, J (1997) Spirituality in management education: a guide to resources, *Journal of Management Education*, 21 (1), pp 121–39

Newstrom, J and Scannell, E (1991) *Still More Games Trainers Play*, McGraw-Hill, New York

Newstrom, J and Scannell, E (1998) *Games Trainers Play*, McGraw-Hill, New York

Niederman, F and Volkema, R (1999) The effects of facilitator characteristics on meeting preparation, set up and implementation, *Small Group Research*, 30 (3), pp 330–60

Nin, A (1966–1976) *The Diary*, Vols1–V1, Harcourt Brace, New York

O'Connell, T, Wachtel, B and Wachtel, T (1999) *Conferencing Handbook: The new real justice training manual*, Piper's Press, Pipersville, USA

Oncken, B (1989) *Managing Management Time: Who's got the monkey?*, Prentice-Hall, Englewood-Cliffs, NJ

Owen, H (1992) *Open Space Technology: A user's guide*, Abbott Publishing, Potomac, USA

Owen, H (1997) *Expanding Our Now: The story of open space technology*, Berrett-Koehler, San Francisco

Owen, H and Stadler, A (1999) *Open Space Technology*, Berrett-Koehler Communications, San Francisco

Parkes, C M (1977) *Bereavement*, Penguin, Harmondsworth, UK

Patnode, D (ed) (1989) *Robert's Rules of Order: Original 1876 text by Henry M Robert*, T Nelson, Nashville, TN

Paulus, P B and Yang, H C (2000) Idea generation in groups: a basis for creativity in organizations, *Organizational Behavior and Human Decision Processes*, 82 (1), pp 76–87

Pearson, C S (1991) *Awakening the Heroes Within: Twelve archetypes to help us find ourselves and transform our world*, Harper, San Francisco

Pearson, D (undated) *Playback Theatre: A methodology for education*, unpublished paper, Perth, Western Australia

Pearson, M (2002) Mapping the group, communication with the author, September 18

Peavey, F (2001) *Strategic Questioning: An experiment in communication of the second kind*, Crabgrass, San Francisco

Pedler, M, Burgoyne, T and Boydell, T A (1986) *Manager's Guide to Self Development*, 2nd edn, McGraw-Hill, Maidenhead, UK

Pepys, S (1983) *The Diary of Samuel Pepys, Vols 1 and 2*, ed H B Weatley, Random House, New York

Peters, R G, Covello, V T and McCallum, D B (1977) The determinants of trust and credibility in environmental risk communication: an empirical study, *Society for Risk Analysis Journal*, **17** (1), pp 43–54

Pierce, V, Cheesebrow, D and Braun, L M (2000) Facilitator competencies, *Group Facilitation*, **2** (2), pp 24–31

Pike, R W and Jones, P (1994) *Creative Training Techniques Handbook: Tips, tactics and how-to's for delivering effective training*, 2nd edn, Lakewood Books, Minneapolis, MN

Polanyi, M (1966) *The Tacit Dimension*, Routledge and Kegan Paul, London

Polanyi, M (1969) *Personal Knowledge: Towards a post-critical philosophy*, Routledge and Kegan Paul, London

Priest, S and Naismith, M (1993) A model for debriefing experiences, *Journal of Education and Outdoor Leadership*, **10** (3), pp 20–22

Progoff, I (1975) *At a Journal Workshop: The basic text and guide for using the intensive journal*, Dialogue House Library, New York

Progoff, I (1992) *At a Journal Workshop: Writing to access the power of the unconscious and evoke creative ability*, Tarch, USA

Radnor, H (2001) *Researching Your Professional Practice: Doing interpretive research*, Open University Press, Milton Keynes, UK

Rae, L (1986) *How to Measure Training Effectiveness*, Gower, Aldershot, UK

Rainer, T (1985) *The New Diary*, Angus and Robertson, London

Reason, P and Heron, J (1981) *Co-Counselling: An experiential inquiry (1)*, University of Surrey, Guildford, UK

Reason, P and Heron, J (1982) *Co-Counselling: An experiential inquiry (2)*, University of Surrey, Guildford, UK

Reddy, B (1994) *Interventions Skill: Process consultation for small groups and teams*, Pfeiffer, San Diego, CA

Reese, R (1997) *A Proactive-Interactive Approach to Bridging Cultural Differences* (6/11) http://csupo.mona.edu~rreese/multicultural.html

Richardson, S (1974) *Pamela: Or virtue rewarded*, Garland, New York

Rifkin, W D (1999) A mime is a terrible thing to waste, *Training and Management Development Methods*, **13**, pp 7.45–7.60

Rittel, H and Webber, M (1973) Dilemmas in a general theory of planning, *Policy Sciences*, **4** (1), pp 155–59

Robert, H M (1979) *Robert's Rules of Order Revised*, William Morrow, New York

Robert, H M (1985) *Robert's Rules of Order, 1876*, Jove Books, New York

Robinson, L (2002) *Pro-Active Public Participation for IRR/SRR in Western Australia: Part 1 Strategic Rationale: Why should communities participate in waste management decisions?*, Nolan-ITU, Manly, Australia

Rochfort, J and Blanchard, A (1996) *Tutoring Across Cultures*, Curtin University of Technology, Perth, Western Australia

Roe, E and McDonald, R (1984) *Informed Professional Judgement: A guide to evaluation in post secondary education*, University of Queensland Press, St Lucia, Australia

Rosenberg, M (1967) *From Now On: A model for nonviolent persuasion*, Community Psychological Consultants, St Louis, MI

Rosenberg, M B (1999) *Non Violent Communication: A language of compassion*, Puddle Dancer Press, Del Mar, USA

Rotter, J B (1975) Some problems and misconceptions related to the construct of internal versus external control of reinforcement, *Journal of Consulting Psychology*, **43**, pp 56–67

Ruete, E (1999) *Facilitation as a Profession* [Online] grp-facl@cnsibm.albany.edu Accessed 3/4/2002

Saint, S and Lawson, J R (1994) *Rules for Reaching Consensus*, Pfeiffer, San Diego, CA

Salmon, G (2000) *E-Moderating: The key to teaching and learning online*, Kogan Page, London

Sarri, R and Galinsky, M (1967) A conceptual framework for group development, in *Readings in Group Work Practice*, ed R D Vinter, Campus, Ann Arbor, MI, pp72–94

Scannell, E E (1994) *Even More Games Trainers Play: Experiential learning exercises*, McGraw-Hill, New York

Schaper, M and Volery, T (2001) *Entrepreneurship and Small Business: An Asia-Pacific guide*, 2nd edn, Vineyard Publishing, Perth, Western Australia

Schein, E H (1987) *Process Consultation, Vol 2: Lessons for managers and consultants*, Addison-Wesley, Reading, MA

Schein, E (1988) *Process Consultation, Vol 1: Its role in organisation development*, Addison Wesley, Reading, MA

Schein, E H (1999) *Process Consultation Revisited: Building the helping relationship*, Addison-Wesley, Reading, MA

Schnelle, E (1979) *The Metaplan-Method: Communication tools for planning and learning groups*, Quickborn, West Germany

Schoemaker, P J H (1995) Scenario planning: a tool for strategic thinking, *Sloan Management Review* (Winter), pp 25–40

Schön, D A (1987) *Educating the Reflective Practitioner*, Jossey-Bass, San Francisco

Schumacher, E F (1973) *Small is Beautiful*, Blond and Briggs, London

Schuman, S P (1996) What to look for in a group facilitator, *Quality-Progress*, **29** (6), pp 69–72

Schwartz, P (1991) *The Art of the Long View: Planning for the future in an uncertain world*, Doubleday Currency, New York

Schwarz, R M (1994) *The Skilled Facilitator: Practical wisdom for developing effective groups*, Jossey-Bass, San Francisco

Scott, B (2000) *Consulting on the Inside: An internal consultant's guide to living and working inside organizations*, American Society for Training and Development, Alexandria, VA

Scriven, M (ed) (1967) *The Methodology of Evaluation*, McNally, Chicago

Shea, G (1992) *Mentoring: A practical guide*, Crisp, CA

Sheehy, G (1977) *Passages*, Penguin, Harmondsworth, UK

Shields, K (1991) *In the Tiger's Mouth: An empowerment guide for social action*, Millennium, Newtown, Australia

Simons, G F (1978) *Keeping Your Personal Journal*, Paulist Press, USA

Simpkinson, C and Simpkinson, A (eds) (1993) *Sacred Stories: A celebration of the power of stories to transform and heal*, Harper Collins, San Francisco

Sitkin, S and Roth, N (1993), Explaining the limited effectiveness of legalistic remedies for trust/distrust, *Organisation Science*, 4, pp 367–92

Skinner, S (2001) *Feng Shui: The traditional oriental way to enhance your life*, Parragon, Bath, UK

Sleigh, J (1996) *Making Team Learning Fun*, CCH Australia, Sydney

Smith, B (1987) Structured diaries, *Training and Management Development Methods*, 1, pp 313–16

Smith, R C (2000) *Mind for Hire: A practitioner's guide to management consulting*, University of Western Australia Press, Perth, Western Australia

Smollett, T G (1983) *Humphrey Clinker: An authoritative text, contemporary response, criticism*, Norton, New York

Sonneman, M R (1997) *Beyond Words: A guide to drawing out ideas*, Ten Speed Press, Berkeley, CA

Spencer, L (1989) *Winning Through Participation*, Kendall Hunt, IO

Spender, D (1996) *Talking Power and Equality*, paper presented at the 28th Annual Conference of the International Community Development Society, Melbourne, Victoria, Australia [Online] http://www.comm-dev.org/conf96/spender.htm

Stanfield, R (ed) (1997) *The Art of Focussed Conversation: 100 ways to access wisdom in the workplace*, Canadian Institute of Cultural Affairs, Toronto

Stein, S and Book, H (2001) *The EQ Edge: Emotional intelligence and your success*, Kogan Page, London

Stephenson, P (2001) *Billy*, Harper Collins Entertainment, London, England

Stewart, I and Joines, V (1987) *TA Today: A new introduction to transactional analysis*, Lifespace, Nottingham, UK

Stewart, J, McGoldrick, J and Watson, S (2001) *Researching Human Resource Development: Philosophy, processes and practices*, Routledge, London

Straker, D (1997) *Rapid Problem Solving with Post-It Notes*, Gower, Aldershot, UK

Strang, H and Braithwaite, J (eds) (2001) *Restorative Justice and Civil Society*, Cambridge University Press, Cambridge, UK

Summerfield, E (1993) *Crossing Cultures Through Film*, Intercultural Press, Yarmouth, ME

Taggart, W J (1989) *Horsley's Meetings Procedure Law and Practice*, 3rd edn, Butterworth, Sydney

Teaching and Learning Committee (1999) *Teaching with Diversity Checklist*, University of Western Australia, Perth, Western Australia

Theobald, R (1998) *Reworking Tomorrow*, Institute of Workplace Training and Development, Wooloowin, Australia

Tomkins, C and McGraw, M J (1988) The negotiated learning contract, in *Developing Student Autonomy in Learning* 2nd edn, ed D Boud, Kogan Page, London, pp 172–91

Tripp, D (1981) Action research and professional development, in *Better Teachers for Better Schools*, ed P Hughes, Australian College of Education, Carlton, Victoria, pp 201–02

Tripp, D (1993) *Critical Incidents in Teaching: Developing professional judgement*, Routledge, London

Trist, E L and Emery, F E (1960) *Report on the Barford Course for Bristol/Siddeley, July 10–16 1960*, Tavistock Document no 598, Tavistock Institute, London

Tseng, A (1991) Discussions with author, ed C F Hogan, Singapore (December)

Tuckman, B W (1965) Developmental sequence in small groups, *Psychological Bulletin*, **63** (6), pp 384–99

Tuckman, B W and Jensen, M A (1977) Stages of small group development revisited, *Group and Organisational Studies*, **2** (4), pp 419–27

Tyson, T (1998) *Working with Groups*, 2nd edn, Macmillan Education, Melbourne

Ukens, L L (1996) *Getting Together: Ice breakers and energizers*, Jossey-Bass, San Francisco

University Associates (1980) Facilitation Skills Inventory, and Goals for Personal Development Inventory, in *Structured Experience Kit*, University Associates, Tucson, AZ [Online] http://www.universityassociates.com/

Van der Heijden, K (1996) *Scenarios: The art of strategic conversation*, John Wiley, New York

Van Gundy, A B (1988) *Techniques of Structured Problem Solving*, Van Nostrand Reinhold

Van Gundy, A B (1995) Creativity in marketing, in *Marketing Encyclopedia: Issues and trends shaping the future*, ed J Heilbrunn, NTC Business Books, Lincoln-wood, IL

Vanier, J (1979) *Community and Growth*, Society of St Paul, Homebush, Australia

Viscovic A (1989) Reflection in adult learning, *Wellington Polytechnic Professional Development Newsletter*, **6** (Nov), pp 8–11

von Oech, R (1992) *Creative Whack Pack*, US Games Systems, Stamford, USA [Online] http://wwwkinecomm.com/java_example2/CreativeWhack PackHelp.html (Accessed 6/6/1992)

Walker, B G (1988) *The Woman's Dictionary of Symbols and Sacred Objects*, Pandora, London

Wates, N (2000) *The Community Planning Handbook: How people can shape their cities, towns and villages in any part of the world*, Earthscan, London

Watkins, G G (1983) *Planning in a Period of Turbulence: Implications for recreation professionals*, Recreation Australia, Perth, Western Australia

Watson, H J, Vallee, J M and Mulford, W R (1981) *Structured Experiences and Group Development*, Curriculum Development Centre, Canberra

Watson, L (1980) *Lifetide*, Bantam Books, New York

Weisbord, M P (1992) *Discovering Common Ground: How future search conferences bring people together to achieve breakthrough, innovation, empowerment, shared vision and collaborative action*, Berrett-Koehler, San Francisco

Wenger, E, McDermott, R and Snyder, W (2002) *Cultivating Communities of Practice*, Harvard Business School, Cambridge, MA

West, E (1997) *201 Icebreakers: Group mixers, warm-ups, energisers and playful activities*, McGraw Hill, New York

Whitaker, D S (1985) *Using Groups to Help People*, Routledge and Kegan Paul, London

Whiteley, A M and Garcia, J E (1996) The facilitator and the chauffeur in GSS: explorations in the forging of a relationship, *Group Decision and Negotiation*, 5, pp 31–50

Wilson, J B (1979) *The Story Experience*, Scarecrow Press, London

Woods, D R (1994) *Problem-Based Learning: How to gain the most from PBL*, Donald R Woods, Waterdown, Ontario, Canada

Woods, D R (2000) An evidence-based strategy for problem solving, *Journal of Engineering Education* (Oct), pp 443–59

Yeomans, P R (1999a) Value management saving the planet: potent paragon or pompous pipedream? in *Hong Kong Institute of Value Management International Conference*, Hong Kong

Yeomans, P R (1999b) Value management: The facts, the fit, the future, *Australian Project Manager* (May), pp 32–34

Zemke, R (1993) In search of … good ideas, *Training*, 30 (52), pp 46–50

Zempe, R (1990) Storytelling back to basics, *Training* (March), pp 44–50

Web sites

Brainstorming: http://www.mindtools.com/brainstm.html

http://www.mindbloom.net

Circlespeak: CircleSpeak@aol.com

Colour flags (multicultural exercise): http://www.class.csupomona.edu/colorfulflags/index.html

http://www.csupomona.edu/~rreese/MULTICULTURAL.html

http://www.csupomona.edu/~rreese/BRIDGING.html

Community participation:

A-Z of effective participation: http://www.partnerships.org.uk/guide/AZpartic.html#Community

Guide to Effective Participation: http://www.partnerships.org.uk/guide/main1.html

Public participation in environmental management (Canadian site): http://www.scarp.ubc.ca/thesis/vanderwal/chap3.htm#s331

Public participation in planning (UK site):

http://www.irs.aber.ac.uk/als/powerpoint/planning7/sld001.htm

Seattle Community Network community participation site: www.scn.org

Youth participation: http://www.hwy-1.net/yp.htm

Consultation: adapting public consultation to different political cultures: http://www.islandnet.com/connor/adapting.html

Drama techniques: International Playback Theatre Network: http://www.playbacknet.org/

Film reviews and parts of scripts: http://www.filmsite.org/

Fractals: www.fractals.com/fractal_gallery/krueger/91.1/2ceab.gut

McMaster six-stage problem solving strategy: http://edweb.sdsu.edu/clrit/ learningtree/PBL/WhatisPBL.html

Murder She Wrote:

http://www.abc.net.au/austory/archivesAustoryArchivesIdx_ Monday29July2002.htm

http://www.abc.net.au/austory/archives/AustoryArchivesIdx_ Monday5August2002.ht

Next step: www.enterprise.net/amb/nextstep/openspace.htm

OECD bookshop:

http://electrade.gfi.fr/cgi-bin/OECDBookShop.storefront/EN/product/ 422001131P1

Open space technique:

http://www.openspaceworld.com/brief_history.htm

Michael Herman's Web site: http://www.globalchicago.net/michael/ index.html

A user's non guide: http://www.globalchicago.net/ost/nonguide/index.html

Chris Corrigan, Canada: http://www.chriscorrigan.com/openspace

Photos: http://www.webshots.com/

Problem solving:

http://www.udel.edu/pbl

www.crabgrass.org/article01.htm

Relaxation techniques: http://www.mindtools.com/page2.html

http://www.mindtools.com/pages/main/newMN_TCS.htm

Restorative justice:

scc.gc.ca/text/prgrm/rjstc/award/info_e.shtml

www.real.justice.org

resources: http://www.realjustice.org/Pages/booksvideos.html

Australian Institute of Criminology RJ site: http://www.aic.gov.au/rjustice/ australia.html

Terry O'Connell's work: http://www.smh.com.au/news/0006/13/pageone/ pageone03.html

www.transformingconflict

www.thorsborne.com.au

Reports on RJ trials: www.aic.gov.au/rjustice/rise.html www.aic.gov.au/ rjustice/rise.html

Robert's Rules: http://www.robertsrules.com

http://www.muc.de/~heuvel/dialogue

http://www.crnhq.org.

St Lukes Innovative Resources: http://www.stlukes.org.au

Scenario planning: www.ashquarry.com

www.cyber.rdg.ac.uk

www.clonaid.com (genetic engineering)

www.wire.com

www.7dimensions.com.au

Storytelling: http://www.thestorynet.com/archive.htm

Australian stories network: http://www.home.aone.net.au/stories/
Aesop's fables Web site: http://www.home.aone.net.au/stories/nd4stori.htm
Six blind men and the elephant: http://www.noogenesis.com/pineapple/
blind_men_elephant.html
Technology:
www.collaborate.com: collaborative technology
www.collaboration-tools.com
www.3m.com/meetingnetwork
www.emoderator.com
www.whatis.com

Videos

The Abilene Paradox (Timmons, 1984)
Australian Story: Murder She Wrote, Parts 1 and 2 (2002)
Blue Eyes and *A Class Divided* (1968) Jane Elliott, IO
Brain Story (two video recordings) Greenfield *et al* (2000) BBC Publications,
London
Collaborative Learning: Working together in small groups (1996) Murdoch University, Perth, Western Australia
Collegial Support Groups: A Facilitator's Perspective (1993) P Klinck, Perth, Western
Australia
Creative and Reflective Journal Processes for Students and Managers (1993) Production
by Clive Jones in conjunction with Christine Hogan and the 'Developing
People at Work' Postgraduate Class. Available from Clive Jones, Curtin
Business School, Curtin University of Technology, GPO Box U1987, Perth,
Western Australia 6001
Creative Training and Presentation Techniques (video and facilitator's guide) (1993)
R W Pike, BBC Training Videos
The Cutting Edge: Exposure (1993) Channel 4, 25 January
DACUM Developing a Curriculum (1987) Produced by Parmelia Productions for
TAFE Western Australia. [2AV] 378.1996 DAC. Available from TAFE National
Centre, Marketing and Promotions, Ms Pat Venning (08) 332 7822. Price
A$25
Dead Poets' Society (1987) Dir. P Weir, Touchstone Videos
Emotional Intelligence: A new vision for educators with Daniel Goleman
Facing the Demons [Online] http://www.realjustice.org/Pages/facingdemons.html
Inside Story: Facing the demons (1999) ABC (2 June), Perth, Western Australia
Learning in Open Space (1991) A Stadler, Abbot Publishing
Mediating Disputes (1992) Produced by Peter Quarry and Eve Ash. Seven
Dimensions, Victoria, Australia
Meetings That Work: The interaction method (1985) Produced for young people,
PEP Resource Unit, TAFE, Royal Street, East Perth, Western Australia
Methods (1965) Hungaro Film, State Film Library, Perth, Western Australia
The Music Paradigm (1999) BBC Worldwide
The Planning Process: Planning for a sustainable environment, Rural Planning, Edith
Cowan University Media Production Office, Perth, Western Australia

Playback Theatre in Action (1995) Media Production Unit, Edith Cowan University, Perth, Western Australia

Scenario Planning, Interview with Dr Peter Schwartz, Ash Quarry Publications

She'll Be Wearing Pink Pyjamas (1998) Film Four International, London (44 171 868 7700)

Treading the Boards: Best practice for women on boards and committees (1995) Department of Industrial Relations, Perth, Western Australia

US WEST Open Space: An open space with 175 people in a work setting (1995) P Holman and J Harris, Open Space Institute

Windmills of Your Mind: Mind mapping and six thinking hats (1997) Curtin Business School, Curtin University of Technology, Perth, Western Australia

Software for mapping problems

Axon Research Singapore (1995) *Axon Idea Processor,* Axon Research, Tanglin PO Box 0398, Singapore 9124

Cedar Software Limited (1995) *Mind Maps Plus* Version 3, Contact Peter Barrett in Scotland, fax 01250 875959

Index